OPEN LETTERS TO LORD CURZON & SPEECHES AND PAPERS

OPEN LETTERS TO LORD CURZON & SPEECHES AND PAPERS

ROMESH CH. DUTT

WITH AN INTRODUCTION BY

D. N. GUPTA
HINDU COLLEGE, DELHI UNIVERSITY

Gian Publishing House

29/6 SHAKTI NAGAR • DELHI-110007 • INDIA

GIAN PUBLISHING HOUSE
PUBLISHERS OF BOOKS ON HUMAN CIVILIZATION
29/6 SHAKTI NAGAR, DELHI-110007

First Reprint in India, 1986

Printed at Goyal Offset Printers, Delhi-110035
and published by Smt. Gayatri Garg
for Gian Publishing House, Delhi-110007

OPEN LETTERS

TO

LORD CURZON

CONTENTS

Introduction

By

D. N. Gupta

INTRODUCTION

The process of Indian people's struggle for liberation from British imperialism began in the second half of the 19th century. What draws one's immediate attention to this struggle is the controversy not only around its nature and class character but also its political objectives and methods of agitation. Since its very inception, its spokesmen and leaders came to be attacked in the contemporary British official and non-official writings on the ground that they consciously or unconsciously represented the interests of the 'microscopic minority',[1] 'the middle class' or 'the educated elite'.[2] They were also accused of representing the interests of the landowning

1 Lord Dufferin, the Viceroy of India, repeatedly characterised the Indian National Movement as that of the 'microscopic minority'. Dufferin to Northbrook, 16 Oct, 1886, *Dufferin Papers, (D.P.)*; Dufferin's minute enclosure to *Home (Public) despatch to Secretary of State* No. 67, dated 6 Nov. 1888; Dufferin, *Speeches* 1884-1888. All references are taken from Bipan Chandra, Lord Dufferin a d the character of the Indian National Leadership, See Bipan Chandra, *Nationalism and Colonialism in Modern India*, New Delhi, 1979; pp. 275-296

2 Dufferin to Lord Cross, 20 March, 1887 (D.P,) The Secretary of State, Lord Cross put the point even more crudely in his *Letter to Dufferin,8 Sept, 1886.* "But there are two distinct classes in India-first the masses, and the next the 'educated natives", (*D.P.*) For reference see, Bipan Chandra, *Ibid;* p. 292. This official view point has been accepted uncritically by many modern scholars. see B.B. Misra, *The Indian Middle Classes*, London, 1961, pp. 346-356. P.C. Ghose, *Indian National Congress 1892-1909*, Calcutta, 1960, pp.41-42. The concept of elite has been systematically applied to the study of early nationalist leadership by Anil Seal. See his, *Emergence of Indian Nationalism*-a study in competition and collaboration in the later 19th century, London, 1968. For a critical evaluation of these assertions, consult Bipan Chandra, *Rise and Growth of Economic Nationalism in India*, New Delhi; 1966, pp, 736-759.

classes against those of the agriculturists.[3] As such it was held that their programme and methods of agitation lacked 'effectiveness' and their action did not enjoy mass support and, therefore, it was of little significance. It was also due to this fact, it was claimed by the colonial administrators, that their basic demands were outright rejected by the imperialists.

Undoubtedly their appreciation of some of the so-called positive achievements of British rule in India and the mild nature of their demands were determined by the fact that British rule did hold, for long, a promise to them, because, "In the material field they were attracted more by the potential than the real more by the hope than the fulfilment...".[4] But with the passage of time when, "they found that their expectations remained unrealised and even appeared to recede farther and farther, they were filled with disappointment and dismay...".[5] Their analysis of the British impact in general and the colonial economic policies in particular led them slowly but gradually to the conclusion that they were injurious to the interests of all the major social classes of India. That they were not able to provide either a 'radical programme' or to mobilise mass support in favour of their politics is altogether a different issue. The reasons for this should not, as has been generally the practice till the present time, be sought in their 'class character', but in their overall understanding of British rule and their initial hopes and expectations from it. What is important is that they were very much conscious of many of the limitations of their work, which they were convinced was of a preparatory nature. For example, Dadabhai Naoroji wrote to D. E. Wacha :

3 Though the charge was again and again repeated by Dufferin and Curzon Bipan Chandra's study of the economic ideas of the early nationalist leadership has established that they, though did not take up the class demands of the peasantry, never opposed any legislation passed in favour of the tenants, See Bipan Chandra, *Ibid*, pp. 416-436,

4 *Ibid;* p. 738.

5 *Ibid;* p. 738.

The very discontent and impatience it (the Congress) has evoked against itself as slow and non-progressive among the rising generation are among its best results or fruits. It is in its own evolution and progress...(the task is) to evolve the required revolution--whether it would be peaceful or violent. The character of the revolution will depend upon the wisdom and unwisdom of the British Government and action of the British people.[6]

Gopal Krishna Gokhale, another leader of this phase of our anti-imperialist struggle expressed the same sentiments when he wrote :

Let us not forget that we are at a stage of the country's progress when our achievements are bound to be small and our disappointments frequent and trying—that is the place which it has pleased Providence to assign to us in this struggle, and our responsibilities ended when we have done the work which belongs to that place. It will, no doubt, be given to our countrymen of future generations to serve India by their successses ; we, of the present generation, must be content to serve her mainly by our failures. For, hard thought it be, out of those failures the strength will come which in the end will accomplish great tasks.[7]

When their success is not measured in terms of their immediate economic and political gains, only then it would be possible for us to do justice to their achievements and understand the nature of their activities in a more scientific and rational manner. As their understanding of British rule matured into a closer analysis of its economic impact on Indian society, they gave up their earlier belief and, "their image of British rule began to take on darker hues".[8] By establishing that the Indian empire was being ruled over and maintained in the interest of the ruling classes of England and not in the interest of the Indian people, they, "made the people of India

6 rom Bipan Chandra, *Rise and Growth of Economic Nationalism in India*. p. 758.

7 Quoted in Bipan Chandra, *Ibid;* p. 759.

8 *Ibid;* p. 738.

conscious of the bond of common economic interests and the existence of a common enemy and thus helped to weld them in a common nationalism".[9] Moreover, by agitating on issues of common interest they imparted political education to the Indian people and prepared them, in the words of Bipan Chandra, for, "modern political and nationalist thinking and activity...".[10] Thus in spite of their many limitations, they definitely, "laid strong and enduring foundations for the national movement to grow upon and deserve a high place among the makers of modern India".[11]

Among the early nationalist leaders who made a serious analysis of the British economic impact on India, R.C. Dutt occupies an important place. "The role of the pioneer in this field was distinctly played by Dadabhai Naoroji and a number of Dutt's contemporaries...it fell to Dutt, however, to present a complete and connected account of the colonial phase of modern Indian history".[12] To a great extent he performed this important theoretical task in a competent manner through his critical writings on the economic history of India during the British period.

Born in the well-known Dutt family of Rambagan in the year 1847, R.C. Dutt was one of the first Indians to get into the Indian Civil Service.[13] Between 1871 and 1882 he served in many districts of Bengal in various capacities.[14] It was during

9 *Ibid;* p. 758.

10 *Ibid;* p. 757.

11 *Ibid;* pp. 758-759.

12 D.R. Gadgil *Introduction to R.C. Dutt's Economic History of India*, New Delhi, 1970 Vol. I, p. xxiii

13 It was in the competitive examination of 1869 that Dutt, along with S.N. Banerjee, Beharilal Gupta, and Sripad Babuji, stood third in the merit list of the successful candidates. The only other Indian who had been successful earlier was S.N. Tagore, an elder brother of the poet, Rabindra Nath Tagore. For the early career of R.C.Dutt, See J.N.Gupta, *Life and Works of Romesh Chandra Dutt*, London, 1911, pp. 10-38.

14 For details of his official career and administrative work see, Gupta, *Ibid;* pp. 39-177. Also R.C. Dutt, *Romesh Chandra Dutt*, New Delhi, 1968, pp. 20-54.

these years that he acquired a first hand knowledge of the conditions and the problems of Indian agriculture. Soon he developed an immense interest in these peoblems. By the time he took over as the Commissioner of Burdwan Division in 1893, his ideas on the agrarian structure had taken a definite shape. Therefore soon after his retirement in 1895 from the government service, he devoted most of his time and energy to the study of the conditions of the Indian agriculturists.

Though his better known and maturer works on the economic history of India were completed after his retirement, when he also took to politics, his *Peasantry of Bengal* published in 1874, was the first manifestation of his increasing interest in the problems of Indian agriculture. It came at a time when the agrarian discontent had already attracted the attention of the British Indian Government. What is significant about this work is that while still in government service, R.C. Dutt espoused the cause of the raiyats against that of the zamindars.[15] He wrote :

> In the face of the crisis that is staring rudely at us, half-hearted legislation would be useless and worse than useless. Our rulers will not, and cannot, once more degrade the raiyat to his pristine position of servitude under the zamindars—the only measure then to heal the ill-feeling between the two classes and to put a stop to the mass of litigation that is eating into the very vitals of an agricultural population, is to raise the status of the raiyats....[16]

Advocacy of the cause of the raiyats in those days and while in government service was definitely a daring act on the part of R.C. Dutt. It was bound to cause alarm in the ranks of

15 It is an important point because of all the nationalist leaders, R.C. Dutt in particular has been accused of representing the interest of the zamindars against that of the raiyats. For details on the controversy and certain useful clarifications, see Bipan Chandra, *Colonialism and Nationalism in Modern India*, pp. 416-436.

16 R.C. Dutt's *Peasantry of Bengal*, first published in 1874. Reprinted with an introduction by N. Kaviraj, Calcutta, 1980. From Gupta, *op. cit*, p. 57.

the zamindars as it actually did. "This bold advocacy for the cause of the raiyats", writes his biographer, "created alarm in the ranks of the zamindars and the great-Kistodas Pal, the champion of vested interests, took the field against the daring iconoclast..."[17]

Despite the fact that in the early years of his official career, R.C.Dutt had given adequate proof of his immense aptitude for facts and figures about economic history, it was only in the late 19th and the early years of the 20th century that he reached the climax of his intellectual and political career. When in 1899, in recognition of his services he was invited to preside over the Lucknow Session of the Indian National Congress he attained the highest political stature a nationalist Indian could hope to get in those days. His 'Famines and the Land Assessments in India' in 1900, two volumes on the 'Economic History of India' in 1901 and 1903 and yet another two volumes of 'Speeches and Papers on the Indian questions' covering a wide range of subjects and published in 1902 and 1904 respectively, further enhanced his intellectual repute and earned him high and universal praise.

Though R.C. Dutt's contribution to the understanding of the British impact on India is recognised through his two volumes on the 'Economic History of India', it was in his Presidential address to the Congress in 1899, five 'Open letters to Lord Curzon' in early 1900 and innumerable speeches and papers that he challenged the accepted official position on the questions of the occurrence and recurrence of terrible famines and the causes responsible for the impoverishment of the Indian peasantry, and that, too, with the help of official facts and figures,

The present collection,divided into three parts, is a compilation of R.C. Dutt's five 'Open letters to Lord Curzon', Curzon's reply in the form of the resolution of Government

17 Gupta, op cit; p. 57.

of India, dated 16 January, 1902;[18] and two volumes of his 'Speeches and Papers on the Indian Questions covering the period from 1897 to 1902. Though the major theme covered in these works is the impact of the land revenue policy of the British on Indian agriculture and the causes of both the famines and the impoverishment of the Indian peasantry, his 'Speeches and Papers on the Indian Questions' also include certain important writings on cultural, religious and political issues confronting Indians during those days. For example, his views on the important role the two great epics—The Ramayana and the Mahabharata-have played in the life of the Indian people and on questions like the separation of the judicial and the executive services and the association of the Indians with the work of administration at all levels, form a significant part of the present collection. These writings, taken together, reflect the multi-dimensional personality of R.C. Dutt and his competence to handle a wide range of problems.

In his five 'Open Letters', he picked up cudgles against Curzon, the then Viceroy of India, on the most important and burning question of the time, i.e; the impact of the land revenue policy of the British on Indian agriculture. He published this collection in 1900 with the objective of making available to the British officials and his countrymen, "an easy handbook on the land question of India, on the conditions of the cultivators, and the incidence of the land tax and the reforms needed to make agriculturists more self-relying and resourceful and famines less and less frequent and less fatal..."[19]

The phenomenon of the frequent occurrence of famines had attracted his attention from the early years of the official career. What drew his attention the most was the fact that

18 For the Resolution of the Government of India, See Part I of the present Volume pp. 85-135, and for R C. Dutt's reply to the resolution, See Part III, pp. 165-200.

19 R.C. Dutt, *Famines and Land Assessments in India*, London, 1900; p. xix

the famines had affected the lives of millions of his countrymen in the various parts of the country. Within a period of 130 years of the establishment of British rule in India 22 famines had occurred at different times. R.C. Dutt's understanding was that there could be some justification of this phenomenon in the 8th or even in the early 19th century because "when an old system of government breaks down and the country passes under a new power wars and disorders are inevitable...",[20] and, therefore, in such situations the irrigation facilities, famine relief work and the overall interests of the agriculturists were bound to be neglected. However, there was no reason why the famines should at all occur in the second half of the 19th century. It was impossible for him to understand why the famines had not disappeared even though, "these causes had longed ceased to operate."[21] After 1857, just in a period of forty years at least 50 million Indians had been the victims of famines in one way or the other. What pained him the most was that the famines were occuring in a country whose, "land is fertile...".[22] The official explanations that the main reasons for the occurence of famines and the impoverishment of the Indian peasantry were either the increase in population or the lack of frugality, sobriety and prudence on the part of the Indian peasantry, did not convince R.C. Dutt. He, therefore, seriously took up the study of the causes of this phenomenon and its remedies.

In his five 'Open letters to Curzon', he began his investigation with a detailed discussion of the various types of land revenue systems, the British had introduced in India. His study led him to the conclusion that the British had made many mistakes in their agricultural policy. Whereas in areas like Bengal and Northern India the cultivators paid as land revenue between 5% to 10% of the gross produce, in the

20 R.C. Dutt, *Open Letters to Lord Curzon;* Calcutta, 1901, p. 15.
21 *Ibid*, p. 16
22 *Ibid;* p. 16.

directly assessed areas like Bombay, Madras and the Central Provinces, the amount demanded varied between 16% and 33% of the gross produce. This heavy assessment along with enhancement at each recurring Settlement to the maximum paying capacity of the cultivators amounted to confiscation of private property in land and transformation of the peasant proprietors into virtual serfs of the state. Hence in the famines of 1877, 1897 and 1899, the parts of India which were over-assessed had suffered most severly. He was also perturbed by the fact that Lord Lytton's policy of setting apart an amount of a crore and a half every year, to be used in case of a famine on famine relief and insurance, had not been actually and strictly followed. He calculated that in fifteen years i.e., down to 1895-96 the expenditure for the purpose set forth was only Rs. 17,644,185/-, whereas the famine grant, at a crore and a half annually, was 22½ crores. Moreover, he noticed that irrigation works were being neglected and a large amount of money was, instead, being spent on the construction of railways. He was opposed to any expenditure on protective railways anymore. On the contrary, he wanted that at least a crore of rupees, out of the total of a crore and a half of the famine grant, should annually be spent on protective irrigation.

Besides the basic flaws in the land revenue policy of the British in India, he also noticed a number of fallacies regarding the land tax in India. One of these was the irrelevant controversy in the official circles whether revenue was a tax or rent. While not going into the details of the controversy and considering it useless from the point of view of the Indian agriculturists he opined that "the land revenue of India is a tax, and a very heavy tax, on the people...".[23] What he was mainly concerned with was the practical impact of the heavy demand on the cultivators rather than the academic aspect of the controversy. As he wrote :

23 R.C. Dutt, Famines and Land Assessments in India. p. 95.

So far as the poor agriculturists of India are concerned, the dispute is mainly a quabble, and often a heartless quabble. Four-fifths of the population of India depend directly or indirectly on the produce of the soil, and if an unduly large share of the produce is taken by the state, so as to leave the cultivators impoverished, it is small comfort to them to learn that some able and ingenious financiers call it a rent and not a tax... . The millions of cultivators who are driven to the moneylenders within two months after they have reaped their harvest in order to meet the State demand, will find little consolation if the curious information be placed before them that learned political economists in Europe give a very special name to that very severe demand. And the six millions of starving men and women and children who have been unable to save anything after paying the State demand in past years and who are crowding to relief centres in this year of drought and failure of crops will fail to appreciate the kindness of able eloquent debators who are ready to prove that the demand was no tax at all... .[24]

Secondly, he said that it was difficult to understand why land revenue in India was estimated on the basis of the supposed gross produce of the entire province because this kind of estimation was full of anomalies. It did not matter to a particular cultivator whether on an average the gross produce was on the higher side or not. "For the practical administrative purpose of fixing the land revenue evenly and moderately in those tracts and those individual cases where it presses hard on the population the supposed average for an all India is of little value",[25] remarked R.C. Dutt.

Thirdly, he challenged the comparison, as was generally done in the official circles to show the light burden of their demand on the peasantry, between the land revenue demand under the Mughals and that of the British. His basic argument

24 *Ibid;* p. 96.
25 *Ibid; p.* 99.

was "the old figures represent an ideal demand which was never collected in full..." and, therefore, "to compare modern figures with those old figures is to compare collection actually made by the British administrators with collection which were never made by Mohammedan administrators."[26] Moreover, even if the taxes under the Mughals were as heavy as under the British, he emphasized that the essential difference between the nature of the two rules should not be forgotten. Whereas under the Mughals the entire collection was spent within the country; under the British a large amount was drained out of the country. As he remarked; "it is obvious that the incidence of heavy taxation is better if the proceeds of the tax flow back to the people themselves, than if a large portion of it is spent out of the country, adding to the capital and helping the trade and industries of a distant land"[27].

Fourthly, he was also critical of the Tory party's policy of discovering a scientific frontier in India which had not yet been found because the whole pecuniary burden of the frontier wars had been thrown on the famine stricken population of India and that, too, "not for the requirements of India but for the requirements of the British Empire in Asia, Africa, and even in Europe..."[28]

With this understanding of the causes of the frequent occurence of famines, R.C. Dutt proceeded to suggest certain important remedial measures. His investigation convinced him that the condition of the Indian cultivators could not be improved without a proper reform of the land revenue system itself, because it was the backbone of the agrarian structure. He divided the remedial measures into two parts :— (a) For the areas where the revenue was collected through the landlords and (b) for the areas where the State

26 *Ibid;* p. 100.

27 *Ibid;* pp. 63-64

28 For details see R C. Dutt, *Speeches and Papers on Indian questions, 189 -19* , Calcutta, 1902, pp. 33-37-Henceforth Speeches and Papers (No. I)

demanded land revenue directly from the cultivators. Whereas for the former he suggested that land revenue demand should be fixed at 1/2 of the rental and 'Saharanpur rules'[29] be universally applied, for the latter he suggested that the land revenue in no case should exceed 1/5 of the gross produce.

R.C. Dutt also suggested that land revenue be fixed on permanent basis in the temporary settled parts of the country. Pending this decision, the settlement should not in any case be made oftener than once in thirty years. Moreover, the Government should see to it that the raiyat was protected from arbitrary enhancement during the settlement operations. He was also opposed to charging of water rates on a uniform basis. His proposal was that the water rates be charged on the basis of the actual use of the water by the cultivator concerned.

Along with these suggestions, he also advocated the right of the cultivators to appeal to an independent tribunal in case of a dispute between him and the Settlement officer. Such a tribunal should in no way be concerned with the fixing and levying of rents and taxes. This led him to raise the plea for the separation of the judicial and the executive services. Supporting his plea with the opinions of Englishmen themselves he put forward his proposals in 1893 in the form of a scheme for the separation of the two services. In addition, in all such cases where the State received revenue directly, Lord Ripon's rule that an increase in revenue be determined solely on the basis of the increase in the prices should be applied uniformally and universally.

R.C. Dutt's investigation into the causes of the famines and the remedies suggested by him sparked a fierce controversy between the imperialist ideologues and the nationalists themselves. The British officials saw the real source of famines in the frequent failure of rains and the consequent loss of crop, but R.C. Dutt blamed the evils of the new land revenue

29 In 1855 'Saharanpur Rules' had reduced the State demand from two-thirds of the rental to one-half.

system of the British. According to him, the evil of over-assessment, particularly in the areas where revenue was directly collected by the Government, was the main reason for the occurence of famines and the impoverishment of the peasantry because it left the cultivators without any means or resources during the failures of crops. He was firm in his conclusion that the failure of crops did not cause poverty but it was poverty which transformed scarcity into famines and that poverty was not God-sent, as was put forward by the British, but man-made and hence controllable and curable.

More than anything else, his plea for the fixity of land revenue on a permanent basis in all parts of India needs some clarification, for it is on this ground that he has been accused of being the spokesman and champion of the cause of the zamindars. This accusation, though started by Lord Curzon, has continued till today in the writings of some Indian scholars like P.C. Ghose and B.B. Misra. Ghose has gone to the extent of writing that in his Presidential address to the Indian National Congress in 1899, R.C. Dutt, "requested the Government to extend the Bengal system to other parts of India."[30] However, contrary to this belief, the early nationalist leaders in general and R.C. Dutt in particular never demanded either the reproduction of the Bengal system or its extension to other parts of the country. What he advocated was the protection of the interests of raiyats which, as he rightly thought, could partly be achieved by the fixation in perpetuity of the land revenue demand of the government. In his opinion a great harm was caused to the interest of the cultivators by continuing the uncertain and fluctuating demand. In his Presidential address he remarked, "Never mind under what system or under what settlement he (agriculturist/cultivator) lives, assure to him an adequate proportion out of the produce of his land...and

30 Ghose; *op. cit*; pp. 41-42, B.B. Misra; *op. cit*; p. 350 and Hira Lal Singh *Problems and Policies of the British Rule in India;* Bombay, 1963; p. 217.

he is saved, and the nation is saved."[31] Dutt further explained his position in his fourth letter to Lord Curzon :

My Lord, there are blessings which have been secured to the Bengal landlord and the Bengal cultivators by the Permanent Settlement and by the successive Rent Laws of Bengal. But I do not wish to be misunderstood. I do not, at the present time, ask for the extension of the Bengal System to other parts of India. I have not made any such suggestions in the three letters which I have had the honour to address to Your Excellency... . What I have asked, my Lord, is that protection be granted to the cultivator of each Province under the land system under which he lives "[32].

On the basis of his understanding of the economic impact of British rule on India, he arrived at certain political conclusions. Perhaps the most important of these was his advocacy for a due share to the people of India in the administration of their country. He was convinced that most of the economic ills were due to the debarment of Indians from any major share in the administration of the country. He was of the opinion that even with the best of intentions, British administrators in India had repeatedly drifted into errors or forgotten their pledges, because the *people themselves had been carefully debarred from any real share in the administration.* In his Presidential address to the Congress he remarked, "Gentlemen, it is possible, to avert distress and deaths from famines, to spread prosperity and contentment and peace, and to evoke the zealous and loyal and spontaneous support of a grateful nation, *only by conceding to the people, with due and proper safeguards, the rights of self-Government. It is not possible without such concession, without admitting the people to a real share in the control of their own affairs, to save*

31 From Bipan Chandra, *Nationalism and Colonialism in Modern India*. p. 426.

32 R.C. Dutt, *Open Letters to Lord Curzon*, p. 65; See also *Speeches and Papers on the Indian Questions*. II, Calcutta, 1904; pp. 17-18.

India from distress and discontent, from impoverishment and famines. Therefore, as an old and faithful servant of the Indian Government, I have thought it my duty to raise my voice and urge the adoption of the better and the wiser course, the only course which can save our country from preventible misfortunes and disasters, and can consolidate the British Rule in India."[33] He wanted that real participation be given to the Indians at all levels from the village to the Executive Council of the Viceroy. He put the following questions to his audience at the Lucknow Session of the Congress:

Am I urging anything unreasonable when I propose that the Viceroy who has the benefit of consulting experienced English administrators in his Executive Council, should also have the advantage of hearing the views and opinions of a few Indian members in the same Council before he decides on questions affecting the interests of the people of India ? Am I urging anything unwise when I propose that the Viceroy, when he considers, measures affecting the condition of the indebted cultivators, the operations of the plague and famine relief, the rules of land revenue settlements, the questions affecting Hindu and Mohammedan customs and manners, should have by him, in his own Executive Council, a few Indian gentlemen who represent the views, the opinions and the feelings of the people ?...[34]

He hammered the point again in his farewell speeches at Calcutta and Bombay in February and March, 1900. For example, at Bombay he said, "Gentlemen, if we could presume to give any advice to his Excellency (Bombay Governor), we would couch it in the very same words ; consider the representations of the people in a liberal and generous spirit..."[35] Not only this, he also wanted the Indianisation of all the higher services of the country liberally. In his

33 R.C. Dutt, *Speehes and Papers I.* pp. 147-148 Emphasis added.

34 R.C. Dutt; *Speeches and Papers* I. p. 143.

35 *Ibid;* p. 174.

Bombay farewell speech, he made the point without any qualification, when he said. "I am not only speaking of the great Civil Service of India, but of all the services—the education service, the medical service, the police service, the engineering service, the post and telegraph services. the jail and forest services-all the great services, of India. By a system of exclusion, unexampled in the history of any civilised country in ancient or modern times, we, the people of India, are virtually excluded from the higher ranks of these services, and all the higher appointments in the services, barring a very small percentage, are held by Europeans..."[36]

Though his contribution to the understanding of the nature of the economic policies of the British in India and his criticism of their political and administrative actions are universally known and fully recognised ; his interest in literary pursuits has not been fully appreciated outside Bengal. It was, in fact, 'literary fame', as he wrote to his brother, that was his 'first love' ; and it remained so throughout his life. Despite his busy schedule and preoccupation with administrative and political problems, he was always able to spare some time for the literary pursuits because he never regarded it, "a task but a recreation and a joy". In his farewell speech at Calcutta he admitted :

"That (literary) work has beguiled my saddest hours, solaced me in lonely hours and refreshed me in the midst of overwhelming work of a different nature...... In my long furloughs, and with the help of many pandits whose learned names graced the pages of my works, I placed before my countrymen in original and in translation, the substance of that vast body of sacred Hindu literature which is the noblest heritage of the Hindu nation. And I did not consider that task complete till I was able, after retirement from Service, to place before the modern world, in a condensed and readable

36 *Ibid;* p. 178.

form, the great epics of India. *This gentlemen, has been the recreation of my life; it has strengthened me and sustained me amidst multitudinous work, and I hope it will continue to help and sustain me in all my labours during the remaining days of my life.*"[37]

His 'Literature of Bengal' ; 'Bengali Translation of the Rig Vedas'; 'History of Civilization in Ancient India'; and 'the Translations of the Epics' are outstanding examples of his passion for literary pursuits and love for Indian culture and civilization. His papers on the two great epics-The Ramayana and the Mahabharata-read before the Royal Society of Literature, London, in 1899 and 1900 and his review of Max Muller's 'Six systems of Indian Philosophy' show his deep understanding and great admiration of Hindu religion and philosophy. He therefore, emphasized the need on the part of the Europeans to have a proper understanding of Indian philosophy and culture. He informed his European audience : "To know the two Indian epics is to understand the Indian people better. And to trace the influence of the Indian epics on the life and manners of the Hindu nation, and on the development of their modern languages, and religious reforms, is to comprehend the real history of the people during three thousand years. As mere literary works, the RAMAYANA and the MAHABHARATA are among the greatest and loftiest creations of the human imagination. And unless I am very much mistaken in my estimate, the two great epics of India, when they are better known in Europe, will take their rank along with the work of Homer, of Dante, and of Shakespeare, as undying works of art, composed for all times, all countries and for all mankind".[38]

Though R.C. Dutt started with the belief that the ills of the land revenue system, the frequent occurence of famines and the ultimate poverty of the Indian agriculture was the

37 *Ibid*; pp. 150-151. Emphasis added.

38 R.C. Dutt, *Speeches and Papers*, I; p. 241.

result of lack of proper understanding on the part of the British people, parliament, anc government, gradually he came to the conclusion that no reform could take place without an adequate participation of the Indians in the administration of the country. His critique of the British land revenue system, his refutation of the accepted official position on the question of Indian poverty, his attack on unnecessary expenditure on frontier wars and its burden on Indian exchequer, and most of all, his advocacy for a real share to the Indians in the administration of the country at all levels as well as Indianisation of all the services, were ideas which were against the established ideology, practices and interests of imperialism. These ideas, howsoever, mildly or aggresively R.C. Dutt might have put forward in his writings and speeches, cut at the very roots of British imperialism in India. This was definitely a great theoretical task which he performed in the late 19th and the early 20th century. The present collection of R.C Dutt's works on various Indian questions will give the readers a fairly good idea of his views on economic, political, administrative, and cultural problems confronting the Indian people during the early phase of their anti-imperialist struggle.

15, University Road, Delhi-7 *D.N.G.*

OPEN LETTERS TO LORD CURZON

FAMINES IN INDIA.

The Reports of the Indian Famine Commissions, published in 1880 and in 1898, tell a melancholy tale. Excluding severe scarcities, often confined to limited areas, there were eighteen famines between 1770 and 1878; and if we add to this list the subsequent famines of 1889, 1892, 1897, and 1900, we have a sad record of twenty-two famines within a period of 130 years of British rule in India.

I. *Bengal Famine of* 1770.—The first great famine in India which attracted the attention of the British nation to the state of things in India was the Bengal famine of 1770. Like all famines, it had its immediate cause in the failure of rains; but the intensity of the famine, and the great loss of life it caused were partly due to the maladministration of the East India Company, and the consequent impoverishment of the people. The Court of Directors deplored the corruption and rapacity of their servants, but were unable to check the evils, until the famine disclosed the state to which the country had been reduced. It was officially estimated by the Members of the Council, after they had made a circuit through the country to ascertain the effects of the famine, that about one-third of the population of Bengal, or over ten millions of people, had died of that famine. The terrible calamity aroused the attention of the British public to Indian administration, and the Regulating Act of 1773 was passed by Parliament to improve the administration.

II. *Madras Famine of* 1783.—There was a famine in Madras in 1783, mainly due to the wars of Warren Hastings with Mysore. The exact loss of life from this famine is not known.

III. *Famine in Northern India in* 1784.—There was a very wide-spread and intense famine in Northern India in 1784, directly due to failure of rains, but aggravated in some places by blunders and maladministration. Oudh was not then under British rule, but British officers had been sent to Oudh to command the Nawab's troops, and, following the mischievous practice of the times, they had farmed the revenues of the country for their private gain. Large numbers of the people were driven to rebellion and were put down with cruel severity. Captain Edwards visited Oudh in 1774 and 1783. In the former year he had found the country flourishing in manufacture, cultivation, and commerce; in the latter year he found it to a great extent forlorn and desolate. Warren Hastings himself witnessed the effects of this famine in Behar, and recorded that: "The distresses which were produced by the long-continued drought unavoidably tended to heighten the general discontent; yet I have reason to fear that the cause existed principally in a defective, if not a corrupt and oppressive, administration. I am sorry to add that from

Buxar to the opposite boundary I have seen nothing but traces of complete devastation in every village." When inquiries were made later in Benares, it was found that one-third of the lands in the State had gone out of cultivation by 1788. The exact loss of lives from the famine of 1784 in Northern India is not known. On the 13th of August 1784, Pitt's Bill for the Better Government of India was passed, and in the following year a nobleman of high reputation and character, Lord Cornwallis, was sent out as Governor-General of India.

IV. *Bombay and Madras Famine of* 1792.—There was famine in Bombay and Madras during Lord Cornwallis's administration, and it was in 1792 that relief works were first opened by the Madras Government for the support of the famine-stricken. The loss of life from this famine is unknown. Lord Cornwallis made a Permanent Settlement of the land revenues with the Zemindars or landlords of Bengal in 1793; and since that date there has been no famine in the permanently settled tracts of Bengal, causing serious loss of life.

V. *Bombay Famine of* 1803.—The wars of Lord Wellesley with the Mahrattas, which prevented much land being sown, and the ravages caused by the army of Holkar and the Pindarees, were the principal causes of this famine. Grain was imported by the Government into Bombay and sold at a fixed price to the public; exportation was prohibited; and public works and hospitals were started in the towns of Bombay and Surat for the relief of those who flocked to those towns. The number of deaths from this famine is not known.

VI. *Famine in Northern India in* 1804.—The wars of Lord Wellesley, the ravages caused by the army of Holkar, and also the early mistakes made by the East India Company's servants in land revenue administration, seem to have aggravated the effects of this wide-spread famine. A part of the dominions of the Nawab of Oudh had been ceded to the British Government in 1801, and blunders were made by the new rulers in the collection of the land revenues. Mr. Dumbleton, one of the early collectors of revenue, said in a letter to the Board of Revenue, that the Settlement of 1802 "pressed beyond a fair demand," and that the severe rates of the Nawab's Government were stereotyped, "*without* the same elasticity in realising."* The Government made large remission of revenue during the famine of 1804, gave loans and advances to landowners, and offered a bounty on grain exported into Benares, Allahabad, Cawnpur, and Fatehgarh.

VII. *Madras Famine of* 1807.—The early endeavours to assess lands in Madras were as unhappy as in Northern India, and when there was a wide-spread failure of rains in 1806, it was followed by a severe and desolating famine. Large crowds of emaciated people flocked into the town of Madras, attracted thither by the existence of a charitable association, and by the hope of obtaining gratuitous help without limit. The Government at the outset declared against any interference with private trade, but in the end they conceived

*Baden-Powell's "Land Systems of British India," vol. ii. p. 14.

it necessary to purchase grain, guaranteeing a minimum price to importers. The number of deaths from this famine is not known. It was during the early part of this famine that Sir Thomas Munro wrote in favour of employing labour, but against gratuitous relief. "The Natives of India are probably as charitable as those of any other country, and the poor may be left to their care. . . . I see no cause to apprehend a famine in the Ceded Districts. I cannot discover that such an event has ever happened in any former period, unless when war was added to an unfavourable season."

VIII. *Bombay Famine of* 1813.—Similar causes led to a similar calamity in Bombay six years later. The Government refused to prohibit export, or to import grain on this occasion, and recorded in a separate minute its adherence to the principles of Political Economy as expounded in Adam Smith's *Wealth of Nations.*

IX. *Madras Famine of* 1823.—A new system of land-settlements, ordered by the Home Government in 1812, was introduced first in Madras and then in Bombay. The system was one of settlements, not with landlors or Zemindars as in Bengal, but with individual cultivators or Ryots; but the fundamental principle, so far as the revenue was concerned, appears to have been the same as in Bengal,—the Government demand on the land was considered to be fixed for ever. There was a famine in Madras in 1823, and a severe scarcity in Bombay in the following year. Mr. Mountstuart Elphinstone, Governor of Bombay, declined after some discussion, to interfere with private trade; in Madras a bounty was offered on all grain imported to the distressed locality. The mortality is unknown.

X. *Madras Famine of* 1833.—The northern districts of the Province suffered most from this famine, specially the district of Gantur, in which the mortality was so terrible that this was known as the Gantur famine. The Government appears to have been taken by surprise, and the severity of the calamity was not recognised till too late. Very little was done to relieve distress, except by the distribution of gratuitous food in the towns to which the sufferers flocked. It was estimated that 200,000 persons died in Gantur out of a population of 500,000. Groups of people died in the streets of Madras, numbers perished in Masalipatam; in Nellore "the roads were strewn with dead bodies."

XI. *Famine in Northern India in* 1837.—The earlier mistakes in land administration were very slowly rectified in Northern India, and a regular settlement was begun in 1833. But the revenue demanded was still excessively heavy, being two-thirds of the rents received by landlords.

There was a failure of rains in 1837 and a famine ensued. "I have never in my life," wrote Mr. John (afterwards Lord) Lawrence, "seen such utter desolation as that which is now spread over the perganas of Hodal and Palwal." Deaths were numerous. In Cawnpur a special establishment patrolled the streets and the river to remove the corpses. The same thing was done in Fatehpur and Agra. In many places the dead lay on the roadside till wild animals devoured the corpses.

The view adopted by the Government was that the Government should offer employment to those who could work, but the relief of the helpless and infirm should be left to the charitable public. The mortality due to this famine was estimated long after by Colonel Baird Smith at about 800,000 ; but the Famine Commission considers this much under the mark

XII. *Madras Famine of* 1854.—A famine visited the northern part of the Madras Presidency and portions of Hyderabad in 1854. Relief was administered only by public works, and for over nine months over fifty thousaud people obtained relief on these works. The mortality from this famine is not known, but the census taken in 1856-57 showed that the growth of the population had received a serious check.

XIII. *Famine in Northern India in* 1860.—The mistake of demanding two-thirds of the rental as the Government revenue, which was committed in the Settlement of 1833-49, was rectified by the "Saharanpur Rules" of 1855, and the Government revenue was fixed at one-half the rental, which is the recognised rule in Northern India to the present day. This gave great relief to the landlords and cultivators alike; and when the East India Company was abolished in 1858, the administration of the Indian Empire came directly under the Crown. The wars of the Indian Mutiny, and the acts of retribution which followed, had, however, greatly interfered with cultivation, and when there was a failure of rains in 1860, it was followed by a famine. The principles of relief were the same as were adopted in 1837, viz, that the duty of the State was to provide employment for those who could work, and of the charitable public to support those who could not. Ten large relief works were opened, and minor works were opened to provide work for those who could not travel. Gratuitous relief at the expense of the charitable public was generally distributed in the shape of cooked food, and this excellent system was introduced at Moradabad by Mr. (now Sir John) Strachey, who was then collector of the district. 35,000 people were employed for ten months on relief works, and 80,000 people received gratuitous relief for nine months. The mortality was high, and Sir A. Cotton estimated it at 200,000 at least. After the famine was over, Colonel Baird Smith was deputed to examine into the causes of famines. He reported that the famine of 1860 was less severe than the famine of 1837 on account of the more lenient land assessments made by the Government, and he recommended a Permanent Settlement of the land revenues, such as had been made in 1793 in Bengal. Lord Canning, then Viceroy of India, strongly recommended such a Settlement; and the Secretary of State for India recorded a memorable Despatch describing the proposal as "a measure dictated by sound policy and calculated to accelerate the development of the resources of India, and to insure in the highest degree the welfare and contentment of all classes of Her Majesty's subjects in the country." If this proposal had been then carried into effect, India would have been spared those more dreadful and desolating famines which we have witnessed in later years. But the interests of the land revenue received greater consideration than the well-being of the people; and after a fruitless discussion of twenty-one years, the proposal of Lord Canning was rejected by the Secretary of State for India in 1883.

XIV. *Orissa Famine of* 1866.—There was a famine in some parts of Madras, and in spite of relief given to 12,000 people in relief works for fifteen months, and to 31,000 people gratuitously for sixteen months, the number of deaths increased by about 450,000. But this famine was most severely felt in Orissa, a part of the Province of Bengal where, generally speaking, no Permanent Settlement of the revenues had been made. The means of communication to Orissa were imperfect; the Government had with difficulty thrown in 10,000 tons of food grain by November 1866; but meanwhile the mortality among those whom this relief did not reach was severe; and it was estimated that one-third of the population of Orissa, or nearly a million persons had died. The inundations of the year caused further damage to the crops, and relief operations had to be resumed in the succeeding year.

XV. *Famine in Northern India in* 1869.—There was a famine in Rajputana in 1869 and cholera and locusts added to the sufferings of the people. The same famine also affected Northern India; 65,000 persons were employed on relief works in the N.W. Provinces for twelve months, and 18,000 persons received gratuitous relief daily. The mortality from the famine was estimated at 1,200,000.

XVI. *Bengal Famine of* 1874.—There was a famine in Behar in 1874; but Behar was permanently settled and therefore comparatively prosperous; and the wise and ample relief measures adopted by Lord Northbrook, then Viceroy of India, were completely successful. 735,000 persons were employed on relief works for nine months, and 450,000 persons received gratuitous relief for six months. The result of inquiries specially made was to indicate that no mortality whatever was due to the famine.

XVII. *Madras Famine of* 1877.—In fatal contrast to the Bengal famine of 1874, the Madras famine of 1877 was attended with serious loss of life. The Ryotwari Settlement of Madras, effected in the early years of the century, had been recognised to be permanent in principle. In 1856 the Government of Madras had declared in its Administration Report, that "the Ryot under this system is virtually a proprietor on a simple and perfect title, and has all the benefits of a perpetual lease." In 1857 the Board of Revenue had declared that "a Madras ryot is able to retain his land perpetually without any increase of assessment, so long as he continues to fulfil his engagements." And in 1862 the Government of Madras, in its letter, No. 241, of the 8th February, had stated that "there can be no question that one fundamental principle of the Ryotwari System is that the Government demand on the land is fixed for ever." Nevertheless, the assessments varied in practice; and the Settlement operations, introduced in

Madras after 1856, made the revenue liable to enhancement at recurring settlements. The serious question attracted the attention of Lord Northbrook when he was Viceroy of India; and during the administration of his successor, Lord Lytton, occurred the severest famine which has visited Madras within this century. Sir Richard Temple was sent as Famine Delegate of the Government of India in January 1877, and he unwisely reduced the wages in relief works to a scale which, in the opinion, of the Sanitary Commissioner, Dr. Cornish, provided less than subsistence for the labourer. Sir Richard Temple stated his reasons thus:—"This rate [two annas per diem] is fixed upon the supposition that it will purchase one and a half pounds of grain per diem, a quantity which is deemed essential for a man while at work.[1] There might indeed be a question whether life cannot be sustained with one pound of grain per diem, and whether Government is bound to do more than sustain life. This is a matter of opinion; and I myself think that one pound per diem might be sufficient to sustain life, and that the experiment ought to be tried." The unhappy experiment was tried and abandoned after three months; and it was also then decided that weakly persons, incapable of performing half the task work, should be supported at their homes. The intensity of the famine decreased when the rains commenced, and the numbers receiving relief fell from 2,218,000 in September, 1877 to 440,000 in December 1877. The loss of life from this terrible famine was estimated at over five millions.

Lord Lytton was succeeded as Viceroy of India by the Marquis of Ripon, and he tried to settle the vexed land question of Madras on an equitable basis. In his Despatch of the 17th October 1882, Lord Ripon laid down the principle that in districts which had been surveyed and settled by the Settlement Department, assessments should undergo no further revision except on the sole ground of a rise in prices. This decision gave the Madras cultivator some fixity of rent after the old right of a *perpetual* assessment had been ignored; it did away with the harassing reclassification of soils and recalculation of grain-returns at each recurring settlement; it left the door open to an increase of the Government revenue on the reasonable ground of an increase in prices; and it was a reasonable compromise which was accepted by the Madras Government itself. It is one of the saddest episodes in the history of Indian administration that this moderate measure, calculated to give some security of rent and tenure to the harassed and famine-stricken Indian cultivator, was rejected by the Secretary of State for India in his Despatch of the 8th January 1885. The Madras cultivator has been deprived of that *perpetual* assessment which he was declared to enjoy in the first half of the century; and he has not obtained that *security of rental* which Lord Ripon and the Madras Government agreed to bestow on him. The interests of the land revenue once again received greater consideration than the well-being of the people.

XVIII. *Famine in Northern India in* 1878.—

There was a famine in Northern India in 1878. The average daily number on relief works for twelve months was 557,000, and in poor houses, 13,750. The relief works were placed under the Public Works Department with little control from the local civil officers, and the result was disastrous. The excess mortality from this famine was 1,250,000.

XIX. *Madras Famine of* 1889.—There was a famine in the Ganjam District of Madras and in parts of Orissa in 1889. Relief works were started in Ganjam, but gratuitous relief to the infirm and the weak was unfortunately delayed with fatal results. When Lord Connemara, the Governor of Madras, visited Ganjam in June 1889, 18,000 people were employed on relief works, and 2300 people had been admitted to gratuitous relief. Lord Connemar recorded that "a large amount of distress, amounting to starvation, existed, and that the most urgent orders and the most prompt action were required if many lives were not to be lost by the most lingering and dreadful of deaths." The number on village relief rose to 93,000 in the first week of August, and 11,000 persons were also daily fed in the kitchens in that month. The mortality in Ganjam during the famine year (Oct. 1888 to Sept. 1889) was high. In Orissa the distress was less, the number on relief did not exceed 3600 in September 1889, but deaths from the combined effects of famine, cholera, and other diseases generally brought on by privation, were numerous.

XX. *Famine in Madras, Bengal, Burma, and*

Ajmer in 1892.—There was a wide-spread famine in 1892, affecting portions of India as remote from each other as Madras, Burma, and Ajmer. The average number relieved in Madras in June 1892 rose to over 87,000 ; in Behar to 47,000, and in Ajmer-Merwara to 34,000. In Burma the number in February was 30,000. In Madras the death-rate was higher than usual ; in Bengal "there were no deaths from starvation."

XXI. *Famine in Northern India, Bengal, Burma, Madras, and Bombay in* 1897.—A more wide-spread and intense famine than had ever before visited India appeared in 1896-97. The number of persons relieved in the different Provinces, when the famine was most acute, are shown in the following table.

N.W. Provinces & Oudh	May 1897	1,062,000
Bengal	June 1897	820,000
Central Provinces	May 1897	567,000
Madras	July 1897	215,000
Bombay	April 1897	478,000
Punjab	February 1897	50,000

The largest number relieved in the months of the acutest distress may therefore be taken at 3,000,000. In the N.W. Provinces and Oudh the famine relief operations were "a conspicuous success." In Bengal the operations were "eminently successful." In the Central Provinces the local authorities "failed to grasp the situation," the operations were inadequate, and the death-rate in the eighteen districts of the Province rose from an average of thirty-three to an average of sixty-nine per thousand in 1897. In Madras the operations were "as a whole adequate and successful" though there was some increase in the death-rate in the affected districts. In Bombay "as a whole the measure of success attained was very great," although there was an increase in the death-rate. In the Punjab, the measures adopted were eminently successful.

Towards the conclusion of their report the Famine Commissioners record the following significant remarks about the labouring classes of India. "This section is very large and includes the great class of day-labourers and the least skilled of the artisans. So far as we have been able to form a general opinion upon a difficult question from the evidence we have heard and the statistics placed before us, the wages of these people have not risen in the last twenty years in due proportion to the rise in prices of their necessaries of life. The experience of the recent famine fails to suggest that this section of the community has shown any larger command of resources or any increased power of resistance. Far from contracting, it seems to be widening, particularly in the more congested districts. Its sensitiveness or liability to succumb, instead of diminishing, is possibly becoming more accentuated."

XXII. *Famine in the Punjab, Rajputana, Central Provinces and Bombay in* 1900.—Of the famine from which India is suffering in the present year it is not possible to give any final figures, either to show the numbers relieved, or to indicate the mortality. In the present month (June 1900) nearly six millions of people are on relief works, and in spite of every effort on the part of relief officers, mortality is high in Gujrat and elsewhere. It is a sad but a significant fact that the last famine of this century is also the most wide-spread and the severest famine that has ever visited India.

One cannot read without a feeling of sadness and of humilation this melancholy record of famines in India under British rule. There were reasons for famines in the last century and in the early years of this century. When an old system of government breaks down, and the country passes under a new power, wars and disorders are inevitable. When the Moghal power broke down in India, and Mahrattas and Afghans contended for supremacy, war and devastation followed. And when the British nation entered into the arena, they too took their part in many wars which impeded culivation and harassed the population of peaceful villages. In the words of Sir Thomas Munro, wars were added to unfavourable seasons to bring on recurring famines in India. We may also add to these reasons the misrule of the servants of the East India Company, and the unhappy blunders which were perhaps inevitable, when a new race of rulers found themselves suddenly called upon to administer the land revenues of a strange and newly conquered country.

But these causes have longed ceased to operate. In 1858, the administration of the country passed from the East India Company to the crown, and since then India has enjoyed profound peace, undisturbed by a single war within her natural frontiers. The land is fertile; the people are peaceful, industrious and frugal; and generations of British administrators have been trained in the duties of Indian administration. And yet famines have not disappeared. Within the last forty years, within the memory of the present writer, there have been ten famines in India, and at a moderate computation, the loss of lives from starvation and from diseases brought on by these famines may be estimated at twenty millions within these forty years. It is a melancholy phenomenon which is not presented in the present day by any other country on earth enjoying a civilised administration.

An explanation is sometimes sought for this phenomenon in the supposed improvidence of the people, in the rapacity of the money-lender, or in the increase of population. A close examination of facts, however, shows the unsoundness of such explanations. The increase of population in India is slow, slower than in England and Wales, slower than in eighteen other countries out of twenty-eight for which figures are available. The peasantry of India are not improvident, they are the most frugal and the most provident of all races of peasantry on earth. And the money-lender is the result, not the cause, of the poverty of the cultivators. In portions of India where cultivators are well off, the money-lender has little influence; where the peasantry are in perpetual poverty, the money-lender saves them in times of difficulty but gets a good grip over their land and property.

If we honestly seek for the true causes of recent

famines in India, we shall not seek in vain. The immediate cause of famines in almost every instance is the failure of rains, and this cause will continue to operate until we have a more extensive system of irrigation than has yet been provided. But the intensity and the frequency of recent famines are greatly due to the resourceless condition and the chronic poverty of the cultivators, caused by the over-assessment of the soil on which they depend for their living.

We have no wars within the natural frontiers of India now, but peace has not brought with it a reduction in the public expenditure or in the public debt. India maintains the most expensive foreign government on earth, and one-third of the revenues of India is sent out of India every year, instead of being spent in the conntry to fructify her industries and trades. Land revenue is the most important item of the Indian revenues, and so it happens that the taxation falls heavily on the cultivators of the soil, and reduces them to a condition of chronic poverty. They can save nothing in years of good harvest, and consequently every year of drought is a year of famine.

It is necessary, for a clear understanding of the subject, to consider the different Provinces of India separately. In BENGAL and in NORTHERN INDIA the cultivators generally pay rents to private landlords, and wise laws have been made to restrict the demands of landlords, though a further extension of these laws may be still necessary. The State-demand from the landlords, too, has been restricted—in Bengal by the Parmanent Settlement of 1793, and in Northern India by the Saharanpur Rules of 1855—and the land revenue realised is between five and ten per cent. of the value of the gross produce of the soil. But in BOMBAY and in MADRAS the State generally collects the land revenue direct from the cultivators; and has not provided adequate protection against over-assessment; and the land revenue realised is often as high as twenty or thirty percent of the actual gross produce. In the CENTRAL PROVINCES, the cultivators pay rents to private landlords, but the rents so payable are fixed by the State, and the proportion of the rent demanded as Government revenue is also fixed by the State. In recent settlements the Government revenue has been raised to an oppressive degree.

Such, briefly, are the land administration arrangements in the five different portions of the Indian Empire, and if we examine somewhat closely the death-rates of the famines which have occurred in India within this generation, *i.e.*, within the last twenty-five or thirty years, we shall find that deaths have generally been most numerous, and famines have been most intense and fatal, in those places where the cultivators are least protected against over-assessment. In 1874 there was a famine in Bengal which caused no loss of life; in 1877 there was a famine in Madras, and over five millions of the population perished. In 1892 there was a general famine in many parts of India; there was loss of life in Madras, but in Bengal "there were no deaths from starvation." In

1897 there was also a general famine ; in Bengal and Northern India the relief operations were successful in preventing loss of lives ; in the Central Provinces the deaths were more than double the normal rate. And in the present famine the distress is most severe, and the deaths most numerous, in Bombay and the Central Provinces.

There is no people on earth animated by a more loyal and sincere desire to contribute to the resources of the Government according to their power than the people of India. They desire that the revenues of the Government should increase with the increasing prosperty of the people. But they also demand that the revenues of the Government be not increased by over-assessing the soil and impoverishing the people. Any endeavour to increase the revenues of India by over-assessment of the soil is both unjust and unwise—unjust because the soil in India is now virtually the only means of the nation's subsistence, and unwise because the revenues of India and the trade with India will not increase in the long run if the people are impoverished.

FIRST LETTER TO LORD CURZON.

THE CENTRAL PROVINCES.

My Lord,—I had the honour, in course of the interview which Your Excellencey granted me, to place certain facts and figures relating to settlements in the Centrtal Provinces before Your Lordship. I take the liberty of noting those facts somewhat more fully and clearly in this letter, and hope they will receive such consideration from Your Lordship as they may seem to deserve.

2. The first regular Settlement of the land, after the Provinces came under British administration, was effected after 1860. Moved by sincere desire to improve the condition of the people of the newly-conquered Provinces, Lord Canning's Government expressed itself, in letter No. 2279, dated 28th June 1860, in favour of long leases and light assessment. And para 24 of the Settlement Code modified the old rule of demanding sixty-six per cent. of the landlord's assets, and fixed fifty per cent. of the assets as the proper and equitable Government revenue.

3. Unfortunately the intentions of the Government were not carried into effect in the Settlement which followed. Two mistakes were made. In the first place the rents payble by cultivators to landlords (Malguzars, were fixed too high; and in the second place the

revenue payable by Malguzars to the Government was fixed too high.

4. Under the old Hindu Law, one-sixth the gross produce of the soil was recognised as proper and equitable rent, and for thousands of years the cultivators of India have paid at this rate. Some Hindu or Mahomedan sovereigns occasionally demanded a higher rate of rent, but in the olden days there were various ways of evading such demands, and it may be safely asserted that no higher rent than one-sixth the gross produce was ever actually realised in any province of India. At the present time the Zemindars of Bengal make their own arrangements with the cultivators, and in no District is the general average of rent higher than *one-sixth the gross produce*, while in many Districts it is considerably less. In the North-Western Provinces also, where the Zemindars are now allowed to make their own arrangements with the cultivators, the rate of rent is about *one-fifth the gross produce*. (*vide* Sir Antony Macdonnell's evidence before the Currency Committee,—answers 5737 to 5740).

5. The principle, however, which was adopted in the Settlement of the Central Provinces after 1860 was that *one-half the net produce of the soil* should be paid by cultivators as rent to landlords. The net produce was ascertained by deducting from the gross produce the supposed cost of cultivation. Calculations about the actual cost of cultivation can never be accurately made, and the errors committed by Settlement Officers were not always in favour of cultivators. The result

was that about one-third of the gross produce was deducted as the cost of cultivation, and one-half of the remainder was fixed as the rent payable by cultivators to landlords. Virtually, therefore, the rent fixed was about at *one-third the gross produce*,—a rate which is unexampled in Bengal or Northern India, and which is double the rate prescribed by the old Hindu Law. *

6. The second mistake which was made was to demand an unduly large share of the Malguzar's assets as Government revenue. The principle that one-half of the Malguzar's assets should be demanded as revenue was repeatedly laid down and insisted upon in the orders of the Government of India, and I have failed to discover under what authority this principle was departed from in practice. As a matter of fact, however, the revenue demanded was sometimes seventy-five per cent. of the Malguzar's assets, a rate which is unexampled in Northern India at the present day, and

* Exception has been taken to these statements. It has been urged by Sir Andrew Fraser that Settlement Officers did not fix the rental in the settlement of 1863, "the matter being arranged by agreement between landlord and tenant"; and secondly that "the rents were not one third of the gross produce." (Note forming an enclosure to Lord Curzon's Land Resolution of 16th January 1902.) On the first point, I may point out, that Sir Andrew Fraser's statement is contradicted by Sir Alexander Mackenzie's Report No. 501 S. dated the 18th May 1887, where it is asserted that at the settlement of 1863 "the rental value of each Mahal was in fact determined by the comparison of a number of statistical references" and that "rents rose in the proceedings taken for rent adjustment after the assessment was given out." On the second point I may point out that there are official records like Mr. Russell's Jubbulpur settlement Report, 1867, shewing that the rent fixed was assumed to be one-third the gross produce. I hope this assumption was wrong, and that so large a proportion of the produce was nowhere taken as rent.

which would be ruinous to the landlords of any poor and agricultural country. A double injustice was thus perpetrated in the first Settlement of the Central Provinces; the rents payable by cultivators to Malguzars were fixed too high; and the revenue payable by Malguzars to the Government was fixed too high.

7. One redeeming feature of the Settlement, however, was that it was made for a long period of thirty years. New lands were brought under cultivation within this period, and as the Government revenue remained fixed, the severity of the Settlement was felt less and less with the lapse of time. The period of Settlement at last expired, and the time came for a new Settlement.

8. It might be expected that the mistakes made in the first Settlement would now be avoided after the experience of thirty years, and that the peasantry of the Central Provinces would receive the same considerate treatment as the peasantry of Northern India. As a matter of fact, however, the Settlement which has been effected in the Central Provinces since 1890 has been felt as more harsh and severe, and has caused more actual suffering and distress, than any previous Settlement in any part of India. The facts that I state have been obtained after careful inquiry from the best sources of information available to me, but Your Excellency's Government will be able to correct me if I am wrong in any particular. My information is, that the rents now fixed can with difficulty be paid even in years of good harvest, that they leave no fair margin

for saving for bad years, and that they can never be realised by Malguzars from year to year. Large tracts of the country, which were previously under cultivation, have gone out of cultivation owing to over-assessment, and instances have occurred in which Malguzars have applied to surrender their estates in order to be relieved of their liability to pay a Government revenue which they cannot pay, and their application has not been granted. The condition of the peasantry and the landlords alike, after this new Settlement, contrasts unfavourably with the condition of the same classes in Northern India; and as the period of Settlement too has been unwisely reduced, there is no prospect, either in the immediate or in the remote future, of an improvement in the condition of the people from a state of hopeless penury and indebtedness.

9. Rents have been enhanced at this last Settlement after very complicated calculations which need not be described in detail in this letter. Briefly speaking, lands were first classified after "crop experiments" and "local inquiry," and the incidence of the old rental for each "soil unit" was ascertained by a process of calculation illustrated in the footnote.* After this *the Settle-*

* A village has 600 acres of first class lands
and 400 acres of second class lands.
Rate of first class soil to second class is 20 to 12.
The old rental of the village is Rs. 1000.
Acres 600 × 20 = 12,000
400 × 12 = 4,800

Total, 16,800 soil units.
Incidence of old rental
per soil unit Rs. $\frac{1000}{16,800}$ = ·95 or nearly one anna.

ment Officer decided on "general considerations" what enhancement he would impose on the village, and having done this, he calculated at what rate it fell per soil unit. The standard unit enhancement rate was then applied to the holding of each cultivator according to the "soil units" comprised in his holding.

10. These complicated calculations were unintelligible to the cultivator, and were moreover made in the dark. What the cultivator did understand was that a general enhancement had been effected over the high rental of the old Settlement; and there was alarm and consternation in the country when the new enhanced rents were proclaimed. I repeat, my Lord, that these rents if enforced will leave the peasantry of the Central Provinces in a permanent state of indebtedness and destitution.

11. The revenue demanded from Malguzars was fixed equally high. Departing from the old rule of demanding fifty per cent. of the landlord's assets as revenue,—a rule which is in force in Northern India,—the authorities of the Central Provinces asked the sanction of the Indian Government to demand fifty to sixty-five per cent. of the Malguzar's assets as revenue. The Government of India in its letter No. 397, dated 31st May 1888, had "some hesitation in allowing in any case so high a percentage as sixty-five to be taken," but nevertheless did grant the permission in some cases, and made sixty per cent. the maximum rate in other cases. If we add to these high rates another twelve and a half per cent. which has been added as rates, it will be easy to see that between seventy and eighty per cent. of the landlord's

supposed assets, *i.e.* nearly one hundred per cent. of his *real* assets, are now demanded by the Government as revenue.*

12. My Lord, the question to which I have ventured to invite Your Lordship's attention is one of life and death to the Indian cultivator in the Central Provinces. The question is not a complicated one but a very simple one. If after the experience of nearly a century of administration it has been found in Northern India that the wisest, safest, and most considerate policy is to let landlords make their own arrangements with cultivators as regards rents, subject to salutary checks imposed by the Government, is it a wise policy in the Central Provinces for the Government to fix after calculations, which are unintelligible alike to landlord and tenant, what rent each cultivator should pay for his holding? If private landlords in Northern India consider one-fifth of the gross produce a fair rent for the lands held by their tenants, is it considerate of the British Government to impose on the poorer peasantry of the Central Provinces a rental of one-third or more of the gross produce? And if the Government of the North

* This requires correction. I have been informed since I wrote the Letter that though sanction was obtained for raising the revenue to 65 per cent. of the rental, nevertheless in practice it was nowhere assessed at above 60 per cent. And the rates were 12½ per cent. on the revenue, and therefore came to between 6 and 7 per cent. on the rental. Making allowance for all this, a total assessment of 67 per cent. on the *supposed* rental leaves little to the landlord out of his *actual* collection; and such an assessment violates the spirit of the Saharanpur Rules laying down half the rental as the Government revenue.

Western Provinces consider forty per cent. of the landlord's assets as fair Government revenue (*vide* Sir A. P. Macdonnell's evidence before the Currency Committee),* will Your Excellency's Government sanction and approve of a State-demand of sixty or sixty five per cent. in the Central Provinces, *plus* twelve and a half per cent. as rates? These are smiple questions which will demand from your Lordship an early consideration, because they affect the well-being of more than ten millions of Her Majesty's Indian subjects, who have suffered most acutely during the famines of 1897 and of the present year, and who are at present the most helpless and resourceless class of peasantry in all India. The main reason of their wretchedness is manifest from the facts stated above. There is not a cultivator in India who does not understand and recognise *three annas in the rupee* out of the gross produce of his holding as a fair and equitable rent,† leaving a fair margin of saving. And there is not a cultivator in India who does not feel *five or six annas in the rupee* of the gross produce as an oppressive and

* Exception has been taken to this statement. Sir Antony Macdonnell has pointed out that though the Government in the N.W. Provinces takes about forty per cent. of the rental, its proper theoretical share is fifty per cent. I accept this correction, but it does not affect my argument, as I have recommended that fifty per cent. of the rental be fixed as the Government demand in the Central Provinces and elsewhere.

† More correctly speaking *three annas in the rupee* should be the *maximum rent*, as was proposed in the Bengal Government Resolution, dated August, 6, 1883. See my views on this point more fully and clearly explained in para 18 (b) of my Fifth Letter.

exhausting rent, impoverishing him in good years, and sending him to relief works in bad years.

13. My Lord, Your Excellency's administration has been marked by a famine which exceeds in its intensity any previous famine known in India. I trust and hope that Your Excellency's administration will also be marked by one of those great remedial measures which permanently ameliorate the condition of the people, and which the grateful population of India cherish and remember from generation to generation. The impoverishment of an Indian Province under British administration is a more serious calamity than any defeat or disaster which has been known in the history of British rule in India; and if Your Lordship be convinced after inquiry that the impoverishment of the people of the Central Provinces is due to any extent to the exhausting rental fixed in those Provinces, as compared with Northern India, I feel convinced, Your Excellency will not lay down the reins of administration in India without removing the cause of their permanent wretchedness, and enabling them to improve their own condition, as the peasantry of Bengal and of Northern India, have been enabled to do.

14. The close of the present famine operations in the Central Provinces may appear to Your Lordship an appropriate time to institute an inquiry, not merely into systems and rules of relief works, but into the general condition of the people, and the incidence of the land revenue and rents, as compared with Northern India. Such an inquiry may elicit facts which are

not now clearly known, and may be fruitful of some suggestions for permanently improving the condition of the agricultural population, an object which Your Lordship is endeavouring to secure by every possible means. No one can be better fitted to superintend, help, and direct such an inquiry than the present Chief Commissioner of the Central Provinces, Mr Fraser, who has already won the esteem of the people by his sympathy and his real desire to secure their interests. The people of the Central Provinces will have confidence in him, and in any other officers whom Your Excellency may entrust with the task. And should Your Excellency consider me fit to represent the views and wishes of my countrymen on the Commission which may be appointed to conduct the enquiry, I shall be prepared, on receipt of Your Excellency's commands, to return to India, to join the work at any time that may be fixed for the inquiry. And I shall ask for no remuneration for my humble services in the conduct of an inquiry needed for the well-being of millions of my countrymen.

12th February 1900.

SECOND LETTER TO LORD CURZON.
MADRAS.

My Lord,—In continuation of my letter of the 12th February I have the honour to submit to Your Excellency this brief note on Land Settlements in the Madras Presidency. The subject has repeatedly come under the consideration of Your Lordship's predecessors, and will probably receive Your Lordship's attention.

2. Madras was one of the first Provinces in India which came under British administration, and while some estates were permanently settled with landlords, in the rest of the Province a *Ryotwari* Settlement was made directly with the cultivators. Sir Thomas Munro, the virtual author of this system, explained the principle of the Settlement in his evidence before a Select Committee of the House of Commons on the 15th April 1812. And his idea was to regard each cultivator as the propietor of his holding, and to make a perpetual Settlement with the cultivators, as a permanent Settlement had been made with Zemindars in Bengal in 1793 by Lord Cornwallis.

3. This was the principle recognised by the Government of Madras for over forty years after the time of Sir Thomas Munro. As late as 1855-56, the Ryotwari system was thus explained in the Madras Administra-

tion Report:—"Under the Ryotwari system every registered holder of land is recognised as its proprietor and pays direct to Government. He is at liberty to sublet his property or to transfer it by gift, sale, or mortgage. He cannot be ejected by Government so long as he pays fixed assessment. . . . The ryot under this system is virtually a proprietor on a simple and perfect title, and has all the benefits of *a perpetual lease*." And in 1857 the Madras Board of Revenue thus described the Ryotwari tenure in a report to Government on the Survey and Settlement then proposed to be introduced:—"A general opinion prevails in England than the Bombay Settlement for thirty years secures a far greater permanency of tenure to the land holder than the present Ryotwari tenure of Madras. This is altogether an error, for a Madras ryot is able to retain his land *perpetually without any increase of assessment*, as long as he continues to fulfil his engagements." The Italics are my own.

4. My Lord, the *first* point to which I desire to invite Your Excellency's attention is that this right of the Madras cultivator to a fixed, perpetual, and unalterable assessment, recognised by the British Government during half a century, has been virtually confiscated by the British Government within the last forty years. This will appear perfectly clear from the following extract from para 4 of the Madras Board of Revenue's Standing Order I., as amended on the 1st July 1895 under orders from the Madras Government. "At each Settlement or resettlement of a District, Government will fix at its

discretion the period for which such Settlement or re-settlement shall be in force. The Collector shall then notify the period in the District Gazette, and explain to the ryots that the new rates will not be liable to alteration during the currency of the settlement period; but that on the expiry of the said period, Government reserves to itself the right to revise the assessment in such manner as may then seem just and proper, either with reference solely to a rise or fall in prices, or with reference also to other considerations such as would require a re-classification of soils or a re-calculation of the grain outturns." I beg, my Lord, to point out that while in 1857, the Madras Board of Revenue recognised the right of the cultivator "*to retain his land in perpetuity without any increase of assessment*," in 1895, the Madras Board of Revenue claimed for the Government the right "*revise the assessment*" at each recurring settlement, and to enhance rents on various grounds.

5. I cannot believe that the British Government deliberately desired on this or on any other occasion to violate a right which it had deliberately affirmed and recognised before. I am inclined to believe that in the Settlement and Survey operations which were introduced after 1857, the real position of the Madras cultivator was lost sight of, and rules were introduced to secure an increase of the land revenue without an adequate consideration of the rights of the cultivator. So far as the Madras cultivators are concerned, there can be little doubt that the rights previously assured to

them have in effect been withdrawn, and the pledges previously given to them have in effect been violated. And at the present time the Madras cultivator, instead of holding "his land in perpetuity without any increase of assessment," is subject to enhancemant at each recurring settlement, and has been reduced to a state of poverty and indebtedness which makes him an easy prey to famines in years of bad harvests.

6. This grave and important matter attracted the attention of Your Excellency's predecessors. Lord Mayo was of opinion that when the quality of soil and the quantity of produce were once determined, there should be no further alterations in the assessments except on the ground of fluctuations in prices. Lord Northbrook was also in favour of a self-regulating system of assessments, and was against the system of repeating valuations at each fresh settlement. The great famine of 1877 occured under Lord Lytton's administration, and is estimated to have carried off five millions of the impoverished population of the Madras Presidency. This calamity hastened a solution of the problem, and Lord Ripon, who succeeded Lord Lytton, proceeded on the lines laid down by his predecessors. In his despatch of the 17th October 1882, Lord Ripon laid down the principle that in districts which had once been surveyed and assessed by the Settlement Department, assessments should undergo no further revision except on the sole ground of a rise in prices. This decision was accepted by the Madras Government in 1883. And while it restored to the cultivators something of

their old right to a perpetual assessment, it conferred on the Government the right to increase the revenue on the reasonable ground of an increase in prices. It was the best compromise which could be effected after the old right had been sacrificed; it gave the cultivator some security of assessment without which agriculture cannot flourish in any part of the world; and it did away with those harassing operations, leading to re-classification of soils and recalculation of grain outturns, which are felt as the most oppressive features of settlement operations in Madras.

7. Unfortunately, after the departure of Lord Ripon from India, his proposal was vetoed by the Secretary of State for India in his despatch of the 8th January 1885. The lessons of the Madras famine of 1877 were to some extent forgotten, the impoverished condition of the peasantry was overlooked, and the proposal to which both the Madras Government and the India Government had agreed, for giving some security of assessments to the Madras cultivators, was disapproved by the authorities in London. For the people of Madras, the despatch of the 8th January 1885 is one of the saddest documents ever issued from London; it reopened the question which had been wisely solved after years of mature deliberation in India; and it has thrown back the Madras cultivators into another era of uncertainty, needless harassment, and unjust enhancements. I venture to hope that this grave question will receive Your Excellency's attention, and that Your Excellency will receive the sanction of the ecretary of State for India to the solution which Lord

Ripon, agreeing generally with the views of Lord Mayo and Lord Northbrook, proposed in his despatch of the 17th October 1882.

8. The *second* point to which I solicit Your Lordship's attention is the manner in which assessments are now revised at each recurring settlement in Madras. The principle accepted is that *one-half of the net produce of the soil* is due to the Government as revenue, and this net produce is ascertained by deducting from the gross produce the estimated cost of cultivation. The calculations are made by Settlement Officers, and are not always in favour of cultivators, and mistakes which are inevitable in such calculations are fatal to successful agriculture. For good lands in Tanjore District the estimated annual cost of cultivating an acre of land is fixed at Rs. 14, as shown in the footnote.* Many of the figures given in the list are very inadequate; and no allowance is made for the feeding and housing of bullocks, or for thrashing and storing the rice, or for conveying it to markets. But what I wish to specially point out is that while Rs. 14

	Rs.	As.	P.
*Value of bullocks	1	5	6
Agricultural implements	1	7	6
Seeds	2	3	0
Coolies for ploughing	1	10	3
Cost of manuring	2	12	0
Coolies for transplanting	1	4	0
Weeding	0	11	0
Watering and watching	0	7	6
Clearing silt from canal	0	3	0
Reaping and stacking	1	6	0
Lowering levels of fields	0	10	3
	Rs. 14	0	0

is fixed as the estimated cost of cultivating an acre of good land, Rs. 6 is all that is allowed for cultivating an acre of ordinary arenaceous sandy soil. Your Excellency is aware that the cost of cultivating poor soil is not always less than the cost of cultivating good soil in proportion to the produce; and every cultivator in India knows that Rs. 6 an acre, corresponding to Rs. 2 the *Bigah* of Bengal measurement, does not cover the cost of cultivation of any kind of cultivable soil in India. The Madras authorities must themselves be aware of this fact. Mr. Meyer says "the tendency to make the cultivation expenses roughly proportionate to the value of the land is one of the weak points of the Settlement Department." Dr. Macleane says in p. 109 of the Manual of the Administration of Madras: "The cost of cattle, implements, seed, the wages of parmanent servants, and the cost of transplanting are taken as constant, whatever the soil." Mr. Master writes in his report on the Western Delta, para 79:—"I cannot ascertain that the outlay on the poorer soil is much smaller than on the richer; indeed, some stoutly maintain that it is larger." And Mr. Bowden, himself a landholder of considerable experience, wrote in his letter of the 5th December 1895 to the Collector of his District:—"The idea that the cost of cultivating an acre of poor land is less than the cost of cultivating a better class of land is purely mythical. So far from this being the case, the poorest land often demands the greatest outlay. Ryots know this well to their cost." Nevertheless, My Lord, the Settlement Department endeavours "to make the cultivation expenses roughly proportionate to the value of the land," and this renders the estimate of the "net produce" of the soil wholly unfair and untrustworthy. Assessments made on such calculations are ruinous to the cultivation of the poorer class of lands, and it has been pointed out by Mr. A. Rogers, one of the greatest authorities on revenue settlements that the Indian Civil Service has produced, that over three millions of acres of cultivable lands are out of cultivation in Madras.

9. Another rule which regulates the assessments made in Madras is that the rent or revenue fixed by such calculations *should not exceed one-third of the gross produce of the soil* where the land is not irrigated at Government cost. I have had occasion to point out in another place that this proportion is excessive, and will necessarily impoverish the peasantry of any part of India. In Bengal, the cultivators do not pay more than *one-sixth* the gross produce to their landlords in a District, if the District average be taken. And in Northern India, according to Sir A. Macdonnell's evidence before the Currency Committee, the cultivators pay about *one-fifth* of the gross produce of the soil to their landlords. I hold it, my Lord, that where the British Government stands virtually as landlords, the Government should be less exacting, and not more exacting, than private landlords in India. And I also hold it, that cultivators living directly under the British Government should be treated more leniently, and not less leniently, than cultivators living under private land-

lords. I feel confident that these views will commend themselves to Your Lordship, and that Your Lordship will condemn both the rule of levying *one-half the net produce* as revenue, and the rule of making that revenue approximate *one-third the gross produce.** There is not a cultivator in India who does not recognise 3 annas in the rupee of gross produce as fair rent. And there is not a cultivator in India who does not consider 5 or 6 annas out of each rupee of gross produce to be an oppressive and impoverishing rate of rent.

10. The *third* and last point to which I beg to invite Your Excellency's attention is the Bill recently introduced in the Madras Legislative Council to enable the Government to levy a compulsory water-rate on all lands within the wet cultivation area, without allowing the cultivators the option to take or to refuse water. The reason assigned in the Statement of Objects and Reasons is that, "where a field is in the midst of wet cultivation, any attempt to exclude the water is frustrated by percolation." Tested by the experience gained in other parts of India, the reason is insufficient.

* It is necessary to explain clearly that the rule of levying *one-half the net produce* is not objectionable, if by net produce is meant the real economic rent. It becomes objectionable when the half net produce is so calculated as to make it approximate to *one-third the gross produce*. The Madras Board of Revenue urge in their Report, which forms an enclosure to Lord Curzon's Resolution dated January 16, 1902, that there has been no rule in existence, since 1856 and 1864, limiting the revenue to one-third the gross produce. But the rule *does* appear in the Standing Information for the Madras Presidency published in 1879. The Madras Government explain that it appeared there by a "misapprehension of the compiler." Was this ever pointed out to Settlement Officers? It is a general complaint throughout the Province that the revenue assessed not unfrequently approximates to one-third the gross produce of the soil.

There are large tracts of country in Behar, in Burdwan, and in Orissa, which are within the irrigation area, but no cultivator is compulsorily assessed on the ground that attempts to exclude the water from his field are frustrated by percolation. A private cultivator who digs a well or a tank to irrigate his field cannot recover a part of the cost from his neighbour even if he proves that his neighbour's field has been benefited by percolation; and the Government should not, by legislation, assume a power which would be considered unjust and wrong in a private individual.

11. A compulsory water-rate has been repeatedly condemned by the highest authorities. In 1870, the Duke of Argyll, then Secretary of State for India, refused his sanction to the Northern India Canal and Drainage Bill because His Grace held that, "to force irrigation on the people would be not unlikely to make that unpopular which could otherwise scarcely fail to be regarded as a blessing." Another proposal made in 1879 in connection with the Bombay Irrigation Act, that all lands commanded by the water of the canals should be taxed, was also thrown out by the Secretary of State for India. There is far less reason for a compulsory rate in Madras than in Northern India, because it was shown in a Memorandum prepared in 1889, and presented to both Houses of Parliament, that while canals paid only four per cent. on their cost in the Punjab and the N. W. Provinces, the irrigation works in Madras paid more than fifteen per cent. on their cost.

It is not stated in the Statement of Objects and Reasons that the revenue has declined in recent years.

12. The High Court of Madras has held that, under the present law, a cultivator cannot be taxed unless he applied for the water. It is proposed in the Bill, not only to alter the law and to make the water-rate compulsory within wet cultivation areas, but also to bar the jurisdiction of the High Court and all Civil Courts in cases relating to assessments of water-rate made by the Collector. My Lord, the people of India have the greatest veneration and faith in the High Courts of Justice, and to bar the jurisdiction of High Courts in the matter of water-rate assessments would create the impression that the Government seeks to uphold an act of wrong-doing by stopping all appeals to Courts of Justice. It is neither fair nor wise that such an impression should be created in India, and it is not necessary that the British Government should shrink, in any particular class of cases, from that appeal to justice which is allowed in all other classes of cases.

13. The suggestions, therefore, which I have the honour to submit to Your Excellency with regard to Madras are these. That your Excellency will find it possible to confer on the Madras peasantry that qualified permanency of assessments which was comtemplated by Lord Mayo and Lord Northbrook, and was proposed by Lord Ripon in 1882 with the concurrence of the Madras Government. That in revising assessments, one-fifth of the gross produce, and not one-half of the net produce, be accepted as the maximum of

revenue.* And that the water-rate within the wet cultivation area be not made compulsory in Madras, as it has never been proposed to make it compulsory in Bengal.

10. I trust and hope that Your Excellency's administration will be marked by these remedial measures for improving the condition of the Madras cultivators. There never has been a time within my recollection, which goes back to the closing years of the East India Company's rule in India, when the people of India suffered so intensely from two such desolating famines within three years, as the famines of 1897 and 1900. And there never has been a time when they deserved a more considerate, a more lenient, a more sympathetic treatment at the hands of their rulers. No Government measures affect the well-being of the masses of the people of India to the same extent as the assessment of agricultural holdings. And should Your Excellency find it possible to place these assessments on a *moderate* and *permanent* basis, precluding harassing surveys and reclassifications of the soil, and permitting the cultivators to save and to improve their condition in the future, Your Lordship's administration will be remembered as a beneficent era in the history of British Rule in India.

20th February 1900.

* See foot-note in page 39. The rule of levying *one-half the net produce* is not objectionable if the net produce is correctly ascertained. In subsequent correspondence, therefore, the limit of *half the net produce* is recommended, and the additional limit of *one-fifth the gross produce* is also proposed.

THIRD LETTER TO LORD CURZON.

BOMBAY.

MY LORD,—In continuation of my letters of the 12th and 20th February last, on the subject of Land Settlements in the Central Provinces and in Madras, I take the liberty to submit for Your Excellency's consideration the facts and circumstances narrated below relating to Settlements in the Bombay Presidency. The distressed condition of the agriculturists of the Deccan and Southern India has often received the attention of Your Excellency's predecessors, and I feel convinced that in the present year of famine the subject will receive Your Lordship's attention, and that every suggestion made with the honest desire of improving the condition of the peasantry of Bombay, Madras, and the Central Provinces will receive Your Lordship's consideration.

2. *Land System in the Deccan under Marhatta Rule.*—The prevailing tenure in the Deccan under the Mahratta rule was the *Miras* tenure, under which the Land Tax was fixed in perpetuity in money or in kind in proportion to the net produce, and settlements were made with Village Communities through their headmen on the joint and several responsibility of the *Miras* holders. When additional contributions were required by the State for prosecuting wars or other purposes, they were levied in the shape of extra cesses or special demands from the Village Communities, and did not disturb

the unity of village life and the permanence of the Land Tax. Extraordinary contributions were frequent in the last years of the Mahratta rule; Village Communities were harassed with unending demands and went largely into debt to meet them; but even then the unity of village life and the permanence of the land assessments were seldom disturbed.

3. *Early Land Settlements under British Rule.*—The dominions of the last Maharatta Peshwa passed under British Rule in 1817; and from that year the land revenue was continuously raised. In 1817 the revenue realised in the newly-acquired territories was eighty *lakhs*, in 1818 it was raised to 115 *lakhs*, and in a few years more it came up to 150 *lakhs*, or a million and a half tens of rupees. The Village Community system broke down under this pressure, and the *Ryotwari* system, introduced in Madras by Sir Thomas Munro, suggested the introduction of a similar *Ryotwari* system in Bombay, *i.e.*, a system of separate settlements with individual cultivators.

4. *Settlement of Pringle and Cruickskank.*—Settlement on the Madras principle was ordered by the Government of Bombay in 1825, and was undertaken by Mr. Pringle, C.S., in the Deccan, and by Captain Cruickshank in Gujrat. But the estimates of produce made were incorrect, the share demanded as revenue was therefore unfair, and the cultivators were reduced to poverty and distress. The settlement operations, both in Gujrat and in the Deccan, were stopped in 1829-30. "Every effort was made—lawful and un-

lawful—to get the utmost out of the wretched peasantry, who were subjected to torture—in some instances cruel and revolting beyond description—if they could not or would not yield what was demanded. Numbers abandoned their homes and fled into neighbouring Native States; large tracts of land were thrown out of cultivation, and in some districts no more than a third of the cultured area remained in occupation." (*Administration Report* for 1892-93, p. 76.)

First Regular Settlement from 1836.—The Government then ordered a general inquiry into the subject, which was conducted by Mr. Goldsmid, C.S., who was subsequently joined by Captain Wingate and Lieutenant Wash. The Joint Report, submitted in 1847, proposed a new Land Revenue Settlement on an improved plan. The proposal was accepted, and forms the basis of what may be called the first regular Settlement in this Presidency, which had commenced in 1836. The principles of this Settlement were these: *In the first place*, it continued the old system of separate settlements with individual cultivators; *secondly*, it instituted leases of thirty years for the short leases which had preceded; and *thirdly*, it abandoned the basis of produce estimates and substituted the estimated value of lands as the basis of assessment. The Settlement, commenced on these principles in 1836, was completed, or nearly completed, by 1872, and showed an increase of land revenue from Rx. 1,533,000 to Rx. 2,031,000, an increase of thirty-two per cent., exclusive of Poona, etc., then under a second Settlement. (*Administration Report* for 1872-73, p. 49.)

6. *Second Regular Settlement from* 1866.—The leases granted at the first Settlement began to fall in from 1866, and a second regular Settlement commenced, and is still proceeding. Out of 27,781 villages in the Province, 13,369 villages have up to date been resettled, and the total land revenue of these villages has increased from Rx. 1,446,000 to Rx. 1,886,000, showing an increase of thirty per cent. (*Administration Report* for 1898-99, Appendix II.)

7. *Third Regular Settlement from* 1896.—The leases granted at the second Settlement began to fall in from 1896, and a third regular Settlement has commenced and is still proceeding. Seventy-eight villages in the Poona Collectorate have been resettled, and the revenue of these resettled villages has increased from Rx. 10,353 to Rx. 13,359, showing once more an increase of thirty per cent.

8. *Undue Enhancement of Land Revenue.*—My Lord, the brief history of Land Settlements in Bombay given above will indicate to Your Excellency one principal reason of the impoverished condition of the Deccan cultivators. The produce of the soil does not increase, either in quantity or in value, thirty per cent. every thirty years, and the endeavour to obtain such an increase in land revenue necessarily leaves the cultivators in a state of greater helplessness and poverty after each Settlement. Much of the best lands in the Deccan was under cultivation in 1836, *i.e.*, after the first twenty years of British rule in that country; new lands brought under cultivation since are less fertile

and less productive; and the disproportionate enhancements of land revenue obtained at each successive Settlement have necessarily impoverished the peasantry and made them more resourceless and helpless in years of bad harvests. The late Sir William Hunter, speaking in the Viceregal Council in 1879 about the Bombay Settlements, said that "the fundamental difficulty of bringing relief to the Deccan peasantry . . . is that the Government assessment does not leave enough food to the cultivator to support himself and his family throughout the year." This fundamental difficulty has not been removed since, and the assessment commenced after 1896 is more severe, and is likely to leave the cultivator more impoverished and resourceless, than the assessment commenced after 1866.

9. *No Check on Enhancements provided in the Revenue Law.*—My Lord, the revenue law of the Province provides no adequate check on these assessments. The assessment made is not based on estimates of the produce of the fields, but on a scientific but thoroughly unpractical appraisement of the intrinsic value of the land, and an examination of the fiscal history of the *Talooka.* Enhancements are made, not merely on the equitable grounds of extension of cultivation and rise of prices, but also on the vague and indefinite ground of improvements effected by the State. A new road constructed, a new line of railway opened, and even the gener advance of the country in times of peace, may be, and are, included under this third head as grounds of enhancement; and it will be obvious to

Your Lordship that the condition of the Deccan peasantry can never improve so long as the Deccan Settlement Officer is armed with this comprehensive power to raise the rental with the general advance of the country. So far as the cultivator of the Deccan is considered, the blessings of peace and the benefits of a civilised administration add to his impoverishment, because improved roads and communications, and the general advance of the country are made a ground of enhancement of his rent. If such roads and communications have increased the prices of the produce, an enhancement of the rental on this definite ground is just and fair. If the roads and communications have not increased the prices of food grains, wherein is the cultivator benefited? and why should his rental be increased because his richer neighbour can travel by rail, or his money-lender has a civil court nearer at hand? All the real advantage which the cultivator secures from the general advancement of the country is shown in the rise of prices, and that is a just and legitimate ground of enhancement of rents. To provide an additional ground for enhancements when the prices have not risen is to tax the cultivator for a benefit which he has not derived, and makes him poorer after each Settlement.

10. *No Equitable Limitations on Enhancements.*—My Lord, there are no equitable limitations to the enhancements which the Settlement Officer is empowered to make. The rule is that (1) the increase of revenue in the case of a *Talooka*, or group of villages, should not exceed thirty-three per cent.; (2)

the increase of revenue in the case of a village shall not exceed sixty-six per cent.; (3) the increase of revenue in the case of an individual holding shall not exceed one hundred per cent. I beg that these checks on the powers of the Bombay Settlement Officer may be compared with the limitations prescribed in the Tenancy Act for the Bengal Zemindar. It is undesirable that the Government should take wider powers of enhancement with respect of cultivators living under the State, than it allows to private landlords in respect of cultivators living under such landlords.

11. *No Judicial Checks on Enhancements.*—Lastly, My Lord, there are no judicial checks on the action of the Settlement Officer. In 1873, an appeal in an assessment suit was preferred in the High Court of Bombay, and the High Court decided the case against the Settlement Officer, and in favour of the plaintiff. Immediately after, a Bill was introduced in the Council to exclude the jurisdiction of the High Court and of all Civil Courts in matters relating to assessments, and the Hon. Mr. Ellis explained the object of the Bill in these memorable words: "It was not expedient that the general policy of Government in relation to the land revenue should be questioned, or that the details of revenue assessments should be questioned by the Civil Courts." The Bombay Revenue Jurisdiction Act was accordingly passed, excluding the jurisdiction of Civil Courts in matters of assessment; and if the assessment is severe or unfair, or the Settlement Officer commits a blunder, the aggrieved cultivator has no independent

tribunal to appeal to from his decision. My Lord, I do not wish to make any reflection against Revenue Officers. I have been a Revenue Officer myself all through my official career, and I speak from personal knowledge when I state that Revenue Officers endeavour to perform their difficult and onerous duties as justly and conscientiously as Judicial Officers, or as any other class of officers in India. But it will appear from a moment's reflection that in the matter of assessment suits the Revenue Officer and the Settlement Officer *are virtually a party to the suit*, and it cannot meet the ends of justice if they are made the final judges in such suits. The failure of justice which often results from this inequitable system is illustrated by the facts I have mentioned in paragraph 8 of my letter to Your Lordship of the 20th of February last; the cost of cultivation in Madras is underestimated by the revenue authorities; and the Madras Raiyat obtains no redress from this injustice because he cannot ask a Civil Court to determine the actual cost of cultivating his field. In Bengal, the Tenancy Act of 1885 permits the cultivator to take his case to Civil Courts; all over India the private citizen and the private trader are permitted by the British Government and by British laws to seek redress, even against the Government itself, in the impartial Civil Courts of the land. But the cultivators of India, the poorest, the most ignorant, and the most helpless class of the Indian population, are debarred (except in Bengal) from seeking redress against the assessment of Revenue Officers; and the assessment becomes necessarily unfair and excessive because it is unchecked by an appeal to an independent tribunal.

12. *Sir Charles Wood's Despatch of* 1864.—It will appear to Your Lordship from what has been stated in the four preceding paragraphs that there is no real check against undue enhancements made by Settlement Officers; that enhancements out of all proportion to the increase of produce and the rise of prices are made in the absence of effective checks; and that this is the real reason of that distressed condition of the Deccan cultivator which Sir William Hunter deplored in 1879, and which every beneficent English administrator in India deplores at the present day. The check on enhancements which was generously provided by Sir Charles Wood, Secretary of State for India, as far back as 1864, has turned out to be ineffective in practice. In his memorable despatch of that year Sir Charles Wood laid down the principle that assessments on lands should not on any account, and under any circumstances, exceed one-half of the net produce of the land, *i.e.*, one-half of the produce after deducting the cost of cultivation. This rule, laid down with the most benevolent intentions, has completely broken down in its application. In Madras the cost of cultivation is underestimated in many cases, and no appeal is allowed to Civil Courts against such underestimation; in Bombay the cost of cultivation is not estimated at all, lands being assessed with an eye to their intrinsic value and their fiscal history.

13. My Lord, it has been a painful task for me to

place all these facts and circumstances relating to Land Assessments in India before Your Excellency; and I have done it because I feel convinced that Your Excellency's Government is animated by a sincere desire to materially improve the condition of the Indian cultivator. There is no race of cultivators on earth who are more loyal, more peaceful, more willing to pay their proper contribution to the State, and more provident and capable of helping themselves if they are allowed the chance. But the continuous enhancement of the revenue at each recurring Settlement, not merely on just, and equitable, and real grounds, but on vague, shadowy, and unreal grounds, precludes the possibility of any improvement in the condition of the cultivator, and takes away from him all motive and all power to effect permanent improvements. It is possible, my Lord, without interfering with the steady increase of the Land Revenue of India, to make that increase commensurate with the improvement in the condition of the cultivator; and I trust and hope Your Excellency's Government will adopt measures to secure this desirable object, viz., to make the increase of the public revenues dependent on the improvement in the condition of the people.

14. We do not ask for anything that is unreasonable or impracticable; we ask for those rules and limitations which experience has proved to be practicable and beneficial in some parts of India. In Bengal the rent does not generally exceed one-sixth of the average gross produce in any district; in the North-West it is about

one-fifth of the average gross produce, according to Sir Antony Macdonnell's evidence before the Currency Committee. We beg, my Lord, *in the first place*, that this limitation, which is generally observed by private landlords in Northern India, be introduced in the Central Provinces, Madras and Bombay, where Government Settlement Officers fix the revenue.* In the North-Western Provinces, again, the Government is satisfied, according to Sir Antony Macdonnell's evidence before the Currency Committee, with forty per cent. of the rents received by landlords from cultivators. We beg, therefore, *in the second place*, that this healthy rule be extended to other parts of India, and that wherever the Land Revenue is obtained from the landlord, one-half of the landlord's assets be fixed as the maximum State-demand. *Thirdly*, in the North-West and in Bombay also, Settlements are made for thirty years; we beg that this rule may be invariably adhered to in all provinces of India, and that no shorter terms of settlement, involving frequent harassment to the people as well as frequent enhancements, be sanctioned under any circumstances. *Fourthly*, we beg that where the Settlement is made directly with cultivators, the rule proposed by Lord Ripon in 1882

* This first rule, recommended by me, has been misunderstood. I intended that one-fifth the gross produce should be the *Maximum Limit* of Government Revenue which should not be exceeded in any single village or field. But the Government took my Rule to mean that one-fifth the gross produce should be *General Standard* of Government Revenue for large Districts and Provinces. Recent enquires shew that the General Standard of rents, levied by Zemindars in Bengal, is one-ninth of the gross produce. The General Standard of Government Revenue, levied from cultivators in Madras and Bombay, should be less, not more.

with the concurrence of the Madras Government be adopted, and that in districts which have been completely surveyed and settled, no enhancements of rents be made in subsequent Settlements except on the sole ground of a rise in prices. *Fifthly*, where water-rates are imposed for irrrigation, we beg that the rates be optional, as it is now in all parts of India; and that it may not be made compulsory until there are stronger grounds for doing so than have yet been shown to exist in the Bill recently introduced in Madras. And, *sixthly and lastly*, we consider it fair, both in the matter of water-rates and of land assessments, to permit the cultivator an appeal to a civil tribunal against the action of the Revenue Officer who is virtually a party to such suits. I do not think that such a permission is likely to foster litigation; the Indian cultivator is not often likely to question the action of the Revenue Officer unless the Revenue Officer has committed a mistake. Such an appeal is necessary to guard against unfairness and undue assessments, for the best and most conscientious amongst us are not free from blunders, and it cannot be the desire of the British Government that such blunders should re[illegible] unchecked precisely in those cases which affect the interests and the well-being of the helpless and voiceless peasant population of India.

6th April 1900.

FOURTH LETTER TO LORD CURZON.

BENGAL.

My Lord,—In continuation of my previous letter on Land Settlements in the Central Provinces, Madras and Bombay, I ask leave to submit the present letter to Your Excellency about Bengal. I have passed all my official life in Bengal districts, and among Bengal cultivators, and I venture to hope that such facts as I am able to lay before Your Lordship about the agricultural condition of the Province will receive Your Lordship's consideration. I will not enter into any matters of controversy; I will endeavour to make my letter a brief and clear statement of facts.

2. *History of the Bengal Zemindars under the Afghan Rule.*—As far back as we can obtain any evidence of a historical nature, we always find the Province of Bengal parcelled out among Zemindars, who were virtually rulers within their respective estates. When the Afghans conquered Bengal, they carved out estates, here and there, for military Commanders and Jaigidars, but left Hindu Zemindars generally in possession of the estates which they had inherited from their fathers. Mahomedan Kazis and Kotwals performed judicial and police work in towns, but within their own estates the Hindu Zemindars were left with their old powers. They levied rents, preserved peace and order, settled disputes, and led large armies. One

of these Hindu Zemindars helped the Afghan Emperor of Delhi, about 1280 A.D., with his own troops against an insurgent chief; and when Bengal became independent of Delhi in the following century, one of the Hindu Zemindars had sufficient influence and military power to make himself King of Bengal, and to leave the throne to his son.

3. *History of the Bengal Zemindars under the Moghal Rule.*—Bengal was once more brought under the rule of Delhi by the Emperor Akbar in the sixteenth century, and Hindu Zemindars continued to hold the same position, and to exercise the same political and military powers, as they had done under the Afghans. We read in the *Ayin-i-Akbari* that the Zemindars of Bengal were mostly Kayests by caste, that the militia force in the province consisted of 23,330 cavalry, 801,150 infantry, 1170 elephants, 4260 guns, and 4400 boats; and that the revenue of Bengal, including Orissa, was Rs. 14,961,483, or in round numbers about Rx. 1,500,000. Similarly Behar had a militia force of 11,415 cavalry, 449,350 infantry, and 100 boats, and paid a revenue of Rs. 5,457,985, or in round numbers about Rx.500,000. (*Ayin-i-Akbari*, vol. ii., Col. Jarrett's translation, pp. 129 and 158.) Roughly speaking, the land revenue of Bengal, Behar, and Orissa demanded from the Zemindars by the Government of Akbar, but perhaps never fully collected, was about two *Krors*. The land revenue of the same Provinces actually collected in 1897-98 was Rs. 39,782 190, or nearly four *Krors*.

4. *Real Position of the Bengal Zemindars.*—My Lord, I have thought it necessary to state these facts because speakers and writers on Indian subjects sometimes make the mistake of supposing that Zemindars were mere middlemen and rent collectors under the Mahomedan rulers, and that they were raised to the status of landlords, in the English sense of the word, by Lord Cornwallis. This is not the fact. Zemindars have not only been *de facto* landlords, but also *de facto* rulers within their own estates, since the dawn of history. They performed the same necessary and useful part in the history of Bengal, previous to the British rule, that the barons of Europe performed, or were supposed to perform, in the Middle Ages. They preserved peace and order within their own estates, repressed crime and punished offenders, adjudicated cases and protected labourers and cultivators, and represented and maintained the royal authority and influence. Their system of administration was no doubt rude, their exercise of power was often arbitrary, and their forces were often engaged in warring with each other, as was the case in Europe down to the eighteenth century. But in spite of all this, the Zemindars of Bengal played a useful and necessary part in the history of those times; they maintained order in the interior where the King or Subahdar had no means and no agency to preserve the peace; they settled disputes, adjudicated cases, and punished crime; and they encouraged learning and arts in their courts. The literature and traditions of Bengal reflect to this day the position and

influence which Zeminders owned in the political and social economy of the province.

5. *Policy of Warren Hastings.*—When the British became the virtual rulers of Bengal in the latter half of the eighteenth century, the Zemindars of Bengal necessarily lost some of their influence and power. Feudalism had died a natural death in Europe, and it was inevitable that such quasi-feudal powers as the Zemindars exercised before should also be withdrawn. Warren Hastings deprived them of their judicial and police powers, and bestowed those powers on newly-created District Collectors and Police Officers. I will not enter into a discussion as to whether this was wisely or hastily done, but it is obvious that the step was inevitable, for under a modern system of rule the functions of the judge and the police can be exercised only by officers of the Crown. But when Warren Hastings imprisoned defaulting Zemindars, sold their estates to outsiders for arrears, or let them out on short leases, he scarcely acted with sufficient regard to the ancient traditions of the province, or to the position which the hereditary landlords had held for centuries among their people.

6. *Policy of Lord Cornwallis.*—Lord Cornwallis acted with a truer appreciation of the spirit of Indian institutions. He did not render back to the Zemindars those judicial and police powers of which they had been deprived; but he wisely sought to secure to them that honoured place which they had held for centuries. With the true instincts of a nobleman, he saw that it

was not good for the people, or for the rulers, that the estates of the ancient houses should pass into the hands of shroffs and money-lenders and other auction purchasers; and with the true instincts of a statesman, he endeavoured to give the Zemindars of Bengal the motive and the opportunity to extend cultivation, to accumulate capital, and to improve the country. All the estates of Bengal were very severely assessed after an elaborate inquiry; but this assessment, made with a strict regard to the interests of the Government, was declared to be permanent, by the famous Regulation of 1793.

7. *Result of the Permanent Settlement.*—My Lord, this Permanent Settlement of the land revenues of Bengal is sometimes condemned by writers who merely look upon it as a loss to the Government revenue. But administrators, who have lived and worked in Bengal districts, and have studied the far-reaching and beneficial results of Lord Cornwallis's policy, do not share this opinion. In the first place, the placing of a limit to the Government-demand in the permanently settled tracts of Bengal has enabled the Government, by subsequent legislation, to limit the demand of the Zemindars themselves from the actual cultivators; and the cultivators of Bengal are therefore more prosperous, more resourceful, and better able to help themselves in years of bad harvest, than cultivators in any other part of India. In the second place, the limitation of the State-demand has fostered agricultural enterprise, extended cultivation, and led to the accumulation of some capital in the hands of private proprietors, a

result which far-sighted administrators wish to bring about in other parts of India. This capital is expended in fostering trades and industries, in supporting schools, dispensaries, and charitable institutions, in excavating tanks and wells, and lastly in supporting the poorer classes in seasons of distress and famine. I may cite here the remarkable instance of the late Maharaja of Darbhanga, who altogether expended a hundred thousand pounds sterling in relief works and in remissions of rent, during the famine of 1897. In the third place, the modest capital accumulated is not retained in the hands of a few exclusive houses in Bengal; it is fairly distributed among intelligent, enterprising, and industrious men in all districts and of all classes; it passes from those who are unworthy to those who prove themselves to be worthy; it encourages professions, education and culture, and it promotes generally the well-being of all classes and thereby indirectly helps the revenues of the country. Fourthly and lastly, the policy of Lord Cornwallis has confirmed the loyalty of the most substantial classes of the people, and through them of the entire people, towards the ruling power. All who have anything at stake look on the British rule in India, not only as a just and enlightened system of administration, but as a Government with which their own interests are intimately associated; as a Government whose permanence means the well-being of the people. In the dark days of the Mutiny of 1857 there was no disaffection in Bengal, and in the words of Mr. Seton Karr, "the Sepoys took to the villages and the jungles, and then they literally melted away before the impassive demeanour, the want of sympathy, and the silent loyalty of the Zemindars." And Your Excellency is aware that in the present year of a British war in South Africa, Bengal Zemindars have been the foremost, among all the loyal communities of India, in their enthusiastic support of the British cause; and that their influence and their example and their exertions have told on all classes of the people, and evoked a general and enthusiastic expression of loyalty througout the country.

8. *Rent Laws for the Protection of Cultivators.*—The Regulation of 1793, making a permanent Settlement of the land revenue payable by Zemindars, contained at the same time a promise to enact laws in the future for the protection of cultivators. This pledge was first redeemed by the Government of Lord Canning by Act X. of 1859, which prohibited the enhancement of rents except on certain well defined and equitable grounds. These provisions of the law of 1859 were upheld by the subsequent Act VIII. of 1868; and lastly the occupancy rights of cultivators were largely extended by the Tenancy Act of 1885, which was drawn up under the Government of Lord Ripon, and passed by the Government of Lord Dufferin. These rent laws of Bengal have given adequate protection to cultivators; and it will be found on inquiry that the rents generally realised by Bengal Zemindars are fair and moderate, and permit the cultivators of the soil to save in good years for years of bad harvests.

9.—*Proportion of Rent to produce in Bengal Districts.* —My Lord, during a period of over twenty-five years that I was employed as a Revenue Officer in different districts in Bengal, I had occasion to make such inquiries for myself; and I found that the rents generally realised by Bengal Zemindars were about one-sixth of the gross produce in some districts, and were even less in others. I have, since then, compared the results of my own inquiries with the figures contained in Sir W. Hunter's "Statistical Accounts of Bengal," published in 1875 and subsequent years, and I note below the figures given in Sir William Hunter's work. The "Statistical Accounts" do not, unfortunately, give the average produce and the average rents for all districts in Bengal; but for almost every district for which figures are available in the work, they have been reproduced by me in the list given in the next paragraph. I have used the letters (a) and (b) to indicate, generally, superior and inferior lands according to their produce.

10. *Produce and Rent in Bengal shown in figures as given in Statistical Account of Bengal.*

District.		Produce per Acre. £	s.	d.	Rent per Acre. £	s.	d.	Proportion of Rent to Produce.
24 PERGANAS ...	(a)	5	2	0	0	18	0	18·7 per cent.
	(b)	2	2	0	0	9	0	
NADIYA ...	(a)	3	3	0	0	7	6	13·8 "
	(b)	0	13	6	0	3	0	
JESSOR ...	(a)	3	13	6	0	9	0	12·3 "
MIDNAPUR ..	(a)	3	15	0	0	9	0	12·0 "
HUGLI ...	(a)	3	12	0	1	1	0	29·4 "
	(b)	1	10	0	0	9	0	

District.		Produce per Acre. £ s. d.	Rent per Acre. £ s. d.	Proportion of Rent to Produce.
HOWRAH	...	(a) 3 8 0	0 18 0	25·0 ,,
		(b) 2 0 0	0 9 0	
BANKURA	...	(a) 2 17 0	0 14 3	25·5 ,,
		(b) 1 14 6	0 9 0	
BIRBHUM	..	(a) 4 3 0	0 18 0	22·7 ,,
		(b) 1 16 0	0 9 0	
DACCA	...	(a) 4 13 0	0 10 6	11·2 ,,
BACKERGANJ	...	(b) 1 16 0	0 5 8	15·7 per cent.
FARIDPUR	...	(b) 1 10 0	0 3 9	12·5 ,,
MYMENSING	...	(a) 5 2 0	0 18 0	17·3 ,,
		(b) 2 14 0	0 9 0	
NOAKHALI	...	(a) 3 5 0	0 9 0	13·8 ,,
TIPPERA	...	(a) 3 12 0	0 18 0	24·5 ,,
		(b) 1 18 3	0 9 0	
DINAJPUR	...	(b) 1 16 0	0 9 0	25·0 ,,
RAJSHAHI	...	(b) 1 13 0	0 9 0	27·2 ,,
PABNA	...	(a) 3 15 0	0 9 0	12·0 ,,
GAYA	...	(a) 3 12 0	0 18 0	21·1 ,,
		(b) 2 10 5	0 9 0	
MANBHUM	...	(b) 1 12 0	0 9 0	28·1 ,,
BALASOR	...	(a) 1 0 0	0 6 0	28·1 ,,
		(b) 0 12 0	0 3 0	

N.B.—All districts for which figures are given in Sir William Hunter's work are included in the above list, except Burdwan, Rangpur and Malda, for which the figures given are obviously incorrect. Rents for Burdwan and Rangpur have been overestimated, and rents for Malda underestimated. The average rent for the twenty districts named above is about twenty per cent. of the produce; and if the value of straw was included in the produce in all districts, the proportion of rent would be still less. *

* As a matter of fact Bengal Zemindars obtain about 11 per cent of the gross produce as rent. See Bengal Government Report, forming an enclosure to Lord Curzon's Land Resolution of 1902.

11. My Lord, the figures given in Sir William Hunter's work, and quoted above, were compiled about thirty years ago. Since then the prices of food grains have risen in Bengal higher than the rents of lands, and the Tenancy Act of 1885 has given a wider protection to cultivators than existed before. If an inquiry were now made, district by district, as to the average produce, including straw, and the average rents of Bengal, the rents now generally realised will be found to be below one-fifth or one-sixth the gross produce in most districts. It will, therefore, appear that the Permanent Settlement of Bengal and the subsequent Rent Acts have secured all the results which they were intended to secure. They have extended cultivation, fostered enterprise and works of public utility, and maintained in Bengal an intelligent, influential, and loyal class of landlords, the strongest supporters of British Rule in India. They have protected cultivators, moderated rents, and enabled the poorer classes to save something in good years for years of bad harvest. They have decreased the indebtedness of the cultivating classes, and enabled them to live in better houses, use better utensils, and save more in agricultural stock and in silver jewellery, than their fathers did before. And lastly, moral advancement has kept pace with material advancement, and the Bengal cultivator of the present day is better read, better informed, more self-reliant, more able to defend his own interests, than he was before.

12. My Lord, these are blessings which have been

secured to the Bengal landlord and the Bengal cultivator by the Permanent Settlement and by the successive Rent Laws of Bengal. But I do not wish to be misunderstood. I do not at the present time ask for the extension of the Bengal system to other parts of India; I have not made any such suggestion in the three letters which I have had the honour to address to Your Excellency. Each Province in India has its own land system under which the people have lived for generations, and with which the people are familiar; and it is possible, under each land system, to afford adequate protection to the cultivator against frequent reassessments, and undue enhancements. What I have asked, my Lord, is that such protection be granted to the cultivator of each Province under the land system under which he lives. I have prayed that where the cultivator pays direct to the State, the impracticable rule of realising one-half the *net* produce or one-third the *gross* produce be abandoned,* and the rule of fixing one-fifth the gross produce as the maximum of rent be adopted. I have prayed that where the revenue is paid by landlords, one-half of their assets be fixed as the Government revenue, as is done in the N. W. Provinces of India. I have prayed that where no Permanent Settlement has been made, the period of

* It is necessary to explain once more that the rule of realizing one-half the *net* produce is neither impracticable nor objectionable, if it is properly worked. Instead of recommending its abandonment, I should therefore have insisted on its being honestly carried out, under the additional safe-guard that the half net produce should in no case exceed one-fifth the gross produce. This I have done in para 18 (*b*) of my fifth letter.

each recurring settlement be fixed at thirty years as in the N. W. Provinces of India. And I have prayed that where districts have been once surveyed and settled, a rise in prices be made the sole ground of enhancement in future settlements, as was proposed by the Marquis of Ripon in 1882. I sincerely trust and hope that these proposals, which are moderate and practicable, and which do not in any way modify the principles of the different land systems in the different Provinces, will find acceptance with Your Excellency's Government.

25th April 1900.

FIFTH LETTER TO LORD CURZON.

NORTHERN INDIA.

My Lord,—In continuation of my previous letters on Land Settlements in the Central Provinces, Madras, Bombay, and Bengal, I take the liberty of submitting to Your Excellency this final letter on Land Settlements in Northern India. The land system in the N. W. Provinces differs somewhat from that in Oudh, and these systems again are somewhat different from the Punjab system; but there is a general resemblance in the systems prevailing in all these three Provinces of Northern India. For in all these Provinces the cultivators generally pay their rents to landlords; and the revenue payable by landlords to the Government, (except where it is permanently settled), is liable to revision and enhancement at each recurring Settlement. I shall, therefore, with a view not to prolong this correspondence, endeavour to compress my remarks and suggestions with regard to all the three Provinces of Northern India within the limits of this letter

2. *Acquisition of the North-Western Provinces.*—The North-Western Provinces came under British Rule at different dates. (*a*) Benares and some adjoining

districts were acquired from the Nawab of Oudh by the treaty of 1775, and were permanently settled in 1795. In this respect they resemble the permanently settled tracts of Bengal, of which I have spoken before, and I shall have no further remarks to make of these districts in the present letter. (*b*) Allahabad and some adjoining districts were ceded by the Nawab of Oudh in 1801. (*c*) Agra and some other districts were conquered by Lord Lake in 1803. Some less important tracts were added in subsequent years.

3. *Early Mistakes in Land Revenue Settlements.*—It may easily be imagined that mistakes were made by administrators who first endeavoured to settle the land revenues. It was the custom in the last days of the Mahomedan rule to fix the State-demand at a very high figure, and then to realise as much of the nominal demand as was possible from year to year. The mistake made by British administrators was to adhere to this high nominal demand, and then to try and realise the whole of it. Some British administrators saw this mistake, and one Collector, Mr. Dumbleton, wrote that the Settlement of 1802 "pressed beyond a reasonable demand," and also complained that the severe rates of the Nawab's government were stereotyped by the British rulers, "*without* the same elasticity in realising." (Baden-Powell's "Land Systems of British India." vol. ii. p. 14.)

4. *Early Settlements,* 1802 *to* 1822.—Proclamations were issued in 1802, that a Settlement would be made for three years ; to be succeeded by another

Settlement for three years ; and this was to be followed by a third Settlement for four years ; after which a Permanent Settlement would be concluded. But before the expiry of the total period of ten years, the views of the rulers had changed, and the idea of a Permanent Settlement had been abandoned. Two fresh Settlements were made for five years each, *i.e.* down to 1822. In the meantime, Mr. Holt Mackenzie submitted his famous Minute, which led to the passing of Regulation VII. of 1822.

5. *Regulation VII. of* 1822, *IV. of* 1828, *and IX. of* 1833.—The three successive Regulations were passed within eleven years, but the mistake of over-assessment was not altogether rectified, and the State-demand was fixed at two-thirds of the rental by the last Regulation. Settlements were accordingly made between 1833 and 1849, and the country remained in a state of perpetual poverity. A terrible famine visited the North-Western Provinces in 1837, and desolated the whole country from Allahabad to Delhi, though it was most intense in the Doab and in the neighbourhood of Agra. The Government revenue was permanently decreased in most districts after the famine.

6. "*Saharanpur Rules*" *of* 1855.—It was not until 1855 that the exorbitant State-demand of two-thirds of the rental was reduced to one-half the rental by the famous "Saharanpur Rules." This is now the general rule in Northern India, and has given considerable relief to the people. When a famine again visited Northern India in 1860, it was less severe

than the preceding one ; and Colonel Baird Smith, who inquired into the causes and effects of the famine, declared that its comparative mildness was due to the moderate demands of the State. Colonel Baird Smith recommended a Permanent Settlement of the land revenue for the improvement of the condition of the people. The recommendation received the approval of Lord Canning and of the Secretary of State for India in 1862 ; but the proposal was long kept in abeyance, and was, at last, unfortunately abandoned in 1883.

7. *Act XIX. of* 1873, *and the Present Method of Settlement.*—The revenue law was much simplified by Act XIX. of 1873, which repealed about fifty Regulations or parts of Regulations, and eight Acts. The assessment of rents, too, which had hitherto been made by Settlement Officers after elaborate calculations and on somewhat theoretical grounds, resulting in much harassment to cultivators and gross inequality of incidence, was now much simplified. The healthy rule was at last adopted, in 1886, that the rents actually received by landlords, as shown in village rent rolls, should be received as the basis of assessment, with necessary corrections. "We do not," says Sir Antony Macdonnell, in his evidence before the Currency Committee, "for the purpose of assessing the Government revenue, make a basis of our own ; we proceed on the basis of actual facts, which have been brought into existence by the operation of the ordinary law of rent, and the arrangement which the landlord has made with his own tenant." (Minutes of Evidence, vol.

i. p. 211). It will thus be seen that, though the North-Western Provinces have not obtained a Permanent Settlement, which would have led to some accumulation of capital and promotion of industries in the country, yet the worst blunders of the early land-settlements have been rectified one by one. In 1855 the revenue was fixed at one-half the rental; in 1873 the Land Revenue Act was simplified; and in 1886 the harassing process of settling rents on theoretical grounds, which still unfortunately prevails in some other parts of India, was abandoned; and the actual rental of the country was accepted, with necessary corrections, as the basis of assessment.

8. *Acquisition of Oudh.*—Oudh was annexed by Lord Dalhousie in 1856, *i.e.* after the land revenue administiation had been reduced to system in the N. W. Provinces, and it therefore escaped some of the worst blunders made in earlier years. The landlords of Oudh were called Talukdars, and out of 23,543 villages in Oudh, 13,640 were settled, in 1856, with Talukdars, and 9903 with Village Proprietors.

9. *Settlement after the Mutiny of* 1857.—After the Mutiny of 1857 all lands were confiscated by the Government by a proclamation in 1858. This summary and somewhat alarming procedure was much criticised in England; and then the estates were re-conferred on the Talukdars with a provision for protecting the rights of subordinate tenants, which provision was entered in the *sanads* or title-deeds which were afterwards issued. The assessment of the

estates of six (reduced to five) loyal Talukdars had been made permanent; the other estates were settled between 1860 and 1878 for thirty years.

10. *Acquisition of the Punjab.*—A portion of the Punjab, between the Sutlej and the Ravi, was annexed after the first Sikh war in 1846. The remainder was annexed after the second Sikh war in 1849. And Delhi and some other districts were transferred from the North-Western Provinces to the Punjab after the Mutiny in 1858. A Board of Administration was formed for the Punjab in 1849; it gave place to a Chief Commissioner a few years later; and after the Mutiny, and after the transference of Delhi and other districts into the Punjab, a Lieutenant-Governor was appointed for the Punjab in 1859.

11. *Settlement in the Punjab; Rates of Assessment.*—Mistakes, similar to those which had been made in the early Settlements in the N. W. Provinces, were made in the Punjab; and British administrators endeavoured to realise the rates at which lands were assessed under the Sikhs. Major Wace said, in his evidence before the Famine Commission of 1878, that "commencing in 1849, with a standard of one-third of the produce, a period of low prices, combined with other considerations affecting the welfare of a newly-conquered and previously much-oppressed country, compelled us to reduce that standard successively to a fourth and a sixth." Even this standard applied only to Lahore and Amritsar Divisions, settled between 1860 and 1872; in later Settlements, one-half the

customary rents was accepted, as in the N. W. Provinces, as the Government revenue. (Appendix III. to Famine Commission's Report, p. 365.) A Land Revenue Act (XXXIII. of 1871) was passed for the Punjab in 1871, and this has been replaced by the present law, Act XVII. of 1887. There are a large number of petty landlords in the Punjab, who cultivate their own lands; and in the Famine Commission's Report (1879) it is stated that fifty-four per cent. of the cultivated area is held by cultivating landlords, and forty-four per cent. by tenants.

12. *Assessment Rules.*—Rules were formulated, under the Revenue Act of 1871, that the Government revenue should not exceed the "estimated value of half the net produce of an estate, or, in other words, one-half of the share of the produce of an estate ordinarily receivable by the landlord in money or in kind." This rule has been reaffirmed and explained by the subsequent rules passed under the Revenue Act of 1887, two of which are quoted below :—

(1) "The general principle of assessment to be followed is that the Government—demand for land revenue shall not exceed the estimated value of half the net produce of the estate."

(3) "In estimating the net produce of cultivated lands of any class, whether occupied by landowners themselves or by tenants, the rents paid in money or in kind on an average of years by ordinary tenants-at-will for such lands in the assessment circle to which the estate belongs, shall be the principal guide."

It is important to note that while the *principle* fixing the Government-demand is the same in the Punjab as in Madras, viz. one-half the net produce, the *practice* is widely different. In the Punjab the usual rent is accepted as the net produce, and the revenue is therefore about half the rental, as in the North-West Provinces. In Madras the net produce is calculated by an elaborate process which is inaccurate in results, and is unjust and oppressive to the cultivators.

13. My Lord, I have in the preceding paragraphs briefly described the land revenue systems and rules of the North-West Provinces, Oudh, and the Punjab; and I crave permission to indicate in a few words the modfiications and the safeguards that seem to be called for. I will not, in the present letter, recommend the extension of Bengal system of Permanent Settlement to Northern India; I will merely suggest improvements which are consistent with the systems prevailing in Northern India, and which will not in any way affect the principle of those systems.

14. *Fair Rents and Secure Tenures for Cultivators.*—The protection of the cultivators is the first object of the Government, and this object is imperfectly secured under the present laws. Sir A. Macdonnell said before the Currency Committee: "Whenever we find a rent-roll which we consider unstable or excessive, we reduce the rental for the purpose of assessment as between the landlord and the Government; we make no interference as between the landlord and his tenant." (Minutes of Evidence, Part I. p. 211). It is necessary to consider

whether such "unstable or excessive" rental should be permitted, and whether a maximum limit of rents in proportion to the gross produce should not be laid down by law in case of ordinary cultivated lands. Some years ago the British Indian Association of Calcutta, representing the large landholders of Bengal, proposed to accept twenty-five per cent. of the gross produce as the landlord's share, as appears from Mr. Dampier's evidence before the Famine Commission of 1878, (Appendix II. p. 72). And when the Bengal Tenancy Bill was framed in 1883, it was proposed to lay down one-fifth the gross produce as the maximum rent. Again, in the Punjab Administration Report of 1898-99 I find that "over two thousand notices (to eject tenants) were issued in Hissar. Most of these were in Sirsa; they show that the people are preparing for the coming Settlement by ejectment of such tenants as might claim to be occupancy tenants." This, I submit, is another case which requires attention, and I venture to hope that the Government will so modify the law as to extend occupancy rights to all settled tenants in Northern India.

15. *Fair Revenue and Long Settlements.*—The principle on which land revenue is fixed in Northen India, viz. at one-half the rental, is fair, and Settlements are generally made for thirty years in Northern India. It is desirable that these rules should be made universal in their application in all parts of India, to prevent frequent harassment of the people. Each Settlement generally secures a large enhancement on the revenue, as will be

seen from the figures given below, and it is necessary

District.	Increase of Revenue due to resettlement.
Budaun ...	27·4 per cent.
Garhwal ...	53·2 "
Unao ...	19·8 "
Partapgarh ...	31·7 "
Rae Bareli ...	24·8 "
Sultanpur ...	24·2 "
Lucknow ...	21·5 "
Hardoi ...	25·5 "
Sitapur ...	28·9 "
Bari Banki ...	30·8 "
Fyzabad ...	29·0 "

Administration Report of N.W.P. & Oudh, 1897-98, *pp.* 7 *to* 9.

District.	Old Revenue.	Increase of Revenue due to resettlement.
Montgomery	Rs. 408,981	Rs. 163,058

Administration Report of the Punjab, 1898-99, *pp.* 23, *and Statistical Table XV.*

therefore to inquire minutely if this is not partly due to undue and excessive enhancements of the rental secured by landlords. There is always the risk of landlords trying to obtain such enhancements of the rental, after they have submitted to an enhancement of the revenue at a new Settlement.

16. *The Imposition of Cesses.*—The difficulty of realising direct taxes in India, principally on account of the poverty of the people, has induced the Government to raise such taxes from the land, along with and in addition to the land revenue. In Bengal, cesses are (6¼ p. c.) levied from landlords and cultivators for roads, and for public works; in Northern India, cesses are levied for Roads, Schools, Post Office, Dispensary, Famines, Patwaris, and Chowkidars, amounting to eight and a quarter per cent.

on the rental; and in the Central Provinces such cesses come up to six and quarter per cent. on the rental. These cesses are assessed on the rent, and paid by landholders with the land revenue; and when the land revenue is enhanced at settlements, the cesses advance automatically. It will be clear to Your Excellency that the object of fixing the revenue at fifty per cent. of the rental is entirely lost if another eight or six per cent. on the rental is added under the name of cesses. The "Saharanpur Rules," which reduced the land revenue from sixty-six and two-thirds per cent. to fifty per cent. of the rental, are thus reduced to a dead letter, and the object of fixing a moderate land revenue is defeated, if the land is once more assessed with various cesses. There may be some reason for assessing the land for works which directly benefit the land, like roads and wells, but there is no reason or justice in assessing the land for schools and dispensaries. The total of cesses in Bengal is one anna in the Rupee, or six and a quarter per cent. of the rental, and this rate should be fixed as the maximum total of all cesses imposed on land, leviable only for works benefiting the land. If a moderate assessment of the land be essentially necessary for the well-being of a nation of cultivators, it is absolutely necessary to guard against indirectly raising that assessment to a material extent, or for purposes not directly calculated to benefit the land.

17. In the last place, I desire, my Lord, to say only one word about the Land Alienation Bill, now under the consideration of the Indian Government. I shall not

anticipate the decision of the experienced administrators who are giving their attention to the matter, nor shall I venture to express an opinion how far some provisions of the nature may be needed in some localities as a temporary measure of relief. All that I wish to urge is that no permanent relief can be given to the cultivators of India by taking away from the marketable value of about the only property which they possess. In Bengal such proposals were under consideration in 1883 and again in 1896, but it was wisely decided that good rent laws and light rental were the soundest means to save the cultivators from the grasp of money-lenders ; and within my experience, good rent laws and light rental have to a great extent freed the cultivators of Bengal from indebtedness within the last thirty years. The cultivators in Northern India, the Central Provinces, and the Deccan, are not less thrity and frugal than Bengal cultivators ; and the same result which has been achieved in Bengal can be produced elsewhere through the same means, viz., light rental and good rent laws, protecting the cultivators from undue and uncertain enhancements.

18. For the sake of convenience I desire briefly to summarise the proposals which I have made in the five letters, of which this is the last ; and as these proposals embody the views of my countrymen generally, I feel convinced they will receive Your Excellency's consideration.

(*a*) Where the State receives land revenue through landlords, and the revenue is not permanently settled, we ask that the "Saharanpur Rules" may be universally applied, and the State-demand be limited to one-half the rental.

(*b*) Where the State receives land revenue direct from cultivators, we ask that the rate be limited to a maximum of one-fifth the gross produce of the soil.* In Madras the old rule, demanding one-half the net produce as revenue, is supplemented by a rule limiting the revenue to *one-third* the gross produce, and this has led to over-assessment in that Province. Having regard to the rates of rent and revenue in all Provinces of India, we ask that the old rule of demanding one-half the net produce be supplemented by a rule limiting the revenue to *one-fifth* the gross produce, wherever revenue is paid to the State direct by cultivators.

(*c*) Where the State receives land revenue direct from cultivators, we ask that the rule laid down by Lord Ripon, of making an increase of prices the soil ground of enhancement at the time of re-settlements, be universally applied.

(*d*) Where the land revenue is not permanently settled, we ask that settlements be made not oftener than once in thirty years.

(*e*) We pray that no cesses be imposed on the rental of the land except for purposes directly benefiting the land; and that the total of such cesses assessed on the

* The maximum of one-fifth the produce should not be exceeded in the case of any single holding. The rate is proposed as a *Maximum Limit*, not for adoption as a *General Standard*.

rental may not exceed six and a quarter per cent. (one anna in the rupee of rent) in any province of India.

(*f*) We pray that where the Government provides water for irrigation, the cultivator may be left—as he has been during the last forty years—the option of paying for the water if he chooses to use it, and that no compulsory water-rate be imposed.

(*g*) And lastly, we pray that in the case of any difference between cultivators and Settlement Officers in the matter of assessment, an appeal be allowed to an independent tribunal, not concerned with the fixing and levying of revenue.

12*th May* 1900.

MEMORIAL OF DECEMBER 20, 1900.

TO THE RIGHT HONOURABLE

LORD GEORGE FRANCIS HAMILTON, M. P.,

Her Majesty's Secretary of State for India.

MY LORD,

In view of the terrible famines with which India has been lately afflicted, we, the undersigned, who have spent many years of our lives among the people, and still take a deep interest in their welfare, beg to offer the following suggestions to your Lordship in Council, in the hope that the Land Revenue administration may be everywhere placed on such a sound and equitable basis as to secure to the cultivators of the soil a sufficient margin of profit to enable them better to withstand the pressure of future famines.

2.—We are well aware that the primary cause of famines is the failure of rain, and that the protection of large tracts of country by the extension of irrigation from sources that seldom or never fail has been steadily kept in view and acted on by the Government for many years past; but the bulk of the country is dependent on direct rainfall, and the pinch of famine is most severely felt in the uplands, where the crops fail simply for want of rain. The only hope for the cultivators throughout the greater part of India is therefore that they should be put in such a position as to enable them to tide over an occasional bad season.

3.—To place the cultivators in such a position, we consider it essential that the share taken as the Government demand on the land should be strictly limited in every Province. We fully agree with the views of Lord Salisbury, when Secretary of State for India, as set out in his Minute of April 26th 1875:—

"So far as it is possible to change the Indian fiscal system, it is desirable that the cultivator should pay a smaller proportion of the whole national charge. It is not in itself a thrifty policy to draw the mass of revenue from the rural districts, where capital is scarce, sparing the towns, where it is often redundant, and runs to waste and luxury. The injury is exaggerated in the case of India, where so much of the revenue is exported without a direct equivalent."

4.—Without going into tedious detail, we consider it very advisable that, in those parts of the country in which the Land Tax is not permanently settled, the following principles should be uniformly adhered to:—

(*a*) Where the Land Revenue is paid directly by the cultivators, as in most parts of Madras and Bombay, the Government demand should be limited to 50 per cent. of the value of the nett produce, after a liberal deduction for cultivation expenses has been made; and should not ordinarily exceed one-fifth of the gross produce, even in those parts of the country where, in theory, one half of the nett, is assumed to approximate to one-third of the gross, produce.

(*b*) Where the Land Revenue is paid by landlords, the principle adopted in the Saharanpur Rules of 1855 whereby the Revenue demand is limited to one-half of the actual rent or assets of such landlords, should be universally applied.

(*c*) That no revision of the Land Tax of any Province or part thereof should be made within thirty years of the expiration of any former revision.

(*d*) That when such revision is made in any of those parts of India where the Land Revenue is paid by the cultivators direct to the Government, there should be no increase in the assessment except in cases where the land has increased in value (1) in consequence of improvements in irrigation works carried out at the expense of the Government, or (2) on account of a rise in the value of produce, based on the average prices of the thirty years next preceding such revision.

5.—Lastly, we recommend that a limit be fixed in each Province beyond which it may not be permissible to surcharge the Land Tax with local cesses. We are of opinion that the Bengal rate of 6¼ per cent. is a fair one, and that in no case should the rate exceed 10 per cent.

We have the honour to be,

Sir,

Your obedient Servants,

24, PALACE COURT, W.,
20th *December*, 1900.

R. K. PUCKLE,
Late Director of Revenue Settlement and Member of the Board of Revenue, Madras.

J. H. GARSTIN,
Late Member of Council, Madras.

J. B. PENNINGTON,
Late Collector of Tanjore, Madras.

H. J. REYNOLDS,
Late Revenue Secretary to the Government of Bengal, and late Member of the Legislative Council of the Governor-General of India.

RICHARD GARTH,
Late Chief Justice of Bengal.

ROMESH C. DUTT,
Late Offg. Commissioner of Orissa Division in Bengal, and Member of the Bengal Legislative Council.

C. J. O'DONNELL,
Late Commissioner of the Bhagalpur and Rajshahi Divisions in Bengal.

A. ROGERS,
Late Settlement Officer and Member of Council in Bombay.

W. WEDDERBURN,
Late Acting Chief Secretary to the Government of Bombay.

JOHN JARDINE,
Late Judge of the High Court of Bombay.

J. P. GOODRIDGE,
Late B.C.S., and formerly Offg. Settlement Commissioner, C.P.

RESOLUTION ISSUED BY THE GOVERNOR GENERAL IN COUNCIL ON THE 16TH JANUARY 1902.

Origin and importance of the inquiry.

THE attention of the Government of India has lately been called, in a special manner, to the subject of the Land Revenue administration of this country, partly by the series of almost unprecedented calamities which have in recent years assailed the agricultural population, partly by a number of representations which have reached them from sympathetic friends of India, who have devoted careful study to the above-named problem. In the course of 1900, Mr. R. C. Dutt, C. I. E., formerly Acting Commissioner of Burdwan, addressed to His Excellency the Viceroy a series of letters (subsequently published in the form of a book) concerning the Land Revenue system of the different provinces, and he submitted certain recommendations as to future policy and action. At a little later date the Secretary of State transmitted to the Government of India a memorial signed by certain retired officers of the Indian Civil Service, formulating a somewhat similar list of suggestions.

2. The Government of India welcomed the opportunity thus afforded to them of instituting renewed enquires into a matter that has, for more than a century, been the subject of anxious discussion. The well-being of the agricultural community in India, constituting as

it does so overwhelming a proportion of the entire population of the Indian continent, and contributing so large a quota to the Indian revenues, cannot fail to be to the Government a matter of the most intimate concern; nor can it be denied that upon the incidence of the Land Revenue collections must the prosperity of those classes in a great measure depend. The question may be recognized therefore as one of the highest national importance, transcending the sphere of party or sectional controversy, and demanding at once the most exhaustive scrutiny and the most liberal treatment. When further it appeared that the main contention submitted to the Government by certain of its critics was that the intensity and frequency of recent famines are largely due to poverty caused by over-assessment—a contention the gravity of which cannot be disputed, seeing that it is tantamount to an arraignment of the policy that has been pursued by successive Indian administrations for an entire century,—and when this general proposition was accompanied by a series of detailed allegations as regards the system of assessment in vogue in the various parts of the country, it seemed to the Government of India that the opportunity should not be lost of definitely examining the grounds for these assertions, and the letters above referred to were accordingly referred to the Local Governments for their consideration and report. Their replies have been received and are annexed to this Resolution. The Governor-General in Council is grateful for the labour which has been bestowed upon their preparation, and he hopes that in the comprehensive review of Land Revenue policy throughout India which has thereby been obtained, may be found a corrective to many current misapprehensions and a source of more trustworthy knowledge in the future.

3. On the present occasion he is, however, less concerned with the individual statements or mis-statements that may have been made with regard to particular areas—the replies of the Local Governments will show that an imperfect acquaintance with facts has been the source of much confusion and misunderstanding—than he is with the larger questions affecting our Land Revenue policy as a whole, and the connection which it is alleged to have with the recurrence and intensity of famine in India.

Alleged connection between revenue policy and famine.

It does not seem necessary to discuss the economic fallacy that any alteration in the system or scale of assessments can permanently save an agricultural population from the effects of climatic disaster. The relation of cause and effect between a good rainfall, abundant crops, and agricultural prosperity, is not more obvious than is that between a bad monsoon, deficient produce, and a suffering people. When the vast majority of the inhabitants of a country are dependent upon an industry which is itself dependent upon the rainfall, it is clear that a failure of the latter must unfavourably, and in extreme cases calamitously, affect the entire agricultural community. The suspension of the rains means a suspension of labour; the suspension of labour means a drying up of the means of subsistence; and the latter is necessarily followed by distress and destitution. There is no industry in the world the sudden interruption or the temporary destruction of which is not attended by impoverishment and suffering; and there is no country in the world, where the meteorological and economic conditions are at all similar to those prevailing in India, that could by any revenue system, that might possibly be devised, escape the same results.

4. Nevertheless, if prevention of the inevitable consequenees of drought be an ideal incapable of attainment, mitigation is minifestly an object worthy of the closest attention of the Government. It cannot but be their desire that assessments should be equitable in character and moderate in incidence; and that there should be left to the proprietor or to the cultivator of the soil—as the case may be—that margin of profit that will enable him to save in ordinary seasons, and to meet the strain of exceptional misfortune. Such aspirations must be even more forcibly impressed upon the Government at a time when, owing to the prolonged continuance of adverse circumstances, the agricultural population has passed through a phase of almost unequalled depression, and needs the fullest measure of encouragement that it is possible to afford. It is with the object of demonstrating how far these objects are capable of being realised under the existing system, or to what extent the latter is susceptible of improvement, that the Governor General in Council now proceeds to examine the general charges that have been brought against it, and the individual modifications that are proposed.

The two kinds of settlement: Permanent and Temporary.

5. By the ancient law of the country—to quote the opening words of Regulation XIX of 1793, by which the Permanent Settlement was created in Bengal—the ruling power is entitled to a certain proportion of the produce of every acre of land unless it has transferred or limited its rights thereto. The procedure by which that proportion is determined is styled a Settlement of the Land Revenue. A Settlement is of two kinds: permanent, by which the demand of the State is made fixed and unalterable for ever; temporary, under which the State demand is revised at recurring periods of greater or less duration. Inasmuch as all agricultural land in India must fall within either the permanently-settled or the temporarily-settled areas, it is desirable to consider what are the criticisms or proposals that have been made with reference to each of these two classes. The permanently-settled districts, as is well known, cover the greater part of Bengal, parts of the North-Western Provinces and Madras, and a few other isolated tracts. At an earlier period, the school of thought that is represented by the present critics of the Government of India advocated the extension of the Permanent Settlement throughout India; and although this panacea is no longer proposed, the Government of India are invited by Mr. Dutt to believe that had such a policy been carried into effect 40 years ago, "India would have been spared those more dreadful and desolating famines which we have witnessed in recent years." It is also stated by the latter in his letter upon

Land Settlements in Bengal that, in consequence of the Permanent Settlement in that province, the cultivators are more prosperous, more resourceful, and better able to help themselves in years of bad harvest, than cultivators in any other part of India, that agricultural enterprise has been fostered, cultivation extended, and private capital accumulated, which is devoted to useful industries and to public works and institutions. The hypothetical forecast above recorded is not rendered more plausible to the Government of India by their complete inability to endorse the accompanying allegations of fact. Bengal, and particularly Eastern Bengal, possesses exceptional advantages in its fertility, in its comparative immunity from the vicissitudes of climate to which other parts of the country are liable, in its excellent means of communication, in its enjoyment of a practical monopoly of the production of jute, and in the general trade and enterprise which radiate from its capital city. But neither these advantages nor the Permanent Settlement have availed to save Bengal from serious drought when the monsoon failure, from which it is ordinarily free, has spread to that part of India. Omitting to notice the frequent earlier famines, that known as the Behar famine of 1873-74 (so called from the part of the Bengal Province most seriously affected) cost the State £6,000,000, while it can be shown that in the famine of 1897 there were at the height of the distress considerably more than ¾ million persons on relief in the permanently settled

Failure of the Permanent Settlement to prevent famine in Bengal.

districts of Bengal, and that the total cost of that famine to the Bengal Administration was Rs. 1,08,04,000, or £720,266 (as compared with a famine expenditure of Rs. 98,28,000, or £655,200, in Madras, and Rs. 1,26,37,000 or £842,466, in Bombay), and this although the daily cost of relief for each person was less (Re. ·081 in Bengal as compared with Re. ·104 in Madras and Re. ·106 in Bombay). If the figures of persons in receipt of relief in the permanently settled districts of Western Bengal were compared with those of the adjoining temporarily settled districts of the North-Western Provinces, where the conditions were closely similar, it would also be found that the percentage was more than half as high again in Behar as in the North-Western Provinces. The Government of India indeed know of no ground whatever for the contention that Bengal has been saved from famine by the Permanent Settlement, a contention which appears to them to be disproved by history; and they are not therefore disposed to attach much value to predictions as to the benefits that might be ensued had a similar settlement been extended elsewhere.

Its influence on the condition of the tenantry in Bengal.

6. As regards condition of cultivators in Bengal, who are the tenants of the land-owners instituted as a class in the last century by the British Government, there is still less ground for the contention that their position, owing to the Permanent Settlement, has been converted into one of exceptional comfort and prosperity. It is precisely because this was not the case, and because, so

far from being generously treated by the Zeminders, the Bengal cultivator was rack-rented, impoverished, and oppressed, that the Government of India felt compelled to intervene on his behalf, and by the series of legislative measures, that commenced with the Bengal Tenancy Act of 1859 and culminated in the Act of 1885, to place him in the position of greater security, which he now enjoys. To confound this legistation with the Permanent Settlement, and to ascribe even in part to the latter the benefits which it had conspicuously failed to confer, and which would never have accrued but for the former, is strangely to misread history. As for the allegation that the Parmanent Settlement has been the means of developing in Bengal an exceptional flow of public-spirited and charitable investment, while the Government of India are proud of the fact that there are many worthy and liberal-minded landlords in Bengal—as there also are in other parts of India—they know that the evils of absenteeism, of management of estates by unsympathetic agents, of unhappy relation between landlord and tenant, and of the multiplication of tenure-holders, or middle-men between the Zeminder and the cultivator in many and various degrees—are at least as marked and as much on the increase there as elsewhere; and they cannot conscientiously endorse the proposition that, in the interests of the cultivator, the system of agrarian tenure should be held up as a public model, which is not supported by the experience of any civilised country, which is not justified by the single great experiment that has been made in India, and which was found in the latter case to place the tenant so unreservedly at the mercy of the landlord that the State has been compelled to employ for his protection a more stringent measure of legislation than has been found necessary in temporarily settled areas. It is not in fine in the Permanent Settlement of Bengal that the ryot has found his salvation ; it has been in the laws which have been passed by the Supreme Government to check its license and to moderate its abuse.

The two classes of Temporary settlements : Zemindari and Ryotwari.

7. It is, however, to the temporary settled districts that the bulk of criticism has been directed, and to this branch of the subject the Governor General in Council will now turn. The two sub-divisions of this category will be successively examined ; the Zemindari tracts (in some provinces called Malguzari and Talukdari), where the landlord pays the Land Revenue to the State, whether he cultivates the land himself or by means of rent-paying tenants ; and the Ryotwari tracts, where the cultivator pays directly to the State.

8. The Zemindari tenure is the prevailing form of land tenure in the Central Provinces, the North-Western Provinces and Oudh, and the Punjab. The suggestions with regard to it, which the Government of India have been invited to consider, are as follows :—

Suggested reforms in Zemindari Settlement examined.

(1) Limitation of landlord's enhancement of tenants' rents.

9. It is nowhere clearly stated, but it may be inferred, that in the opinion of their critics some limit should be placed to the amount of rent which the landlord may take from his tenant. The Government of India

would have been better pleased had greater prominence and a more indisputable enunciation been given to this proposition, since it is one with which they are in cordial agreement. It does not seem to them to be consistent that great stress should be laid upon the share of the produce which should be taken by the Government when it deals directly with the tenant, or with the share of the rental that it should take from the landlord when the latter is the intermediary, while little or no attention is devoted to the rent paid by the cultivator in cases where he happens to pay it to a Zemindar. If it is the interests of the ryot that are at stake, and that stand in most urgent need of protection, that protection is not less necessary when his payments are made to a Native landlord in the form of rent, than when they are made in the form of Land Revenue to the British Government. Such being the logic of the case, it is with satisfaction that the Government of India can point to the fact that the principles here laid down have been, and are still, the basis of the numerous Tenancy Laws which have been enacted by them in recent years. Mention has already been made of the Tenancy Acts in Bengal. Similar legislation has been carried through for the Central Provinces; and in the North-Western Provinces a Tenancy Law has recently been strengthened in the interest of the ryots. The Government of India will welcome from their critics, upon future occasions, a co-operation in these attempts to improve and to safeguard the position of the tenant which they have not hitherto as a rule been so fortunate as to receive.

(2) Limitation of the State's demand on landlords.

10. The next contention is that where the land revenue is paid to the State by the landlord, the principle adopted in the Saharanpur Rules of 1855, limiting the State-demand to one-half of the rent or assets of the landlord, should be unversally applied. Here it seems to the Governor General in Council to be necessary to utter a word of caution, which will be found to apply both to the present and still more to some of the subsequent proposals that will come under examination. These proposals contain the common suggestion of definite mathematical fractions of rent or produce, as the maximum share of Government. The Governor General in Council, while far from denying the possible utility of such standards as general principles of guidance, must guard himself from any acceptance of them as hard-and-fast rules of practice. It is impossible to apply any one criterion to all parts or classes in one Province, much more so to the whole of India. The conditions of uniformity which would alone justify uniformity of treament, are in many cases lacking. A rule of division which would be light in one case might be harsh in another; a proportion of rent or of produce which would leave a wide margin of profit in one part of India might be vexatious elsewhere. While, therefore, general principles may reasonably be formulated in order, as far as possible, to secure unity and continuity of policy, the Government of India would deprecate, in any case, the hasty acceptance of too precise mathematical formulæ, as likely to tie the hands of their officers, and

to produce rigidity, instead of elasticity, in Land Revenue administration.

11. Subject to the above qualification, to Governor General in Council now proceeds to examine the suggestion of a 50 per cent. limitation of the Government share in the landlord's rental. It has already been stated on the authority of Regulation XIX of 1793 that the ruling power in India has always, by the ancient law of the country, been entitled to share in the produce of the soil. Regulation II of 1793 pointed out that the Government share of that produce was fixed by estimating the rents paid by the tenants, deducting therefrom the cost of collection, allowing to the lanlords one-eleventh of the remainder as their share, and appropriating the balance or ten-elevenths, as the share of the State. But if this was the ostensible basis upon which the Permanent Settlement in Bengal was originally made, and if, at the commencement of their fiscal administration, the Government of India thus followed indigenous custom in assessing the revenue, they soon began to moderate the severity of the practice. It is unnecessary to trace here in detial the process of mitigation. It will suffice to say that long before the late century had reached its midway point the demand of the State upon the landlord had been limited to two-thirds of the net assets. About the middle of the century, *i.e.*, before the mutiny, the question of the relative share of the State and of the landlords in the net produce of the soil came again under careful review in Northern India; and

Ancient right of the State to a share of the produce of the soil.

the result of this further consideration of the matter was embodied in what are known as the "Saharanpur Rules" (so called because they were issued in connection with the resettlement of the land revenue of the Saharanpur district of the North-Western Provinces). The Settlement Rules previously in force authorised the demand of two-thirds of the net produce of an estate, or rather its value in money, as the Government share in respect of land revenue. The Saharanpur Rules, issued in 1855, laid down "not that the revenue of each estate was to be fixed at one-half of the net average assets, but that in taking these assets with other data into consideration, the Collector will bear in mind that about one-half, and not two-thirds as heretofore, of the well-ascertained net assets should be the Government demand." These orders have since remained the accepted canon of assessments on landlord's estates in the North-Western Provinces, and they continued to govern assessments in the adjacent districts of the Central Provinces, until the constitution of the latter as a separate administration in 1862. But, for the assessment of the Nagpur district of the Central Provinces, which had been escheated to the Government of India in 1854, assessment up to 60 per cent. of the gross rental had been permitted by separate orders issued in 1860, owing partly to the undesirability of introducing too sharp a revulsion from the practice of the previously existing native administration, partly to the great extent of uncultivated land, which enabled the landlords largely to

The Saharanpur Rules.

increase their incomes while the Settlement was running its course.

Progressive reduction of the State's share under British rule.

12. It is, therefore, an erroneous assumption that what is known as the "half assets rule" anywhere bound the Government to take as its land revenue from a district as a whole no more than 50 per cent. of the actual rental of the land owners. Not only were there no compulsory orders in the matter, but the construction placed on the word "assets" at the time, and for many years later, permitted the Settlement Officer to look beyond the actual cash rental, and to take into consideration prospective increases of income, to assume a fair rent for land held by tenants enjoying privileges as against the landlord, and to consider the profits of *sir* or home-farm cultivation (where the land was held entirely by cultivating proprietors) as well as the rental value of home-farm lands. Hence it arose that the assessments taken, though amounting only to about 50 per cent. of the nominal assets, absorbed as a rule a considerably higher proportion of the realised rental. In recent years, however, there has been a steady movement in the downward direction. In the North-Western and other Zemindari provinces, prospective assets have been excluded from consideration; allowances have been made for improvements made by the landlord, for precariousness of cultivation, and for local circumstances; and the revenue has been fixed at a share of the actual income of the proprietor, his income including a fair rental value for the

lands which he farms himself, or assigns on privileged terms to tenants. The share to be taken as land revenue by Government is thus being brought down in the North-Western Provinces—in the interests of the proprietor—to an average of less than 50 per cent., while in the re-settlement of Oudh, now on the point of completion, the average falls below 47 per cent. In the Central Provinces, which have been for a shorter period under British rule, and where much higher assessments, amounting in some cases to over 75 per cent. of the actual income, were inherited from the Mahratta Government, there has been a progressive reduction of assessment; but it has not yet reached the very moderate level that is common in the North-Western Provinces. In time, as population increases, and more labour and expenditure are devoted to cultivation, the share taken by Government may be expected still further to diminish, and already (as pointed out in the Report from the Central Provinces) three of the districts in the north of the provinces have recently been re-assessed (from a desire to limit the sudden enhancements that result from long-term settlements) at less than 50 per cent. of the rental. In Orissa the gradual reduction of the Government proportion has been even more striking. In 1822 it was authoritatively declared to be 83·3 of the assets; in 1833 it was lowered to 70—75 per cent.; in 1840 to 65 per cent., with a permissive reduction to 60 per cent., while at the re-settlement just concluded, it has been brought down to 54 per cent. In the Punjab, where proprietary cultivation is common, and where the maximum land revenue that may be taken is the "estimated value of half the net produce"—the principal guide to this being the rents that are paid by neighbouring tenants-at-will—the calculations given in the official reply reveal yet lower proportions. Assessments of 45, 39, 35, and 25 per cent, are recorded in particular cases, and the general average is shown not to exceed 45 per cent. of the net income.

13. From this summary it results that, while the standard of 50 per cent. has nowhere been laid down as a fixed and immutable prescription, there has been, and there is, a growing tendency throughout temporary settled zemindari districts to approximate to it, and in special circumstances a very much lower share is taken. It does not appear to the Government of India to be necessary to issue fresh regulations upon a matter in which their general policy is so clear, and where, save in exceptional cases, to be justified by local conditions, uniformity of practice is now so common.

Suggested reforms in Ryotwari Settlements: Revenue to be a definite share of gross produce.

14. The Governor General in Council now passes to the consideration of those parts of the country where, under temporary settlements, the ryotwari or peasant proprietary form of tenure prevails, and where the cultivator pays directly to the State. The principal illustrations of this category are the greater parts of the presidencies of Madras and Bombay, and the Provinces of Burma and Assam. The recommendations that have been made with regard to these areas will now be examined. It should be noted,

however, that there is not complete identity between the two forms of the first recommendation that falls to be noticed; for whereas the memorial sets forward the proposition that "the Government demand should be limited to 50 per cent. of the value of the net produce, after a liberal deduction for cultivation expenses has been made, and should not ordinarily exceed one-fifth of the gross produce, even in those parts of the country where, in theory, one-half of the net is assumed to approximate to one-third of the gross produce," Mr. Dutt, when speaking for himself, urges that "the impracticable rule of realising one-half the net produce or one-third the gross produce be abandoned, and the rule of fixing one-fifth the gross produce as the maximum of rent be adopted." It appears, therefore, that whereas Mr. Dutt as a signatory of the memorial does not contemplate the complete abandonment of the net produce standard, he yet, when petitioning on his own behalf, describes it as impracticable, and urges its disappearance. Moreover, in the latter capacity, he advocates a further mathematical criterion, namely, that while the maximum of one-fifth the produce should not be exceeded in the case of any single holding, the average land revenue for a whole district, including wet and dry lands, should be limited to one-tenth, as alleged to be the case in Northern India.

Danger of arithmetical standards.

15. These fractional standards illustrate the remarks which were made a little earlier as to the danger of laying down hard-and-fast lines; and they also

indicate the arbitrary and inelastic nature of the system which the Government of India are now invited to introduce. When Mr. Dutt suggests the analogy of Northern India, which is under an entirely different form of tenure, he appears to confuse rent with revenue, for he has elsewhere said that in Bengal and Northern India the average rents paid by the cultivator to the landlord are equivalent to one-fifth or 20 per cent. (not 10 per cent.) of the gross produce; whereas he here recommends that in Southern India the average proportion should be limited to one-tenth, or 10 per cent. Why there should be this distinction is not made clear.

Impracticability of the suggestion that the land revenue should be fixed at a share of the gross produce.

16. The Government of India believe it to be an entirely erroneous idea that it is either possible or equitable to fix the demand of the State at a definite share of the gross produce of land. There is great practical difficulty in ascertaining what the average produce is. It is dependent upon a number of varying factors, such as the industry and resources of the cultivator, the nature of the crop, the capacity, security, and situation of the holding, and the chance of the seasons. The share of the gross produce which a crop can afford to pay must stand in close relation and in inverse proportion to the amount of expenditure which has been required to grow it, and this will vary very greatly, for instance, in the cases of sugar-cane and of wheat. In zemindari districts, accordingly, rental value, and not produce, has for the last 50 years been adopted as the basis of assessments, although the

latter have commonly been checked by comparison with produce, with the result, as a rule, of showing that, judged by that standard, they were unreasonably low. In the ryotwari provinces of Madras and Burma, the attempt has been made to fix assessment rates in accordance with produce, but the rules giving effect to this principle fence it round with so many qualifications as practically to involve its abandonment. It is now nearly 40 years since the alternative standard of half the net produce was introduced in Madras, the reason being that the gross produce standard, while it favoured the more fertile, pressed with extreme severity upon the poorer lands. But even the standard thus adopted has not been worked up to in practice. There and elsewhere the net produce has been valued at much less than the current money rates, the outturn per acre deduced from crop experiments has heen notoriously underestimated, and liberal deductions have been made for unprofitable cultivation, distance from markets and vicissitudes of season, so that the rates in actual use for assessment are considerably below the nominal share. There has been a similar reduction in the theoretical measure of assessment, which is also one-half of the net produce, in Burma ; and the last assessment report received from the Hanthawaddy district shows that the assessment actually imposed fall short of a quarter (not one-half) of the net produce by nearly 20 per cent. The truth is that assessment of land revenue is subject to so many complicated and varying conditions that any attempt to educe it to an exact mathematical proportion either of gross or of net produce would not only be impracticable, but would lead to the placing of burdens upon the shoulders of the people, from which, under a less rigid system, if sympathetically administered, they are exempt. Nor must the influence of the personal equation be ignored. Those who are familiar with the realities of assessment know well that among Settlement Officers there is a growing inclination towards leniency of assessment; and that this spirit is encouraged by the avowed policy of Government, of the considerateness of which the progressive reduction of the State demand already indicated affords conclussive proof. The more the officers of Government know of the people, and the more intimate their mutual relations become, the less likelihood is there of severity in the enforcement of public dues. In no official relation does a member of the Public Service come into such close contact with the people as in Settlement work; and it cannot be his desire to aggrieve those among whom he is spending some of the most laborious years of his life, or to initiate a Settlement which, after a short interval, will break down. Every natural instinct and every recent injunction of the Supreme Government urge him to reasonableness and moderation.

Its effects if adopted.

17. Nothing, indeed, can be more clear than that, while the net produce rule itself calls for, and is habitually subject to, modifications in the interest of the cultivator, the gross produce standard recommended by the memorialists would, if systematically applied lead to an increase of assessment all round. The Report

from the Central Provinces shows that the proportion to produce of the gross rental ranges from one-sixth to one-fourteenth, and that the enforcement of any such standard would double the liabilities of the ryots. The Bengal Report gives statistical reasons for believing that rents are generally much below one-fifth of the gross produce, and indicates that ryots on Government temporarily settled estates are, judged by this standard, better off than under proprietors with a Permanent Settlement. The Madras reply says that, "if Government took one-fifth of the real gross produce from its ryots, it would fully double its present land revenue, exclusive of cesses, but inclusive of the total charge for water." In the ryotwari tracts of the Punjab the proportion taken by Government nowhere exceeds one-fifth of the gross produce, and is more often one-seventh or one-eighth, or even less. Similar conclusions are borne out by the Report of the recent Famine Commission (paragraphs 261—268), in which it is stated, as the result of special enquiries, that in the Central Provinces the incidence of land revenue is less than 4 per cent. of the average value of the produce, that in Berar it is about 7 per cent., in Ajmer about 10 per cent., in the Hissar district of the Punjab 3½ per cent., in other parts of the Punjab 7 per cent., except in the Delhi district, where it is 10 per cent. ; in the Deccan probably above 7 per cent., in the Punch Mahals 5 per cent. ; and in Gujrat alone (where the profits on cultivation are very high) 20 per cent. ; or the equivalent of the one-fifth pleaded for in the memorial. Since then it has been conclusively established that, under the existing practice, the Government is already taking much less than it is now invited to exact, and since the average rate, so far from showing an inclination to enhancement, is everywhere on the downward grade, the Governor General in Council is unable to accept a proposal which could only have consequences the very opposite of those which are anticipated by its authors.

The term of settlement. Suggested minimum of 30 years.

18. The next recommendation to which the attention of the Government of India has been drawn is that no term of settlement in temporarily settled districts should be for a shorter period than 30 years. The history of settlements may briefly be summarised as follows. In Bombay the 30 years' term was introduced by the Court of Directors so far back as 1837. From there it was extended to Madras and the North-Western Provinces, where it has been the standard period for the last half century. The same principle was followed in an extension of the Orissa Settlement in 1867, and in confirming most of the Settlements made in the Central Provinces between 1860 and 1870. But it never came into general use in the Punjab, where, in the greater part of the province, the shorter term of 20 years has been the recognized rule. The question was exhaustively examined in 1895, when it was finally decided by the Secretary of State that 30 years should continue to be the ordinary term of settlement in Madras, Bombay, and the North-Western Provinces, that in the

Punjab 20 years should be the general rule (30 years being admitted in some cases), and in the Central Provinces 20 years also. A 30 years' term has been adopted for the recent re-settlement of Orissa. In backward tracts, such as Burma and Assam, and in exceptional circumstances such as exist in Sind, shorter terms are permitted. The reasons for this differentiation are familiar and obvious. Where the land is fully cultivated, rents fair, agricultural production not liable to violent oscillations, it is sufficient if the demands of Government are re-adjusted once in 30 years, *i.e.*, once in the lifetime of each generation. Where the opposite conditions prevail, where there are much waste land, low rents, and a fluctuating cultivation, or again where there is a rapid development of resources owing to the construction of roads, railways, or canals, to an increase of population, or to a rise in prices, the postponement of re-settlement for so long a period is both injurious to the people, who are unequal to the strain of a short enhancement, and unjust to the general tax-payer, who is temporarily deprived of the additional revenue to which he has a legitimate claim. Whether these considerations, justifying a shorter term of settlement than 30 years, apply with sufficient force to the Punjab and the Central Provinces at the present time; and, if they do apply at the present time, whether the force of their application will diminish with the passage of time, are weighty questions to which careful attention will be given by the Government of India upon a suitable occasion.

Considerations which determine the term of Settlement.

Improvements in procedure rendering re-settlement less disturbing.

19. It may further be pointed out that many of the objections at one time urged to revisions of settlement have become, or are fast becoming, obsolete. The process of re-settlement itself is more rapid and less disturbing than was formerly the case. Where the re-settlement of a district thirty years ago lasted for six or eight years, the work is now, in a large district, usually completed in about four years and often in less. The improvement in the village records, and their punctual correction and maintenance up to date, have to a large extent obviated the necessity for detailed surveys, and for those local enquiries by subordinate officers which were in former times a fruitful source of harassment and extortion to the agricultural community. The aim of the existing policy is to exclude underlings from all connection either with the work of assessment or with the preliminary investigations leading up to it, and to devolve upon the Settlement Officer and his gazetted assistants all the negotiations with the people. The Government of India and the Local Governments will always be ready to carry this policy to further developments, their object being to simplify the maintenance, correct and up to date, of the village papers, and thereby to secure an authentic record of the rights and privileges of the people, as well as a trustworthy instrument for the speedy determination of the fair claims of the Government on the land.

20. Again, the principle of exempting from assess-

Exemption of improvements from assessment.

ments such improvements as have been made by private enterprise, though it finds no place in the traditions of the past, has been accepted by the British Government, and is provided for by definite rules, culminating, in the case of the Bombay Presidency, in legal enactments which secure to the cultivator in perpetuity the whole of the profit arising not only from such irrigation works as private wells or tanks, but from the minor improvements which would count for an increase in assessment under a system of reclassification of the soil. The Madras ryots have a recognized right to enjoy for ever the fruit of their improvements, and the exemption of wells, irrigation channels, and tanks which are private property is provided for by executive orders. Minor improvements are also protected, as in Bombay, by the permanent recognition of a land classification once fairly effected. In zemindari provinces, where the revenue is temporarily assessed on estates as a whole, and not on each particular plot of land composing them, the State has not similarly surrendered its right to all share in improvements in which the capacity of the soil plays a part with the industry or outlay of the cultivator. But the principle followed has been that additional assessments should not be imposed on these grounds until the private labour or capital expended upon them has had time to reap a remunerative return. In the Punjab and Bengal the term of exemption has been fixed, without reference to the term of settlement, at 20 years for masonry wells, 5 years for canal distributaries, and 10 years for other irrigation works. In the North-Western Provinces and the Central Provinces, irrigation works not constructed by Government are freed for the term of settlement next following their construction, the average period of exemption being 45 years in the former and 30 years in the latter provinces. The rules of all provinces provide for the grant of longer terms of exemption in special cases. This summary of existing procedure reveals a variety in practice which it is not possible to reduce to complete uniformity. It is the intention, however, of the Government of India, in consultation with the Local Governments, to take the whole matter into consideration, with a view to the framing of rules that may stimulate the expenditure of private capital upon the improvement of the land, and secure to those who profit by such opportunities the legitimate reward of their enterprise.

Effects of long as against short settlements in increasing resources of the people.

21. The question of the effect upon the domestic life of the community of long as against short settlements has been the subject of much discussion. It may be regarded as certain that long-term settlements leave more money to the people, however large be the revenue enhancement at the close. On the other hand, short-term settlements, which are the familiar practice of Native Rulers, excite less discontent, when not associated with inquisitorial proceedings. An increase of liabilities which comes once in a generation is said by some to be more acutely resented than which has been rendered familiar

by more frequent repetition. Upon this point it is difficult and perhaps unnecessary to pronounce: attention should, however, be called to a concession made by the Government with a view to reducing its own share of the produce, and leaving more to the landholder. Formerly the basis of assessment was the anticipated average yield of the land during the coming period of settlement. Now it is the actual yield at the time of assessment, so that the landowner enjoys to the full any new advantages that may accrue either from his own outlay or from outside circumstances, in the interval before the next revision is made. Assessment upon actual, as distinct from prospective, assets has thus become a cardinal principle of the land revenue policy of Government.

Suggested limitation of Government enhancements to rise in value due to (1) State improvements, (2) rise in prices.

22. In the foregoing paragraphs a partial answer has been given to the next prayer of the memorialists that in ryotwari tracts "there should be no increase in assessments except in cases where the land has increased in value, (1) in consequence of imprvements in irrigation works carried out at the expense of Government; (2) on account of a rise in the value of produce, based on the average prices of the thirty years next preceding such revision." The first of the above provisos is not included in Mr. Dutt's independent recommendation, which is to the effect that no enhancement be anywhere permitted at a new settlement except on the ground of an increase of prices. The entire contention will now be examined.

The principle that the State in India has a right to share in the produce of the land carries with it the right to share in any increment of the produce or its value. In the case of increments resulting from the expenditure of private labour or capital, this right, as has already been pointed out, has been altogether waived in some provinces, and materially limited in others. But it can scarcely be contended that such a surrender should equally apply to improvements produced by the growth of population, by the gradual development of the country, by the introduction of new staples or by an increase in the productivity of the soil and in the value of its produce, more particularly if the latter are themselves the result of an expenditure upon irrigation or communications that has been incurred by the State. The concession to the landlord or the tenant of a complete monopoly of the profits of all improvements of the soil in perpetuity whether created by himself or not, would be a doctrine not merely economically unsound, but without any foundation in native custom or any precedent in history. What happens in practice is this: in Zemindari areas the claims of Government to a share in the increasing value of the land are adjusted by a periodical settlement with the landlords for its portion of the rental, subject to a not infrequent sacrifice, in the interest of the tenants, of the fractions which might fairly be claimed. The possibility of making prices the basis of assessment in these tracts was carefully considered, and was finally negatived by the Secretary of State in 1885. Some interesting information may be derived from the Bengal Report as to the inequality of assessment which has resulted in that province from the non-interference of Government during the past century; and from this may be deduced how uneven a settlement would become that was only liable to revision by an all round enhancement or deduction. Whatever be the case as regards Zemindari districts, it is now, however, urged that in Ryotwari areas no ground of enhancement but a rise in price should in future be allowed. Attention has already been called to the limitation that has been placed by Government upon the discretion of its officers in respect of changes in land classification as a possible basis of enhancement. In Bombay no change in a classification once definitely accepted is permitted by the law. In Madras, though the Government of India, acting under the instructions of the Secretary of State in 1885, have declined to give a pledge against future revisions of classification, they have intimated their cordial acceptance of the principle that the existing classification, if found to be in the main equitable, shall, on re-settlement, not be disturbed. In these circumstances, to deny the right of the State to a share in any increase of values except those which could be inferred from the general tables of price statistics—in itself a most fallacious and partial test—would be to surrender to a number of individuals an increment which they had not themselves earned, but which had resulted, partly from the outlay of Government money on great public works, such as canals and railways, partly from the general enhancement of values produced by expanding resources and a higher standard of civilisation.

Limitation of cesses on land.

23. The concluding proposal, which it is the duty of the Governor-General in Council to examine, and which, in slightly different shapes, finds a place in both memorials, is that no cesses should be imposed on the rental of land, except for purposes directly benefiting the land, and that a limit should be fixed beyond which it may not be permissible to surcharge the land tax with local taxation. These cesses, which are levied for the construction and repair of roads, the upkeep of schools and dispensaries, and other similiar duties appertaining to Local Government Boards, are generally assessed on the assets or rental value, since the land revenue would, in many provinces, be an unfair basis of distribution. The rate in force in Bengal is $6\frac{1}{4}$ per cent. on the rental, and this rate is taken as a fair standard by Mr. Dutt when speaking for himself. When associated with the other memorialists, he admits that the maximum rate may be as high as 10 per cent., a proportion which, as a matter of fact, is nowhere exceeded. But before going into this question, the Governor-General in Council desires to record an emphatic dissent from the opinion that primary education is not a proper object of local taxation, and that such taxation should be limited to objects directly connected with the land. The aim of local taxation is the benefit of the community, and the spread of elementary education amongst the cultivating classes is the surest preventive of the carelessness which allows so large a proportion of the increased value, that settled government and improved communications have given to the

produce of agricultural industry, to slip through the fingers of the people.

Present incidence of Local Rates.

24. In the Ryotwari provinces of Bombay and Madras and in Coorg the incidence of the Local Rates (for roads and schools) is precisely that in force in Bengal. This comparison involves the assumption that Ryotwari revenue is the equivalent of rent; but, as a matter of fact, the extent to which sub-letting prevails in Ryotwari provinces indicates that the revenue is substantially below the rental value, and the Local Rates are consequently below the Bengal level. In Lower Burma the Local Rates amount to 10 per cent. and in Assam to 8·3 per cent. on the Ryotwari revenue. Though higher than elsewhere, they are within the maximum suggested in the memorial. In the Punjab they are equivalent to 5·2 per cent. on the rental value. In no other province do they exceed 4 per cent. In the North-Western Provinces they are charged at 6 per cent; but two-fifths of the proceeds are devoted to the maintenance of the village watch, which in Bengal and other parts is a charge upon special contributions assessed and collected apart from the Local Rates.

Responsibility of village communities of maintaining rural officers.

25. It may be objected, however, that the rates which are levied for Local Self-Government purposes are not the only extra charges imposed upon the population, and that count should also be taken of the sums payble by them for

the remuneration of the village officers—the watchman, the headman, and the accountant. The support of this village staff has been a charge on the community from time immemorial. In the Central Provinces and Bombay watchmen are still remunerated, according to ancient custom, by grants of land or by fees collected by them directly from the people. Elsewhere they are supported by the proceeds of a cess to which in some provinces non-agriculturists not unreasonably subscribe. The headman is a functionary of more importance in Ryotwari than in Zemindari villages, and, except in Madras, Sind, and Coorg, his remuneration in Ryotwari provinces has been accepted in whole or in part as a charge upon the land revenue which he collects. In the Zemindari provinces, the proprietor of a village is also its headman, but where there are several sharers in the proprietorship of a village, one or more of their number represent the remainder, and have a right to a commission on the revenue payable through them, the rate being generally 5 per cent. This represents a communal arrangement of very long standing. The village accountant's functions have been of late years considerably modified by his employment in the maintenance of a connected system of agricultural statistics for his village. This addition to his duties has been acknowledged in some provinces by grants towards his remuneration from the public revenues, but elsewhere than Bombay, Berar, Burma, and Assam, a cess provides, at all events, a part of his salary. The Governor-General in Council does not consider that these customary contributions towards the maintenance of the staff of village officers can be classed as local taxation without some important qualifications. The commission paid in Zemindari areas by proprietors to their representatives is in no sense a tax, and it is necessary, of course, to exclude from the watchman cess the contribution made in some provinces by non-agriculturists before adding it to the charge on the agricultural population. Assuming, however, that, subject to these deductions, the maintenance of village officers should be accounted as taxation, it is a noteworthy fact that in no provinces but Sind, Madras, and Coorg does local taxation exceed the maximum limit suggested in the memorial, the incidence in these provinces being respectively $12\frac{1}{4}$, $10\frac{3}{4}$, and $13\frac{1}{2}$ per cent. on the Ryotwari revenue. There can be little doubt that it would be substantially lower if calculated on the true rental value. The general conclusion of the Government of India is that there is no reason for thinking that local taxation, if properly distributed, is on the whole either onerous or excessive, while, as a general rule, it already falls short of the limit which the memorialists would propose to fix. But there are grounds for suspecting that the distribution is often unfair; and that the landlords shift on to the tenants that share of the burden which is imposed by the law upon themselves. In the present backward condition of so many of the people, it is not possible effectively to redress this injustice: and the question presents itself whether it is not better,

General conclusions as to burden of local taxation.

as opportunities occur, to mitigate imposts which are made to press upon the cultivating classes more severely than the law intended. The Government of India would be glad to see their way to offer such relief.

Illegal cesses exacted by landlords.

26. But the burdens of which complaint is made are by no means confined to the legal cesses, which, after all, are few in number and strictly limited in amount. There are also, in some Zemindari tracts, a number of practically unauthorized village cesses, of which no mention has been made by the critics of the existing system, but which are well-known to all those who are familiar with the economy of rural life in India. In many cases these unrecognized and often undesirable imposts exceed the total of the cesses levied under the British administration. Their imposition was prohibited by the Regulation of 1793, and ever since that date has been steadily discountenanced by the Government of India, as vexatious to the ryot and detrimental to the successful cultivation of the soil. Their complete suppression by the action of Government is not practicable in the present state of education among the agricultural classes. But the subject is one to which the friends of the ryot might appropriately devote their concern, and in which their exertions might be of much use in supplementing the opposition of Government to a wholly illegimate form of exaction.

27. The Governor-General in Council has now reviewed the particular suggestions of Mr. Dutt and the

Detailed examination of alleged connection of revenue assessments with the famine-resisting resources of the people.

memorialists. There remains to be noticed the underlying idea by which they have all alike been animated, and which, in some parts of the former's writings, has found definite expression. It is the theory that the amount of the land revenue taken by the Government of India, in one form or another, from the people is mainly responsible for famine, with its corollary that, were the assessments diminished, famine would be less frequent, or that at least, when they do occur, they would cause infinitely less suffering. The Governor General in Council does not believe that countenance to this theorv can be derived either from the recorded facts of history, or from the circumstances of the present day. The evidence that has been aduced in this Resolution testifies to a progressive reduction of assessments, extending throughout the last century, and becoming more instead of less active during its second half. If then the severity of famine be proportionate to the weight of assessments, the famines in the earlier part of the 19th century ought to have been incomparably more serious than towards its close; whereas the contention is familiar that the reverse has been the case. Again, the contention that in recent famines the parts of India that suffered most severely were the parts that were most highly assessed, finds (with the exception of Gujarat, which has not been seriously famine-stricken for a century and was soft and unprepared) no support in fact, and was expressly disowned by the recent Famine Commission. It is conclusively disproved in the case of the Central Provinces by the evidence of the Chief Commisioner that, in the famine of 1899—1900, the districts which felt the famine pressure most acutely were those which had been exempted from paying the revised assessments, introduced at the previous revision; while the districts that suffered most from the famine of 1896—1897 were those in which there had been no enhancement for 40 years.

Agricultural losses resulting from famine.

28. The fallacy in question is the result of an imperfect appreciation of the smallness of the land revenue compared with the enormous losses resulting from a widespread failure of crops. It has been estimated that in the Central Provinces the agricultural classes have lost 40 crores of rupees, or more than 26 millions sterling during the past seven years—an amount equivalent to the total land revenue of 50 years; while seven years' land revenue would be required to recoup the State for its famine expenditure in these provinces since the year 1896. Similar calculations could be made with regard to the other famine-smitten provinces. It is clear that no reduction of the land revenue demand, short of its total abolition and not even its abolition itself, could enable any community to hold up its head against a calamity so vast and so appalling.

Probable effects of an abatement of the land revenue on the resources of the people.

29. It is not of course disputed that if the Government were largely to abate its demand, and if the amount of such abatement were fairly distributed amongst the cultivating

classes and were saved up by them, instead of being thoughtlessly spent, or absorbed by an increase of population, or appropriated by a particular section, a reserve would be created that might enable those classes better to withstand the losses caused by failure of the rains. But, unfortunately, neither in the past nor in the present circumstances of the country can any warrant be found for the belief that the revenue so relinquished by Government would constitute a famine relief fund in the hand of the people. Experience has shown that excessive leniency of the kind in question re-acts prejudicially upon the industry of the agricultural classes, while it encourages the transfer of the soil to money-lenders and middlemen, who swallow the profits intended for the cultivators, and reduce the latter to a condition resembling serfdom. In illustration a reference may be made to Behar, which is permanently settled at a very light revenue, estimated as equivalent to a concession of at least 80 lakhs of rupees a year to the inhabitants. These advantages, however, have been monopolised by the land-owning section of the community, while the Behar tenants remain among the most heavily rented in India; and as the experience of two famines in the last 30 years has shown, have displayed the least capacity of resistance to the shock.

The classes which suffer from famine.

30. An additional source of error lies in the conception, which is erroneous, that it is from the rent-paying or revenue-paying classes of the agricultural community that the sufferers in famine and

the recipients of famine relief are principally drawn. An inspection of any relief works on a large scale, while it will show that the poorer sections of the tenant class are not unrepresented, will also demonstrate that the great majority are not ryots, but labourers on the land, whom the land revenue assessment practically in no way affects.

Theory of connection between land revenue and famines rejected by famine Commission, 1901.

31. It is noteworthy that the theory which has here been examined, meets with no encouragement at the hands of the latest expert body that has enquired into the facts of the case, *viz.*, the Famine Commission of 1901. After stating what was, in each of the provinces visited by them, the pressure of the land revenue on the soil—in figures which have already been cited—they concluded by saying that except in Bombay, where they regarded it as full, the incidence of land revenue is low in moderate years, and that it should in no way, *per se*, be the cause of indebtedness. It is unnecessary, on the present occasion, to discuss what are the secondary causes of famine—for as to the primary, there can be no dispute—and of the poverty and indebtedness which famine brings in its train. But it is manifest that any one who shuts his eyes to the industrial and economic forces that are at work in India at the present time, and that are patent upon the surface of agrarian life, who does not take into account the ever-increasing sub-division of holding (arising from the land-hunger of the peasant population and the inveterate reluctance of the ryot to move even to the smallest distance from his natal place),

the decilne of industrial occupations other than agriculture, the rack-renting to which tenants are subjected by the more inconsiderate class of landlords and especially by middlemen of various degrees, the usurious rates of interest demanded by the money-lending class, the speculative expenditure upon litigation, the proneness to extravagance on festival occasions, and the numerous payments, in the form of petty bribes, among the ryots themselves, but who concentrates his entire gaze upon one aspect alone of their poverty, will carry away a most distorted impression both of the malady which he has set himself to diagnose, and of the remedies which it is in the power or is the duty of Government to apply.

Three possible causes of hardship requiring attention.

32. Before concluding his examination of this problem, the Governor General in Council desires to notice three aspects of the land revenue question involving three possible causes of hardship to the poorer landholder, which seems to him to be of much greater importance than the criticisms which he has so far been engaged in examining. The first of these is the pitch of enhancement, the second is the levy of the same assessment in bad years as in good, on the assumption that savings in the one will meet the losses of the other; the third is the effect of local deterioration upon land revenue payments.

(1) Large and sudden enhancements of rerevenue.

33. That revenue enhancements must often be large is of course the direct consequence of long-term settlements, and it is, no doubt, because their dis-

turbing effect furnishes an argument for shorter settlements, that a reference to it has not been found in the fore-front of attack. There can be no question of the hardship which a family must experience in finding its income suddenly reduced by a third or even more, as may happen, for instance, when at the end of a term of settlement it is enjoying 75 per cent. of the assets, and re-settlement is made at 50 per cent. the question in the aspect now under consideration is not really affected (as is sometimes assumed) by the grounds on which the enhancement is made: a heavy addition to the assessment is as disturbing if justified by a large increase of cultivation as if resulting from a rise in valuation rates. It may be argued that a family in such a case has profited largely by the enjoyment of income which it would have lost under a shorter term settlement; that it should have saved from its surplus to meet the eventual curtailment of its means; and that the State will find long-term settlements exceedingly disadvantageous if it is not only to lose all increment during their currency, but is also to forego part of its dues at their close. But the question must be considered from a practical point of view, and with reference to the conditions of human nature. The State cannot without hesitation call upon people suddenly to effect a great reduction in their domestic expenditure, however well-justified in theory its demand may be. A man will look more to the actual increase of his obligations than he will to the arithmetical standards by which it is justified or determined. If for 30 years he has been paying a land revenue of Rs. 1,000 and is called upon to pay Rs. 2,000 upon resettlement, it is small consolation to him to be told that, while the former sum represented 50 per cent. of his former assets, the latter only amounts to 47 per cent. of his assets as they now stand. A reduction in percentages is far from compensating him for an enhancement of burdens.

The remedy applied.

34. To meet such cases, the Government of India desire to lay much stress upon the principal of gradual and progresive enforcement of sudden increases of other than moderate dimensions. The mitigation of a large enhancement by spreading its imposition over a term of years has been a recognised feature in the settlement procedure of Upper India for a long time past, but has not till recently been brought systematically into practice. In 1895 the Government of India, with the concurrence of the Secretary of State, drew general attention to the advisability of making larger use of progressive enhancements. In the North-Western Provinces, very complete effect has already been given to this principle. Similar rules have recently been used in the resettlement of the Seoni district in the Central Provinces, and the expediency will now be considered of prescribing it for general guidence in those provinces. The rules of this subject contained in the Bengal settlement code are of particular application to ryots and tenure holders; but they admit the use of progressive assessments in the Orissa settlements, though they lay down no definite scheme of progression, and, as a matter of fact, progressive assessments were most liberally granted in those settle-

ments at a loss to the state of nearly 8 lakhs of rupees. In the Punjab, the use of progressive assessments has been discouraged on the ground that, though an appropriate means of easing an enhancement to a large landholder, they are not suitable to the circumstances of the petty proprietors who hold a very large proportion of the land in that province. Large increases in the demand have been commonly avoided by under assessment. But it seems open to question whether an expedient which has proved serviceable in other parts of India might not be usefully adopted in the Punjab, and the point will be considered, though the effect of of progressive assessments in this province would be to raise, not to lower, the Government revenue. Turning now to Ryotwari settlements, a rule of the Madras Settlement Code limits to 25 per cent. the enhancement which may be imposed at once, the balance being imposed by annual instalments each not exceeding 12½ per cent. on the original assessment. This gives a ryot six years in which to accommodate himself to the doubling of his assessment. In the Bombay Presidency also the levy of substantial enhancements is distributed over a term of years, and the maximum enhancement may not exceed double the former amount. Deviations from these rules have, however, apparently been permitted. The procedure of Ryotwari Settlements renders it difficult for an assessing officer to pay close regard to the circumstances of individuals in framing his proposals, and there is, therefore, the greater need of general rules to obviate hardships in particular cases, even if it be conceded that men who cultivate their own land can support a heavier percentage enhancement than those who subsist upon rental receipts. The question is one that calls for, and will receive, further consideration.

35. The question of varying the revenue demand to meet the character of the season is similar to the preceding, in that it involves depature from the theory of settlement at the cost of some revenue to the State. In theory the Government revenue represents the sum that may fairly be demanded on an average of seasons, and it is assessed in the belief that cultivators will save from the surplus of good years to meet the deficit in bad. It is manifest, however, that, in tracts where the chances of a bad harvest are high, it must be exceedingly difficult to make allowances for crop failure in framing the assessment rates. And it is also clear that the agricultural classes have not, as a rule, yet learnt to regard a good harvest, not as an occasion for larger expenditure, but as a means of insurance against failure of crops. In truth, to a poor family a short harvest must be a severe calamity. The assessment may absorb but a small share of the gross produce of its land. But its circumstances depend on the net produce, on which the assessment is in higher proportion, and it is obvious that on inferior land a substantial deficiency in the outturn may leave no net produce whatever, so that (in the absence of savings) the assessment can only be paid by borrowing or by stinting the necessaries of life.

(2) Exaction of a fixed demand where produce fluctuates.

When such a deficiency is frequent, the rigid demand of the land revenue must add very materially to the hardships endured by a poor and uneducated people.

36. In tracts where great variations from the average of produce are not very frequent, such a demand may be suitable enough, its simplicity and educative effect compensating for the hardship that may be felt in individual cases. But where the produce of the land is liable to great and frequent fluctuations owing to failure of irrigation or vicissitudes of season, there is reason to apprehend that a fixed assessment may ruin people before it teaches them. The revenue system of several provinces—notably those of Madras and the Punjab have recognised the necessity of special arrangements for the remission of revenue for failure of crops on lands capable of being supplied by state irrigation works. In Madras no revenue is charged upon irrigable land the produce of which has not matured owing to the failure of water-supply; and in the Punjab this principle has received a further development, a deficiency of produce, not amounting to total failure, entitling the ryot to a proportionate abatement of the assessment rate. This system entails an elaborate procedure of crop inspection and throws much responsibility upon native subordinates. But it has worked well, and is being extended. Unirrigated lands in the Ryotwari provinces of Burma and Assam are ordinarily exempt from payment of assessment if left unsown; but these provinces afford almost the only exceptions to the rule that lands

Necessity for greater elasticity.

which are dependent upon the rainfall pay a fixed assessment irrespective of their produce. During the past twenty-five years the advantages, for lands of this description, of a more elastic system of collection have been urged at various times on the Government of India by very high authority, and have been carefully debated with Local Governments. The weight of opinion has been against change; but this seems to be due partly to the idea that remissions in some years would be balanced by an increase of assessment in others, and partly to the difficulty contemplated in appraising the loss sustained by each of thousands of small holdings. The Government of India freely admit that a fluctuating assessment, in the sense of an assessment without a definite maximum limit in cash, and annually varying with the outturn of the crops, is exceedingly difficult to work with fairness, throws an undesirable amount of power into the hands of subordinate officials, and lacks the influence for thrift which has been the desire of Government to secure in its land revenue policy. It would be a retrograde step, and would imply a reversion to the methods of Native rule. But these objections would not apply so forcibly to a system under which the produce of particular harvests would be taken merely to justify the reduction of a standard demand, when such produce falls below a point at which relief is, for general reasons, pronounced to be necessary. Experience, gained on a large scale during the past years of distress, indicates that when crop failure affects an entire village, or other separately assessed area, the difficulty of dealing with holdings individually may possibly be met by working from aggregate to detail, by accepting the village, or other such area, as the unit for calculating the amount of reduction to be given, and leaving it to subordinate officials of approved character merely to distribute this amount according to the degree of the loss sustained by individuals. Where a landlord is interposed between the ryots and the Government, his assistance will often be of value in making this distribution, as it is in the interest of his rental collections that it should be fair. Such a system will no doubt offer difficulties of its own and careful supervision would be indispensable. But the Government of India are not satisfied that, in certain well-known tracts of insecure land, where crops are liable to violent fluctuations in produce, some such plan is not required in the interests of the people, and the question of its introduction will receive fresh consideration. It would be essential that the working of the system should be under the supervision of European officers of experience, at all events during the first years following its introduction.

(3) Expediency of meeting local deterioration with prompt relief.

37. In a country of the size and diversity of India exceptions must occur to the general rule of agricultural progress, and localities are to be found where the conditions are those of actual deterioration. The Governor General in Council has in mind not only the losses of population and of produce which are the unavoidable consequences of severe famine, but the circumstances of tracts and villages

which lose ground owing to such special causes as the effect of decimating epidemics of malarial fever or other conditions, whether connected or not with vicissitudes of season. For some years past the Government of India have insisted upon the importance of the early detection of cases of local deterioration, and have committed to Provincial Departments of Land Records and Agriculture the conduct of systematic enquiries to this end. But the information thus collected has not always been fully utilized, and there have been cases in which a reduction of revenue was not granted till the troubles of the people had been aggravated by their efforts to provide the full fixed demand. It is no doubt true that any alteration of the assessment is in conflict with the terms of the original contract, by which the landholder has undertaken a liability for loss in return for an expectation of profit. But in this matter the interests of the Government are identical with the interests of the people, and it is unwise to exact from impoverished persons a revenue which they really cannot pay, merely because they are under an engagement to pay it. The Governor General in Council is convinced of the desirability of granting prompt relief in these cases, whether they involve tracts or single villages, even though such a course may involve a departure from the strict principles of settlement. The amount of revenue which the concession will cost to the State will be insignificant compared with the advantages obtained in assisting and encouraging an afflicted population.

38. In the review of their land revenue policy which

Summary of propositions established.

has now been brought to a close, the Government of India claim to have established the following propositions, which, for convenience sake, it may be desirable to summarise before concluding this Resolution :—

(1) That a Permanent Settlement, whether in Bengal or elsewhere, is no protection against the incidence and consequences of famine.

(2) That in areas where the State receives its land revenue from landlords, progressive moderation is the key-note of the policy of Government, and that the standard of 50 per cent. of the assets is one which is almost uniformly observed in practice, and is more often departed from on the side of deficiency than of excess.

(3) That in the same areas the State has not objected, and does not hesitate, to interfere by legislation to protect the interests of the tenants against oppression at the hands of the landlords.

(4) That in areas where the State takes the land revenue from the cultivators, the proposal to fix the assessment at one-fifth of the gross produce would result in the imposition of a greatly increased burden upon the people.

(5) That the policy of long-term settlements is gradually being extended, the exceptions being justified by conditions of local development.

(6) That a simplification and cheapening of the proceedings connected with new settlements, and an avoidance of the harassing invasion of an

army of subordinate officials, are a part of the deliberate policy of Government.

(7) That the principle of exempting or allowing for improvements is one of general acceptance, but may be capable of further extension.

(8) That assessments have ceased to be made upon prospective assets.

(9) That local taxation as a whole, though susceptible of some redistribution, is niether immoderate nor burdensome.

(10) That over-assessment is not, as alleged, a general or widespread source of poverty and indebtedness in India, and that it cannot fairly be regarded as a contributory cause of famine.

The Government of India have further laid down liberal principles for future guidance and will be prepared, where the necessity is established, to make further advance in respect of—

(11) the progressive and graduated imposition of large enhancement;

(12) greater elasticity in the revenue collection, facilitating its adjustment to the variations of the seasons, and the circumstances of the people;

(13) a more general resort to reduction of assessments in cases of local deterioration, where such reduction cannot be claimed under the terms of settlement.

Conclusion.

39. In thus defining their policy, the Government of India would not desire to claim for the land revenue system of

British India an exactitude or a freedom from blemish to which it cannot pretend. Historically it owes its immediate origin to practices inherited from the most decadent period of Native rule, and its form to changes made slowly, and not without mistakes, by men who were aliens to the country, and could only with difficulty, and by slow degrees, assimilate the requirements or enter into the feelings of people. Where habit and precedent count for more than wisdom, there has been need for caution in reform ; and logical completeness or simplicity could not be expected of a system born amid such surroundings, applied to such manifold conditions and to so heterogeneous a population, and subject, in the various stages of its development, to considerations of practical expediency rather than of abstract symmetry or scientific perfection. Indeed the one claim which the Government of India would decline to make for the land revenue system of this country is that it can properly be regarded as a science at all. In no country can land valuation be so described; and India, in spite of records, estimates, and tables, is no exception to the rule. A part of the weakness of the criticisms which have been directed against it, arises from the erroneous assumption that it can be regulated by fixed laws, or shaped by arithmetical standards. Assessments cannot be dictated by the theorist in his study ; they elude dogmatic treatment, and can only be safely worked out by the Settlement Officer in the village and on the fields. While they may admit of statistical analysis, they are liable to be hampered by premature statistical definition. The true function of

Government is to lay down broad and generous principles for the guidance of its officers, with becoming regard to the traditions of the province and the circumstances of the locality, and to prescribe moderation in enhancement, and sympathy in collection. Above all it is its duty to exercise discrimination in the choice of the agents whom it employs for this most critical and responsible of tasks. The Governor General in Council acknowledges with gratitude the services that have been rendered to Government in this respect by a long line of devoted and capable officers, and he believes that the existing system, if pursued upon the lines that have been indicated, is both well suited to the present conditions of the country, and compatible with its future development, and that the revenue which it provides, and which is more lenient in its incidence than at any previous stage of Indian history, is capable of being levied from the people with surprisingly little hardship and without discontent.*

* *Four Replies* to this Resolution will be found in the concluding portion of *Speeches and Papers Part II.*, included in this volume. A fuller exposition and history of the Indian Land Revenue Policy will be found in my *Economic History of India* (1757 to 1837) and my *India in the Victorian Age* (1838 to 1900).

LETTER FROM LORD GEORGE HAMILTON,

Secretary of State for India.

Dear Mr. Dutt,

I have to thank you for your letter and enclosure which pressure of business has alone prevented me from answering.

I am fully in sympathy with all disinterested efforts to improve our system of Land Revenue and Assessment; and to my mind the great advantage of the discussion you and others inaugurated was that it shewed that a wide and general misapprehension prevailed as to the principles governing the action of the Revenue Officers in fixing and resettling Land Revenue payments. You suggested five principles but Lord Curzon shewed that three of these had been for many years in force. You now call my attention to two other principles, not adopted, as you say, by Government.

But I demur to the statement. The original proposition made in the Memorial of the 20th December 1900, Para. 4 (*a*) was that the Government Demand should in Ryotwari Districts be limited to 50 per cent. of the value of the *net* produce. Lord Curzon, while shewing that a rigid application of an exact mathematical test was impracticable, did prove that 50 per cent. was far in excess of the assessment in practice.

The second suggestion is in much the same category. The Government cannot definitely lay down, unconditionally and in all circumstances, a rigid adherence to the principle contained in Para. 4 (*d*) of the same Memorial. But in practice, the Ryot is allowed the benefit of all improvements made by him in general, and is, as far as possible, exempt from a reclassification of soils, and is reassessed mainly with reference to prices.

I fully appreciate the beneficent motive prompting your action, and the moderation of the language you employ in advocating changes ; but it does seem to me that you have hardly made sufficient allowance either for the difficulties which Government have to encounter in giving wholesale effect to general principles, or sufficiently grasped the tendency and effect of the actual systems of assessment now in force in different parts in India.

Believe me,
Yours very truly,
GEORGE HAMILTON.

July 31, 1903

REPLY TO LORD GEORGE HAMILTON,

Secretary of State for India.

MY LORD,

I am greatly indebted to you for your kind letter of the 31st July, and for the consideration you have given to my paper on the "Peasant Proprietors of India." Your Lordship will perhaps permit me to make one or two remarks on points raised in your letter.

It has been stated in this letter that three out of the five principles we urged in our Memorial of December 1900 had been for many years in force in India. Permit me to point out that, though we are thankful to Lord Curzon for generally accepting these three principles, they have not hitherto been in force in all parts of India, and are not yet universally in force.

(1) We urged that settlements should be made for 30 years, where the Land Revenue is not permanently settled. Your Lordship is aware that the existing rule in the Punjab and the Central Provinces is to make settlements for 20 years only. These Provinces have been for half a century under British Rule; and if your Lordship will *now* extend to them the 30 years settlement rule, the people of those Provinces will be saved much hardship in future, and will enjoy the same security in respect of term of settlement which has been extended to Northern India, Madras and Bombay.

(2) We urged that the Land Revenue, where not permanently settled, should be limited to half the *actual* rental. We are thankful that Lord Curzon has accepted the principle generally, but it is not yet universally in force. I enclose a copy of "Notes on the Land Revenue Policy," issued only last year by the Hon'ble Rai Nehal Chand Bahadur, a landlord in Northern India, and a Member of the Legislative Council of Agra and Oudh. In page 11 of the Notes your Lordship will find some rules issued by the Board of Revenue in 1901, by which the settlement officer is directed to reject the actual rental when it is low, and to base assessments on his own estimate of what the rental should be. This is teaching landlords to be severe when they are inclined to be lenient; and no administrator of Northern India,—certainly not the Right Hon'ble Sir Antony Mac Donnell,—will approve of such a policy on the part of the Government. We shall be thankful if Lord Curzon, in accordance with the general principle which he has affirmed, *now* thinks it desirable to direct Local Governments to cancel such rules, and to substitute rules for basing the land assessment on the *actual* rental in all cases.

(3) We recommended a limit for the Local Cesses imposed on the land, and Lord Curzon has expressed a desire to reduce these Cesses when possible. The budgets during the last two or three years have shewn large surpluses, but none of the Cesses imposed on the soil since 1871 has yet been reduced or abolished. The agricultural population of India will be grateful if

advantage is *now* taken of these prosperous budgets to reduce some of these Cesses. And Lord Curzon's administration will be remembered with gratitude if it gives some relief in this way to the poor agriculturists of India, who are more heavily taxed than any other section of the people, and who cannot speak for themselves.

My Lord, I have dwelt on these three points in order to shew that our recommendations were not made under any "general misapprehension," and that the principles we urged had not been in force in all parts of India, and are not yet universally in force. We do hope that Lord Curzon's general affirmation of these three principles will *now* lead to their being carried into practice; and it is with this view that I have taken the liberty of again troubling your Lordship on this subject.

With regard to the other two points we urged, I do not intend to say much in this letter. Your Lordship says that 50 per cent. of the value of the nett produce is far in excess of the present assessment in the Ryotwari tracts. If an enquiry were made from village to village in Madras and Bombay, and if the actual produce reaped by cultivators were ascertained, as I did ascertain it in some villages last winter, it would be found that the present assessment is far in excess of 50 p. c. of the nett produce in many individual cases. In this matter we are agreed as to the principle; and I only ask that some simple method may be adopted to give redress to every cultivator in whose case the principle is violated. If no cultivator is assessed at a sum exceeding half his nett produce, no alteration will be made in the settlement. If some of them are so over-assessed, justice will be done which is now denied to them.

And in the matter of enhancements too, the cultivator needs such protection. If he can shew that his assessment has been increased without any reasonable grounds, he should obtain relief. I do not necessarily suggest a reference to Civil Courts. But a District is resettled once in 30 years; it is not too much to ask that after such re-settlement a high Revenue Officer, other than the Settlement Officer, should be appointed, say for one year only, to hear the objections of cultivators, and to give them relief, (1) if they have been assessed at more than half the nett produce, or (2) if their assessment has been enhanced without reasonable grounds. This simple method would, without encouraging litigation, and without militating against the existing principles and methods of assessment, give the Madras and Bombay cultivator hope and heart, and a confidence in the justice of British land administration.

My Lord, I have lived and moved much among Indian cultivators. I see things as they see; I feel as they feel; I ask for them the simple method of redress which they would ask if they could speak. I place myself in the position of one of those millions of men among whom I moved last winter. His assessment, say of Rs. 50, has been raised to Rs. 60, he does not know, why. Permit him a reasonable time and opportunity to stand before an independent tribunal and to say, if he can say this with truth: "My field yields me Rs. 150 in good years; I don't save more than Rs. 100 after paying the expenses of cultivation; my assessment was Rs. 50 before; the enhancement of Rs. 10 in the assessment is unjust. Come and see my field, and my wretched home and starving children if you like, estimate my produce yourself if you wish it, but do justice to a poor man who has no other redress."

My Lord, this is not a hypothetical case. Many a poor cultivator appealed to me in words like these, last winter, forgetting that I was a mere visitor and not a judge. And in many a case did I find that a poor cultivator, who barely got 150 rupees in average years, and scarcely saved 100 rupees after the expenses of cultivation, had been assessed at 60 Rupees or more. And I honestly feel that it would be a greater glory to the British Rule to bring justice to that poor man than to achieve geat military and political triumphs.

You have very kindly expressed your appreciation of the motive which has prompted my action in this matter, and the moderation of language I have always used in advocating changes. Permit me to state in this connection that I am sincerely greateful for the uniform courtesy and kindness which I have received, both from yourself and from Lord Curzon, throughout this long debate which has now lasted for nearly four years.

And it would greatly add to my satisfaction if I could feel that my moderate and dispassionate appeal for my poorer countrymen has led to some practical good,—some effective method of securing to them those rights which, in principle, are conceded to them. And, I may add it would do some good, if I could convince my countrymen that a moderate and dispassionate appeal obtains a hearing and secures justice under British Rule. Unfortunately a different impression is spreading. My endeavours, humble as they are, are known in India, and are almost universally believed to lead to nothing. A sullen despair and discontent prevail among the agricultural classes, which deepen with their indebtedness, and which contain germs of political danger in the future. Nothing on earth, I honestly believe, can induce the peasantry of Bengal to join in a disturbance against a Government which has conferred on them rights which they value, and which they know how to defend. But small causes may, I apprehend, lead the wretched peasantry of Madras and Bombay to join in worse disturbances than were committed in Poona in 1875.

My Lord, it is worth while trying to convert the cultivators of southern and western India into hopeful, resourceful and self-relying men, confident in their rights, and confident in the justice of the British Rule. This is what has been effected in Bengal within my memory, through the Legislative Acts of Lords Canning, Lawrence, Ripon, and Dufferin,—the Rent Acts of 1859, 1868, and 1885. And this *can* be effected in Madras and Bombay by the same simple method—giving an effective redress to every individual cultivator, (1) against a revenue-demand exceeding half his net produce, and (2) against any enhancement without specific and reasonable grounds.

I remain, my Lord,
Ever yours truly,
Romesh Dutt.

54, Parliament Street, S. W.
August 3, 1903.

my countrymen that a moderate and fixed assessment might obtain a hearing and secured justice under British Rule. Unfortunately a different impression is spreading. My endeavours, humble as they are, are looked in India, and are almost universally believed to lead to nothing. A sullen despair and discontent spreads among the agricultural classes, which increases with their indebtedness, and which contains germs of political danger in the future. Nothing on earth, I honestly believe, can induce the peasantry of Bengal to join in a disturbance against a Government which has conferred on them 1793, which they value, and which they know how to defend. The same [illegible] may, I apprehend, lead the wretched peasantry of Madras and Bombay to join in those disturbances which were committed in Poona in 1875.

My Lord, it is worth while trying to convert the cultivators of southern and western India into cheerful, resourceful and self-relying men, confident in their position and confident in the justice of the British Government. What has been effected in Bengal within recent years through the Legislative Acts of Lord Canning, Lord Lawrence, Lord Lytton, Lord Ripon and Dufferin—the Rent Acts of 1859, 1869 and 1885. And this can be effected in Madras and Bombay by the same method in those—giving an effective redress to every individual cultivator (1) against any Land Revenue demand exceeding half his net produce, and (2) against any enhancement without specific and reasonable grounds.

SPEECHES AND PAPERS

ON

Indian Questions,

1897 to 1900

CONTENTS.

I. FAMINES IN INDIA.

[*Reprinted from the Fortnightly Review, August* 1897.]

SIXTY years ago, in the very year in which Her Majesty the Queen ascended the throne, her Indian Empire, then managed by the East India Company, was desolated by a great famine. The calamity was confined to the North-Western Provinces of India, but the sufferings of the people, as described by eye-witnesses, were truly heartrending. Villagers lay down in hunger by the wayside, and died with that silent resignation which is more terrible than the wildest excesses and disorder. And famished men and women in the last stage of exhaustion were attacked and devoured by jackals when they were unable to resist or even to escape. There was practically no organization for famine relief in those days, and Lord Auckland's Government could do little to mitigate the sufferings or prevent the deaths of the people.

Scarcely a quarter of a century had passed away when the same Provinces were once more desolated by another severe famine in 1860. Men still in their middle age remember that terrible year, which claimed more victims in India than the Mutiny, which had recently been quelled. The Government of Lord Canning did what it could to afford relief to the sufferers, and subscriptions were raised in all the towns of British India for this purpose. But in the absence of an organized plan of operation the relief afforded to the sufferers was neither adequate nor very efficacious. A Commission was then appointed to inquire into the causes of the calamity, and we will refer further on to some of the recommendations made by this Commission.

Only six years after this a still more terrible famine broke out in the Province of Orissa. The Government of the day had not taken adequate precautions in time, and when the extent of the distress became fully manifest it was almost too late. Shiploads of rice were hurriedly sent to the suffering Province, but the means of communication were inadequate, and the people in the interior perished in large numbers. Calcutta was flooded by starving men and women with children in their arms, and never did the native population of that great town distinguish themselves in a higher degree by their benevolence and charity than on this memorable occasion. Rich men's houses were converted into relief centres, high officials and merchants went from door to door to collect subscriptions, and tens of thousands of sufferers from Orissa, who had come to Calcutta for refuge, were fed, clothed, and saved by private charity. Those who witnessed the scenes of 1866 are not likely ever to forget them; they are still fresh in the memory of the present writer after a lapse of thirty years.

The next great famine was in Behar in 1874, and this was the first famine in which the relief operations undertaken by Government were adequate, and loss of life was prevented with complete success. The bitter experience of 1866 had left sad recollections, and the Government of 1874 determined to do all that it was possible to do to prevent a repetition of the same scenes. To Lord Northbrook, then Viceroy and Governor-General of India, belongs the credit of having first combated an Indian famine with complete success. The famine was confined to Behar and to parts of Bengal, and the present writer, then a young officer, took his share in the work of famine relief.

A far more terrible famine visited Madras only three years later. In 1877, while Lord Lytton was proclaiming to the great Darbar of Delhi that Her Majesty had assumed the august title of Empress of India, the dark cloud of famine had cast its shadow over the province of Madras. The precautions taken on this occasion were not commensurate with the extent and intensity of the calamity, the operations of relief were not adequate, and the dire calamity counted its victims by the million. Never within the memory of living men, never within the present century, has there been destruction of life so terrible and so great as in the Madras famine of 1877. And when at last that great calamity had subsided and a census was taken, it was found that over *five millions of people* had been swept away. A population equal to the population of Ireland had disappeared under the desolating breath of the famine of 1877.

These figures enable us to some extent to conceive the extent and magnitude of human suffering and death caused by an Indian famine. When we read of the havoc of war or of pestilence in these days, we lament the death of thousands, probably tens of thousands, of our fellow-beings. The Crimean War, one of the most disastrous of modern wars in the loss of life which it involved is said to have cost about two hundred and fifty thousand human lives. The Madras famine claimed *twenty times* the victims of the Crimean War.

The Government of India now awoke to the magnitude of the recurring calamity to which the people of India were subject, and they devised means to prevent a repetition of the scenes of 1877. A Famine Fund was created, partly for the construction of canals and protective railways, and partly as a sinking fund which would enable the Government to borrow with greater facility in years of distress. Much has been said of late of this Famine Fund, and any further remarks on the subject are unnecessary. As Lord George Hamilton stated in the House of Commons, two-thirds of the amount which was proposed to be devoted to famine insurance has been so devoted within the last twenty years. This is eminently satisfactory, and India is better prepared to-day by her railways and canal systems to meet a famine than she was before. But nevertheless one feels a regret that the whole of the amount which was proposed to be devoted to famine insurance in India was not religiously applied to this sole purpose.

Twenty years have elapsed since the famine of 1877,

and within this period there have been famines in Northern India, in Madras, and elsewhere. But in the year 1896 the autumnal rains failed nearly over the whole of India except in the south, and in the present year, therefore, famine has appeared in Bombay and in Bengal, in the North-West and the Punjab—*i. e.*, over a larger area than was ever desolated by famine in any single year, within this or any preceding century, of which any records have been left to us.

Of the preparations which have been made to meet the present famine, and of the endeavours which every official in India, from the highest to the lowest, is making at the present moment to save human life, I need not speak. Ample details are being published day by day in the shape of message and correspondence from India, and my own testimony would add but little to the information now before the British public. Nevertheless, as an Indian myself, and as an official who was engaged only a few months ago in making inquiries into the state of crops and the condition of the people in one of the afflicted parts of India, I consider it my duty to say a word or two, if only for the information of those Englishmen who have come forward so generously to help my countrymen in this time of their sore distress and need. I desire, therefore, to bear witness to the anxious care and solicitude with which the prospects of crops and the condition of the people have been watched by officials in India since the failure of the last autumnal rains; to the inquiries which have been made since to ascertain the stocks of food grain, the outturn of harvests, the requirements of the people, and the probable deficit in the food supply; and to the plans which have been organised with wisdom and carried out with industry to find out distress by means of test relief works, and to relieve it with all the resources under the command of the Government of India and the Provincial Governments. So far as the resources of India and the watchful care and industry of officials in India can save lives and relieve distress, those great objects shall be achieved in the present year.

My present object, however, is not to discribe the relief operations which have been adopted in India in the present year, but rather to impress on my readers the fact that famines are a recurring event in India, and that each year of famine, in spite of the most careful relief measures, is attended by sufferings and deaths to an extent of which it is not possible to form an adequate conception in Europe.

It is, therefore, incumbent on us to consider, calmly and dispassionately, what precautionary measures can be adopted to protect the people of India from the worst effects of such dire calamities. Indian questions are unfortunately often discussed with much heat and passion, and before we have proceeded very far in the clear understanding of a question it is clouded by unseemly charges on one side and on the other. But if ever there was a question which required a thorough and calm and dispassionate inquiry, it is the question of protecting the people of India from famines. For Englishmen of all parties are equally interested in this great question, as they are interested in the welfare of their Indian Empire and the safety of their Indian fellow-subjects.

Replying to Sir William Wedderburn, in course of a discussion in the House of Commons, Lord George Hamilton said: "I agree with the hon. baronet that the opportunity this famine affords ought not to be allowed to pass without our taking every opportunity to inquire into and ascertain the best methods of protecting the people of India from the recurrence of similar calamities." To suggest the best methods for securing this object, in so far as my experience and my knowledge of the condition and wants of my countrymen enable me to do so, is the object of this paper. It is certainly possible to provide remedies which will lessen the force of famines, or prevent them altogether; and it is incumbent on us to find and to apply such remedies, in order to protect the people from preventible destitution, suffering, and death.

Protective railway works have been constructed all over India. There is no part of the country to which food cannot be transported by rail at a few days' notice. Two hundred million pounds have been spent on railways, and 20,000 miles are open to traffic. No more lines should be constructed out of the public revenues, or under a guarantee of profits from the revenues.

On the other hand, Irrigation works have been neglected. Only twenty million pounds have been spent on irrigation works. Out of 200 million acres of cultivated land in India, only 20 million acres are protected. This is not as it should be. It is possible to construct canals only in level tracts of the country and in the basin of large rivers; but storage tanks and wells can be constructed every where. The whole country could have been covered by such works within the last sixty years, since the famine of 1837. The Famine Commission of 1880 drew special attention to this, but their advice has been neglected. It is to be hoped that more attention will be paid to Irrigation after the present famine, so that such wide-spread calamities may be impossible in the next generation.

But more important administrative measures are needed to rescue the agriculturists of India from their chronic state of poverty and indebtedness. The first and the most obvious means of improving their material condition is a reduction of the public expenditure, and a corresponding reduction of the taxes which press heavily on those classes. All Indian administrators within the last quarter of a century have contemplated with something akin to alarm the steady growth of expenditure in India, and the corresponding growth of taxation.

The expensiveness of the present system was well described over ten years ago by Mr. Cotton, now Chief Commissioner of Assam, when he stated that India could no more afford such a system than the English farmer could plough with race-horses or the Indian cultivator with elephants. On this point all authorities are pretty well agreed; but no practical steps have yet been taken to give effect to this reduction in expenditure desired by all.

Sir Henry Fowler, when discussing the question of the present famine in the House of Commons, remarked :—"If it should prove to be the fact, notwithstanding the surplus of which the noble lord (Lord George Hamilton) has spoken, that this famine will entail, as I am afraid it will, a very considerable charge upon the revenues of India, for the loss from the land revenue will be considerable, I think that it is time for this House, and I am sure this House will be representing the people of the country—in the same spirit in which it made contribution in the case of the Afghan War to the Indian Exchequer—to make an Imperial contribution to the Exchequer of India in aid of the taxation of India." I am convinced my countrymen will appreciate the spirit in which this suggestion was made. But, nevertheless, if I am capable of forming a judgment in the matter, it is not in this shape that a contribution from the British Exchequer will be most acceptable to them. India has always paid for her internal administration, and if the financial relations between England and India were adjusted on a proper basis, India would not stand in need of donations from the British Exchequer for her internal administration.

The reference which Sir Henry Fowler made to the contribution made on the occasion of the Afghan War suggests the true and only method in which England could grant relief to India with justice, and India could receive it with dignity. India now pays not only for her internal administration, not only for the army and defensive works within her own limits, but also for the maintenance of England's Empire in Asia outside the limits of India. Burma, including the Shan States, is as large as France, and borders on the dominions of France and China. British possessions in the wilds of Beluchistan, Afghanistan, and Chitral extend for hundreds of miles beyond the natural limits of India, and the expensiveness of the occupation and defence of these places is alarming. Little income is derived from the Shan States of Burma, or from Beluchistan, Chitral, or Afghanistan, and India is bled for much of the cost of maintaining these portions of England's Asiatic Empire. England is the richest country in the world, India is one of the poorest. And yet India is made to pay for England's possessions and wars in Asia beyond her own natural boundaries.

Forty years ago, when India passed under the direct rule of the Crown, a pledge was given that the cost of wars outside India would not be charged to India. Within the period of forty years the limits of England's Asiatic Empire (miscalled India) have been extended to the frontiers of China in the east, and have been pushed forward into Afghanistan, Beluchistan, and Tartary in the west; and the cost of these outside extensions has been charged to India. And within this period the expenses of India have so enormously increased that every responsible Indian statesman has been filled with anxiety, and every method of taxation, bearing more and more severely on the people, has been tried, with poor and ghastly results. We seem to be coming back in despair to taxes which every civilised country has discarded. A scheme to re-impose tolls on roads and to levy a tax on every marriage is now under the consideration of the Bengal Government.

At such a time of need India can legitimately ask England to contribute a share of the vast military expenditure required to sustain her Asiatic Empire. It may be possible to ascertain roughly what proportion of the military expenditure of India is incurred for England's imperial purposes, and the defence of her distant possessions in Africa and in Asia. As the people of England are disposed, judging from Sir Henry Fowler's speech, to give some substantial relief to India out of the English Exchequre, the shape in which such relief would be most acceptable as well as most equitable would be the contribution of this proportion of the military expenditure which India is no longer able to bear alone.

A Commission is now sitting to make a proper adjustment of expenditure as between England an India. Much valuable evidence has been recorded by this Commission, but I will in the present article refer to the evidence of one witness only. Sir Henry Brackenbury is the military member of the Council of the Viceroy of India, and his opinion may be supposed, therefore, to reflect to some extent the opinion of the Indian Government. I take the liberty, therefore, of quoting a part of his evidence from an Indian paper.

"In the first place, I would say that the army in India is largely in excess of the requirements for the preservation of internal order of India. The strength of the army in India is calculated to allow of a powerful field army being placed on or beyond the Indian frontier, in addition to the obligatory garrisons required for keeping order in India. The necessity for maintaining in India the powerful field army in addition to the obligatory garrisons is caused by the approach of a great military Power into a position which enables her directly to threaten Afghanistan, to which we are under treaty obligations, and indirectly to threaten the security of India itself. The foreign policy of India is directed entirely from England by Her Majesty's Government, and it is part of British foreign policy generally—indeed, the object of British foreign policy as I believe it to be—to secure Great Britain's rule over her Empire. If we desire to maintain British rule in India only for India's sake, then I think it would be fair to make India pay to the uttermost farthing everything that it could be shown was due to Britain's rule over India. But I cannot but feel that England's interest—or Britain's interest—in keeping India under British rule is enormous. India affords employment to thousands of Britons, India employs millions of British capital, and Indian commerce has been of immense value to Great Britain. Therefore it seems to me that India, being held by Great Britain not only for India's sake but for Great Britain's sake, the latter should pay a share of the expenditure for the purpose. And in estimating what that share should be, I think that England should behave generously to India, because, in the first place, England is a rich country and India is a poor country."

This is a stronger argument than mine, and it is urged by a high authority who has a claim to be heard. The facts and arguments urged by the military member of the Viceroy's Conncil will no doubt appeal strongly to the minds of all thoughtful Englishmen ; and the sad events which are taking place in India before our own eyes in the present year will plead eloquently for a fresh adjustment of the great military expenditure which is necessary for the maintenance of England's Empire in Asia.

For the rest, if England undertakes to pay, not a fixed sum as is sometimes proposed, but a fixed proportion of the total military expenditure now incurred in

India, it will be possible for her to control that expenditure better than it can be controlled in India. From the nature of things, there can be no authority in India able to control any military expenditure which the Viceroy and the Commander-in-Chief consider it necessary to incur; and practically, therefore, there is no control over such expenditure. No doubt every official in India, from the Viceroy and the Finance Minister to the humble district officer, exerts himself to keep down expenditure within the lowest possible limits. But, nevertheless, the most conscientious spending department would be all the better for some efficient control.

I have confined my remarks to military expenditure, as it is that which presses most severely on the resources of India. If India could obtain some relief in that direction, her other expenses could be easily adjusted. The enormous "Home Charges," too, ought to be somewhat curtailed, and the annual drain from India which is impoverishing the country should be reduced.

The second remedy for improving the condition of the agricultural classes which suggests itself to me is a salutary and needful change in our administrative system. This is a very large subject, but I propose to deal with it briefly, and in a general manner. Hard and fast rules and regulations, framed no doubt with the most benevolent objects, often bear hardly on the agricultural classes. Our law courts, which are in themselves excellent institutions, are often taken advantage of by the money-lender to rivet his chains on the indebted cultivator. Both in civil and in criminal matters the people are compelled to travel to distant and expensive courts, and taught to depend on tutored evidence to win their cases, true or false. Litigation is eating into the vitals of the agricultural population, and no adequate endeavours have been made to organize village institutions for settling village disputes. All power is centralised in district authorities far removed from the homes of most villagers, and no real power is left in the hands of village elders and village unions. I have known an instance in which the people of a village had to wait for days or weeks before they could remove a tree which had fallen across a village path and obstructed the road: they could not do this without orders from the police! Centralisation of power has been carried too far, and has crushed all life out of village organizations.

There is great room for improvement in this direction, and much can be done to save villagers from litigation in our law courts, and ruin through indebtedness. Courts of conciliation should be organized to settle village disputes, and other measures should be adopted to save villagers alike from our expensive law courts and from the tricks of rapacious money-lenders. Agricultural banks should be opened to help substantial tenants, and every endeavour should be made to enable them to stand on their own legs.

The third remedy which I have to suggest relates to land assessments. Over eighty per cent. of the population of India are dependent on agriculture, and it is no exaggeration to state, therefore, that the well-being of the people of India depends on the wisdom and moderation with which lands are assessed. The Indian Government, and all the local Governments, are no doubt animated by a desire to proceed with moderation in making assessments. But, on the other hand, it should always be borne in mind that the land revenue bears a fairly large proportion to the total revenues of India, and an endeavour is naturally made, at every settlement, to raise the land revenue to some extent, in order to obtain a substantial increase in the general revenues. And when it is added that these settlements are made in the same Province and in the same district again and again in a century, and that at each settlement Government expects and does obtain a substantial increase in revenue, it can be understood that the margin of profit left to cultivators can never increase, however much agriculture may flourish in the country.

Thanks to the generous policy of Lord Cornwallis, the greater part of Bengal is free from the increasing demand from the produce of the land. No single act of the British Government that can be named has done so much for the prosperity and well-being of the people as the permanent settlement of the land revenue of Bengal effected by Lord Cornwallis in 1793. Cultivation has largely increased since that year, and prices have risen, but the profits have remained with the people of the country, and the landlords of Bengal are at the present day among the most contented and loyal classes of people in India. And as the landlords are not subject to increasing demands on the part of the Government, they themselves have been stopped by three successive Acts from obtaining increase of rent from cultivators, except on the most reasonable grounds. The result is that the Bengal cultivator is more prosperous and better able to stand the effects of droughts and of bad harvests than the cultivator in any other part of India. There never has been a serious famine in Eastern Bengal within the memory of living men, or since the permanent settlement of 1793. And when there was a famine in Western Bengal (Behar) in 1874, the measures taken for relief were more completely successful in saving life than any other relief operations that have been undertaken, before or since, in any other part of India. And lastly be it added, that in the present calamitous year, when the whole of India (except the extreme south) has suffered, the number of men on relief works in Bengal is, in proportion to her population, less than the number of men in the North-West or in Bombay. The worst cases of distress, starvation, and high mortality are reported not from Bengal, but from the other afflicted Provinces.

Those who know India well know that the peasantry of Bengal are better able to take care of themselves in the worse times than the peasantry of other Provinces. Many instances of the self-reliance of the Bengal cultivators must occur to every administrative officer who has served in Bengal, but I will mention only one instance, which appears to me to be as good as any other. In 1876 a cyclone and a storm-wave, over twenty feet high, broke on the south-eastern coast of Bengal, swept away two hundred thousand poeple, and utterly destroyed the corps in many parts. It was a year of much suffering and sorrow and death. Dead bodies lay thick on the ground as on a battle-field : some hung on the trees to which they had been lifted up by the wave, and some were floated in and out by every changing tide. The huts of the villagers were utterly demolished and swept away, and men and women and children lived under trees or under the most imperfect shelter which had been hastily constructed. A good deal of their cattle and property was also destroyed, and rest was floated up and down into other villages. Each villager was content to lose what he lost, and kept what he got, so that there was a sort of redistribution of property such as would have delighted the soul of the most thoroughgoing Socialist. To add to the horrors of the year, a cholera epidemic, the like of which I have never seen, and never wish to see again, visited the afflicted parts and carried away tens of thousands of the surviving villagers.

Amidst these appalling calamities the agricultural classes of South-Eastern Bengal showed a resourceful self-reliance which astonished me and every other administrative officer on the spot. From the branches of the innumerable areca-nut trees which grow in these parts they constructed temporary huts for themselves and their families. They searched up and down the country for their lost property and cattle, and recovered what they could find. They gathered in what remained of the much injured harvest, and this served them for a few months. They travelled long distances, sometimes twenty or thirty miles, to obtain cholera-pills and other drugs from the doctors whom Government had sent to the spot, and did what it was possible to do to lessen the force of that dreadful epidemic. After their store of rice was exhausted, they sold their brass utensils and the silver jewellery of their women, and imported boatloads of rice from other parts of Bengal. They constructed new villages and new markets all over the land, resumed their old industries, and kept off famine by their own industry and resource. As the executive officer in charge of one of the worst tracts during this calamitous year, I undertook some measures for the relief of helpless women and children who had lost their relations. The able-bodied people needed no relief, and asked for none. From the 31st October, 1876, when the storm-wave broke on the land, to the 31st of August, 1877, by which date the autumnal harvest began, the people of South-Eastern Bengal, who had lost their houses, property, and crops, saved themselves from a famine by their own resources. And this was the year when the unfortunate and resourceless peasantry of Madras succumbed to a famine—the worst which has been known in India in this century.

It is needless to multiply instances. From an experience of over twenty-five years, spent mostly among the peasantry, I am able to state—and those who know India best will agree with me—that if the object of the permanent settlement of 1793 was to create a thoroughly loyal class of landlords and a prosperous class of peasantry in Bengal, that object has succeeded beyond all expectation.

The distinction which we perceive to-day between

the condition of the Bengal cultivator and the condition of the North-West cultivator was perceived by Lord Canning as long ago as 1860, and that great statesman did not fail to discover its true cause. After the famine of 1860 Lord Canning appointed a Commission to inquire into its causes. Colonel Baird Smith, R.E., was the distinguished President of the Commission: he found after a careful inquiry that the famine of 1860 had been less disastrous than that of 1837, and he attributed this to the greater fixity of the public demand from the soil in the later than in the former date. Convinced of this fact, he had the courage to recommend a permanent settlement for the North-Western Provinces or for all India. I quote his words below :—

"Such having been the results of the protracted fixity of the public demand, the security of titles, the general moderation of assessments, the recognition and general record of rights, the inference seems irresistible that, to intensify and perpetuate these results, we must proceed still further in the same healthy and fruitful direction. The good which has been done by partial action on sound principles is both a justification and an encouragement to further advances; and entertaining the most earnest conviction that State interests and popular interests will alike be strengthened in an increasing ratio by the step, the first, as I believe, the most important measure I have respectfully to submit is the expediency of fixing for ever the public demand on land, and thus converting the existing settlement into a settlement in perpetuity."

Such a liberal and statesmanlike recommendation was not lost on Lord Canning. A Government resolution was published, which set forth the views of the Government in the following terms :—

"His Excellency in Council sees no reason to doubt that the measure would be in every way beneficient. He believes that the increased security of fixed property and the comparative freedom from interference of fiscal officers of the Government will tend to create a class which, although composed of various races and creeds, will be peculiarly bound to British rule, while, under proper regulations, the measure will conduce materially to the improvement of the general revenue of the Empire."

The different Provinces of India were thus about to obtain, under Lord Canning, that great boon which Bengal had obtained under Lord Cornwallis. The Secretary of State approved of the Viceroy's proposal, and sent a despatch which concluded in the following terms:—

"After the most careful review of all these considerations, Her Majesty's Government are of opinion that the advantages which may reasonably be expected to accrue, not only to those immediately connected with the land, but to the community generally, are sufficiently great to justify them in incurring the risk of some prospective loss of land revenue in order to attain them; and that a settlement in perpetuity in the districts in which the conditions required are or may hereafter be fulfilled is a measure dictated by sound policy, and calculated to accelerate the development of the resources of India, and to insure in the highest degree the welfare and contentment of all classes of Her Majesty's subjects in the country."

India was thus on the eve of obtaining a great boon, when her hopes were dashed to the ground by the death of one man. Lord Canning, who had held firm sway over India during the unexampled disasters of the Mutiny, and whose moderation and sympathies for the people of the country had won him the name of Clemency Canning, left the country in March, 1862 with a shattered constitution, and died in the following June. England honoured the hero who had saved India by interring his remains in Westminster Abbey, and India mourned, with good reason, the loss of one whose large-hearted wisdom did not animate his successors.

After the death of this benevolent ruler, Indian officials formed a different opinion on the question of permanent settlements. Some of them reported that if assessments could no longer be periodically raised in future, it would be, so far, a prospective loss to Government and a sacrifice of land revenue. These counsels prevailed ; the idea of a permanent settlement was finally abandoned in 1883, and the North-Western Provinces are subject to increase of land revenue at each settlement.

What is stated of the North-Western Provinces is true also of Bombay and Madras and the Central Provinces of India. Periodical settlements take place in these Provinces, and each settlement means a fresh increase in the rental. Settlement officers, at least in the higher grades, do not consciously make excessive demands ; on the contrary, they desire to be moderate and fair. The settlement operations of the Province of Orissa went on before my own eyes during the whole of the last year, and I willingly testify to the moderation and fairness of the young settlement officer who presided over these operations. But, nevertheless, the anxiety to have some increase in the revenue animates all officers from the highest to the lowest, and every increase in the revenue is a corresponding decrease in the resources of the people, and their capacity to provide against years of bad harvest. The share of the produce from land generally left to the people enables them to live well enough in good years, but it does not enable them to provide against bad times. It is for this reason that we hear of frequent evictions of cultivators in the Southern Provinces, and it is for this reason also that immediately after a bad harvest the tenants of the North-West Provinces, Madras, and Bombay succumb more hopelessly than cultivators in Bengal.

More than a hundred years have elapsed since the time of the permanent settlement in Bengal. Within this time repeated settlements have taken place in the other Provinces of India and rents have been raised; and the increase in the prices of food grains has not benefited the cultivator in those Provinces as it would benefit the English farmer, and it has benefited the Bengal tenant. Railways and other causes which have led to a rise in the price of wheat and rice in India have largely and steadily added to her land revenue, and have not conduced to make the condition of the rice-grower and the wheat-grower more prosperous. The ever-recurring settlement sweeps away all increase in profits; and, even in this disastrous year, when famine has thrown its dark shadow over the land, the harassing and ceaseless settlement operations are still going on in some parts of India, securing an increase in the Government revenue, and leaving the classes dependent on land a smaller margin of profit than before the settlements.

I have dwelt long on this question because there is no other question which so directly and vitally affects the condition of the mass of the people as this, and because it is often overlooked by those who are not familiar with the details of Indian administration. Land is the source of living of four-fifths of the population: leave them a good margin of profits from land and they are prosperous; sweep away all increase in the profits from land into the Imperial treasury at every settlement, and they are impoverished and helpless.

If, then, it be desired to insure to some extent the Indian cultivator against recurring famines, it is necessary to insure to him the future profits from land. In the words of a former Secretary of State, "A settlement in perpetuity in the districts in which the conditions required are or may hereafter be fulfilled is a measure dictated by sound policy." But if the settlement officer is constantly among the agricultural population, pruning away every increase in the profits from land once in thirty years, or once in fifteen years, it is idle to talk of improvement in the condition of the agricultural population.[1]

(1) Since the above was written I am glad to find that the proposal of a permanent settlement of the land revenue, at least in certain parts of India, has the support of the singularly well-informed and talented writer on Indian Affairs in *The Times*, the well-known Sir William Hunter. "Shrewd observers assert that the absence of a permanent settlement operates as a discouragement to improvement, and that, as a matter of fact, the Government pays dearly for its power to raise the rent by checking the prosperity of the people. . . . The main fact remains that the Government has given a distinct and a repeated promise (of permanent settlement), and that the time has come to redeem it. The request for the fulfilment of that promise is not made by political agitators, but by a body of loyal proprietors who have done their utmost to strengthen the hands of the Government in all times of need, and who believe that fixity of tenure more than any other measure will enable them and their tenants to resist famine."—*The Times*, 27th April, 1897.

The present year is a memorable year in the history of of the British Empire. British subjects, whether they live in Europe or in America, in Africa or in Australia, are rejoicing over the celebration of the long reign of their gracious Sovereign. In India alone a voice of lamentation is heard. Ten times within these sixty years India has suffered from terrible and desolating famines, and the last famine is, in the area affected, the worst known in the history of the country. But out of evil cometh good. And if this great calamity which has overtaken Indian cultivators through the length and breadth of the country brings about a more liberal policy of land settlements, and secures for India generally the great boon of a perpetual settlement which Lord Cornwallis bestowed on Bengal and Lord Canning proposed to bestow on other Provinces, the three hundred millions of the Queen-Empress's Indian subjects will have truly cause to bless her name and to cherish memory. It will be an act worthy of the gracious Sovereign and the gracious occasion. And the story will be handed down among the Indian peasantry from generation to generation, that the great Empress who, by the grace of God, lived to reign sixty years in England, bestowed the great boon of fixity of rent to the cultivators of India because she loved them well, and was distressed to see them suffering from famine and hunger.

Fourthly and lastly, I would suggest some administrative action to encouarge and revive the ruined industries of India. A nation which depends entirely on agriculture cannot but be poor; and it would be a wise and statesmanlike policy to diversify the occupations of the people of India, and thus add to their resources. It is a large subject which requires full treatment in a separate article ; and I therefore content myself by merely mentioning it in this place.

I conclude this article by summarising the suggestions made above. My suggestions are few and simple and, I venture to hope, practicable. They are ; *firstly*, a contribution from the British Exchequer towards the military expenses of her Asiatic Empire and a reduction of the annual economic drain from India ; *secondly*, a reform in the administration and the removal of certain causes which are palpably leading to the impoverishment of the cultivators ; *thirdly*, a settlement in perpetuity of the revenues derived from the soil ; *fourthly*, encouragement of Indian industries and manufactures.

My first suggestion contemplates a contribution, which I venture to think is a just and equitable one, from the British Exchequer towards the maintanence of the British Empire in Asia. And my third suggestion contemplates a possible sacrifice of prospective increase in the land revenue of India, although such sacrifice is likely to be more than compensated in other ways if the condition of the agricultural classes is bettered. To those statesmen who shrink from the idea of the smallest concession and the smallest sacrifice my appeal will be made in vain. But I may point out to them that no great result has been achieved without some sacrifice, and that the condition of the peasantary of India cannot be improved by the trick of a conjuror. A famine Code is an excellent thing, but it prescribes the method of treatment when the disease is on us, and is not a preventive. A Famine Fund is also an excellent provision, but it means additional taxation on the people. The true remedy for famines, therefore, is some measure which will directly decrease expenditure, and will leave something more with the cultivator than he is now allowed to keep. No remedy can be generally efficacious which does not achieve these two objects—decrease in India's expenditure, and increase in the resources of the masses. You cannot eat your cake and give it to the poor. And unless you are prepared to make some reduction—some concession and sacrifice—it is idle to talk of improving the condition of the peasantry of India.

Much has been said of the increase of population in India. But India is not the only country in which population increases. The population of the British Islands was twenty-five millions when the Queen ascended the throne; it is now forty millions, not counting ten millions more who have found homes beyond the seas. The population of India, excluding annexations, has not increased at half this rate. On the other hand, trade and commerce have increased in India, railways and canals have been opened, wastes have been brought under cultivation, and the resources of the country have been developed during these sixty years. The increase of population has not been greater than the increase in cultivation. The increase in population affords no explanation, therefore, for the recurring famines of India.

Let us have done with such generalizations, and go

to the root of the matter. Let us, or those of us who can do so, mark the condition of the Indian cultivator in his home, and find out what causes impoverish him and make him unable to save. The reason is not a want of frugality, or of sobriety, or of prudence. The Indian peasant is the most sober, the most frugal, and the most prudent peasant on the face of the earth. The reason is, that at each settlement the rent payable by him is increased, and his capacity to save is decreased. The reason is that, with no savings of his own, he goes to the money-lender under every pressure, and our Civil Courts, with their hard-and-fast rules, only cast him deeper into the meshes of the money-lender. The reason is that in every petty dispute, civil and criminal, he is compelled to have recourse to distant and expensive law courts. The reason is that he has to pay many taxes in order to maintain England's Empire in Asia.

If, having our eye still on the condition of the Indian cultivator, we desire to remove or lessen one by one these causes which impoverish him, we find that some improvements in the administration must be effected, and some concessions and sacrifices must be made. If we are prepared to make these concessions and sacrifices, we can better the condition of the Indian peasant. If we are not prepared to make any concessions and sacrifices, then this terrible year of suffering and death will have passed away without teaching us any useful lesson, and without leading to the removal of those causes which have intensified famines in India during the last sixty years.

II. LIBERALISM AND PEACE.

[*Speech delivered at Swindon on January, 29, 1898, in support of the Liberal Candidate Lord Edmond Fitzmaurice.*]

A LARGE and enthusiastic meeting was held at Swindon in support of the Liberal candidate for the Cricklade division, Lord Edmond Fitzmaurice, brother of Lord Lansdowne late Viceroy of India, but a true Liberal in English politics. The candidate himself, Lord Edmond, spoke on home politics, and Mr. Romesh Dutt, C.I.E., spoke on Indian affairs for nearly an hour. No full report of the speech was published ; the following summary of the speech is taken from *India*.

Mr. Dutt said that he considered it an honour and a privilege to appear in support of the Liberal party and of the liberal candidate Lord Edmond Fitzmaurice. He appeared before them, not altogether as a stranger, but as a British citizen, and as one who was proud to call himself a subject of their beloved Queen. The name of the Oueen of England was cherished with affection and love in all the colonies and dependencies of England's world-wide empire, but nowhere did it evoke greater loyalty and affection than among the millions of India. (Cheers.) Nor was this merely a passive sentiment. In times of action the people of India had ever risked their lives for their Queen, side by side with the bravest soldiers whom these islands had sent out, as was proved by the incidents of the present war. (Cheers.) What was the secret of this loyalty? What was the secret of the British ascendancy in India? Military people sometimes asserted that India was conquered by the sword and held by the sword. (Cries of "No, no.") He was glad that this assertion was so emphatically denied, because a falser assertion was never made. He maintained without hesitation that India was won by good government and was held by good government. (Prolonged cheers.) In the last century when the central power of Mogul Emperors had gone to pieces, when lawless freebooters swept through the country, when State warred against State and tribe warred against tribe, the British Power appeared on the scene as the one Power which could give the country peace and rest and settled government and a just administration. The people saw this and felt this, and spontaneously gave their support to this Power. In Bengal, in Madras, in Bombay, in the North-West, the silent and efficacious support of the people, and not victories on the battle-field, had helped the rise of the British power, and maintained British power in India. To this day, the silent and efficacious support of the people supported the government, which in spite of blunders and mistakes meant to be just to the people. All administrative officers knew this. He himself had taken his humble share in the work of administration under the Government of India for over twenty-five years; he had charge of Indian Districts with areas of four to six thousand square miles, with populations of two to three millions;

situated hundreds of miles from the nearest seat of the army, and having for his support only a few subordinate civil officers, and a body of police less than five hundred strong. But under these circumstances he felt perfectly secure in the exercise of his power and authority, because of the silent and efficacious support of the people among whom he worked, and who knew that whatever his blunders were, whatever the blunders of the Government were he was trying honestly to promote their welfare, secure peace and do justice between man and man. (Cheers.) India was thus held not by the sword but by good government. If the government turned unwise and foolish and oppressive, the seventy thousand British troops could not hold together a population of over two hundred millions for a single generation—not for a single decade. (Cries of "No, they could not.") And if the Government were wise and recognised the claims of the people for reforms and popular privileges, nothing could sever India from England. (Cheers.) Looking back to the history of the past forty years, he maintained that, generally speaking, whenever the Liberals had been in power for a long period, India had enjoyed peace and good government, and whenever the Tories had been in power for a long time, India had drifted into foolish and unjust annexations, into sinful and disastrous wars. (Loud cheers.) He pointed to the period of sixteen years since the abolition of the East India Company, from 1858 to 1874, during which the Liberals were in the power at home with brief interruptions, and during which India enjoyed peace under wise rulers like Lord Canning and Lord Lawrence, Lord Mayo and Lord Northbrook. He pointed to the next period of six years, 1874 to 1880, when the Tories were in power, and when an unwise Viceroy was sent out to carry out an unwise policy which ended in disaster and war. He pointed to the third period of 1880 to 1885, when the Liberals were in power, and India enjoyed peace once more under the beneficent administration of Lord Ripon, than whom no better or greater Viceroy had ruled in India. And he pointed to the last period, 1885 to the present date, when the Tories were in power with brief interruptions, and during which successive Viceroys,—Lords Dufferin, Lansdowne, and Elgin,—had wasted the revenues of impoverished India in making unprofitable annexations and useless forts beyond India, in weakening the frontier and making enemies of friendly tribes. (Cries of "Shame.") Mr. Dutt then referred to the calamities which had crowded on India in the year of the Queen's Diamond Jubilee-famine, plague, and a needless and iniquitous war. Amidst these complications, in the face of the vast expenditure which had to be incurred for the relief of the famine and the prosecution of the war, India expected some help, some relief from the British Exchequer The Chancellor of the Exchequer had given some hope of relief about a month ago, and had then turned round and said that the Indian Government did not want the money from the British Exchequer. The reason of this sudden change had leaked out through a paper in India, which had mysterious access to the views of the

Indian Government. That paper had said that Parliamentary interference in Indian concerns had done mischief in the past, and it was undesirable to let the British workman pay for the Indian war, lest he enquired too minutely into the causes and the necessity of the war! It came to this, that the Indian Government were so afraid of the British public enquiring into Indian wars and Indian administration that they would rather have no help from the British Exchequre than ask for help which might be followed by enquiry. (Cries of "Shame.") But he hoped that the British public would enquire into Indian questions, and he hoped that his hearers would support that great Liberal party which had in the past identified itself with peace and domestic improvement in India.

There was loud and prolonged cheering for nearly a minute when Mr. Dutt resumed his seat, and when he left the room a few minutes later to catch the train for Oxford, the audience left their seats, shook hands with him, and followed him with cries of "God bless your countrymen!"

III. FRONTIER WAR AND FAMINES.

[*Speech delivered at Oxford on March 7, 1898.*]

On Monday evening a public meeting was held in the Corn Exchange under the auspices of the Oxford Liberal Association, when Mr. Romesh Dutt, C.I.E., was invited to deliver an address on the question of "Frontier War and Famines in India." Among those present were Professor Sidgwick (who presided), Professor Macdonell, the Sheriff Mr. Cooper, Alderman Downing, Councillors Dodd, English, Moore, and J. H. Saltor, Messrs. J. Massie, S. Ball, Snow, A. M. Bell, Norman Smith, Grubb, A' Bear, Wintle, Watts, Jackson, Miss Weld, Mrs. Peters, Miss Goodwin, &c. The following summary of the speech is taken from the *Oxford Journal.*

The lecturer at the outset described the Lawrence policy of the Liberal party, and the Lytton policy of the Tory party, and said that, without going into details, if they looked back upon the history of the past forty years, they would find that whenever the Liberals were in power in this country they had tried to maintain what was known as the Lawrence policy, and endeavoured to promote the peace and happiness of the people of India; but whenever the Tory party was in power for any length of time, they had followed the Lytton policy, and had tried to discover a scientific frontier in India which had not yet been found! He did not make this as a sweeping statement, but it was a fact that the Liberal Government had always been more or less mindful of the needs of the country, while the Tories had always aspired to foolish expeditions and conquests. He was glad to tell them this quest after an undiscoverable frontier had at last come to an end, and that Lord George Hamilton had at last accepted the Lawrence policy with regard at least to the greater part of the Indian Frontier. The question arose however, now that the war was over, who was to pay the cost of this war that had taken place? The war had been imposed upon India not by the policy of India but by the Imperial policy of England, and question was, if the Imperial Exchequer should not meet the expense. They would remember that seventeen years ago, during Mr. Gladstone's administration, the same question was debated in the House of Commons, and Mr. Gladstone and his cabinet with a sense of fairness and of justice came to the conclusion, that as England was responsible for the war of 1878, she should bear at least a portion of the cost; and five millions were contributed by this country to the cost of that Afghan War. (Applause). The same reasons still held good, and they all expected that, in view of the special calamities under which India was suffering, the Tory Government would have the justice at least to contribute some share of the expense of the late war. But no, that was not the Tory policy. Their policy was to run the empire on the cheap, and to go to war and make other countries pay for it! Wisely, England had so far avoided wars in various parts of the world; she had avoided war in China, in Crete, and in South and West Africa. He said wisely, because he was always glad to see war avoided as long as it could be avoided, consistently with the honour of the nation. (Hear, hear). In two places only had England gone to war—on the frontier of India, and on the frontier of Egypt, but in both cases they made other countries pay, while England had declined to contribute anything towards the cost. If the nation wanted war, and thought its honour was involved, the nation ought to be prepared to make the sacrifices; but to make war from a spirit of Jingoism and make other nations pay, was a proceeding which would not have the approbation of Englishmen. (Applause). He asked them as men of ordinary common sense, was it possible that India in the present year should meet the enormous expenditure incurred by this war on the frontier? From their own admission, between five and six millions had been spent in consequence of the famine;—was this a year in which India should bear the burden of a war without some assistance? He said emphatically it was not, and the reason England was not asked to pay any share of the cost was this, that when an Englishman paid, wanted to know the reasen why. And it would be difficult indeed for the most ingenious Cabinet Minister to find out a reason for this unnecessary and senseless war. (Hear, hear). The speaker then referred to the effects upon India of the famines of 1837, 1860, 1866, 1874, 1876, and of 1896, and remarked that the last famine was more wide-spread than any previous famine that had occured in the present century. The civil officers did their very best to relieve the sufferers, and when Englishmen undertook to do a thing, they knew how to do it, and did not spare themselves. All this was very satisfactory, but the deeper question arose, why should there be so many famines in India, why such a terrible death-rate from starvation? They never heard of such famines in any other civilised country of the world. They sometimes heard of scarcity, but they never heard in any civilised country of famines so desolating, so destructive of human life and so frequent as in India. He had seen this question answered in various ways, but the answers were both unsatisfactory and untrue. It was sometimes said the population of India increased beyond the ordinary rate of increase in Europe, and that when a population increased to such an extent, they must make up their mind to die by famine. But the population did not increase at a larger rate or even at the same rate as the population of these islands. It was also said that the peasantry of India were wreckless and unthrifty, and that one could not help people who would not help themselves. But he (the speaker) knew of no peasantry who were so sober, frugal, and so absolutely parsimonious, as the peasantry of India. No, the real reason lay in the fact that the expenditure of the Indian Government, with its wasteful wars and a vast army, was far more than the population of India could bear. Quite four-fifths of the population depended entirely on agriculture; therefore if they so adjusted taxation as to leave a fair margin of profit to the agriculturists, the people would be prosperous. But if they raised the land tax from time to time so as to leave no margin to the people, nothing could save them from poverty and indebtedness, and from famines whenever there was a bad harvest. All this talk about improving the material condition of India was idle mockery. If they were earnest in their desire to improve the condition of the people of India, two things were necessary; first, the reduction of expenditure, and secondly, a reduction of taxation on land on which and which alone the people lived. A strong, good government always secured peace and economy; feeble and fussy governments suffered alternately from panic and vain-gloriousness. The speaker therefore appealed to them to administer India again as it had been administered by wise statesmen in the past, and to renew the policy of men like Lord Canning, Lord Lawrence and the Marquis of Ripon. (Applause).

On the proposition of Mr. Ball, seconded by Mr. Dodd a hearty vote of thanks was accorded to the Lecturer, and a similar compliment was paid to Professor Sidgwick for presiding.

IV. NEW IMPERIALISM IN INDIA.

[Speech delivered at the Sixth Annual Conference of the Women's National Liberal Association, on May, 17, 1898.]

THE Sixth Annual Conference of the Women's National Liberal Association was opened on Tuesday morning in St. Martin's Town Hall, London. There was a large attendance, the hall being well filled. Lady Hayter presided at the morning session, and among those on the platform were Mrs. Bryce, Miss Shaw-Lefevre, Miss Orme, Mrs. Grimwade, Mrs. Crossley, Mrs. Reeves, Sir Francis and Lady Evans, Mr. and Mrs. Byles, Sir Arthur Hayter, Mr. Ellis Griffith, M.P., Mr. Herbert Paul and Mr. Romesh Dutt. C. I. E. The following report of Mr. Dutt's speech is taken from *India*.

Mr. Dutt said: I consider it an honour and a privilege to be asked at this great annual gathering to say a few words on India, and I respond to the call with the utmost satisfaction, because there never was a time probably within this generation, when Indian affairs demanded your attention more urgently, and when my countrymen needed a larger share of your help and your sympathy. You are aware that last year, at the very time when the people of this country, and the people of British colonies and dependencies all over the world, were celebrating the Diamond Jubilee of the reign of their beloved Queen, India was passing through a series of calamities which find no parallel in the previous history of the country. A famine, wider in the area affected than any previous famine of which there is any record, desolated the fairest provinces of India. A plague, unprecedented in its extent and virulence, half depopulated for a time our fairest towns, and has travelled from Poona to Bombay, and from Bombay to Calcutta. And, as if these natural calamities were not sufficient, the Government brought upon themselves a disastrous war with tribes living beyond the Indian frontier, who are our best friends if we leave them alone,—(Cheers),—and who are our worst enemies if we interfere with their tribal independence, (Cheers). But it is not of these great calamities that I wish to speak this morning. The famine happily is over, and the one consoling incident connected with this famine is the sympathy and the help which were exhibited by the people of this country with their fellow subjects in India. You ladies and gentlemen, sent out from your private purses over half-a-million of English money for the sufferers in India ; it was a kind act, which has not been forgotten, and will not be forgotten, by the people of India. But though the famine of the past year is over, the question will arise in thoughtful minds why India is afflicted by such frequent famines under British rule. It was the tenth great famine which has visited India within the sixty years of Her Majesty's reign, and these ten great famines have swept away more than ten millions of the population of India. It is a sad chapter in the history of British rule in India, and the lesson which these famines teach us is that so long as an ever-increasing land tax is raised from the poor cultivators of the soil, their condition can never improve, and they can never be safe from famines and deaths in the future. We in India are not now a great manufacturing nation, nor are we a great commercial nation; but we are a great agricultural nation, and four-fifths of the population of India subsist directly or indirectly on agriculture. If the Government of India places some reasonable limits on the Land Tax, the cultivators can save something in good years to meet the calamities of bad years, as they do in Bengal. But if the Government of India continuously enhances the land revenue at each recurring settlement as they are now doing, the cultivating classes must necessarily be impoverished and indebted, and must perish in large numbers at each famine. Nowhere probably during the last year was the famine severer and more fatal than in the Central Provinces of India. And yet while the people were dying by the ten thousand, the settlement operations were proceeding, and the revenue was being enhanced. One of our best friends in the House of Commons, Mr. Samuel Smith (Cheers) asked the Secretary of State for India, if, in view of the famine from which those Provinces have lately suffered, he would postpone for a few years the introduction of the enhanced assessment. The Secretary of State for India declined to do so. (Shame). If policy like this is pursued in India there can be no improvement in the condition of the masses, and no protection from poverty, starvation, and deaths from famine. The frontier war too is happily over, and I need not say much about it except to remind you that the present Government which brought on the war by reversing the Chitral policy of their predecessors have had the kindness and the generosity to throw the whole pecuniary burden of the war on the famine-stricken population of India! If there had been a frontier war in any of the self-governing colonies of England under similar circumstances, do you think England would have sent the bill of costs to the colony for payment? And is it fair or just or righteous that the famine-stricken people of India should be treated differently because they are not self-governing, because they trust in the good faith and honour of England? Far different was the treatment which we received from the Liberal Government of that just and great and righteous statesman, whose name is as lovingly cherished in millions of grateful hearts in my own country, as it is in this country where he has lived and worked. (Prolonged cheers). Seventeen years ago, Mr. Gladstone was in power when the Afghan war was concluded, and with that fairness and sense of justice which were a part of him he contributed five millions of money from the English Exchequer towards the cost of that war. Contrast that action with the ungenerous and unjust decision of the present Government, which is distributing doles to all its friends and supporters, but cannot make a contribution which India demands with justice. But I turn from the subject of the frontier war, to the internal administration of India. You would expect naturally that in a year in which we have suffered so much from an accumulation of disasters and calamities, we would at least receive some sympathy and considerate treatment at the hands of the Government. The fact, however, is that a change has come over the spirit of the Indian administration, and New Imperialism is signalizing itself in India by measures of coercion and acts of confiscation. I can remember the administration of India from the time when it passed from the Company to the Crown, forty years ago, and I do not exaggerate when I state that among all the dark periods of British rule in India within these forty years, there was not a darker period for repressive legislation and for coercive measures than the present. You have heard how two respectable and honoured citizens of Bombay were deported by the Government, and were kept in confinement for nine months without a trial, and that even now they have not been released from all restrictions. You have heard of the prosecution instituted against the Indian Press, and of the monstrous sentences passed by Indiah judges on editors of newspapers, sentences which have shocked public opinion in this country as well as in India. And you have heard of the Acts recently passed by the Indian Government to virtually gag the Press of India—in spite of the opposition of all classes of the Indian Community. I will not go into the details of these Acts, but I may merely allude to one or two of their clauses to give you an idea of this strange Draconian law. One clause is that if an Indian speaker or writer says or writes anything, in this country, which may bring the Government of India into contempt, that

Indian speaker or writer may be prosecuted for it—not here, not before a British judge or British jury, but on his return to India, before an Indian magistrate, who is also the head of the police. We in India have the very highest respect for authority and for the Government, but I am not sure that it is possible even to mention some of its recent doings without exciting some feelings other than respect! And if what I have said this morning has excited in the minds of my fair listeners any unamiable feelings towards the Government, I may look forward to the pleasure and the luxury of a prison home when I go back to India, whether it be six months hence or six years hence. (Laughter). Another clause is that magistrates are empowered to demand security from editors of news papers, and in default to imprison them with hard labour. (Shame). Imagine how much of the liberty of the Press would remain, even in this country, if every Police Magistrate were empowered to require security for good behaviour from editors of London and country papers, and in default of such security to cast the editors into prison. Such a suppression of the Press would be a folly and misfortune in England; it is ten times more a folly and a misfortune in India. For in this free country you have the House of Commons and a hundred free institutions to give expression to your sentiments. In India we have no House of Commons and no free institutions, and to suppress Press would be to suppress the only possible expression of public opinion. It would render despotism more despotic, it would silence criticism and suppress public opinion, it would endanger the empire. For if there be dissatisfaction in the land with certain measure of the Government, is it not far better and far safer that the people should speak it out—(Cheers)—and that you should know it—(Cheers)—that you should try to remove it—(Cheers)—than that the dissatisfaction should work in the dark and end in a catastrophe? This is the just, the statesmanlike, and the true Liberal policy, and this was the policy of the great Liberal leader who is departing from us. Twenty years ago the Tory Government were unwise enough to pass a law to gag the Vernacular Press of India. But when Mr. Gladstone came into power, I need hardly say the foolish Act was expunged from the Statute Book of India. And the people of India confidently trust and believe that when a worthy successor of Mr. Gladstone will come once again into power, the Gagging Act now passed will once more cease to disgrace the Statute Book of India. (Cheers.) Ladies and gentlemen, I have one more word to say before I conclude. You are all aware that the present Government has declared its intention to demolish the self-government of London, and to destroy the great municipal powers enjoyed by the London County Council. You know how arduously the Tory leaders strove to influence the London elections in their favour, and how the great people of London have given the Government an answer whose import cannot be mistaken. And if the Government still persists in bringing forward a Bill, you may be quite sure that it is for the sake of appearances, and for gracefully retiring from the attitude they were unwise enough to take up. So, gentlemen, the thunderbolt which was so assiduously manufactured for London by the Tory Government has really fallen on our devoted heads in Calcutta. Twenty-two years ago the Municipality of Calcutta received a constitution by which two-thirds of the members of the Corporation were elected by the tax-payers. The system has worked well, and the people receive this limited right. But, the present Government sickens at the very idea of working through the people, and by means of a popular institution, and they have introduced a Bill in the Bengal Council, virtually taking away all real power from the elected Municipal Commissioners of the Capital of India! A blow is aimed at the root of self-government in Calcutta, and it is dreaded as the beginning of the end of all municipal self-government in India! Ladies and gentlemen, I thank you sincerely for the kind attention with which you have listened to me. Do not adopt this New Imperialism,—this method of coercion and repression—that will not save your Indian empire. Continue the policy which you adopted in the past, of trust and confidence in the people, of accepting the help and co-operation of the people in the management of their concerns, (Cheers,)—and the empire of India will be based on the firmest of all foundations, the affection and the loyalty of a great nation. (Loud cheers.)

V. DEATH OF MR. GLADSTONE.

[*Speech delivered at Derby on May*, 20, 1898.]

THE annual meeting of the National Reform Union was held at Derby on May 20, in the Temperance Hall. On account of the death of Mr. Gladstone only formal business was done and the annual report adopted. The Hon. Philip Stanhope, M.P., who presided, then spoke of the services which Mr. Gladstone had rendered to his country, and the loss sustained through his death. Mr. F. Maddison, M.P., spoke on behalf of the labour party, and he was followed by Mr. Romesh Dutt, who spoke on behalf of India. The following summary of his speech appeared in *India*.

Mr. Dutt said; I feel it a mournful duty to add a few words on this sad occasion, at the death of one whose name is as lovingly cherished in millions of grateful hearts in my own country as in this land where he lived and worked. (Cheers.) For the loss which has been sustained at the death of Mr. Gladstone is not a loss to England alone; it is a loss to the whole British Empire, and a loss to the cause of humanity. (Cheers). Your country, sir, is rich in illustrious men, whose genius has shed light and lustre in all parts of the world, men whose burning thoughts and burning words have raised a joyous echo in the remotest corners of the earth for freedom and for justice. But I doubt if even in this illustrious land there has lived within this century a man whose heart yearned more truly and nobly for the oppressed and the suffering than Mr. Gladstone, or whose voice pleaded more eloquently for right and for justice. For half a century Mr. Gladstone's name has been identified with the cause of right and justice, and has been cherished by nations of the earth far beyond the limits of the British Empire. In Italy, in Greece, in Armenia, in Crete, in Bulgaria, in Montenegro, wherever nations have struggled against oppression and wrong, Mr. Gladstone's voice has made itself heard, Mr. Gladstone's influence has made itself felt. (Loud cheers). Sad recollections come to one's mind on the present mournful occasion. I had the great good fortune, sir, to be in this country thirty years ago, when the great election of 1868 brought the Liberals to power. And I had the proud privillege of seeing Mr. Gladstone when he sat as Prime Minister in the House of Commons for the first time. You know the noble results of that brilliant administration (1868-74), one of the noblest administrations of this century. The Irish Church was disestablished, the first Irish Land Act was passed, and a system of national and compulsory education was organised for this country. (Cheers). I was again in this country, in 1886, and was present at those great debates in the House of Commons which followed Mr. Gladstone's introduction of his first Irish Home Rule Bill. One again, in 1893, I was here, and was a silent and admiring witness to that prolonged and persevering fight by which the venerable statesman succeeded in getting his second Home Rule Bill passed by the House of Commons. Then Mr. Gladstone retired from the scene of his labours to well-earned repose, but he never, to the last day of his life, ceased taking a lively interest in what he considered to be right and just. One private incident I wish to mention, because it illustrates the characteristic sympathy of Mr. Gladstone for the people of India. Last year, when Mr. Gladstone was living in retirement at Hawarden, I had the honour of sending him a copy of a small book on "England and India," in which I had indicated some needed reforms in the methods of Indian administration. The book had little interest for the general reader, but it had great interest for Mr. Gladstone, and I had the proud privillege of receiving a letter from him in his own handwriting, in which he thanked me for the gift, and expressed a hope that my little work would have some effect in awakening Englishmen to their duties towards their Indian fellow-subjects. (Cheers). But I do not wish to dwell on these personal recollections. I desire rather to refer in a few words to those great services which Mr. Gladstone has rendered to my country and to my countrymen. Not once or twice, but repeatedly, did the great and venerable statesman turn from the turmoil and bustle of British politics to render services to India, which have drawn towards him the hearts of my countrymen. In referring to some of these services, I will carefully avoid all political controversy, which is unsuited to this solemn occasion, and I will remember your injunction, sir, to exclude all discussion of party politics. I will barely mention one or two facts, and let the facts speak for themselves. You have all heard, ladies and gentlemen, of the frontier war into which India drifted during the last year, and which has been happily brought to a close. Twenty years ago India drifted into another such war with Afghanistan, during the administration of Lord Beaconsfield. As you all remember, Lord Beaconsfield's Government fell, and Mr. Gladstone came into power in 1880; he terminated the Afghan war; and with that sense of justice and fairness which was a part of him he decided that as the Afghan war was more an Imperial than an Indian war, a portion of the cost of the war should be contributed by England. Five millions of English money were contributed from the Imperial Exchequer towards the cost of that war. I need hardly remind you that the decision of the present Government with regard to the recent frontier war has been different; the whole cost of this last war has been charged to India. I will cite another instance. Under Lord Beaconsfield's administration the Government of India thought fit to pass an Act to restrict the liberty of the Vernacular Press of India, a liberty which it had enjoyed under British rule for half a century or more. As I said, Mr. Gladstone came into power in 1880, and the Press-gagging Act was expunged from the Statute Book of India. On this point too, the decision of the present Government had been different; they have passed two new Acts this year to restrict the liberty of the Press in India. Permit me to cite yet one more instance illustrating the spirit of Mr. Gladstone's legislation for India. Within the same brief period of Mr. Gladstone's second administration, to which I have already referred, and which lasted from 1880 to 1885, a noble and well-beloved Viceroy, the Marquis of Ripon, laid the foundation in India of what is known as local self-government. District boards and local boards were created; members were elected to these boards by the people, and they were entrusted with the management of roads, primary schools, dispensaries, and other local institutions. Tax-payers in towns were allowed to elect representatives, and Municipalities were allowed to elect chairmen. On this point also the spirit of Mr. Gladstone's administration differs from that of the present administration, for a Bill has been introduced this year by the present Government to take away from the Municipality of Calcutta those powers of self-government which it has enjoyed for many years past. Ladies and gentlemen, I need not allude to other instances, nor shall I on this solemn occasion discuss the current politics of India. India has fallen upon evil times, and we are passing through dangers which threaten to overwhelm us and wrest from us those humble rights and privileges which we have enjoyed in the past. We are filled with alarm, but not with dispair. Standing—if I may say so—by the grave of the greatest statesman of this century, we cannot think that wise Government is dead even in the dependency of India. The great heart of England is sound to the core—(Cheers)—and England, which is just and true to her colonies all over the world, cannot be unjust and untrue to India—at least, as long as England can cherish and love and venerate the name and the memory of Mr. Gladstone. (Prolonged cheers.)

VI. THE NEW SEDITION LAW.

[*Speech made at a Conference of Indains held in St. Martin's Town Hall, London, on June* 20, 1898.]

THE following report of Mr. Romesh Dutt's speech is taken from a published report of the proceedings. He moved the following resolution.

"That this meeting condemns the new Sedition Law of India, (1) which makes invidious distinctions between different classes of Her Majesty's subjects; (2) which seeks to restrict the free discussion of Indian measures by Her Majesty's Indian subjects in England, by threats of prosecution on their return to India; (3) which takes away the liberty of the Press that has been enjoyed in India for over half a century, and substitutes a method of repression unworthy of the British Government; (4) which empowers magistrates in India, who are heads of the police, to demand security for good behaviour from editors of newspapers, to refuse such security when offered, and to send the editors to gaol with hard labour, *without trial for any specific offence*; (5) and lastly, which is based on suspicion and distrust against the people, and is thereby calculated to alienate the people and weaken the foundations of the British Empire in the East."

Mr. Dutt said: I feel some hesitation in rising to move this resolution because, as you are aware, I have spent the best years of my life in the service of the great Indian Government, and I feel a pardonable pride in having done my humble little in serving the cause of good government in India. (Cheers.) I felt, therefore, some hesitation in accepting an invitation to speak on the subject of the blunders of the Indian Government. But the blunder on this occasion has been so serious, and is liable to be followed by consequences so disastrous, that I felt I should not be doing my duty towards my countrymen, or to the Government which I have served so long, if I did not on this occasion raise my warning voice against this unwise piece of legislation. (Loud cheers.) The idea of gagging the Press of India is not a happy one, not even a new one. As most of you are aware, about twenty years ago another Indian Viceroy, Lord Lytton, who waged another frontier war, conceived the idea of silencing criticism in India by means of gagging Act. He gagged the Vernacular Press by an Act in 1878, and you know what followed. The Liberal Government came into power two years after, and that Act was expunged from the Statute Book of India—(Cheers)—by that great and righteous statesman whose recent death has caused sorrow and lamentation in India as well as in England. Once more, now, we have a Viceroy who has passed another law, gagging this time not only the Vernacular Press but the whole Press, English and Vernacular, Native Indian and Anglo-Indian. I shall be very much surprised if this act remains very long on the Statute Book. I feel perfectly sure that, if the universal sorrow which has been manifested at the death of Mr. Gladstone indicates some appreciation of those righteous principles which guided his life, then there is not the remotest doubt that the leaders of Liberal thought in England will take an early opportunity of removing from the Statute Book an Act which is a disgrace to British Legislation.

(Cheers.) With these few remarks I think I will now at once go into some of the details of the Bill. You know that, about this time last year, a hint was received by some members of the House of Commons that it was contemplated to pass an Act to silence criticism in India and to gag the Press. The Leader of the Opposition put a question to the Secretary of State for India, asking him whether, before such an Act was passed, he would give the House of Commons an opportunity of knowing and discussing the details of the measure. Lord George Hamilton replied that the Indian Government was primarily responsible for the maintenance of peace in India, and the Indian Government, therefore, should have the initiative on all Indian measures. I particularly invite your attention to this reply, because I am going to show from the Blue-book which I hold in my hand that Lord George Hamilton has not acted in accordance with this statement. He has not allowed the Indian Government to act on its own opinion with regard to this Act, but he has in some respects forced the Indian Government to go further in the methods of repression than the Viceroy intended or desired to do. Soon after this, Parliament was prorogued, and the House did not re-open until February. Then the question was raised by one of our truest friends in the House of Commons, Mr. Herbert Roberts—(Cheers)—who discussed this proposed law in an eloquent and convincing speech. I will not repeat all the remarks he made on that occasion, but there is one sentence which I wish to read, because it truly describes the nature of the Act which has since been passed. He said, "The result of the new law, if passed, will be to open up an endless vista of prosecutions against editors of newspapers in India." Another member who sits on the Government side of the House, Mr. Maclean, said, "You can govern India by your justice and generosity, and in case of need by force of arms, but you will never do it by preventing the free expression of opinion among the people." (Cheers.) What was the reply of Lord George Hamilton? He assured the House that the law was under the consideration of the members of the Viceroy's Council, and that it was not then the proper time to discuss it in the House of Commons. He said that after the law had been passed it would be published, if desired, and opportunity would then come for discussion. The papers have since been published, but no opportunity for discussion has been given; nor will it be given until the closing days of August, when the Indian budget will be discussed, as usual, before empty benches. (Cries of "Shame.") I am not at all surprised at this unwillingness of the Government to discuss it, because the Act contains provisions so antagonistic to the principles of British law that the most powerful Government we have known for many years may well hesitate to bring it before the House of Commons. The law consists of two amending Acts. One amends the Penal Code, and the other amends the Criminal Procedure Code. With regard to the Penal Code, section 4 is repealed and the following is substituted for it. "The provisions of this code apply also to any offence committed by any native Indian subject of Her Majesty in any place without and beyond British India." That means that if any Native Indian subject of her Majesty criticises, in a way which the new law forbids, the acts of the Indian Government in this country, in this town of London, or in this hall this evening, the Indian Government takes the power to prosecute that Indian gentleman, not in this country, not before an English magistrate or an English jury, but when he goes back to India, four, five or six years hence. Then he will be taken before an Indian magistrate who is also the head of the local police. (Cries of "Shame.") In every civilised country the law declares that an offence shall be tried in the country in which it has been committed, but the Indian Government, in its anxiety to get all native Indian subjects within the clutches of the Indian law, have provided that, wherever the supposed offence is committed, the Government will wait until the supposed offender goes back to India, and will then haul him before an Indian magistrate, who is the head of the local police, in order to get him convicted. (Renewed cries of "Shame.") And mark, that this provision has been made specially to apply only to Native Indian subjects of Her Majesty. Therefore, if an Englishman should be so misguided as to write something in newspapers here, or to speak something which might increase the ill-feeling between race and race in India, there is no provision for prosecuting him in India. But if an Indian subject tries to reply to him in a manner calculated to have the same effect, then he can be prosecuted when he goes back to India. Is this in conformity with the promises and pledges so often given of equal justice to all classes of Her Majesty's subjects? (Cries of "No.") Now let me pass on to the main alteration made in the Penal Code, and that is the definition of the words "disaffection." The word was carefully defined by a lawyer whose name is as well-known in India as in this country, I mean Sir James Fitz-James Stephen. (Cheers.) He defined it so as not to include such disapprobation of the measures of the Government as is compatible with a disposition to render obedience to the lawful authority of the Government. That means that whatever our criticisms are—and I trust that all British subjects in all parts of the world will always criticise the acts of the Government, and so help the cause of good administration (Hear, hear)—so long as those criticisms are consistent with a desire to render obedience to lawful authority, there is no sedition. Will you believe it, that this most necessary and important provision has been struck out in the present law? And will you believe it, that the provision has been so struck out not because the Viceroy of India considered it necessary to do so for the safety of the Empire, but against the wishes and against the recommendation of the Viceroy by mandate of the Secretary of State for India? (Cries of "Shame.") The Viceroy said in his despatch that it was not necessary to amend Section 124A, since the highest courts in India had laid it down that the section did in substance reproduce the law of sedition in force in the United Kingdom. He added, "we consider that it is not necessary or desirable to amend the section. It might be possible by redrafting it to make its meaning more clear, but we think it unwise to undertake any revision of it so long as the interpretation hitherto placed upon it by the Courts in India is maintained." To that Lord George Hamilton replied, "I have come to the conclusion that the section should be revised, and that being so it seems better to make the alteration simultaneously with the change of jurisdiction." Not only that, but Lord George Hamilton also sent out a suggestion of what the definition should be, namely, that "disaffection includes all feelings of ill-will." (Laughter.) So, if the remarks have just fallen from our Chairman about the currency question have excited in you any feelings of ill-will—that is disaffection! If the remarks which I have the misfortune of making with regard to the new sedition law are exciting in you any feelings of ill-will—that is sedition! If the remarks which my esteemed friend Mr. Bose may make later on about the proposed Municipal law for Calcutta excites any feelings of ill-will—that is sedition! And if the remarks of my esteemed friend Mr. Khalil about the Indian frontier war produces such an effect on your minds—that is sedition! (Loud laughter.) This is how the Act was proposed to be altered, and although the Viceroy did not desire it, although he thought it "unwise," yet it is probably not known to you that legislation in India is to a great extent carried on by "mandates" from this country, and the Viceroy had virtually to accept the orders of the Secretary of State for India. (Cries of "Shame.") The definition finally adopted was that "disaffection includes disloyalty and all feelings of enmity." It leaves the offence dangerously vague and undefined. I have now only a few other remarks to make about the important changes in the Criminal Procedure Code. One of the most startling of these is that which classes the editors of newspapers with vagabonds, professional thieves, and professional burglars—(Laughter)—in so far that a magistrate is empowered to demand from them security for good behaviour, to refuse such security when offered, and to send them to gaol with hard labour, without any specific offence having been proved. (Cries of "Shame.") For you will understand that if any specific offence is proved proceedings are brought under the Penal Code. If no specific offence is proved, then, on vague information, on vague stories heard by the Magistrate, he can fall back on the Criminal Procedure Code, and send an editor to prison with hard labour. The Government of India had hitherto empowered the Magistrates to take this course with regard to notorious bad characters. I myself, as an Indian Magistrate, have exercised this law for about 20 years. When I found crime increasing, and the universal suspicion of villagers pointing to a particular man as the author of the crime, I have called on that man to give substantial security for his good behaviour, and on his failing to do this I have sent him to gaol with hard labour. This law has so long been reserved for habitual offenders, for notorious thieves, burglars, and extortioners. It has now been extended to editors of newespapers. (A Voice: "A downright shame.") Can you conceive a county Magistrate in this country calling upon the editor of the *Times* or the *Daily Chronicle*, the *Daily Newes* or the *Manchester Guardian* to give security for good behaviour on the strength of information he had received, and on the editor failing to satisfy the Magistrate in regard to security, sending him to gaol? (Laughter.) There is one other amendment to which I wish to allude. Hitherto all these offences relating to sedition have been tried by experienced judges. Now, this important class of offences are to go before district officers—men of high education and responsible position, no doubt, but men who represent the Government in their districts, and who are mainly responsible for the peace of their districts. So that virtually it comes to this, that the man who is the head of the police and the virtual prosecutor in all criminal cases, is to try editors or bind them down for good behaviour. I can only say that this condition of the law reminds me very strongly of the law which prevailed in England 200 or 300 years ago for stamping out witchcraft. They took an old woman suspected of being a witch and threw her into a deep pond. If she floated, that was considered a proof that she was a witch, and she was burned at the stake; if she sank, that proved that she was innocent, and she only died of drowning. (Loud laughter.) So in the case of editors, if any specific offence is proved against them, they are convicted and sent to gaol under the Penal Code. If no specific offence is proved against them then they are not convicted, but are sent to gaol for failing to furnish security for good behaviour under the Criminal Procedure Code.

("Shame.") I have only to add a word or two. I have told you that I have passed the best years of my life in the service of the Indian Government, and for many years I was in charge of important districts which in area and population far exceed the limits of an ordinary county in this country. Being thus isolated, as a Government official, in the midst of vast populations, I felt that my own security, and the security of the Government which I humbly tried to represent, rested on the confidence of the people in the justice and fair play of the British Government. It is with deep regret that I have to say that I can hardly remember any time—and my memory goes back to the time of the Mutiny—when the confidence of the people of India in the justice and fair play of English rulers was so shaken as it has been within the last two years. (Cheers, and a Voice: "Very true.") It is a calamity that this should be so. It is a grave calamity that the very foundation of British rule in India, our confidence in the justice of English rule and English administration, should be shaken; but it is a still greater calamity that the British Government itself should in this Sedition Law show its weakness and its want of trust in the people. (Cheers.) In the interests of my countrymen and of the Government of my country, I do ask those men who shape our destinies to turn back from this policy of coercion and repression, and to turn to that policy of conciliation and trust and confidence in the people by which the British Empire in India has been established, and by which alone it can be maintained. (Loud cheers.)

VII. THE CALCUTTA MUNICIPAL BILL.

[*Speech delivered at a great meeting in Manchester, on November* 22, 1898. *The Bishop of Hereford presided.*

THE following summary of Mr. Dutt's speech is taken from *India*. Mr. Romesh Dutt said : They had listened with pleasure and instruction to the eloquent speeches which had explained and insisted on the duty of Englishmen to deal with native races in all parts of the British Empire, with justice and equity. For himself, coming from India, he could say that he had listened to them with gratitude. Such eloquent advocacy of just and fair dealing was needful and beneficial ; and there never was a time within this generation when it was so needful as at the present day. In India it would almost seem as if we were going backwards from the path of progress which we had trod so long, and that the rights and privileges accorded to the people by wise statesmen in the past were about to be withdrawn under the influence of a New Imperialism ! The Empire of India was built up by the co-operation of the people, by Indian soldiers who had fought side by side with English soldiers, and by the help of races and nations who had rallied round the only power which could give the people peace and security and civilised government. But lately they had passed through evil times ; the famine of the last year was the tenth great famine which had marked the Queen's reign in India; and these ten famines were estimated to have carried off ten or twelve millions of their Indian fellow-subjects. But what was perhaps even more alarming than the famine was the change which had come over the spirit of British rule in India, and the want of trust and confidence in the people which betrayed itself in measures of coercion and repression. There can be no wise and successful administration in India with its vast population without the advice and help and co-operation of the people themselves. (Applause.) It was not the officers who went out to India who were to blame; he had himself had the honour to belong to the great Civil Service of India for 26 years of his life, and he would say this; take the Indian Civil Servants with all their faults, they were as fine a body of administrators as they sent out to any part of the world. It was not the men, it was the system which was to blame—(Applause)—and the system was not improving with the lapse of time, but was becoming more distrustful, more unsympathetic, and more despotic under the perfervid Jingoism of the present day. He would give them one illustration of the manner in which popular administration had succeeded in India in the past, and how, nevertheless, the present Government seemed bent upon withdrawing popular rights and privileges, and reverting to methods of despotism and distrust in the people. Twenty-two years ago, when India was under the administration of Lord Northbrook, the ratepayers of Calcutta were allowed the right of electing two-thirds of their Municipal Commissioners, the remaining third being appointed by the

Government. We in this country should not consider it a great concession to the metropolis of India to allow it to elect two-thirds of their Municipal Commissioners; but they in India were thankful for small mercies, and during the last twenty-two years they had cherished this as one of the most valued rights they had secured under British rule in India. How the elected Commissioners had done their municipal work was a matter of history, they had cleansed the city, improved the drainage and extended the water supply, and in the words of Sir Antony MacDonnell, one of the most successful administrators of India, they had worked with a zeal which rose to the level of devotion. Men who had entered young had grown grey in the service of the town; and the best educated and most patriotic citizens took a pride in their work, and in their position as representatives elected by their townsmen. Calcutta was not an ideally sanitary town yet, but Calcutta was nevertheless one of the healthiest places now in Bengal, the value of land had doubled, and thousands of people came to the city annually from the surrounding country to improve their health. More than this, when a few cases of plague were recently imported into Calcutta from Bombay, they were promptly stamped out, partly through the superior sanitary arrangements of Calcutta, and partly through the zealous and devoted exertions of the elected Commissioners of the city. (Applause.) They would think that after this good work of twenty-two years, after saving the town from the horrors of a plague, the ratepayers of Calcutta had deserved some extension of their rights and privileges, some broadening of the scheme of self-government in the city. But would they believe it, at the present moment there was a Bill before the Bengal Council virtually withdrawing from the citizens the right of self-government ! It was a wanton measure of injustice to the people of Calcutta, and it was felt as a confiscation of the people's rights. He had had enough experience of Indian administration to know what the result of the change would be ; they could not administer the concerns of 860,000 people, which was the population of Calcutta, without the co-operation of the people themselves and the good work which had been done in the past in the metropolis of India would be ruined. He appealed to them on behalf of his countrymen and not to ruin Indian administration by rejecting the willing and zealous co-operation of the people themselves. (Applause.)

[The following note on the past history of Calcutta was referred to by the speaker in course of his speech.]

Commissioners appointed by the Government, 1856. They failed. Act XXVIII. of 1856 vested the administration of Calcutta in three Commissioners who "shall be appointed by the Lieutenant-Governor of Bengal, and shall be removable at his pleasure." The Commissioners so appointed by the Government failed to improve the town, and Mr. (afterwards Sir John) Strachey thus describes the town in 1863 :—

"With regard to the northern or native division of Calcutta which contains some hundred thousand people, it is no figure of speech but the simple truth to say that no language can adequately describe its abominations. In the filthiest quarters of the filthiest towns that I have seen in other parts of India or in other countries, I have never seen anything which can be for a moment compared with the filthiness of Calcutta. This is true not merely of the inferior portions of the town, or of the byeways and places inhabited by the poor classes, but it is true of the principal thoroughfares and of the quarters filled with the houses of the richest and most influential portion of the native community. If a plain unvarnished description of the northern division of Calcutta, bordered by the horrible open drains in which all the filth of the city stagnates and putrifies, were given to the people of England, I believe they would consider the account altogether incredible."

Justices of the Peace appointed by the Government, 1863. They failed. Act. VI. of 1863 was then passed by which the Government handed over the administration of the town to Justices of the Peace appointed by itself. The Justices did something to improve the town, and introduced water-works, but failed to improve it effectually. Dr. Payne, the Health Officer of the town, wrote thus in 1876:—

"It is impossible to conceive a more perfect combination of all the evils of crowded city-life in the primitive filthiness and disorder than is presented in the native portion of Calcutta. Dirt in the most intense and noxious forms that a dense population can produce covers the ground, saturates the water, infects the air, and finds in the habits and incidents of the people's lives every possible facility for re-entering their bodies; while ventilation could not be more shunned in their houses if the climate were arctic instead of tropical. If then Calcutta be not a deadly place, filth in its utmost intensity must be innocuous, and sanitation a pretentious sham."

Election System introduced in 1876 as a remedy. Act IV. of 1876 was then introduced by

SIR R. TEMPLE, then Lieutenant-Governor of Bengal, and passed into law. It provided that the Corporation of Calcutta was to consist of 72 members, 48 of whom were to be elected by the ratepayers and the remaining 24 appointed by the Local Government.

How the Election System worked between 1876 and 1884. In 1884 a Commission was appointed "to enquire into certain matters connected with the sanitation of the town of Calcutta." Two of the members of the Commission point out defects (which have since been remedied), but did not recommend any constitutional changes. On the contrary they suggested the inclusion of the suburbs of Calcutta within the town, which has since been done. The third member of the Commission, Mr. H. J. S. Cotton, now Chief Commissioner of Assam, thus spoke of the Corporation :—

"The Corporation of Calcutta as a representative body commands the confidence of the vast majority of the ratepayers; it has already done very much in the direction of sanitary reform; it has not retrograded in giving effect to a single sanitary improvement; stimulated by the healthy action of public opinion and profiting by the greater experience gained year by year, it has afforded, by the systematic enterprise of the past three years, the most solid guarantee that it will continue to advance on the path of the progress.

Favourable Opinion recorded in 1890 by Sir Steuart Bailey, then Lieutenant-Governor of Bengal. The amalgamation of the suburbs was effected by Act II. of 1888, which provided that the Corporation would consist of 75 members, 50 of whom were to be elected by the ratepayers, 15 to be appointed by the Local Government, and 10 to be elected by

European commercial bodies, and the Port Commissioners. How well the Commissioners, thus variously elected and appointed, worked with their Chairman is shewn by the following extract from a resolution recorded in 1890 by Sir Steuart Bailey, then Lieutenant-Governor of Bengal, on the retirement of Sir Henry Harrison, who had been Chairman of Calcutta for 9 years.

"For 9 years he was Chairman of the Corporation, and the useful administration of the affairs of the municipality during this long period, the firm financial credit of the Commissioners, the innumerable sanitary reforms effected, specially the extension of the water-supply and the conservancy of *bustees*, the increase in material prosperity in the city which, in consequence of these reforms, has shown itself in so marked a degree that the value of land in Calcutta generally may be said to have doubled, the re-organisation and re-construction of nearly every department of work, the hearty zeal and co-operation with which the Commissioners as a body now unite with the Executive to advance the welfare of the city—and attitude for which they were not always distinguished, but which is in itself the best testimony to the capacity of a chairman—the methodical and systematic development of civic administration in all departments, are a sufficient and lasting tribute to the manner in which Sir Henry Harrison has discharged the duties of his responsible, difficult, and thankless office. His name will always be honorably associated with the growth of municipal institutions in the Metropolis."

Favourable Opinion recorded in 1893 by Sir Antony MacDonnell, then Lieutenant-Governor of Bengal. The Municipal Commissioners of Calcutta, the majority of whom were elected by the ratepayers, continued to effect sanitary improvements in their great city; and the opinion recorded by Sir Antony MacDonnell in 1893 is a valuable testimony to their zeal, efficiency, and devotion :—

"Sir Antony MacDonnell has perused with much interest the report reviewed in the preceding paragraphs ; it records the execution of much useful work, especially in the direction of sanitation and of structural improvements, such as the extension of drainage and water-supply and the improvement of the *bustees* ; and for their share in carrying out these measures, the thanks of the Lieutenant-Governor are due to the executive officers of the Corporation, the Engineer and the Health Officer The Commissioners themselves have, as a whole, displayed a care and attention to their duties which is very meritorious, and has in some cases risen to the level of devotion.

Favourable Opinion expressed in 1898 by Sir John Woodburn, present Lieutenant-Governor of Bengal. The Municipal Commissioners of Calcutta, the majority of whom are elected by the rate-payers, have continued up to the present day to perform their work with efficiency and zeal, and will appear from the following words spoken in November last by the present Lieutenant-Governor :—

"They are entitled to all the credit—and it is a high one —of realising the value and necessity of the great schemes which have been drawn up for their approval, such as those for the drainage of the city and the construction of Harrison Road. They have not shrunk from the heavy taxtion which was needed to bring these beneficent projects into effect, and I have myself had evidence of the high public spirit and laborious circumspection which many members of the Corporation bring to the discharge of their municipal duties. These are qualities which not in Calcutta alone have elicited my respect, and it is a pleasure to me to have this opportunity of acknowledging them.

VIII. THE CURRENCY QUESTION.

Evidence given before the Currency Committee on November, 30, 1898.

PRESENT :

The Rt. Hon. SIR HENRY H. FOWLER, G.C.S.I., M.P. (in the Chair).

Sir JOHN MUIR, Bart.
Sir FRANCIS MOWATT, K.C.B.
Sir DAVID BARBOUR, K.C.S.I.
Sir CHARLES CROSTHWAITE, K.C.S.I.
Sir ALFRED DENT, K.C.M.G.
Mr. ROBERT CAMPBELL.
Mr. EVERARD HAMBRO.
Mr. W. H. HOLLAND.
Mr. F. C. LE MARCHANT.

Mr. ROBERT CHALMERS, *Secretary.*

[*Examination of witness, Mr. Dutt, by Sir Henry Fowler, Chairman.*]

10,628. You were selected for the Indian Civil Service at the open competition held in London in 1869?—That is so.

10,629. You joined the service in 1871?—That is so.

10,630. Will you tell us your experience in the Indian Civil Service?—After serving in the lower grades, I held appointments as District Magistrate and Collector between 1881 and 1894 in various districts in Lower Bengal, and as Divisional Commissioner in Burdwan and Orissa Divisions between 1894 and 1897 after 26 years' service.

10,631. The Departments that you were in did not deal specifically with either currency or accounts?—No.

10,632. But they gave you the opportunity of studying the condition of the agricultural labouring classes?—Yes.

10,633. And it is with that experience and your knowledge of Indian affairs that you approach this question?—That is so.

10,634. I will first ask you what you thought of the closing of the mints. Had you any opinion at that time on that point?—We were not consulted. I hardly knew anything about it.

10,635. You were in India when the step was taken?—No; in 1893 I was in this country on furlough.

10,636. You are aware, I suppose, that the rupee had been steadily falling for a large number of years?—Yes.

10,637. At the time when the mints were closed in 1893, they were closed on the ground of the fall of the rupee being a very serious danger to the financial position of India?—I heard that vaguely in this country.

10,638. Since you have been here, you have thoroughly mastered the new proposals of the Indian Government?—In a general way, yes.

10,639. Will you just say, in your own language, what you would like to say first as to the effect of those proposals?—The first effect is likely to be this, that it would lead to general increase of taxation in India. Because all the taxes are paid in rupees, and, by closing the mints, the value of the rupee has been enhanced, and, if the same number of rupees are taken now as were taken before, it means a real increase in taxtion.

10,640. Have you any figures as to what the raising

of prices has been? When you went to India in 1871 the price of silver was $65\frac{5}{16}d.$ an ounce, and the average rate at which the Secretary of State sold his bills was 1*s*. $10\frac{3}{4}d.$ per rupee?—Yes.

10,641. The rate began to fall, I think, materially in 1878 or 1879, and, when the mints were closed in 1892-93, it had gone down to 1*s*. $2\frac{1}{2}d.$?—That is about it.

10,642. That is a fall of 8*d*. in the rupee in those years?—Yes.

10,643. Did the proposals of the Government of India to arrest the fall of the rupee have the effect of raising its value?—Yes, I think it was 1*s*. 2*d*., if I remember rightly, in 1893, and it is now nearly 1*s*. 4*d*., so that within this last five years the value of the rupee has been enhanced by 2*d*. as compared with gold. With regard to the fall from 1871 to 1893, I may be allowed to explain that the Indian Government and the Provincial Governments got a natural increase in their revenue in consequence of the fall. The land revenue and other revenues went up in this way. The prices in rupees rose all round; the prices of food grains rose, and, as the Government in its recurring settlements made that a ground of enhancement—because the Government as landlord is entitled to an increase of rent if the price of the produce rises—there was a natural increase in land revenue. Then also with regard to the income-tax; as the incomes, estimated in rupees, went up, the Government got an increase of the income tax; so that, while there was a fall in the value of the rupee from 1871 to

1893, Government was directly, and in a natural way, getting an increase in the revenues as estimated by the rupee.

10,644. When you talk of an increase in the income-tax, will you explain that further?—Suppose a man's income in 1871 was 1,000 rupees a year. If his real income remained the same, then, by the falling of the rupee, his income as valued by the rupee would be something like 1,200 rupees.

10,645. What do you mean by his real income?—His income estimated by the produce of the country. I am speaking of people outside those in Government employment—not members of the Government service. I am speaking of merchants and traders, agriculturists, and farmers—people outside Government employ.

10,646. You think there was such a rise in prices that, practically, profits were increased to that extent?—Profits as estimated by the rupee. If a man's real profits remained the same, the value of the rupee having fallen, his profits, as estimated by the rupee, must have risen. If his income was 1,000 rupees in 1871, and if the rupee had in the meantime depreciated 8*d.*, his income in 1893, as estimated by the rupee, must have risen, and, therefore, the Government would get an increase in the income-tax obtained from that man.

10,647. Do you mean that they would get more rupees?—They would get more rupees. The depreciation of the rupee has not been a loss to Government, because in this way there is a general increase in taxation without making the burden heavier on the people—there is a general increase in taxation as estimated by the rupee.

10,648. Do you think that in India itself—I am not talking now of external trade or payments out of India—the internal trade has increased?—There has been an increase in the price of food grains within my experience. Between 1871 and 1893 there was a considerable rise in the price of rice.

10,649. Was that accompanied by an increase in wages?—To some extent; and the landlords were able to increase their rents, and the Government in all cases, except where there were permanent settlements, were able to increase their land-revenue on the basis of an increase of rents.

10,650. What would have been the position of things if the rupee had remained stationary?—Then the increase of the land-revenue would not have been so marked, as estimated by rupees. I will try to explain myself in this way. Suppose the Government land-revenue of a district not permanently settled was 3 lakhs in 1871. In the 22 years between 1871 and 1893, the prices of food grains rose; where rice sold at 1 rupee 8 annas per maund in 1871, it sold in 1893 at, say, 2 rupees per maund. In the same way there is an increase in the prices of wheat, barley, jawar, and bajra, and all the principal staple foods of India; there was a general increase of prices in all food grains. Therefore, when the Government came to revise the settlements, it found that there was a general increase in the prices of food grains all over the country, and obtained a legitimate increase of probably a lakh of rupees solely on the ground of increase in prices. If there had not been that increase, the Government might have raised the land-revenue a little, but certainly not so much, if prices had remained stationary.

10,651. I was dealing with the connexion between the falling of the rupee and the rise of prices. Do you consider, for instance, the opening up of the European markets to wheat is a factor ?—It is a very small factor.

10,652. Do you think the increased consumption of rice is a factor ?—I do not think so, for there has been an increased cultivation. I think the main reason of the rise in prices is that the rupee has depreciated between 1871 and 1893. And the land-revenue, as estimated in rupees, has increased.

10,653. Supposing, instead of the Government arresting by their action the fall of the rupee, they had allowed the fall to go on, and that the rupee had gone down to *6d.*, what do you think would have been the effect of that ?—I hardly think it would be possible ; but, if it did go to *6d.*, it would not have made any difference, because the land-revenue would rise at the very next settlement ; the rise in the prices of food grains would be so considerable that, without any effort on their part, the Government would get a natural increase in the income-tax, and a natural increase in the proceeds of almost every tax in the country.

10,654. (*Sir F. Mowatt.*) You are assuming that the prices would immediately follow the fall of the rupee ? —Yes.

10,655. It is on that assumption that your opinion is founded?—Either immediately or within a short time; and my experience during the last 26 years in Bengal has been that, as the rupee has gone down, prices have risen.

10,656. (*Chairman.*) Will you apply that now to the salt-tax?—I do not remember the incidence of the salt-tax.

10,657. The salt-tax is now $2\frac{1}{2}$ rupees per maund. That is a fixed sum?—The Government would be quite justified in increasing the tax in proportion to the fall of the rupee.

10,658. Then take the excise duties and apply the same argument—I mean the duties on spirits and liquor. I want to see where you think the Government income would rise?—In this way. On the liquor distilled in Bengal the Government imposes a duty of something like 2 rupees for each gallon distilled. When the rupee depreciated and food grains all rose in price, the Government would be justified in imposing 2 rupees 8 annas, or 2 rupees 12 annas, or 3 rupees.

10,659. That is dealing with what the Government might do, but that is not what has actually occurred. I understand your point to be this, that automatically, by the reduction in the value of the rupee, the revenue has increased?—In most cases, excepting in those cases where the Government imposes an arbitrary sum, in which cases the Government has the power to increase that sum, and it would be justified in increasing that sum in correspondence with the fall of the rupee.

10,660. Now, your next point, I think, is that the Government have improperly appreciated the currency?—That is my argument, and I find that that argument was taken up, as no doubt this Committee is aware, in 1879 in a letter to the India Office, by the Treasury. I have an extract from that here. This question was discussed in 1879, and the India Office received a letter from the Treasury from which I will read this extract: "In general, the object of such Governments"—this is in reference to those Governments which have depreciated the currency in order to reduce their liabilities—"has been to diminish the amount they have to pay to their creditors. In the present case the object of the Indian Government appears to be to increase the amount they have to receive from their tax-payers. My Lords fail to see any real difference in the character of the two transactions." That is in a letter dated 24th November 1879. The proposal of the Indian Government to raise the value of the current coin of India, and thus to obtain from the ratepayers a really larger revenue, without ostensibly increasing the tax, appears to me to be open to the same objections. The injustice and the hardship are none the less real and none the less oppressive by reason of the fact that, instead of raising the amount of taxes 30 or 40 per cent, the proposal is to raise the value of the rupee to the same extent, or to keep the value of the rupee high to the same extent. Such a proposal does not disguise the real increase in taxtion, and does not minimise either its pressure or its arbitrariness.

10,661. Your first objection is that practically this means a general increase of taxtion ?—Yes, over and above the natural increase.

10,662. Then in the next place, you object to it with especial reference to the land revenue ?—Yes ; the Government of India is the receiver of land-revenues in India. It receives fixed revenues from landlords in Bengal, and rents from actual cultivators in most other parts of India. I assume that, when the value of the rupee is artificially raised, or artificially kept up to that point to which it has already been raised, the Government will not be disposed to make a proportionate reduction in the amount of its rents and land-revenues.

10,663. But what do you say about the fall that has already taken place in the value of the rupee since these rents were fixed ?—Do you mean in Madras or Bombay ?

10,664. Anywhere ?—In consequence of the fall of the value of the rupee, the rents have already been increased, as I explained just now.

10,665. That would not apply in the first place to the permanent settlements ?—No, I am speaking of other places. Settlements are continually going on.

10,666. In individual cases ?—In some parts settlements have taken place ; in others, settlements are going to take place ; so that, if there has been a rise in prices through the fall of the rupee, the Government has either got the advantage of it, or is going to get the advantage of it. But, by increasing the price of the rupee, you, not automatically but suddenly, raise the land-revenues all over India. Take Bengal, for instance, where the revenues are permanently settled; some zemindar has engaged to pay, say, 50,000 rupees as the revenue of his zemindary, and he has paid that sum since the permanent settlement—since 1793; now the rupee is raised from 1*s*. 2*d*, to 1*s*. 4*d*., it may possibly go higher, but it has been raised from 1*s*. 2*d*. to 1*s*. 4*d*. Therefore, in place of the 50,000 rupees which he has been paying since the permanent settlement, by raising the rupee 2*d*. you impose a real addition to the amount of revenue paid by him.

10,667. But you must go further back. When the Cornwallis settlement was made, the rupee was worth really more than 2*s*. The Government, of course, have lost by that?—In the permanent-settlement tracts the Government have lost and the people have gained, and the agriculturists have greatly benefited by that. The condition of the Bengal agriculturist has greatly improved on account of the rise in prices, and the Government has derived advantage from the increased prosperity of the cultivators.

10,668. But do you not think the zemindars have increased their rent?—To some extent they have, but the great benefit is derived by the Government themselves, and not by the landlord. In other parts of India—leaving out those places where the revenue has been permanently settled—the land-revenue has adjusted itself, or is going shortly to adjust itself, according to the rise of prices. Now by suddenly increasing the value of the rupee, there is a further increase in land-revenue. In Madras, for instance, the land-revenue of a district may have been 3 lakhs of rupees; it will be 3 lakhs of rupees now, but of rupees of an enhanced value. Therefore, by this action of the Government, there is a sudden increased demand by the Government over and above the natural increase which it has received already. In order to explain this better, I have prepared this table of figures, which has been placed before every member of the Committee, which will show that in nearly every division in India there was a fall in the prices of food grains immediately after the closing of the mints, in the Punjab, in the North-West Provinces, in Bengal, in Bombay, in Madras, in Assam, and in the Central Provinces. I have compiled these figures from the book called "Prices and Wages in India," annually published by the Government of India; and I have given the reference to the pages from which I have compiled my figures. [*For this Table, see Appendix.*]

10,669. You say there has been a fall in prices since the closing of the mints?—Immediately after the closing of the mints.

10,670. (*Mr. O'Conor.*) The prices of 1892 were extraordinarily high. (*Witness.*) I have taken 1893-94 together, and 1894-95 together, and I find that in every division almost there has been a fall in prices. I have taken division by division, in order to show that there is not only a fall in the different provinces, but that there is a fall in prices all over India in almost every division. I cannot myself explain that in any other way excepting by imputing it to the closing of the mints. I was in Bengal myself in 1892, 1894, and 1895 (I was absent in 1893), and the fall in prices in 1894-95 was certainly not owing to any abundant harvest, because there was scarcity in some parts of Bengal in those years, and there was scarcity in the North-West Provinces, so that naturally you would expect that prices would range high in 1894 and 1895. Instead of that, prices apparently fell in all parts of India. What I am driving at is this, that, although the prices fell, the cultivators had to pay the same amount in rupees. When they sold their wheat, say, at 13 seers for the rupee, they paid a certain rent; when prices fell to 15 or 16 or 17 seers the rupee, they got less by the sale of their wheat, but they had still to pay the same rent. In other words, it was an indirect increase in the rental all over.

10,671. (*Chairman.*) Supposing prices had risen?—The zemindars would have very soon got an increase.

10,672. But take the other parts of India, where there are no zemindars?—Then the Government would have got an increase in the next settlement. The cultivators would have got an advantage for some few years, and then the Government would have had its own share.

10,673. Sooner or later, you say, it would amount to raising the land-revenue?—Yes, according to the rise in prices.

10,674. Then you say that there is another and a still graver objection to the proposal. Will you explain that?—The millions of agriculturists and labourers in India are indebted to moneylenders and mahajans, and the debt is, in many cases, reckoned in rupees, and not in grain. To artificially enhance the value of the rupee, or to fix the value at the rate to which it has been already artificially raised, is to increase the indebtedness of the cultivators and labourers of India to moneylenders and mahajans. The measure serves to add to the profits of the prosperous classes who feed on the distresses of the poor, and to add to the weight of the millstone which the poor and indebted classes carry round their necks. Throughout the bazaars and money markets of India, the effect of raising the value of the rupee is to add to the profits of the rich moneylender, and to enhance the liabilities of the poor cultivator who has a debt. I may only add to this, that even this point was touched upon in that Treasury letter to which I referred just now. In paragraph 20 of that letter from the Treasury to the Indian Office, dated 24th November 1879, there is this passage :—"This relief"—that is the relief to those people who get their pay from the Government—"will be given at the expense of the Indian taxpayer, and with the effect of increasing every debt or fixed payment in India, including debts due by ryots to moneylenders." That is exactly the point I have tried to explain.

10,675. What was the state of things when that proposal was made? The then value of the rupee was 1*s*. 8*d*., and the Government proposed, did they not, that it should be at once raised to 2*s*.?—Yes.

10,676. Is it not against that proposal that the Treasury letter is directed?—I believe that is so, and I think what we are doing now is much the same thing.

10,677. That was a distinct proposal to raise the

value of the rupee, which had been for a long time, and was then, about 1s. 8d., to 2s. At the present time the proposal is to prevent any further fall?—But it has been raised by the closing of the mints from 1s. 2d. to nearly 1s. 4d., and the proposal is to keep it at that.

10,678. Assuming it to be fixed at 1s. 4d., that would be raising it, that is what you mean?—Yes, then I was referring to paragraph 18 of the same letter, in which the Lords of the Treasury go on to say, "It alters every contract and every fixed payment in India." Virtually what it is proposed to do now would have very much the same effect. If the value of the rupee is kept at its enhanced rate by the action of the Government, it really adds to the indebtedness of the cultivator to the moneylender. The cultivator's income estimated in rupees has gone down; it went down during those two years, 1894—95, but then, of course, prices rose again during the famine years. I have not taken famine prices into consideration, but it stands to reason that, if the value of the rupee is artificially raised, the income of the cultivator, estimated in rupees, must fall, but his indebtedness to the moneylender, where it is reckoned in rupees, remains the same. Where he is indebted to the extent of 100 rupees to the moneylender, the moneylender will claim his 100 rupees, although the 100 rupees now represent a larger quantity of rice or wheat than before. Probably the whole produce of the field was 100 rupees before, now the produce of the field would not amount to 100 rupees, but the cultivator is still indebted to the extent of 100 rupees; so that, reckoned by his income, (and the income of the cultivator is in the produce of the soil) his indebtedness to the mahajan is increased all round.

10,679. You assume that prices fall as soon as the exchange value of the rupee is raised?—I assume that, because it must be so; and because our experience of those two years shows that it has been so in the past. In the years 1894—95, from the figures that I have given, it is clear that immediately after the closing of the mints the value of crops went down all over India; and it stands to reason that, if the value of the rupee is enhanced, the value of everything, estimated in rupees must fall. When the rupee is artificially raised, the value of everything must fall. Therefore, by the sale of the produce of his field, whether it is rice or wheat, the cultivator will get, in the number of rupees, less than he got before.

10,680. What have you to say about silver hoarding?—Before leaving this, I would ask permission to say that I think it is sometimes stated that the indebtedness of the agriculturists to the moneylenders is in grain and not in money. I wish to explain that it is so in some cases, but in many cases the indebtedness is in money. In many cases that I know of, in Bengal villages, the debt is estimated in rupees, and the debt is not contracted all of a sudden. Just after the harvest, probably, the cultivator pays off his debt, and then he goes on borrowing 5 rupees or 10 rupees from time to time. When he has to marry a son or daughter, or has some domestic expense of some kind, he goes to the moneylender and gets money advanced till the harvest time comes, and then much of the debt is cleared off. But what I want to point out is that much of his indebtedness is in rupees. There is a portion of it in grain, but much of the cultivator's indebtedness, in Bengal at any rate, is in rupees. Therefore, to that extent, his indebtedness is increased by your artificially adding to the value of the rupee.

10,681. You are assuming that the debt has all been contracted at one specific period and is all going to be paid off at another?—It is annually contracted or runs on.

10,682. But, for instance, during the last 12 months the rupee has been at 1*s*. 4*d*. In 1893 it was at 1*s*. 3*d*. nearly, and in 1894 it was 1*s*. 2½*d*. Then it went down to 1*s*. 1*d*.; then it began to rise, and now it is at 1*s*. 4*d*., you may say. But the people who contracted those debts contracted them when the rupee was worth 1*s*. 4*d*. or more, and that extends back?—But the debt is renewed from time to time.

10,683. It is renewed in rupees?—Yes, with the interest, and it is paid off also in the harvest time, if there is a bumper crop.

10,684. I want you to explain this. Supposing it is an annual loan; suppose a man raises money on his crops and pays his debt when the crops are sold, he pays and receives according to the then rate?—Yes.

10,685. The injustice would arise if the man borrowed when the rupee was worth 1*s*. and had to pay it off when the rupee was worth 1*s*. 4*d*.; but that cannot occur in one year?—The practice is not uniform. Sometimes the loan is annual, sometimes it is for two or three years.

10,686. But so far, with the exception of three or four years between 1892 and the present time, the rate was always above 1*s.* 4*d.* ?—Yes.

10,687. Every liability in India, prior to 1892, was raised on the basis of more than 1*s.* 4*d.* ?—Yes.

10,688. Therefore—I am assuming this for the sake of argument—fixing the rupee at 1*s.* 4*d.* would not be an injury, on your hypothesis?—For those old debts, no.

10,689. Nor would it be for those debts contracted in the last two years when the rupee was at 1*s.* 4*d.* ?—I did not know it was 1*s.* 4*d.* in the last two years.

10,690. It has been steadily rising. Your argument, whether sound or unsound, would only apply to debts contracted in the three years 1894, 1895, and 1896?—Yes.

10,691. And to settlements made in those three years?—Yes, and a great portion of the settlements and debts now current among the agricultural population of India are of those years. The civil law is that, unless a debt is revived within three years, it lapses, and most of the current agricultural debts in India are of the last three years, and those debts have been virtually increased by enhancing the value of the rupee.

10,692. Now will you come to the matter of trinkets?—All that the poor people in India can possibly save in years of good harvest is saved, not in savings banks, which do not exist in India for the poor, but in silver jewellery and trinkets for their women. Practically, all the spare wealth which the cultivating and labouring classes have in India is in this form; and, in years of scarcity and famine, all this silver, or a great part of it, is sold in the affected districts in order to procure food grains. The proposal of the Government of India is virtually one to confiscate about a third of the poor man's savings in India. The value of the rupee being artificially raised, the silver bangle or bracelet in which the cultivator has invested all his savings sells for less than what it cost, and thus, by one stroke of the pen, the Government of India reduces what is really the national wealth of the poor in India, in order to meet its own liabilities on somewhat easier terms. No proposal likely to affect in a similar manner the savings of the poor could be entertained for a moment in England; and it is possible to conceive that, if such a proposal was made in a poor continental country like Italy, the masses would rise in rebellion from one end of the Peninsula to the other. The Indian Government is stronger and more absolute than the Government of Italy, and the responsibility, therefore, of saving the interests of the poor, and of taking no action injuriously affecting the savings of the poor, is all the greater.

10,693. How if the savings were hoarded in rupees? —There is very little of that.

10,694. We will not go into the quantity of it, but what is the proportion?—Of course that would increase in value, but there is a very little saving in rupees in Bengal. I have been in a great many districts in Bengal, and practically all the wealth of the cultivating classes is in the silver jewellery of the women. I have been in districts that were affected by scarcity and famine. I remember that, after the great storm wave and cyclone in 1876, I was sent to a place where the cultivators had practically lost all their paddy and rice. Previous to the calamity the people in this place had been very well off, and for nine or ten months they supported themselves by buying shiploads of rice, paying for it by the proceeds of the sale of the jewellery of their women. That was in 1877. The cyclone was in 1876, and this distress was in 1877. I happened to be sent to the island which was most seriously affected by this cyclone and storm wave. On the greater part of that island the crops were totally destroyed. If such a thing had happened in other parts of India it might have been followed by a famine, but here the cultivators were very well off, and their women had a quantity of jewellery, and, as a matter of fact, they brought out these silver ornaments in order to raise money to tide over their temporary difficulty. I did not see that they brought out hoarded rupees; in fact, the hoarding of rupees is rather the exception in Bengal.

10,695. In the case of ornaments bought previous to 1893, what would be the difference between the value at the time of purchase and the value now?—They paid one rupee for a tola of silver, which is the rupee weight. They take the silver things to the bazaar, and now they get 10 annas for the tola. That is, where they find the difference.

10,696. The price is regulated by the market value of silver ?—The value to the cultivator when he purchased his ornaments was about 14 to 16 annas per tola. Now, for the first time, a difference is made between the price of silver and the coined silver.

10,697. No ; the difference that is made is this, that you cannot take silver and have it coined ?—The result is that there is a great difference between the price of silver and coined silver.

10,698. The bazaar price is what ?—About 10 or 11 annas per tola. In the last 20 or 30 or 40 years, when the cultivator went into the bazaar to buy silver, he paid at the rate of 14 or 15 or 16 annas per tola. They have always made their purchases of jewellery for their women at this rate. Now, if they go to sell their silver ornaments, they get a third less. Therefore it is virtually a confiscation of a third of what they have paid for their jewellery, which, as I have explained, represents the savings of the people of India.

10,699. You say that "the proposals of the Government of India are calculated to add to its own liabilities." Will you explain that ?—There I was referring to the rupee paper—the Government Securities, as we call them in India.

10,700. You contend that it will increase the charge for interest on those securities ?—Yes, it virtually raises the value of the securities, because the rupee is raised.

10,701. You say, "the debt of the Government of

India is partly in rupees, and, by adding to the value of the rupee, you add to the debt ?"—Yes. The indebtedness is mainly to moneyed classes in England, and the net result of the proposals, therefore, will be to add to the indebtedness of the people in India to the money-lenders of England. Where the Government borrowed a thousand rupees of small value, the Government now virtually tears up the old bond and executes a new one for a thousand rupees of enhanced value.

10,702. That again will only apply to the borrowing that has taken place in those three years, and the bulk of the rupee debt was contracted before. Therefore the Government gains now ?—Yes, my remark applies to what took place in the last three years.

10,703. You say, "the proposals of the Indian Government mean a general increase in the pay and perquisites of all officials who are paid in rupees." Will you explain that : do you draw there any distinction between the incomes that have to be remitted out of India, and the incomes that are spent in India ? I will tell you why I want to ask this question. The evidence that has been given here is that inside India a rupee goes now as far as it used to go, practically ; that there has been no appreciable difference made in the internal value of the rupee ?—It goes further, I should say, from the prices which I have quoted here.

10,704. We have had evidence to the effect that, for all practical purposes, that is so ; that is, if I have an income of 1,000 rupees a month and I have to spend that in India, that 1,000 rupees will go just about as far as it would have done 10 years ago?—Well, there has been a fall in the price of food grains and that means an increase of pay to those who get the same number of rupees as before.

10,705. Suppose I have in India an income of 1,000 rupees per month or 12,000 rupees a year, and if I am obliged to remit 600*l.* a year to England for the maintenance of my family, then at a shilling rate I should not have much left?—I was referring only to what is spent in India. I say the proposals of the Government of India mean a general increase in the pay and perquisites of all officials who are paid in rupees. There, of course, I refer to all officials, including those who are natives of India, and who spend their pay in India. I say the poorer and indebted classes, who deserve relief at the hands of the Government, are crushed by an addition to their taxes, by an addition to their indebtedness, and by a reduction of their savings, while to the fortunate classes who are in the Government service, or who draw their pensions in rupees, the Government makes a real donation in the shape of an unearned increase to their pay and perquisites.

10,706. The gist then of this is that you regard raising the value of the rupee as adding to the national debt of the people of India and to the high price which their foreign administration costs?—Their administration generally, because I am referring to the native employees also.

10,707. Then will you tell us how you think these proposals have an effect on the manufacturers of India?

—On that point I should premise that my information is second-hand, because I am not personally engaged in manufacture or trade; but I have consulted men engaged in trade, and they tell me that the raising of the value of the rupee artificially dislocates trade, and has injured manufacture. I have heard from merchants engaged in Bombay in the cotton industry, that the cotton industry is in a miserable state just now, especially in competition with the produce from China and Japan, and they impute that, directly or indirectly, to the closing of the mints. It is well known that many of the manufactures of India have been all but ruined—within the memory of living men—by an unequal competition with the steam and machinery of Europe. I have myself, within the period of my service, visited villages of weavers almost deserted, and relapsing into jungle, manufactories of various Indian dyes, which have been closed and abandoned, and industries in metal and in leather, which are declining. It is useless to complain of this, it is useless to expect, in these days of free trade, that any sort of protection would be extended to the dying industries of India by the British Government. But it is not unreasonable to expect that the Government will refrain from taking any direct action calculated to further repress the declining Indian industries. If India had representative institutions, the representative of the cultivators and manufacturers and exporters would have unanimously raised their voice against artificially raising the value of the rupee. In the absence of such representative institutions, the Government of India represents the interests of the people, and a moral obligation rests on the Government not to sacrifice the interests of the people to the demands of special classes, however strong and however influential. British trade is prospering with other Asiatic countries having silver currencies; why should British traders demand, in the case of India, a fixed ratio between gold and silver, which they cannot demand from other Asiatic countries? The people of India do not ask for it; the people of India will not profit by it; the people of India are likely to lose in a variety of ways, as indicated above, by the artificial raising of the value of the rupee. And the Government of India, naturally representing the people, and standing forward as the protectors of their welfare, should reject a scheme which the people do not want, and cannot profit by. What I ask is that no further impediment should be placed in the way of manufacturers by the closing of the mints, and by the direct or indirect consequences arising from that. It is my opinion, derived from merchants, both in Calcutta and in Bombay, that the closing of the mints has very seriously affected the cotton industry of Bombay, the sugar industry in Bengal and in Northern India, and several other industries in India, and especially industries which are affected by the products of those countries which had silver currencies, like China.

10,708. You think it has affected the competition with China?—Yes.

10,709. Do you regard it as giving a bonus to China as against India?—That is the opinion of the merchants I have consulted.

10,710. You say, "The proposal of the Government of India is not the natural or the proper remedy for that increasing drain which is annually flowing from India to England, in the shape of pay, and pensions, and allowances"? The allowances are paid in England in gold, and, instead of reducing its gold obligations, which is the natural and proper remedy, the Government seeks to adopt the unnatural and desperate and dangerous remedy of converting all its revenues in India into gold. Let us suppose the case of an Indian landlord, who gets his rents from his estate in rupees and has to pay an agent in London in gold. What would courts of justice and equity think if the landlord preferred suits to realise his Indian rents in gold, on the ground that he has to pay one London agent in gold?—His prudent and proper course would be to minimise his London expense, and, similarly, the natural and proper remedy for the difficulties of the Government of India would be to carry on the administration of India, as far as it is consistent with efficiency, through the instrumentality of the children of the soil, whose pay and pensions have not to be defrayed in gold. I say that an endeavour ought to be made, as far as is compatible with efficient administration, to reduce its expenditure; to have as much work done in India by the natives as possible, and, I think, with the spread of education in India, it is possible now to utilise the people of India to a larger extent than is done now under the existing rules. Under the existing rules, the higher services in all departments are recruited from England, and, therefore, from among Englishmen; not only the Indian Civil Service, which includes the Executive and Judicial services, but also the Engineering Department, the Postal Office Department, the Opium Department, the Forest Department, the Medical Department, and the Education Department. In all those departments--I do not know why, but it is a fact—the higher posts are almost invariably filled by Englishmen. The result, of course, is that there is a greater drain from India to this country. When these people retire from the various services, their pensions have to be paid by India, and remitted to this country. My idea is, even from this financial point of view, it is now desirable that, education having spread in India, a greater proportion of the higher posts in the service should be allotted to the people of India.

10,711. At reduced payments ?—Reduced gold payments—at reduced payments in the first instance, and also reduced gold payments.

10,712. You think, generally, that there might be a great reduction of expenditure ?—Yes.

10,713. Both military and civil ?—Yes.

10,714. Then you say, "the proposal of the Indian Government withdraws the natural check which now exists against extravagant expenditure and unlimited borrowing in England." I do not quite follow that. First of all, you can borrow in England at a very low rate of interest ?—Yes.

10,715. Is it an advantage to India to have English money spent in productive works in India ?—If the Government have to borrow, it is certainly an advantage to be able to borrow at low rates; but, I say, an earnest attempt ought to be made to reduce our public debt, as has been done in England during the last 50 years.

19,716. What is the public debt of India?—The debt has gone up by 63,598,000*l.* sterling in the last 20 years.

10,717. Would you define what you mean by "the debt" of India?—I am speaking of the total debt, including railways. I will distinguish that afterwards.

10,718. But that is all important. Of course, where we have made such very large and successful efforts in this country to reduce our debt, the debt is represented, so to speak, by nothing—there is no property against that debt.; it was a debt incurred for public purposes at the time, and there was no reproductive return upon it. Therefore, it is a burden upon the taxpayers of the country, and we have a sinking fund; and when we reduce the debt, as you very properly say, that is an advantage to the country. But let me put this extreme case: Suppose this country had to take over the whole railway system of Great Britain, and had to pay 1,000,000,000*l.*—which, I suppose, is a very moderate estimate—would you say that the debt of his country was increased by 1,000,000,000*l.*?—I will take the two things separately, as you desire.

10,719. If you please. I wanted to be quite clear, because my impression is that for the year 1898-99, the year we are now in, the charge for the debt proper of India is a lower figure than it has ever been since the Mutiny. I have the figures here from the parliamentary return ; 15 years ago, the charge, in 1884-85, was Rx. 3,907,848. This year the interest on debt is Rx. 2,448,000 ?—I take the figures for the last 20 years, according to Sir Henry Waterfield's evidence before this Committee. He says, "the total increase of debt in this country within this period is 63,598,000*l*." Against that he shows a total capital outlay on public works of 61,036,000*l*. sterling. If you take that completely away from both sides, the debt within the last 20 years, which have been years of continuous peace inside India, has not been reduced at all, according to Sir Henry Waterfield's evidence. He says, what we have spent on productive works—in which he includes, I suppose, railways, canals, and irrigation works—is more than covered by the debt that we have incurred in this country. We have spent on public works about 61 millions, we have borrowed 63½ millions. So that, if we deduct all that has been spent upon public works, and so forth, and on the other hand all that we have borrowed in England, our net indebtedness, instead of being reduced, as has been done in this country, has increased in India by 2½ millions in these 20 years.

10,720. But the fall of the rupee alone involved the Indian Government in borrowing 6,000,000*l*. sterling ?—But the fall of the rupee has directly increased the revenues of the Indian Government.

10,721. Dividing the debt into the debt in India and the debt in England, the excess of assets in India (such as railways, irrigation works, loans to corporations, &c.) over the debt in India is Rx. 29,489,000. As against this, there is a balance of liabilities over assets, so far as the debt in England is concerned, of 55,675,000*l*. So that, when the Secretary of State put his Budget before the House of Commons last session, the real debt of India, which represents the Mutiny and all the military operations that have taken place in India, is the difference between the liabilities of 55,675,000*l*. in England, and the assets of Rx. 29,489,000 in India. You can hardly find a parallel to that state of things. All I want is, that you gentlemen, who influence public opinion—quite legitimately—amongst your own people, should not think that your country is as poor as it is sometimes supposed to be?—I should like to learn that from you.

10,722. The interest upon the debt of India is this year only 2½ crores?—Will you allow me to take these two things separately? I will leave out of consideration railways now, and I will say that, taking Sir Henry Waterfield's figures, there has not been any reduction in the public debt of India in the last 20 years. Those 20 years have been years of uninterrupted peace, during which there has been a great deal of reduction of the public debt of England; and, I say, there ought to have been a very considerable reduction in the public debt of India.

10,723. Do you say there has been a period of uninterrupted peace for the last 20 years?—Yes.

10,724. What do you say to the Afghan war?—That only cost 3,000,000*l*. You mean the war last year?

10,725. No, I mean the Afghan war.—That is 20 years ago.

10,726. Since 1880 the English Exchequer has voted 5,000,000*l.* towards the cost of that war? – I know. It was a war outside India.

10,727. At any rate, you cannot call it a period of uninterrupted peace?—Leaving out the expense of the Afghan war, which was a war outside India, we have made no reduction in the public debt of India, and we ought to have made a reduction. An endeavour ought to have been made during those years of peace to bring down our public debt, so that we might borrow again when it was necessary to do so. And I further say that the people of India—say one financial representative from each of the five great Provinces—ought to be consulted by the Government; they should form a committee, and some place should be found for them in the Viceroy's Executive Council, in order to advise Viceroy and the Finance Minister in preparing every year's Budget. A systematic endeavour should be made to reduce the net public debt in every year of peace. That is my first contention. My next point is with reference to railways.

10,728. You say: "Every fresh loan contracted in England by the Indian Government is hailed in this country as a further opening for profitable investment; every fresh order for tools and machinery and rails pleases great English manufacturers; every new line opened in India is a new opportunity for English capitalists and manufacturers." Do you not think all those things a great advantage to India?—The first lines of railway were a great advantage to India, and they would have been cheap if we had had to pay twice the amount that we have paid for them; but the new lines which are being added now, from year to year, are not so much for the benefit of the country. I remember the condition of India 20 years ago. At that time all the main lines had been opened. The new lines that have been opened since have not added much to the development of trade; they have been constructed, rather, with regard to local interest. Take one of these newly opened lines in Bengal, which connects North Behar in Assam. The great mass of the cultivators and traders of Bengal did not ask for that line, and have not, as far as my information goes, benifited by that line.

10,729. Who have found the money for that line? —I do not know.

10,730. Do you refer to the Assam-Bengal Railway? —Yes. Nobody travels that way—that is, in the natural course of trade; the trade is all between Calcutta and the northern part of Bengal. The line may be for the interest of some particular class, but we do not know why the line was laid down. We are never consulted in these things.

10,731. But is not that a matter for the people who find the money? In this country there have been railways made from nowhere to nowhere, but, after all, the loss, if their is a loss, is the loss of the people who put their money into the line?—Exactly; but in the case of India, it is the people of India who put their money into the line.

10,732. No?—We are held liable for the guaranteed profit, which comes to the same thing.

10,733. (*Sir J. Muir.*) Is there a guarantee in the case of the Bengal and Assam line?—I believe so.

(*Sir C. Crosthwaite.*) There is a guarantee, I think, in the case of the Assam-Bengal Railway.

10,734. (*Chairman.*) But the capital was all found in this country?—The capital was found: but, so far as the Government gives a guarantee, we, the people of India, are responsible for finding the guaranteed profits from our taxes.

10,735. The guarantee comes in if the traffic is not sufficient to pay?—Yes. A second instance, I would say, is the line from Assam to Chittagong. That goes over a very wild and hilly country, and I doubt if it will ever pay. It certainly has not devolped and will not develop, the trade of that part of the country, because there hardly any produce at all in that part of the country.

10,736. (*Mr. Campbell.*) Has that a guarantee?—I have no information, but I believe it has.

(*Sir C. Crosthwaite.*) It is part of the Assam-Bengal line.

10,737. (*Chairman.*) Let us assume, for the sake of your argument, that the Indian Government have not always sanctioned the best railways, as the English Parliament has not always sanctioned the best railways. We are now dealing with the development of railways throughout India by English capital. Is not that to the advantage of the people of India?—Certainly; but I say that what we are doing lately is different from the main lines that had been constructed before. By 1878 the whole of the trade of India had found proper and legitimate outlets, and the money which has been spent since has not to the same extent developed trade.

10,738. Then how do you explain the increase in traffic, the tonnage and the passenger revenue?—That is mostly along the main routes constructed before.

10,739. The traffic must be taken a · whole. Taken as a whole, the system of Indian railways, i. ng the railways which are not productive, shews a urn on the capital cost of about five per cent.?—But d by the last Railway Administration Report, wh I have no doubt the Committee have seen, that the t loss to the State up to that date was 57 crores of rupee out of which about one-half, $28\frac{1}{2}$ crores, had been lost in the last 20 years. I do not condemn railways; we wanted railways to develop India, and we must pay for them, even if it is a losing concern; but what I object to is the unlimited extension of railways at an increasing charge to the taxpayer, after all the main lines have been opened out.

10,740. What do you mean by unlimited extension?—I mean what is going on now.

10,741. But there is no unlimited extension. Government sanction has to be obtained?—No doubt there is the engineer's report and the Government inspector's report, and all the rest of it, but what I object to is that the people themselves are not consulted.

10,742. I do not want you to think that these railways in India are sanctioned without considerable caution—indeed, I think a great excess of caution.

I believe that the interests of India would be much better met if the Government gave a freer hand in the construction of public works: and, if English capital goes out there at a low rate of interest, I do not think India has any ground of complaint?—But all this is adding to [illegible] indebtedness, and it is a losing concern, accord[illegible] your own showing—according to the last report published for the year 1897-98. We have lost 57 [illegible]s of rupees, and, of that, 28½ crores have been lo[illegible] within the last 20 years. We should not abandon [illegible] railway system altogether, but we should be cautious, [illegible]nd I think the representatives of the people should be consulted before any new lines are sanctioned. There is a railway now under consideration from Mandalay up towards China. Well, it will probably be years and years before that will pay, and at the same time we have either to pay for the construction of it, or to guarantee some profit to the capitalists out of our taxes. These are matters in which, I say, we ought to be consulted. The whole thing is being overdone—to the advantage of the capitalists and manufacturers of this country, and to the loss and disadvantage of the people of India, who are not consulted. That is my contention.

10,743. Now is there any other point that you want to bring forward? You say, "the only check which now exists is that the interest of the capital so borrowed has to be paid in gold." In some cases it is the fact, is it not, that the interest on the capital is paid in rupees?—Yes, if you wish to borrow;

but the point I wish to make is this: that an attempt ought to be made to reduce our expenditure.

10,744. That is really not before this Committee: We have to consider the question here, whether it is desirable to introduce a gold standard and gold currency into india, and whether it is desirable to have a stable rate of exchange?—What I have said would come directly under that, because the necessity for adopting a gold standard, or for giving a gold value to the rupee, would disappear to a great extent, if the expenditure were so reduced as to make our income meet our expenditure. The loss of which the Indian Government complains would not exist if more economy were practised, and the expenditure of India were reduced.

10,745. Have you considered that, if no step was taken, and the rupee went to its bullion value, and assuming that silver went no lower, you would require at the present rate of expenditure in India something like an increased income of 12 crores?—I have heard that stated. I find, in the first place, that a great portion of that 12 crores could be knocked off by a little economy.

10,746. You think that, by economical arrangement the 12 crores could be saved?—A considerable portion of it; and the remaining portion could be met by the natural increase of revenue which the very fall of the rupee would give rise to, as I have explained.

10,747. Then, taking your opinion as a whole, you would face that emergency and let the rupee go to bullion price?—Yes. I would have no hesitation whatever about that, because I am convinced that the revenues estimated in rupees would rise, as they have risen in the past, with the fall of the rupee; and, secondly, that a good deal of saving could be effected if we practised economy in India.

10,748. For all those reasons that you have very clearly put before us, you are opposed to the proposals of the Government of India?—I am strongly opposed to them.

10,749. Do you upon this question represent the views of the Indian National Congress?—No, I do not belong either to the Indian National Congress or to its British Committee.

10,750. But you do represent a mass of native opinion that you feel justified in bringing before us?—Yes.

[Sir John Muir, Bart. remarked: "The evidence which you have just given has struck me as very important. Could we obtain evidence from others of the Natives of India? We have had difficulty in getting at information from the Natives of India. It appears to me most desirable that we should have that evidence."

Mr. Dutt suggested that witnesses should be called from India, and mentioned the names of Messrs. Rojoni Nath Roy, Seraj-ul-Islam, B. L. Gupta, I.C.S., Sita Nath Roy, A. M. Bose, R. D. Mehta and Perojsha Mehta None of these Indian witnesses however was called or examined.]

IX. CONGRESS AT LUCKNOW.

[*Presidential speech, December* 27, 1899.]

Acceptance of the Chair.

WHEN in October last I received through my friend, Mr. Bonnerjee, your kind invitation to preside at this meeting of the Indian National Congress, I confess, I received it with some degree of surprise and some degree of misgiving. I happened to be then engaged in the pleasant task, to which I have cheerfully devoted most of my spare time during the last fifteen years, of trying to interpret to my countrymen and to modern readers generally some of the literary heritage which has been left to us by our forefathers ; and, I confess, the prospect of a sudden change from the desk to the platform somewhat alarmed me. Nor was the alarm altogether groundless ; for when I read the speeches made from this platform in past years by some of the ablest and most eloquent men that our country has produced during this generation, I felt grave doubts whether you were altogether wise in your choice in asking me to preside in the present year. However, I felt the great honour you did me in imposing the task upon me ; I feel the high honour as I stand to-day among so many who are so well qualified to perform this task ; and for better or for worse, I have accepted your kind proposal and am amidst you to-day. And if you will listen with some indulgence to the plain words of a plain man, I will try to convey to you in a few words some practical suggestions, on the administrative questions of the day.

I need hardly tell you that these questions have received my attention and my consideration for years past; I have spoken and written on them during the last two years; and during the preceding twenty-six years I had constantly to deal with many of them in official correspondence. It is perhaps known to all of you that the Government of India and the Local Governments permit and encourage the utmost freedom to all officials in the expression of their opinions in official correspondence on the administrative questions which constantly come up for discussion. It is in the course of such discussions that the men in the Civil Service come to know and to respect each other's opinions, and are often brought in closer contact with each other. And as we are holding this present meeting of our Congress in the North-West of India, I recall to-day with pride that it was in the course of a discussion of this nature over the Bengal Tenancy Bill which was pased into law in 1885, that I had the pleasure and the privilege of first knowing that sympathetic ruler and that distinguished statesman whom you now claim as Lieutenant-Governor of these provinces, but whom we in Bengal are proud to claim as originally of the Bengal Civil Service.

Gentlemen, I often felt it my duty in the course of these official discussions to suggest reforms on the basis of accepting in a larger degree the co-operation of the people of India in the administration of the country.

And although I have ceased to be an official now, I still consider it my duty to do what lies in my humble power to advise and help the Government of the day in the great task of a good and successful administration based on the co-operation of the people. And it is because this is precisely the object of the Indian National Congress—it is because it is your aim and endeavour to sustain and help British administration based on popular co-operation—that I find myself amongst you to-day, and in complete unison with you in views and aspirations.

The creed of the Congress.

Gentlemen, I have perused a great portion of the Congress literature as published in a handy volume by the enterprising publisher Mr. Natesan; and to those who desire honestly to know the aims and aspirations of the educated men of India, I can honestly recommend a persual of this valuable publication. An honest critic will find in this volume—from the first page to the last—a sincere desire to support and sustain the Government by the co-operation of the people, to strengthen the hands of the Government by fair criticism, to help the Government by keeping it informed of the views and aspirations of the people. These are services which would be useful and valuable to administrators in any country in the world, and these are services which are doubly valuable in India where the people are not represented in any of the Executive Councils and Secretariats where executive and legislative measures are first put into shape. For remember, gentlemen, that there are generally two sides to every question which comes up for discussion, and it is desirable and necessary that both sides should be properly represented and heard before the question is decided. It is no disrespect to the Civil Service of India to say that it represents, ably and fairly, the official side only of Indian questions. I have had the honour of passing the best years of my life in the Indian Civil Service, and I shall be the last person on earth to question either the ability, or the honesty of purpose, of those able and hard-working men who form that magnificent service. I have pleasant recollections of the years which I have passed in complete accord and friendliness with my colleagues in that service, of the fair and handsome treatment which I received from my seniors, and of the loyal and zealous co-operation which I received from my juniors; and I will say this, that take the Indian Civil Service with all its faults and all its shortcomings,—for hard work and honesty of purpose there is not a finer body of administrators in the world. Nevertheless, it must be admitted, and it is no disrespect to the Indian Civil Service to say it, that that service represents only the official view of Indian questions, and does not and cannot represent the people's views. There are two sides to every question, and it is absolutely necessary for the purpose of good government and of just administration that not only the official view, but the people's view on every question should be represented and heard. There are local bodies in different parts of India which give expression to the people's views on local questions; but this National Congress is the only body in India which seeks to represent the views and aspirations of the people of India as a whole in all large and important, and if I may use the word, Imperial questions of administration. Therefore, this National Congress is doing a service to the Government the value of which cannot be over-estimated, and which, I feel certain, is appreciated by the Government itself. It is a gain to the administration to know what we feel, and what we think, and what we desire,—though our demands cannot always be conceded. It is a help to responsible administrators to know in what direction our wishes and our aspirations tend, though they may not always agree with us. I honestly believe therefore that you are helping the cause of good administration and of good government in India by your deliberations year after year, and I trust and hope that you will continue to carry on these deliberations in the future, as you have done in the past, with good sense and moderation, with loyalty to your rulers, and with fidelity to the real interest of the people. We cannot fail in this endeavour; the future is with us; and looking at the progress of nations all over the British Empire in every part of the world, I, for one, feel confident that we, too, are destined to move onwards as a portion of that great Empire, and that we, too, shall secure some measure of progress and self-government under the imperial rule of England. This is the creed of the Congress as it is mine, and it is, therefore, gentlemen, that I feel it an honour to find myself amidst you to-day. And consistently with this principle, my speech to-day will be, not one of criticism, but mainly and essentially one of practical suggestions to which the Government will, I humbly hope, give such consideration as they may seem to deserve.

Famine of 1897.

Gentlemen, it is a little over two years ago you celebrated in India, with every demonstration of loyalty and good feeling, the sixtieth year of the reign of the Queen-Empress. I happened to be in England on that day; and I witnessed with joy and gratification the august procession in London—Her Majesty driving in state through a circuit of six miles, preceded and followed by representatives of every portion of the British Empire, and cheered by half a million of loyal Englishmen who lined the circuit. Every contingent from every land was cheered as it accompanied the Queen, and I can tell you that none was cheered more loudly and more heartily than the Indian contingent—the Indian princes and rajas, distinguished by their graceful dress and noble demeanour, their manly bearing and their soldier-like appearance. It was a great and imposing and gratifying sight, but it was clouded by one dark shadow. The British public felt, British newspapers wrote, and British statesmen spoke, that while every self-governing colony represented in that procession was prosperous and happy, India, alone, with its vast population, was even then suffering from a famine which had spread over a larger extent of country than had ever been visited by famine in any single year. Questions were asked why there should be such famines in India when famines were unheard of in any other well-governed country in the world, and doubts were expressed if British rule in India had been altogether a blessing for the poor cultivators and labourers of India.

But, gentlemen, the famine of 1897 was not the only calamity of that year; it was accompanied by a war outside our frontiers which cost us some millions and many brave lives, and it was accompanied by a plague the ravages of which are not yet over. In the midst of those calamities the Government thought it necessary to adopt rigorous measures, and the Government thought it wise to restrict that liberty of the Press which we in India had enjoyed for over sixty years. It is not my intention to-day to dwell on the sad occurrences of 1897, the saddest year in its accumulation of calamities since the time that India passed from the hands of the East India Company to the Crown. Nor is it my intention to revive to-day the discussions which were held in this country and in England when the unfortunate Sedition Bills were passed into law.

Sedition Law of 1898.

I recall with sadness the debates which took place in the Viceroy's Council and in the House of Commons when these Bills were passed into law. It was my privillege to hear those debates in the House of Commons, and I think I only echo the general feeling of all educated men in this country when I acknowledge our debt of gratitude to those who so ably but so unsuccessfully fought for us both in the Viceroy's Council and in the

House of Commons. I do not desire to renew these discussions, but now that the fight is over, and the Bills have been passed into law, I often ask myself if there is a single Englishman in this country with an intimate knowledge of the country and its people who honestly thinks that the reactionary measure was needed, or that it is answering any useful purpose, or that it has strengthened the Government and increased its reputation and credit in the eyes of Europe. Gentlemen, the measure was based on a blunder—the blunder of connecting sedition with the spread of education. The truth is precisely the reverse of this. English education has not only not produced sedition in the land, but it has been the strongest weapon by which the Government has stamped out real sedition in this country within the last fifty years. In the dark days of 1857 and earlier, there was real sedition in the land,—a real wish in some dark and obscure corners to overturn this great Empire. That desire was born of ignorance and lurked amidst ignorant classes, and the Government has successfully stamped out that feeling by the spread of education. There never was a greater imperialist among the Governors-General of India than Lord Dalhousie, and Lord Dalhousie strengthened and fortified the Empire by giving effect to the famous educational despatch of 1854, and spreading education through vernacular schools. There never was a stronger upholder of British dominion in its darkest days than Lord Canning, and Lord Canning established the Universities of Calcutta,

Bombay, and Madras. The same policy has been pursued by successive Viceroys during the last forty years with the same object and the same effect, and wherever education has spread, sedition in India is dead. And if real sedition still lingers in any corner of India, it is in the darkness of ignorance, not in the sunlight of education and free discussion. If I were disposed to foment sedition in India I would desire in the first place to suppress all free discussion, suppress all newspapers, and suppress all public meetings, as a burglar puts out the lights of a room before he commits burglary. And I make bold to add, gentlemen, that if you had been inspired by hostile feelings against British rule in India, you would have worked in the dark, and not come forward from all parts of India, year after year, to openly and loyally place your views before the ruling power. Educated India has practically identified itself with British rule, seeks to perpetuate British rule, is loyal to the British rule, as Lord Dufferin said, not through sentiment, but through the stronger motive of self-interest; because it is by a continuance of the British rule that educated India seeks to secure that larger measure of self-government, that position among the modern nations of the earth, which it is our aim and endeavour to secure. Gentlemen, if you had a single representative in the Viceroy's Executive Council, if you had one Indian member to take a part in those deliberations in the Executive Council which resulted in the Sedition Law, you could have explained these matters then and there. But it is a penalty which all Governments constituted like the Executive Councils of India have to pay, that they have to decide questions after hearing one side only, and not other. Only one view is properly represented before them, and not the other; and the ablest, the most just, and the most conscientious of judges will make mistakes, if they base their decisions on evidence produced by one party, and not the other.

Only one word more before I leave this subject. I regret as much and as sincerely as any man in India the bitterness of tone which sometimes pervades journalism in this country. Five years ago, as officiating Commissioner of Burdwan, I had occasion to write on this subject, and if I allude to my report now, it is because the report was printed and published in the *Calcutta Gazette*, and is thererore not an official secret. I said on that occasion, and on many succeeding occasions, that differences in opinion must always exist between the English newspapers and the Indian newspapers in this country. English newspapers hold that an absolute government is the best and only possible government of India, and that any system of representation or self-government is a mistake. The Indian papers hold on the other hand that there can be no good government in a large and civilised country like India, and no satisfactory solution of those great problems like famine and the impoverishment of the humbler classes, without some co-operation of the people themselves in the control of the administration. It is possible, I said, to hold and maintain these opposite views without studied contempt and sneer on the one side, and bitterness of tone on the other side. And those journals which introduce this element of contempt and hatred in the discussion of administrative questions are creating difficulties for the British Government, and sowing seeds of evil in India. It is by some degree of sympathy, some degree of good feeling and neighbourly courtesy and not by Sedition Laws that the relations between the different sections of the Indian community can be improved. As one who has passed the best years of his life in administrative work, I have noticed that every improvement in the tone of the English press is warmly responded to by the Indian press, and that every want of kindliness and good feeling adds to the difficulties of administration and weakens British rule in India.

Calcutta Municipality.

But I pass over this subject, because it is not my object to-day to make my speech a criticism of the Sedition Law, or of other measures already passed. I wish also to pass over with very few remarks the controversies relating to recent municipal laws, and to the Calcutta Municipality. These controversies are fresh in your minds, and the subject will, no doubt, receive ample justice from other speakers before we have closed our proceedings. To me one most consoling feature in the history of this unfortunate measure is the help rendered to our cause by so high an authority as the Right Honourable Sir Henry Fowler. It was my privilege to be a listener in the House of Commons on the memorable night when the late Secretary of State spoke from the Liberal front bench, supporting Mr. Herbert Roberts, and condemning the virtual withdrawal of that boon of self-government which it is the proud boast of England to have conferred on the metropolis of India. Gentlemen, even Sir Henry Fowler has spoken in vain—at least, for the present—but we are none the less greatful to him for his strong advocacy of a just and righteous cause, the cause of self-government in India. Nor are we less grateful to those who have fought the same battle in this country, foremost among whom stands Raja Binay Krishna Deb, a worthy scion of a worthy house which has been loyal and friendly to British rule in India since the days of Clive and Hastings. To our friends who fought in the Legislative Council, and to others who were true to the cause of our progress is due our warmest acknowledgment and our deepest gratitude. Gentlemen, their example, their endeavours and their sustained effort will live in the memory of our countrymen, and will find a place in the history of our country. A constitutional battle so fought is not fought in vain, and our children and our children's children, to whom we shall hand down the heritage of a loyal and constitutional agitation for self-government under the imperial and progressive rule of England, will look upon the closing of the nineteenth century as an epoch in the history of the land, and will draw new inspiration from the example of the men of this century who have lived and worked and fought—not in vain. There are defeats which are more glorious than victories; and the defeat which we have sustained will strengthen our hearts, freshen our hopes, and nerve our hands for new endeavours.

With regard to the actual result of this battle, I do not know if there is any class of men in Calcutta who in their hearts like it much. I have asked myself if there is any Englishman familiar with the history of the Calcutta Municipality who thinks that the new measure will improve administration, promote sanitation, or secure the willing co-operation of all classes of citizens. I do not know if the officials of Calcutta who have done so much in the past to foster municipal self-government will contemplate with gratification the ruin of the noble edifice which they built up after the labours of a quarter of a century. I do not know if the European merchants of Calcutta, who are busy, practical men, and have lived in amity and good feeling with the Indian population, will like the idea to spread over the country that wherever English trade prospers not only Indian manufactures, but Indian political and municipal rights, too, must be sacrificed. I do not know if the new City Fathers of Calcutta contemplate with joy their prospects of success, or the odium of a failure, with difficult sanitary problems before them, and a poor, inadequate, almost beggarly income. What the elected Commissioners have done in the way of sanitary reforms with this poor income is a matter of history. Gentlemen, I remember Calcutta some forty years under the administration of Government officials, when we as school boys had to walk to school by open drains and reeking filth. I remember Calcutta as it was under the Justices of the Peace, some thirty years ago, with its awkward tale of waste and jobbery. And I have seen year after year the improvements effected, the sanitary reforms done, the wasteful expenditure cut down, and every department of the office brought to order, by the elected Commissioners within the last twenty-five years, by some of the best men whom our country has produced, and who have given years of their life to this patriotic work. Their work has been consistently recognised in past years by successive rulers of the land, but it is necessary to give a dog a bad name in order to hang it; and it was reserved for Sir Alexander Mackenzie who was a friend of self government under the administration of Mr. Gladstone and Lord Ripon, to end his career in India by giving the self-government system in Calcutta a bad name and then effectually strangling it. Gentlemen, I feel sad whenever I think over these matters, and I feel sad when I recollect that this thing has come to pass in the first year of Lord Curzon's administration. I honestly believe that no Viceroy ever came out to India with a more sincere desire to work for the good of the people, and with the help and co-operation of the people. I honestly think that his Lordship in Council gave a most careful consideration to the question before he issued his own proposals; and if that Council had contained a single Indian member to represent the Indian view of the question, and to explain the true history of the municipality during the last forty years, I am persuaded Lord Curzon would have taken the same view as Sir Henry Fowler has taken, and would have effected the needed reforms in the Calcutta Municipality and strengthened the executive, without virtually sacrificing self-government. But our difficulty and our danger lie in this, that great administrative questions are discussed and settled in Executive Councils where we are not represented and not heard. I do not say that the official view is necessarily wrong, and that our view is necessarily right; but I do say that both views should be fairly represented before the tribunal which shapes our destinies. I do not say that we have more knowledge or more experience or more ability than the high officials who represent the official view of the question, but I do say that we view questions from a different point of view, and that there should be a constitutional channel for the representation of our views in the Executive Councils of the empire. For when the Executive Councils have decided a question, the thing is done—the Legislative Councils simply carry out the official mandate with unimportant alterations, as the Bengal Council has done in the case of the Municipal Bill.

Famine of 1899.

But, gentlemen, I must extricate myself from this subject and pass on at once to the great calamity which now stares us in the face, the famine, from which millions of our countrymen are suffering even now; and with your permission I will devote all my remaining time to this one great subject—which appears to me to be one of paramount importance—the famines of India, and the condition of our poorer classes. Gentlemen, you are aware of the prompt measures which have been already adopted by the Government of Lord Curzon for the relief of distress in British territory and for helping Indian Princes to relieve distress in Native States during this time of trouble and anxiety. And those of you who have had experience of relief operations in previous famines will feel confident that Englishmen when they have once put their hand to the plough, will not leave the work half done. It is with a pardonable pride that I recall past days when I myself was employed along with my English colleagues in famine relief operations, or in providing against impending famines, in 1874, in 1876, and in 1896; and judging from my past experience, and judging from the measures adopted this year, I feel confident that no effort, no expenditure, no means humanly possible, will be spread by a benevolent Government to save life and to relieve distress among the millions of our suffering countrymen. And in the face of that calamity it behoves us all, it behoves this National Congress, to do all we can to strengthen the hands of the Government, to offer our help according to our capacity and power, and to place our suggestions before the Government, not in a spirit of criticism, but in a spirit of loyalty and co-operation, for the relief of the present distress and for the prevention of such distress in future.

Alleged causes of Famines.

It is in this spirit that I suggest that the time has come when it is desirable to take some effective measures to improve the condition of the agricultural population of India. Their poverty, their distress, their indebtedness, all this is not their fault. Sometimes it is asserted that the poverty of the people and the famines which we witness in India, and in no other well-governed country on earth, are due to the over-increase in population. Gentlemen, this is not so. If you go into figures you will find that the population does not increase in India as fast as it does in many European countries like Germany and England. And if you read the paper written by Mr. Baines, the late Census Commissioner of India, in the first volume of the British Empire Series recently issued in London, you will find the Census Commissioner himself admits that the growth of population in India is not so fast as that in Germany or in England.' Sometimes again it is asserted that the poverty of the Indian agriculturist is due to his own improvidence, wastefulness, and folly. Gentlemen, this is not so. Those who have passed the best portion of their life among the Indian cultivators, as I have done, will tell you that the Indian cultivator is about the most frugal, the most provident, the most thoughtful about his future among all races of cultivators on earth. If he goes to the money-lender it is not because he is in love with the money-lender, but because he has nothing to eat. If he pays 25 or 37 per cent. as interest on loans, it is because he cannot get loans on lower interest on such security as he can offer.

We are all aware that the Government of India are at the present time endeavouring to safeguard the interests of the cultivators in the Punjub and elsewhere from the claims of money-lenders on their land. I do not wish to speak on the merits of the Bill, because I never wish to say a word or to express an opinion on inadequate information, and the information I have been able to gather about the condition of the Punjub tenants is not yet as full and complete as I could wish it to be. All that I can say is that this idea, that the condition of cultivators can be improved, not by helping them to save, but by restricting their right of sale and mortgage, is an old idea which has been found utterly unsound in Bengal. The policy was advocated when the Bengal Tenancy Bill was under discussion fifteen years ago ; I myself took my humble part in strongly resisting the policy ; and if I remember correctly, the able Revenue Secretary of Bengal, who is now the Lieutenant-Governor of these Provinces took the same view. I allude to these views because they are no secret, and will be found published in the *Calcutta Gazette* of that year. The absurdity of relieving the cultivators by virtually taking away from the market value of the one property they have on earth was strongly exposed, and the idea of placing any restrictions on mortgage and sale of lands was ultimately abandoned.

Curiously enough, the question was mooted again in Bengal only three years ago, showing what vast importance is attached to official views and ideas formed in close council chambers. The fear was entertained that land was slipping away from the hands of the cultivating classes to the hands of the money-lending classes, and that to restrict the right of sale and mortgage was the only remedy. I happened to be then acting as Commissioner of Orissa, a part of Bengal, which is not permanently settled, and where the condition of the cultivators is worse than in other parts of Bengal. If the free right of sale or mortgage has worked evil in any part of Bengal, it must have done so in Orissa. But I was able to show from the records of half-a-century that, although the right of sale and of mortgage had been freely exercised, land had not slipped out of the hands of the cultivating classes, and that to take away from the market value of the land was not the best way to help the cultivators. Fortunately, the greatest revenue authority of Bengal, Mr. Stevens, who afterwards acted as Lieutenant-Governor of Bengal, took the same view, and the idea of helping the cultivators by decreasing the market value of their land was once more abandoned. I do not wish, gentlemen, to generalise on these facts; I do not wish to infer that what would be needless and mischievous in Bengal and Orissa may not be needful and useful for the time being in some parts of India where matters may have reached a more acute stage. But what I do wish to emphasize is that such remedies cannot permanently improve the condition of the cultivators; that in order to improve their condition, we must make it possible for them—as it is possible in Bengal—to save in good years against failure of harvest in bad years.

Real Cause of Famines and the Remedy

Gentlemen, the real cause of the poverty of cur agricultural population is simple and even obvious, if we have the courage and the honesty to seek for it and to grasp it. It is not over-population, for the population does not increase faster than in European countries, does not increase faster than the area of cultivation. It is not the natural improvidence of the cultivator, for those who know the Indian cultivator will tell you that with all his ignorance and superstition, he is as provident, as frugal, as shrewd in matters of his own interest, as the cultivator in any parts of the globe. The real cause of his wretchedness and indebtedness is that except in Bengal and a few other tracts, the land assessment is so heavy that the cultivator is not able to save in good years enough to meet the failure of harvests in bad years. All our village industries, like spinning and weaving, have been killed by a free competition with the steam and machinery of England. Our cultivators and even our village industrial classes therefore virtually depend on the soil as the one remaining source of their substance. The land assessments should therefore be made in a liberal and even a generous spirit. There is every desire in the high officials to make the assessments in a liberal spirit, but as the people have no voice in controlling these assessments, they are found in the actual working to be often illiberal and harsh. They do not leave the cultivators enough to be able to save; and cultivators therefore fall victims to famine whenever the harvests fail.

Bengal.

The old Hindu law, based on the actual experience of thousands of years, sanctioned one-sixth of the gross produce of the land as the maximum rent. The experience of modern times confirms the wisdom of this ancient rule. In Bengal, where the Permanent Settlement and the land laws of 1859, 1868 and 1885 save the cultivators from the undue enhancements, the average rent paid by cultivators to landlords does not exceed one-sixth the gross produce in any district, and falls far short of it in eastern districts. The result is that Permanently Settled Bengal, which suffered from the most terrible famine in the last century, has been generally free from destructive famines in recent times. The famines of Behar in 1874 and 1897 were comparatively mild, and there was no loss of life. Extend the Bengal rule to other parts of India, make one-sixth of the gross produce the maximum rent leviable from cultivators in other provinces, and the problem of preventing famines in India is solved.

North-Western Provinces.

In the North-western Provinces and Oudh the cultivators are generally speaking, not safeguarded by a Permanent Settlement. Each new assessment means an increase in Government revenue. Let us find out in what position the actual cultivator is left by such settlements. The system of settlements in the North-western Provinces has often been described, but I have never seen a more lucid account of it, within a brief compass, than in the evidence of Sir Antony Macdonell before the Currency Committee which lately sat in London. Read His Honor's answer to questions Nos. 5737 to 5740, and you have a clear account of the North-west settlements in a nut-shell. There are two salient facts which

I will place before you from this account. In the first place the Government allows the landlords to make their own arrangements with the cultivators, and then demands one-half of what the landlord actually gets, after making certain reductions. In the second place, under these arrangements the landlords are actually getting about 20 per cent. of the gross produce in money, and the Government share is one-half of that, or ten per cent. of the produce. Gentlemen, these arrangements are better than those in many other parts of India, and you may be sure the rules are worked considerately, and even leniently, by a ruler who yields to none in India in his real sympathy for the actual cultivator. But nevertheless I should have been relieved to learn that the 20 per cent. of the gross produce represented the maximum limit of rent, and not the average rent. Without such a maximum limit the cultivator has no assurance against over-assessment and undue enhancement. And a landlord who has submitted to an increase of the Government demand at a settlement has the temptation to reimburse himself by raising his rents—as a squeezed sponge fills itself when thrown into the water—to be squeezed again at the next settlement, thirty years later. Adopt the ancient Hindu rule, which is virtually still the rule in Bengal; make one sixth the actual produce—or even one-fifth the actual produce—the maximum-limit of rent under all circumstances, and you make the cultivators of these provinces as prosperous as they are in Bengal, and the problem of disastrous and fatal famines is virtually solved.

Madras.

The state of things is far worse in Madras. Some portions of the Madras Presidency are permanently settled, but in the greater portion of the Province the revenue is not permanently settled; there is no class of landlords, and the Government demands as revenue one-half of the net produce of the land, *i. e.*, of the produce after deducting the cost of cultivation. For a clear, and luminous, and brief account of how this system has worked I would refer you to the speeches made in recent years by the Raja of Bobbili, the Hon'ble Subba Rao and by Mr. Venkataratnam, himself a large land-holder, and President of the Godavari District Association. They point out that the rights of the Madras cultivators have not been strengthened, as in Bengal, by successive Acts within this half-century, but have been weakened by successive measures of the Government. They point out that in 1857, the proprietary right of the cultivator with fixity of assessment was admitted by the Government; that in 1882 under Lord Ripon's administration a virtual pledge was given that no enhancements would be allowed except on the equitable ground of a rise in prices; and that at the present day these pledges are ignored, these safeguards are withdrawn and enhancements are actually made on the ground of reclassification of soils as well as of rise in prices. More than this, I read a passage in the Madras Standing Information of 1879, that the land-tax estimated at one half of the net produce should not exceed 40 per cent. of gross produce where the land is irrigated at Government cost, and should not exceed 33 per cent. of the gross produce in the case of lands not so irrigated. When I read a rule like this, I am filled with bewilderment and pain. Let me mention, gentlemen, that when the Tenancy Bill of Bengal was under discussion in 1884, I had the honour to recommend that 20 per cent. of the gross produce—which is a little over the old Hindu rate—should be fixed as the maximum of rent payable by a cultivator. My proposal was accepted by the then Revenue Secretary of Bengal who is now the honoured ruler of these North-west Provinces and Oudh. The proposal accordingly found a place in the Tenancy Bill drafted by the Government of Bengal, but it was not ultimately passed into law, because in many parts of Bengal, the zemindars were getting much less than 20 per cent. of the produce; and to frame a rule about maximum rent might induce landlords in all parts of Bengal to screw up the rental to that maximum. The argument was good, and I was not sorry that my proposal was rejected. But it is somewhat curious that while the Government declined to fix for *private Zemindars in Bengal* a maximum rent of 20 per cent. of the produce, there is actually a rule in their Standing Information Book fixing 33 and 40 per cent. of the gross produce as the maximum land-tax or revenue *realizable by the Government!* Are you surprised that under the circumstances there should be such repeated and disastrous famines in Madras, and that as pointed out by Mr. A. Rogers—late of the Indian Civil Service and a high authority in revenue matters—a great deal of land is out of cultivation because cultivators cannot pay the tax that is demanded by the State? The rule in Madras is as I have said before, to demand one-half the net produce—*i.e.*, the value of the produce after deducting the cost of cultivation. Gentlemen, if this means one-half the economic rent, as Sir Charles Wood desired it to be in his despatch of 1864, then the tax should not exceed one-sixth the produce of any field, and should, for the whole Province, be about one-tenth the average produce as it is in Northern India.

Bombay and the Punjab.

Gentlemen, I have not time to-day to go over the land-revenue arrangements in other parts of India—of the Bombay Presidency or of the Punjab. In Bombay we have generally the same system as in Madras, the Government generally receiving the tax direct from the cultivators. But the settlement officers in Bombay take into consideration what has been paid by cultivators in previous years without difficulty, and do not endeavour to estimate the field produce at all;—under such a system, where is the security to the cultivator, where is the motive to save? In the Punjab the land-system is somewhat similar to that of the North-Western Provinces; but you will find on examination that neither in Bombay nor in the Punjab is the cultivator assured an adequate proportion of the produce of the land he cultivates; and without such assurance his condition cannot be improved and he cannot be saved from famines merely by tinkering with his relations with his money-lender. I am not discussing to-day the merits of the different systems prevailing in the different Provinces of India—the *Zemindari* system of Bengal, the *Talukdari* system of Oudh, the *Mahalwari* system of the North-west, the *Malguzari* system of Central India, or the *Ryotwari* system of Southern India. Nor am I discussing the desirability of extending the Permanent Settlement to all parts of India as was recommended by Lord Canning in 1860, though I myself think, that would be a wise and a generous measure to which the Government is pledged by its many promises in the past. I am not entering into these subjects in order to avoid all discussion, all controversy; and I am laying down a proposal which must receive universal assent without any controversy—*viz.*, that the cultivator should be assured an adequate share of the produce of his land if he is to be saved from indebtedness and poverty, distress and famine. I have confined myself to the actual condition of the cultivator and incidence of the land-tax on the cultivator, for in India the cultivator is the nation. Never mind under what system or under what settlement he lives, assure to him an adequate proportion out of the produce of his land, and he is saved, and the nation is saved.

Central Provinces.

But before I leave this subject I must say one word about the Central Provinces of India, which have suffered so disastrously in the famine of 1897, and which is suffering once more under the famine of 1899. The

Central Provinces have suffered more from recent famines than any other part of India because the land-revenue settlements have been more severe and more harsh, not in their intention, but in their actual operation, than any other part of India. I constantly heard in England, as I have no doubt you constantly heard in this country, of the disastrous results of the recent revenue settlements in that Province, initiated by Sir Alexander Mackenzie. But I will not mention here what I have heard, I will limit my remarks entirely to the facts contained in official reports, and stated in the House of Commons by the Secretary of State for India in reply to questions put to him in March last year, by one of the truest friends of the Indian cultivator, Mr. Samuel Smith.

Gentlemen, there is a healthy rule, generally followed in the North-Western Provinces, that settlements are made for thirty years, because it is undesirable to harass the people with frequent enhancements and frequent settlement operations. Sir Alexander Mackenzie departed from this rule, and ordered the present settlement for twenty years, save in a few backward tracts, where I suppose still shorter settlements have been made. There is another healthy rule, followed in the North-Western Provinces, that the land-revenue is fixed at one-half the rental received by landlords. Sir Alexander Mackenzie cancelled this rule, and the Government revenue is now fixed at 50 to 60 per cent. in the recent settlement. Add to this certain local rates, and the Government demand on the Malguzars comes to nearly

70 per cent. of their supposed collections. I ask every impartial man, every fair-minded administrator, why settlements have been made in the Central Provinces for twenty years or less when settlements are made in the North-West for thirty years? I ask every responsible ruler why the Government should demand 60 per cent. from the Malguzar of the Central Provinces when the Government, receives only about 40 per cent. in North-West according to the evidence of Sir Antony MacDonnell? These differences in figures may not mean much to the theoretical statesman, but they mean life and death to the Indian cultivator. Every tampering with the settled rules in land settlements, every lowering of the period of settlements, every increase in the proportion of the Government demand means the further impoverishment of the cultivators, means increased wretchedness and indebtedness in ordinary times, increased deaths in famines. Why gentlemen, this very experiment was tried in these North-Western Provinces; the Government demand at first was not half but two-thirds of the assests of the landlords; and that rule created a degree of suffering to the people greater than all the wars of the first half of this century. That rule was ultimately abandoned in 1855, and the Government demand was fixed at one half the rental of the landlord; and is it fair that we should go back in the Central Provinces to the old rule which our experience has taught us here to be harsh and cruel to the cultivators? If the people had any control over the executive action in the Central Provinces, the tampering with the

old established settlement rules would not have been allowed. If the people had been represented in the Viceroy's Executive Council to press these matters, no Viceroy of India would have permitted such departure from the usual settlement rules, a departure which has been disastrous in its consequences on the condition of the people and increased the deaths from famines in the Central Provinces.

Gentlemen, I have detained you longer on this subject than I had intended, but the importance of the subject is my excuse. I state my deliberate opinion, based on a careful study of the question for thirty years, that the land-revenue arrangements in India are responsible, not for bringing on famines, but for deepening the effects of these famines; and secondly, that if the position of the cultivator was assured, if the demand from him were fixed within equitable and fixed limits, loss of lives could be prevented on the occurrence of famines, as it has been prevented in Bengal. British administration has done much for us; it has given us internal peace, it has given us education, it has brought us nearer to western civilisation. But British administration has not performed all its duty so long as the country is desolated by famines, unheard of in any other civilised and well-governed country. My conviction is, and I lay it loyally before the Government, that these frequent and acute famines are mainly owing to the cause that *our village industries are gone, and our village lands are over-assessed.* My conviction is, and I lay it loyally before the Government, that this enormous loss of lives is preventible, and could be avoided through more considerate land settlements, assuring to the cultivator in every province an adequate proportion of the food that he produces.

Military Expenditure, National Debt, Currency, Industries, Services.

Gentlemen, there are various other causes of the poverty of India under British Rule which I have not touched upon to-day, and which I do not wish to touch upon, because they have been discussed ably, eloquently, and repeatedly by yourselves at previous meetings of this Congress, and some of them will be discussed again this year by other speakers. There is the question of the enormous Military Expenditure, and the maintenance of a vast army out of the resources of India, not for the requirements of India, but for the requirements of the British Empire in Asia, Africa, and even in Europe. There is the question of the National Debt, which, in Great Britain, has been reduced by about 175 millions since 1860, and which has gone up by over 100 millions in India within this period, causing an increasing drain out of the revenues of India for the payment of interest in England. There is the question of the Currency which has been lately settled by the Currency Committee in a manner not conductive to the interests of the millions of cultivators whose debts have been increased, and savings depreciated. There is the question of encouraging and helping the Industrial Classes ruined by unfair competition, a question which has been ably and exhaustively dealt with by one of the most learned and thoughtful writers of our generation, the Hon'ble Mr. Justice Ranade of Bombay. And there is the question of the possible saving in expenditure by the larger employment of the educated people of India, not only in the Indian Civil Service, but in the higher grades of all services, Educational and Medical, Police and Engineering, Post Office and Telegraph. Three generations of Indians have been educated in English schools and colleges in India; they have proved their fitness and capacity in every place they have held; and yet they are virtually Uitlanders in their own country so far as a real control over administration is concerned.

I pass over these and other cognate subjects because I have no time to deal with them, and because you have often dealt with them eloquently and exhaustively, and will deal with many of them again. I will only repeat that it is perfectly possible to cut down expenditure, to moderate land assessments, to revive industries, and to prevent deaths from famines, if there is a real and honest determination to rule India for the good of the people and with the co-operation of the people. Gentlemen, I wish with your permission to add one or two words on this last subject, *viz.*, the desirability of enlisting the co-operation of the people in the work of administration,—the desirability of bringing the administration in closer touch with the people, and bringing our rulers in closer touch with ourselves. This is desired by every enlightened and far-sighted ruler as well as by ourselves; and this is calculated to improve the administration and to make British rule in India stronger and more popular. A commencement has been made in this direction since the days of Munro and Elphinstone and Lord William Bentinck; and what I will suggest is not a new departure, but a progress on the lines already laid down. I do not myself believe in new departures and novel experiments in administration; having passed the best years of my life in administration I naturally have more faith in gradual and cautious progress on the lines which have already been laid down.

Village Unions.

Gentlemen, I will begin with villages—because, as I have already said, in India villager represents the nation. In village administrations there is no touch between the rulers and the people, the only link between the administrators and the people in civil administration is hated link of the police. It is a misfortune and an administrative mistake that our District officers should have so little direct touch with the villagers and their natural leaders, and should work so entirely through the police. If there is distress in the land, the police makes enquiries; if there is cholera epidemic in the land the police distributes cholera pills; if a village tank has given way or the the village water-supply dried up the police reports and organises help; if a tree has been blown down and obstructs a village path, (I have seen instances of this myself), the villagers are powerless to help themselves until the police comes and removes the obstruction. It seems to be a mockery that the very country which was the first to organise village communities, village Panchayets, and village self-government, and cherished these institutions for 3,000 years, should be rendered so absolutely helpless, and should be ruled through the undesirable agency of the police. Gentlemen, the mistake has been discovered and Village Unions have been formed or are in the course of formation in most Provinces in India. Make these Village Unions real centres of village administration in so far as is consistent with good Government. Parcel out each Sub-division into twenty or thirty Village Unions, entrust the Union Committees with the charge of village roads, village tanks, village drainage, village education, and village hospitals, and send over to them all petty civil and criminal cases, not for judical disposal, but for amicable settlement. A great deal expensive litigation and bad feeling in villages can thus be stopped, a great deal of useful work can thus be done, and what is more, the natural leaders of the village population will thus come in touch with the Sub-divisional and District administrators, and will form the agents of village administration in so far as they are fit to take that position. An un-sympathetic system of rule through the police will thus be replaced by a rule with the co-operation of the people themselves.

Municipal Towns.

From the subject of Villages I come to the subject of Municipal Towns which are receiving a great deal of attention now. Gentlemen, I consider it of primary importance that we should insist on efficient municipal administration, and that power should be given to the

Government to ensure such efficient administration if the Municipal Commissioners are slack. Such power is retained by the Government in England, and it is more necessary that such power should be retained by the Government in India. But having provided for this, I am of opinion that the work should be done through the elected Commissioners and not through the officials or secretaries appointed by the Government. The latter system ruins self-government, and is not needed. I have myself supervised the work of every Municipality in a District as a District-Officer, and I have supervised the work of all the Municipalities in a Division as a Divisional Commissioner. The Municipal Commissioners were sometimes zealous and sometimes slack, sometimes they went the right way and sometimes the wrong way ; but I have never found them obstructive ; I have never found them averse to sanitary improvement or general progress ; I have never found them other than amenable to reason and advice. With some tact and patience and sympathy we can get all that we want to do through the men elected by people themselves ; and it is unwise and undesirable, it is a confession of our own incompetency and want of sympathy, to try to replace the elective system by men appointed by the Government to do Municipal work in the small District towns of India. The aptitude of Self-Government in towns and villages is, in India, a heritage of three thousand years, and to seek to ignore it is an administrative blunder, and a confession of our own incompetency.

District Boards.

Coming next to the subject of District Boards, the question is often asked why non-official chairmen should not be appointed over these Boards. The reason, gentlemen, in the generality of cases, is that non-official gentlemen who know their own villages and estates well, have not the same knowledge of the District as a whole as the District Officer. We must, above all, insist on efficient work being done—and generally the District Officer is the only man who can in the ordinary course of his tours supervise and secure efficient work throughout his District. At the same time I would not make any hard and fast rule; and where we have retired Government servants or private gentlemen who know their Districts well, and who have the capacity and the time for administrative work, it would be a gain and not a loss to our administration to see such gentlemen appointed chairmen of District Boards; and I sincerely hope to see a beginning made by the Government in this direction. Another question which is often discussed in connexion with District Boards is the poverty of their income. This, gentlemen, is a real and a grave evil; and it has become not only desirable but necessary that for large provincial schemes of irrigation and drainage the resources of the District Board should be supplemented by provincial grants. You are aware how much good is done in these provinces by a system of irrigation-wells; and there is no reason why the work of the maintenance of a sufficient number of such wells and of other works for the prevention of famine should not be made over to the District Board on allotments made by the Provincial Government. In Bengal the crying evil is bad drainage, which causes that malaria which is the curse of one half of the province. There is no reason why a provincial grant should not be made to every District Board for the proper drainage of the District. Gentlemen, I have said it elsewhere that the money spent on one needless trans-frontier war, if spent in improving the drainage of Bengal, would save millions of the people permanently from one of the direst curses of the present age. My advice is, make the District Boards real agents of beneficient administration with the co-operation of the people ; don't strangle them by the shackles of officialism ; don't starve them by want of funds.

Provincial Legislative Councils.

And now, gentlemen, I come to the important subject of Provincial Legislative Councils, and on this subject also my suggestion will be to proceed on the lines already laid down and not to take a new departure. The object of allowing District and Municipal bodies to elect members of these Councils was to allow the views of the people to be represented, and I think every responsible administrator in India will admit that this wise step has improved and strengthened the legislative machinery of the Government. Even when the views of the elected members are rejected—and they are often rejected—even then the expression of their views is a gain to the cause of administration. The time has now come when a fuller scope may be given to this expression of our views and the representation of our opinions. Half-a-dozen members, elected under somewhat complicated rules can scarcely give expression to the views of a province with a population of thirty or forty millions or more. Is it too much to hope that in the not remote future the Government will find it possible to permit every District to be represented by its own member? I do not object to the number of official and nominated members being also increased; I do not object to the Councils sitting five days or six days in the week instead of one day; and I do not object to the head of the Government reserving the power of vetoing a measure, even against the views of the majority of the Council, in urgent cases as the Queen of England has theoretically the power to refuse her consent to a measure passed by both Houses. With these safeguards, I would suggest an expansion of the Provincial Councils on the bases of each District being represented by its member, so that there may be an adequete expression of the people's opinions and views on every question. We do not wish for the absolute control of the administration of the country, but we do demand an adequate means of placing our views before the Government before it decides on questions affecting our welfare.

Provincial Executive Councils.

But, gentlemen, the Legislative Councils deal with legislation only, there are large and important measures of administration which do not come within the scope of these Councils. The weakness of the present system of Government is that in the decision on these administrative measures the people have no voice and are not heard at all. To take one instance out of hundreds which will no doubt suggest themselves to you, the people of the Central Provinces of India had no constitutional means of declaring whether the revenue settlement should be for twenty or thirty years ; whether the Government demand should be 50 per cent. of the Malguzars' assests, or 60 per cent.; and the decision to which the Government arrived without the constitutional advice of the people has been disastrous. Gentlemen, this defect can be rectified, this weakness may be removed. There are Executive Councils in Bombay and in Madras; similar Executive Councils may be formed in the North-West Provinces and the Punjab, in the Central Provinces and in Bengal, and at least one member of the Executive Council should be an Indian gentleman with experience in administrative work, and representing the views of his countrymen. It is usual for a member of an Executive Council to have a portfolio, *i.e.*, to have one department of work assigned to him ; and the work which I would assign to the Indian member is Land Revenue, Agriculture and the Industries. There is no department of work in which an Indian member can make himself more valuable to the voiceless millions of cultivators and artisans. The addition of one Indian member will not weaken Provincial administration. It will strengthen such administration, make it more sympathetic and bring it into somewhat closer touch with the people.

The Viceroy's Executive Council.

And, gentlemen, am I aspiring too high when I hope for similar seats for Indian members in the cloudy heights of Simla? Am I urging anything unreasonable when I propose that the Viceroy who has the benefit of consulting experienced English administrators in his Executive Council, should also have the advantage of hearing the views and opinions of a few Indian members in the same Council before he decides on questions affecting the interests of the people of India? Am I urging anything unwise when I propose that the Viceroy, when he considers measures affecting the condition of the indebted cultivators, the operations of the plague and famine relief, the rules of land-revenue settlements, the questions affecting Hindu and Mahomedan customs and manners, should have by him, in his own Executive Council, a few Indian gentlemen who represent the views, the opinions and the feelings of the people? An Executive Council cannot be much enlarged without loss of efficiency but surely the Viceroy's Council could make room for three Indian gentlemen, one to represent Bengal and Assam, another to represent the North-west and the Punjab, and the third to represent Bombay, Madras and the Central Provinces. The selection should rest, of course, with the Viceroy himself, for anything like election into an Executive Council would be absurd; and the three Indian members should be entrusted with the departments of Agriculture, Industries and Land Revenue of their respective provinces. The wise and magnanimous Akbar entrusted his Land Revenue arrangements to a Todar Mall; and the British Government may consider it wise and statesmanlike to avail itself of the experience of Indian gentlemen in controlling Land Revenue Settlements and generally in improving the condition of the voiceless and impoverished cultivators and manufacturers of India. I myself think that the administration of the country would be vastly improved by such representation of Indian opinions in our highest Councils and that the Government of India and the Government of the Provinces would be brought in closer touch with the people.

Progress in the future.

And now, gentlemen, it only remains for me to thank you once more for the great honour you have done me by electing me to preside on this occasion, and for the kind and patient hearing you have given me. I have been somewhat of an optimist all my life, I have lived in that faith and I should like to die in that faith. The experiment of administration *for the people*, not *by the people* was tried in every country, in Europe in the last century, by some of the best-intentioned sovereigns that ever lived, who are known in history as the Benevolent Despots of the 18th century. The experiment failed because it is an immutable law of nature that you cannot permanently secure the welfare of a people if you tie up the hands of the people themselves. Every country in Europe recognises this truth now, and England foremost of all. Every English colony has obtained a system of self-government, and from being discontented and disaffected they are now the strongest supporters of the British empire. And a system of complete Self-Government in local affairs was conceded to Ireland by the present Government less than two years ago, when Lord Curzon was a distinguished member of that Government. The conditions of india are different, and I admit freely and fully that we want a strong centralised Government here ; and if the moderate scheme I have proposed tended in any way to weaken the Indian Government, the proposal, gentlemen, would not have come from me. But I have discussed the subject with many eminent Englishmen now in England and possessing vast experience in Indian administration, and I have asked them to reject my scheme if they thought it would weaken the Indian Government instead of greatly strengthening it. Gentlemen, I have never been told in reply that the scheme would weaken the Government. It is isolation, it is exclusiveness, it is want of touch with the people, which weakens British rule in India, and my desire is to strengthen that rule by bringing it in touch with the people, by enlisting the zealous co-operation of a great and loyal nation.

Permit me, gentlemen, to refer for a moment to my own experience as a District Officer. You are aware that a District Officer is liable to frequent transfers ; and I was sometimes in charge of districts where 75 per cent. of the people were Hindus, and at other times of districts where 75 per cent. were Mahomedans. I may remark in passing that everywhere I received the cordial co-operation of the people in my administrative work, and the sympathy and support which I received from Mahomedan zemindars and the Mahomedan population generally enabled me to administer with some degree of success such vast and difficult districts as Backergunj and Mymensing. But what I wish specially to mention is that in these Mahomedan districts the Government always employed a number of able Mahomedan Deputy Collectors to advise and help the District Officer in his work; and in all questions relating to the social and economic conditions of the Mahomedan people, and to their public feelings and religious sentiments, I received the most valuable help and advice from my Mahomedan colleagues in the work of administration. Gentlemen, the duties and responsibilities of a District Officer are humble compared to the manifold duties and high responsibilities of a Viceroy or the Governor of a Province; and I therefore often ask myself if those statesmen do not sometimes feel, as we, humble District Officers, always felt, that it would help and improve administration to have a few true representatives of the people by their side and in their Executive Councils. And I cannot help replying to myself that the advice and help of some Indian colleagues would greatly strengthen the hands of wise and sympathetic statesmen in solving the great problems which lie before them, none of which is more momentous and more pressing than the condition of the Indian agriculturist and the Indian manufacturer.

Gentlemen, from whatever point of view I examined the question, whether in the light of European history, or of the spirit of British institutions, or of the requirements for good government for India, I feel convinced that to associate the people of India more largely in shaping the administration of the country is not only the wisest but the only possible path before us. It is true we have not been moving onwards in this path in recent years; we have actually stepped backwards in these years of misfortunes and calamities and panic; we have even been deprived of those rights and privileges which we secured in years of wise and sympathetic administration. But such years of retrograde movement come to all nations from time to time, even to those who are most advanced. Remember England at the close of the last century, when to talk of political reforms was punished as sedition and crime, when coercive measures were passed to stop public meetings, when reactionary laws were enacted to restrict the liberties of Englishmen. The panic passed away after the Napoleonic wars were over, and the Reform came in 1832. The reactionary period through which we are passing will end before long, and wise English statesmen will perceive in the future, as they have perceived in the past, that England's duty and England's interests are the same in India, to consolidate British rule by extending, not restricting Self-Government, by conciliating, not alienating a vast and civilised nation.

Gentlemen, it is possible to avert distress and disasters and deaths from famines, to spread prosperity and contentment and peace, and to evoke the zealous and loyal and spontaneous support of a grateful nation, only by conceding to the people, with due and proper safeguards, the rights of Self-Government. It is not possible, without such concession, without admitting the people to a real share in the control of their own affairs, to save India from distress and discontent, from impoverishment and famines. Therefore, as an old and faithful servant of the Indian Government, I have thought it my duty to raise my voice and urge the adoption of the better and the wiser course, the only course which can save our country from preventible misfortunes and disasters, and can consolidate the British Rule in India.

X. FAREWELL SPEECH IN CALCUTTA.

[*Delivered in the Town Hall on February* 23, 1900, *in reply to an Address presented by the citizens of Calcutta.*]

FRIENDS AND COUNTRYMEN,

I am unable to find words to adequately express my feelings on an occasion like this. You overwhelm me by your kindness and by your cordial appreciation of the humble services which I have attempted to render to the cause which we all have at heart. Your kindness and your appreciation will live in my memory through years of future toil and endeavour. I shall remember that you did not forget your humble fellow-worker, who shared your aspirations and shared your endeavours during years of absence from his country ; and I shall remember that on his return amidst you, you extended to him the hand of kindly appreciation and of brotherly love. There are ties which are stronger than the ties of blood, and they are the ties of a common country, common aims, and common endeavours. These are the ties which bind all castes and creeds in India as one united people, and these are the ties which will nerve our hands and strengthen our hearts in our future endeavours.

It is not possible for me, gentlemen, to refer to the various matters which you have dwelt upon in your kind Address, nor is it possible for me, to make an adequate reply to all that you have stated. You will permit me therefore to confine my reply to only one or two salient points in your Address, and to say a few words on our present situation.

Literary Work of Educated Indians.

You have alluded in flattering terms to that humble literary work which has been, not a task, but a recreation and a joy to me during the last 30 years. That work has beguiled my saddest hours, solaced me in lonely hours, and refreshed me in the midst of overwhelming work of a different nature. I remember the solitary evenings when I was encamped in the midst of the rice-fields of Dakkhin Shahbazpur, a sea-washed island in the mouth of the Ganges, when I read Grant Duff's inspiring work on the History of the Mahrattas, and spent my nights in dreaming over a story of Sivaji. I remember the days when I travelled over Tippera, and occasionally crossed over to Hill Tippera, with Tod's spirited History of Rajasthan in my knapsack, and when I ventured to compose a story of Pratap Sinha. I remember how, after weary days spent over official work and official bundles in the heavy District of Mymensingh, I sought recreation and rest admist the countless volumes of European and Indian scholars who have written on Indian Antiquities, and I conceived the idea of writing a connected history of Civilisation in Ancient India. In my long furloughs, and with the help of many Pandits whose learned names grace the pages of my works, I placed before my countrymen, in original and in translation, the substance of that vast body of Sacred Hindu Literature which is the noblest heritage of the Hindu nation. And I did not consider that task complete till I was able, after my retirement from service, to place before the modern world, in a condensed and readable form, the great Epics of India. This, gentlemen, has been recreation of my life; it has strengthened me and sustained me amidst multitudinous work, and I hope it will continue to help and sustain me in all my labours during the remaining days of my life.

Gentlemen, other and more gifted men than myself have devoted themselves to literary work during this half century, and surveying their work as a whole, it is possible to discern a certain direction which our literary work has taken. In one word, all the greatest works of the half century, about to close, centre round the cardinal idea of *Service to our Mother Land.* Till the middle of this century, we were taught to regard our ancient religion as a system of superstition, our ancient history as fable, and our own languages as unfit for ambitious literary endeavours. That we have outlived those times, that we have discarded those degrading notions, is due to the endeavours of our own countrymen, to that band of noble-hearted and patriotic men who explained to us our ancient religion, elucidated our ancient history, created our modern literature. The venerable Vidyasagar led the van of progress, and explained to us, when we were little children, what was great and glorious in our ancient religion and literature. The talented Madhu Sudan Datta turned away from fruitless compositions in English to his native language, and constructed that splendid fabric of Epic Poetry which is now the pride of his countrymen. And the inimitable Bankim Chandra devoted a well-spent life in creating a body of literature which strengthens and inspires us, while it charms and fascinates. These were the pioneers of our contemporaneous literature, and I know of no truer patriot and no truer servant of his country than these gifted men who taught us to regard our country's religion and history and literature with a legitimate and manly admiration. For, gentlemen, that nation has no future which has no faith in itself; that nation will know no progress which is not conscious of its own strength; and our first and greatest indebtedness for the progress of this half century is to those who have taught us to have faith in ourselves. That progress has not been altogether perfect. We have great sins to answer for. No one knows, better than ourselves, our little weaknesses, our petty jealousies, our vanity and disunion, our self-seeking and selfishness. But making every allowance for our sins—and they are many—we may still confidently declare that in the broad results we have made a distinct progress in this half century. We stand farther ahead than where we were fifty years ago. We feel more strength in our endeavours and more faith in our hearts than we did fifty years ago. And we have more confidence in our country's cause than we had fifty years ago. To those who were the first pioneers in this progress is due our utmost gratitude and our loving homage. And we, who humbly follow in their footsteps, shall do well to remember that literature itself adds to its own title to glory, if it is consecrated by the love of mother land. If following the great masters of this generation, we too succeed in contributing towards this end, and in inspiring in our children a firmer faith in our country's religion, a loftier admiration of our country's history and a manlier pride in our country's literature, our own literary work, humble and poor as they may be, shall not have been done in vain.

Administrative Work of Educated Indians.

Gentlemen, you have alluded in flattering terms to my administrative work during more than a quarter of a century. I look back with pleasure on those long years of my life during which I worked in friendliness and perfect good feeling with other members of the great Civil Service of India. Gentlemen, we understand them better, and they understand us better, when we work together with the same common object, and to the same common purpose. We learn to appreciate their hard work and devotion to duty, and they learn to appreciate our fitness for serving our own country. I can look back through long years to those days when I served under men for whom I still feel the highest admiration, and something more than admiration—men like Sir Charles Stevens, sometime Lieutenant-Governor of Bengal, like Sir Antony MacDonnell, now Lieutenant-Governor of North-West, and Sir Steuart Bayley, now Member of the India Council. It is a pleasure to work and agree with such men, it is a pleasure even to differ from them in opinion. For, gentlemen, not unoften we discussed in perfect friendliness our opposing views, and I may say the value of the admission of Indians in the Civil Service consists in the fact that they represent the views of their countrymen which do not often coincide with Official views. The weakness of the Civil Service lies in the fact that, with all its ability and honest work, it is not in touch with the people and does not know the people. And I look forward to the admission of more Indians in the Service to counteract this defect, and to make the administration of the country more sympathetic, more efficient, more in touch with the people.

Political Creed of Educated Indians.

Gentlemen, you have also alluded in exceedingly flattering terms to the humble endeavours I have made to advance the political cause of our country. Our political aim and endeavour, as I understand them, and as you all understand them, may be described in two words. We identify ourselves with the British rule and pledge our support to that rule at every sacrifice. And we demand under the British rule a larger share in the administration of our own concerns. This is my creed, and this is your creed, and there is not an educated Indian at the present day who does not in his heart subscribe to this creed. Educated India has identified itself with the British rule, and educated India seeks, through the continuance of the British rule, that larger measure of self-government and representation which it is our aim and endeavour to secure.

Self-government, under necessary control and supervision, is the secret of good government among all civilised communities. "It is an inherent condition of human affairs," says the greatest political thinker of this century, the late John Stuart Mill, "that no intention, however sincere, of protecting the interests of others, can make it safe or salutary to tie up their own hands." This is a truth which has been illustrated in every page of the administration of India within the present century. There is no civilised country in the world in which the administrators are inspired with a more sincere desire to promote the material welfare of the people than India, and there is no civilised country in the world where that desire has been so imperfectly fulfilled, because the people have not been consulted, and have had no voice in the control of their own affairs.

I do not propose this evening to go over the entire field of Indian administration. But the attention of the whole country is at the present moment directed to the great famine which is desolating the western portions of India, and I wish, with your permission, to say a few words on the land-revenue administration of the last 40 years, which is mainly responsible, not in bringing about this famine, but in deepening and accentuating its disastrous effects.

Land Administration during 40 years.

Gentlmen, when the history of the Land Revenue Administration of India during these 40 years is fully written, it will be found to be one of the strangest and saddest in the annals of mankind. Forty years ago, India was desolated by a great famine, and I remember the days when as a school boy I heard harrowing accounts of death and starvation in Northern India, when as school boys we were asked to contribute our humble mite for the relief of suffering and distress. The years of famine was at last over, and Lord Canning, who was then the Viceroy of India, sought to introduce some remedial measures, such as would permanently improve the condition of the people and make them more prosperous and resourceful.

Lord Canning's scheme of Land Settlement.

You know that an enquiry, instituted by Lord Canning, was made under the guidance of Col. Baird Smith, and that a recommendation was made that the Permanent Settlement of the Land Revenues, which had secured prosperity to the peasantry and the landlords of Bengal, should be extended to other parts of India. Lord Canning had the courage to place this recommendation before the Secretary of State for India, and the Secretary of State recorded a memorable resolution, describing the proposal as "a measure dictated by sound policy and calculated to accelerate the development of the resources of India, and to insure in the highest degree the welfare and contentment of all classes of Her Majesty's subjects in the country."

Had Lord Canning lived 5 years longer, India would have received this covered boon. But the great statesman died in 1862, and then followed one of those long and fruitless controversies which have so often ruined the best intentions, and marred the noblest objects of Brit'sh rulers in India. The controversy went on for twenty years between the Secretary of State's Council and Viceroy's Executive Council in India, and the strangest part of it is, that the people of India, whose welfare it was intended to secure, were not consulted and not informed as to what was going on. Gentlemen, we are not a race of savages, incapable of understanding our own material interests, nor have we been wanting in experienced and moderate and trusted leaders, commanding the confidence of the Government and the confidence of the people. In Bengal we had wise and thoughtful men like Ram Gopal Ghose, and Digambar Mitter and Kristo Dass Pal, and other provinces produced even more eminent men, like Madhava Rao and Dinkur Rao, who virtually ruled kingdoms, and secured order and prosperity out of chaos and misery. If these men had been consulted, if these men had seats in the Executive Council of the Viceroy, and even in the Council of the Secretary of State, if these men had been allowed to plead the cause of their suffering countrymen and to represent facts in their true light, the decision on Lord Canning's proposal might have been other than it was. But by a strange irony of fate, a strange exclusiveness on the part of the British Government, the leaders of the Indian nation were not consulted with regard to a measure intended to secure the welfare of the Indian nation, the long controversy was carried on among alien administrators secretly and in the dark, and in the end the interests of the people, who were not represented and not heard, were sacrificed. The proposal for a Permanent Settlement was rejected in 1883, and the policy of continuing recurring settlements and recurring enhancements of revenue was continued to the impoverishment of the nation. Gentlemen, at the present moment we are hearing a great deal of the poverty of the Indian peasantry, and it was only last week that the present Viceroy of India raised his voice in this very hall for raising subscriptions for the relief of suffering and distress. Our sincere gratitude is due to that kind-hearted nobleman, who is struggling in the midst of appalling difficulties to relieve the suffering and distress of our countrymen; but I will say this—and few who know the revenue history of the country will contradict me—that if Lord Canning's noble remedial measure had been passed after 1860, it would have been unnecessary for Lord Curzon to appeal to the generosity of the Indian nation for a distress so intense and so appalling in 1900.

Lord Ripon's Scheme of Land Settlement.

Gentlemen, I have brought down the history to 1883. Permit me to narrate the subsequent events in a few words. The Marquis of Ripon was our Viceroy from 1880 to 1884, and while His Lordship consented to the abandonment of the original proposal of a Permanent Settlement, he at the same time made a fresh proposal in a modified form. Looking at the harassing nature of the recurring settlements in Madras, Lord Ripon, in his Despatch of the 17th October, 1882, made a proposal that in all Districts which had been once surveyed and settled, the assessment should be regarded as final and permanent, subject only to variations on the sole ground of rise or fall in the prices of food grains. You will see that this was not a Permanent Settlement such as Lord Canning had proposed ; it permitted the future increase of land-revenue on the ground of a rise in prices ; but subject to this one condition it was a Permanent Settlement of the land assessment and saved millions of cultivators from repeated and harassing surveys and reclassification of soils. Gentlemen, this equitable proposal was cordially accepted by the Madras Government in 1883, and for a time there was some hope again for the oppressed and impoverished cultivators of India.

But History repeats itself, at least in the revenue administration of India, and Lord Ripon's proposal had the same history as Lord Canning's previous proposal. For two or three years, Lord Ripon's proposal was under the consideration of the India Office at Whitehall. We, the people of India, knew nothing of it, our leading men were not informed, our representative men were not consulted. In the prolonged discussions which took place in the dark and secret chambers of Whitehall, we were not permitted to express our views or to plead our cause ; in the equally dark and secret chambers of the Viceroy's Executive Council, our voice was not heard, and our eyes could not penetrate. While our attention was engrossed in a *Legislative* measure known as the Illbert Bill, an *Executive* proposal of far greater importance, because concerning the well-being or poverty of millions of our suffering and voiceless cultivators, was discussed by our alien rulers, here and in

England, and they did not think it worth their while to consult the leaders of the nation for whose welfare the proposal was meant. The result followed which might have been expected. So long as Lord Ripon remained at the helm of affairs in India, the India Office held its silence. Lord Ripon retired from India in December, 1884, and in January, 1885, came the reply from the India Office vetoing Lord Ripon's fair and moderate proposal. Gentlemen, I know of no sadder incident in the history of British rule in India than a decision like this, arrived at by the India Office at Whitehall, rejecting the moderate and beneficent proposals of the Indian Government, and condemning the population of India to continued poverty, misery and indebtedness. I repeat that if we had representatives in the Viceroy's Executive Council and in the Council of the Secretary of State, if we had been permitted to represent our interests and our wishes when Lord Ripon's proposal was secretly debated, the decision on the proposal might have been different. Madras would have been saved from harassing and repeated surveys and unjust enhancements; and if the proposal had been extended to Western India, Western India would have been free from the present famine in its intense form.

Mr. Cotton's scheme of a Land Settlement.

One more word on this subject, and I have done. There are still some administrators among us who are inspired by the benevolence of a Canning or a Ripon, and who place the happiness of the people before the interests of land-revenue, and one of such administrators is now the Chief Commissioner of Assam. That Province, Gentlemen, has vast possibilities in the future, for most of the cultivable land in the Province is still waste grass-jungle. But it requires capital, it requires enterprise, and it requires leadership to bring the vast country under cultivation, to import cultivators, to build huts and villages for them, to supply them with ploughs and bullocks, to dig tanks for them, to do all that a far-sighted and benevolent Zemindar can do when he wishes to reclaim waste lands. Some sort of a Permanent Settlement is necessary to induce capital and enterprise, and the Chief Commissioner of Assam recommended some sort of a Permanent Settlement for Assam in order to open up the country. But the prospect of private Zemindars reaping the future benefits from the extension of cultivation in Assam did not commend itself to our rulers, and Mr. Cotton's proposal has been virtually disallowed. Much regret is often expressed by responsible rulers at the want of capital and enterprise in India. Gentlemen, if some of these fine words could be translated into deeds in the land-revenue department, if measures were adopted which would help enterprise in our cultivators, and lead to accumulation of capital in the hands of our landlords, India would not be so utterly resourceless as she is to-day. And I repeat, gentlemen, that if we had been represented in the Viceroy's Executive Council, if we could have taken a share in the discussions which took place in that Council over

Mr. Cotton's beneficent proposal, if we could have represented there the interests of the people for whose good all righteous Governments exist, the decision on the proposal might have been different from what it is. But we are not admitted to these secret discussions, the people are not allowed to speak in those Councils which shape the administration and decide on the fate of the Indian nation, and the result is that the land-revenue administration of India during these 40 years has, in spite of the best intentions, been fatal to the welfare of the nation.

General Administration during 40 years.

You will pardon me, gentlemen, for dwelling so long on the subject of land administration. Land is virtually the one means of subsistence left to us as a nation after our various industries have been killed by an unequal and unfair competition, and land-administration concerns our well-being as a nation more intimately than administration in any other department. And blunders in land administration are mainly responsible for the frequency and intensity of recent famines. I do not wish to take up your time by reviewing the administration in other departments; but you will find on examination that, in every department, the administration, inspired by benevolent intentions, and carried on with undoubted ability, has failed to safeguard the interests of the people, because it has chosen to tie up the hands of the people. England and India have both enjoyed uninterrupted internal peace during the last 40 years; within this period the financiers of England, working under popular control and inspired by the genius of a popular leader like Mr. Gladstone, has reduced the public debts by over a hundred and seventy millions; but in India our finance ministers, working without the control of the people, have added to the people's debts by over a hundred millions sterling. England pays the whole or a part of the cost of the Imperial troops maintained in every self-governing English Colony; we, in this country, have in the midst of our distresses and famines to pay for the entire army, European and Indian, maintained in India, not merely for the defence of India, but for the safety of the British Empire in Asia and Africa. Every self-governing English Colony has taken measures to protect its infant industries against unfair competition; in India our ancient industries have been ruined, and no adequate measures have yet been taken by the Government to revive, as far as may be, those ancient industries on modern lines. Every self-governing English Colony protects its own interests against foreign labourers, in the most complete and efficacious manner, and you know the harsh laws of Natal against Her Majesty's Indian subjects who wish to work there for a living. In India cheap labour is free from the danger of foreign competition, but we are virtually excluded from the higher ranks of all services. From a Parliamentary return issued in 1892, it appears that nearly one-fifth of the revenue of India went in the payment of salaries to Europeans; and since 1892, the posts open to the people of the country have not been widened, but rather contracted under an ungenerous and reactionary policy especially in the Education and the Engineering Departments.

Gentlemen, I bring no charge against any class or individuals for these disappointing results of the last 40 years of British rule. I have said repeatedly, and I firmly believe, that there is a sincere desire in the higher administrators to promote and safeguard the interests of the people, and many of them, whom I have the honour of knowing, are men who are incapable of passing an order which they consider detrimental to the good of the people of India. But the most beneficent desire fails in its object, unless it is accompanied by a willingness to concede to the people some share in the control of the administration. Good administration in a great and civilised country is an impossibility, unless the people are allowed a share in the administration, and therefore, gentlemen, we ask for and demand a share in the control of the administration of our own concerns.

Lord George Hamilton on the Congress.

This is the claim which you have put forward loyally before the Government for years past, and this is the claim which I repeated in my Presidential speech at Lucknow in December last. I explained our common object as clearly and as forcibly as my knowledge of the English language enabled me to do, and while I expected my proposal to be criticised, I certainly did not expect it to be misunderstood. Nevertheless, I find that my proposal has been misunderstood by so high an authority as the Secretary of State for India, Lord George Hamilton. In a speech which His Lordship made recently in London, he used these words in reference to my speech.

"I read the other day a remarkable speech by no unfriendly critic of British Administration in India. He admitted frankly and fully that British Administration had conferred great benefits on India, and that it was conducted *for* the people, but he wished to substitute another phase, that Government in India should be conducted *by* the people."

Gentlemen, I feel flattered by the kind and complimentary remarks made by so high an authority about my speech, but I wish to point out once more, as I have already pointed out elsewhere, that nowhere in my Lucknow speech did I propose to substitute the present form of Government by another phase, a Government conducted entirely by the people. *Theories*, as such, have no attraction for me ; I always endeavour to find out what is *practicable* under existing circumstances ; and all that I claim under the existing circumstances of India, is that we should have a voice, a share, in the control of administration of our own concerns. This I stated distinctly in my Lucknow speech, and this I repeat on the present occasion.

Exclusive Rule unexampled in History.

Gentlemen, History records scarcely any example of a great and civilised nation permanently placed under a system of government which allowed them no share in the control over their own concerns. In ancient India, the entire village administration was in the hands of village communities or local landlords, and though there was no representation in its modern forms, kings and potentates listened to the wishes of the people and the leaders of the people in deciding on great questions of administration. In ancient Europe the policy of Imperial Rome was inspired by the same spirit, and you no doubt recollect the eloquent words in which Gibbon has described the treatment of conquered provinces by Rome :—

"The grandsons of the Gauls, who had besieged Julius Cæsar in Alesia, commanded legions, governed provinces, and were admitted into the Senate of Rome. Their ambition, instead of disturbing the tranquillity of the State, was intimately connected with its safety a. greatness."

The history of Moghal Rule in India may also be described in almost the same words, and we can truly say :—

"The grandsons of the Hindus who had fought against Babar in the field of Fatehpur Sikri, commanded legions, governed provinces, and were admitted into the Councils of Akbar. Their ambition, instead of disturbing the tranquillity of the State, was intimately connected with its safety and greatness."

Shall we for ever continue to describe British Rule in India in words the reverse of this? Shall we for ever have to say :—

"The grandsons and great-grandsons of those who

helped the British in the field of Plassy and Wandewash, of Laswari and Assye, were excluded from the command of armies, from the government of provinces, from the Council of the Secretary of State for India, from the Executive Council of the Viceroy, from the Executive Councils of the Indian Provinces ?"

Future Prospects.

Gentlemen, the prospect before us is not inspiring. We are living in reactionary times ; we have achieved nothing of late ; we have lost a great deal of what we possessed before. I have felt this, as well as any of you ; I have made my humble endeavours against the tide of reaction ; I have struggled to save the wrecks of our established rights ; I have seen the object of my endeavours snatched away from me almost at the moment of triumph ; I have been beaten, defeated, swept away by the overwhelming tide. It would be idle to pretend that I did not feel the disappointment as bitterly and acutely as any one of you ; but I can truly declare before you that I have never, in bitterest moments of disappointment, been filled with despair. Our cause is so just, our demands are so moderate, our claims are so much in consonance with all wise governments, ancient and modern, that they are bound to triumph. We desire the continuance of the British rule in India ; we desire a strong and centralised British Government to maintain order and peace in this vast Empire ; but consistently with these objects, we desire admission in the Councils of the Empire, and a share in the control over the administration of our own concerns. These are just and righteous and reasonable concessions, which the British nation shall not refuse, and which we are bound to obtain, if we are true to ourselves.

[*The following was the text of the Address to which the above speech was a reply.*]

We, the residents of Calcutta in public meeting assembled, beg to convey to you our deep sense of gratitude for the many services rendered by you to the cause of our country.

Being one of the earliest among our countrymen to enter into the Indian Civil Service, you have had a long and distinguished official career. As a Revenue and Settlement Officer, as the head of the Executive of many first-class Districts, and finally as the administrator of an important Division of these provinces, you won not only the admiration and confidence of the Government under which you served but also the respect and gratitude of the people over whom you ruled.

We are aware that one of the principal reasons of your early retirement from the Indian Civil Service was desire to be more useful to your country and an anxiety to direct the attention of our rulers to the aspirations and grievances of the people of India from a position of greater freedom. The way in which you have employed your time since your retirement has fully justified the wisdom of that step. You have, within a short time, done much, through the press and the platform, to inform and enlighten public opinion in England on some of the most momentous questions of Indian administration—particularly about the recent change in the law of sedition in India and the Calcutta Municipal Bill. You have also sought to explain Indian questions to Members of the English Parliament and have made timely representations to the India Office regarding them. While helping in the election of some members of the British House of Commons, you have availed yourself of the opportunity thus afforded of pleading the cause of your countrymen before the English people. You have also spoken to crowded English audiences on several occasions on Famine and Land-assesment in India, and have been earnestly endeavouring to impress upon the authorities the close relation the one bears to the other. For these services and labours, so disinterestedly and ungrudgingly rendered, your grateful countrymen elected you President of the 15th Indian National Congress, the highest office in the gift of the people of this country.

Your services to literature have been no less conspicuous. You have considerably enriched our national literature by your works of fiction, presenting an important period of our past history in a most vivid and attractive form. By your scholarly and faithful translation of the Rig-Veda, you have helped to diffuse a wider knowledge of its treasures among our countrymen. Your masterly exposition of Ancient India in your historical works and your rendering of our great national epics into English verse have served to interpret to the nations of the West the India of the past and to evoke an interest in the India of the present.

In conclusion, we earnestly and sincerely pray that long may it be given to you to serve your country with the devotion and zeal you have hitherto evinced in her cause.

We Remain,

Sir,

Your Grateful Fellow-Citizens.

XI. FAREWELL SPEECH IN BOMBAY.

[*Delivered in the rooms of the Presidency Association on March* 14, 1900]

MR. PRESIDENT and Gentlemen,—I feel the great honour done to me by this Association in conveying to me their kind wishes and farewell greetings on the eve of my departure for Europe, and I sincerely appreciate the manner in which the Chairman has alluded to my humble services in the cause which we have all at heart. Nothing inspires me with greater confidence in our cause, and greater faith in the future, than to find that educated and patriotic men in all parts of India, living at a distance of a thousand miles or more from each other, join in the same endeavours, and devote themselves to the same cause—the cause of a loyal devotion to the British Rule—and loyal endeavours introduce reforms and extend self-government for the improvement of the administration and the welfare of the people. This is the purpose which animates educated men in all parts of India, which I have visited within the last three months, in Madras, in Calcutta, in Lucknow and last though not the least, in the enlightened city of Bombay. And these endeavours, which are always needful, are specially so at the present moment, when our country is suffering from a severe pestilence and a wide-spread famine, and when we, the people of India, should do all we can to loyally help the Government by co-operating in the measures undertaken for relief, and by submitting our advice and suggestions, based on our knowledge of the condition of our suffering countrymen.

The New Governor of Bombay.

Amidst all these disasters and calamities, you have worked in Bombay in a spirit of moderation, which has earned for you a graceful recognition from the kind-hearted nobleman who was lately the Governor of Bombay. You have chosen to forget the early mistakes of his administration, you have recognized the qualities of his generous heart, and you have parted with him with sincere expressions of good wishes and loyalty. And you have extended a cordial welcome to the nobleman who has now come in your midst, and who brings with him the best traditions of good government—of government for the good of the people of India. Gentlemen, it is now more than thirty years since the time when I was living in England as a young student, and when Sir Stafford Northcote was the Secretary of State for India. In those early days I learned to entertain a sincere and genuine admiration for Sir Stafford Northcote's conscientious zeal for the good of the people of India, which I have never since forgotten in life. I do not often use the language of vain compliments, but I am expressing to you my candid and honest opinion, when I state that within the last thirty years there has been no Secretary of State for India, Nobleman or Commoner, Conservative or Liberal, who has worked with a more single-hearted devotion for the good of the people of India than Sir Stafford Northcote. I am expressing to you my candid and honest opinion when I state that, great and valuable as have been the services of all Secretaries of State for India, there has been no Secretary of State within my life-time who brought to the performance of his duties a higher and more sincere regard for the good of the people. This, gentlemen, is high praise when it is honestly spoken, not by political colleagues in England, but by the people of India, and this high praise was won by Lord Iddlesleigh. And let us hope and trust, this high praise will be won by his son whom you so cordially welcomed to these shores only the other day.

Representations of the People.

Gentlemen, you have all read the account, which appeared in the papers, of a dinner which was given to Lord Northcote on the eve of his departure as Governor of Bombay; and you have all read the speech which the present Secretary of State for India made on that occasion. Lord George Hamilton was good enough to refer on this occasion in complimentary terms to my Presidential speech at the Lucknow Congress in December last; and if his Lordship somewhat misapprehended our aims and aspirations, I do not wish to dwell on the fact on this occasion. Our aim and our aspiration under the British Rule is not to change the present form of Government, as Lord George Hamilton supposed, but to maintain and strengthen the present system of Government by popular support and by some representation of popular opinion. I wish on the present occasion rather to refer to the other portion of Lord George Hamilton's speech, in which his Lordship urged on his Excellency, the new Governor of Bombay, to consider the representations of the people in a generous and liberal spirit, to reject them when they are impracticable, and to accede to them when they are practicable, and moderate. Gentlemen, if we could presume to give any advice to his Excellency, we would couch it in the very same words ;—consider the representations of the people in a liberal and generous spirit, reject them when they are impracticable, accede to them when they are reasonable and moderate. Our complaint in the past has been that our representations, whether reasonable or unreasonable, have not been heard at all ; that the Government has been guided entirely by official opinions which were sometimes sound and sometimes influenced by causeless panic ; and that the most moderate and practicable representations of the people have received virtually no hearing and no consideration in the work of administration performed ostensibly for the good of the people.

Executive Council of Bombay.

What are our representations ? It is not possible for me this evening to enumerate them all within the time at my disposal but I will mention a few to indicate their drift and their purpose. You have in this Presidency an

Executive Council formed of trained and experienced English administrators who help the Governor by their advice and deliberations in the affairs of the State. Our humble representation is, appoint one experienced, and moderate Indian in that Council to represent the views of the people, and specially to represent the interests of the millions of cultivators and the industrial population who form the bulk of the people. This would be not introducing a new form of Government, but strengthening the present system of Government by bringing it in touch with the people. This would be, not taking away the control of affairs from the hands of the present rulers, but conceding to us a humble share in that control, so that our opinions may be heard and our views represented in that secret Council Chamber which shapes the destiny of the nation. Is there any Ruler of Bombay who would not feel himself better informed and more in touch with the people if he had by his side an experienced representative of the people to help him and advise him in the management of the affairs of the people? Is there any Governor of Bombay who would not feel himself stronger for such advice and support at all times, and specially in times of famine and pestilence and panic? And if this is a moderate and reasonable and practicable suggestion, may we not expect that his Excellency the present Governor of Bombay will find it possible within his term of office to consider it, in the words of Lord George Hamilton, in a liberal and generous spirit, and make his rule both stronger and more popular by acceding to it?

Legislative Council of Bombay.

You have in this Presidency a Legislative Council, partly consisting of members elected by popular bodies. The object of this elective system was to obtain some real representation of popular opinion in matters of legislation affecting the well-being of the people. Those who have watched the legislative work of the last seven years will be unanimously of opinion that the admission of elected members has improved the work of the Council, and has secured a more careful consideration of the views and wishes of the people, at least in the minor details of the laws which are enacted. All that we ask for now is that after seven years of a successful experiment the principle may be extended further, and that every district in the Province may be represented in the Council. Indian districts are so vast in area, so varied population, and present such a variety of conditions of agriculture, industries and trade, that some representation of the local needs and circumstances of each district is necessary for the purposes of good administration and useful legislation. We have no objection to a corresponding increase in the number of official members, but we desire that each district may have a chance of being heard through its own member before Legislative Acts are passed. And if this be a moderate and reasonable and practicable suggestion, may we not expect that his Excellency the Governor may take it into his favorable consideration, and may even find it possible to give partial effect to it before he lays down the reins of administration ?

Separation of Judicial and Executive Services.

You have in this Presidency, generally in each district a Judge who is the head of important judicial work and a Collector who is the head of the revenue and executive work and of the police. You have asked that the whole of the judicial work be placed under the Judge, and that no portion of it be kept under the officer who is the head of the executive and of the police. You have represented that to place subordinate Judicial officers under the officer who is the head of the police, not only leads to occasional failure of justice, but oftener leads to the suspicion of injustice which, in a country like India, should not be tolerated. Is there anything unreasonable in this prayer? Do not the highest judicial authorities in England, including men who have had long experience of Indian administration, condemn the present system and demand a separation of the Judicial and executive functions as perfectly feasible and likely to be beneficial in India? And may we not expect then that his Excellency the Governor of Bombay, in accordance with the sound advice of the Secretary of State for India, will give a favourable cosideration to this representation of the people, and mark his administration of an important Province of India by giving effect to this representation?

Admission of the people to the Higher Services.

You have in this Province, as elsewhere in India, the higher ranks of all the Civil Departments of the State filled under a system, which virtually excludes the people of India from getting a fair share of the appointments. I am not speaking only of the great Civil Service of India, but of all services—the educational service, the medical service, the police service, the engineering service, the post and telegraph services, the jail and forest services—all the great services, of India. By a system of exclusion, unexampled in the history of any civilised country in ancient or modern times, we, the people of India, are virtually excluded from the higher ranks of these services, and all the higher appointments in these services, barring a very small percentage, are held by Europeans. I have said, this is a state of things unexampled in the history of any civilised country, for I can call to mind no instance, in ancient or modern history, in which the rulers of a civilised and great country so entirely excluded the people of the country from all the higher ranks of the civil administration. The British nation do not desire this act of injustice to be perpetrated and continued. Her Majesty the Queen-Empress has declared in the most solemn manner her desire to admit all her subjects to all offices without distinction of race, caste or creed; and yet the rules of admission to the Civil services have been framed so, as to virtually exclude us from holding a reasonable share of the high appointments in our own country. From a parliamentary return issued in 1892, it appears that nearly one-fifth of the revenues of India went in the payment of salaries to Europeans drawing more than a thousand rupees a year. You have asked that this unjust and ungenerous rule of exclusion should be modified, and that after we have been educated for three generations in English schools and colleges, we may now be permitted, under more equitable rules of admission, to have a fair share of those appointments for which we have proved our fitness. Is this representation unfair or unreasonable? If they be not so, if they be reasonable and moderate, may we not expect his Excellency the new Governor of Bombay will signalize his administration by modifying the present system of exclusion, and admitting us to a fair share of those high appointments to which our claim is recognized by our Queen and Sovereign?

Relief to Cultivators by moderate and fixed Land Assessments.

But, gentlemen, I turn from these and many other subjects, on which you have from time to time submitted your representations to the Government, to that vaster subject which is at present engaging the attention of his Excellency, the poverty and distress of the agricultural population, and the famine which is desolating Western India at the present moment. If there is one subject which should be above the sphere of party controversies, and should appeal to the humanity of all, it is the subject of those famines which are desolating the country so frequently in recent years. And if any of you, gentlemen, have visited relief centres as I have recently done, and seen hundreds and thousands of starving and tottering men and women, our brothers and our sisters, crawling along the roads, resting under trees, lying down on the wayside perhaps to die before the hand of relief can reach them, you will have felt, as I felt, that this calamity, this overwhelming scene of human suffering and distress and death, cries to Heaven for a permanent redress. The way in which a permanent redress can be provided, and the condition of the agricultural population of India can be improved is not unknown to the authorities. In Provinces like Bengal, where private zemindars make their own arrangements with ryots, the cultivators do not pay more than one-sixth the gross produce of their lands as rent, and in many districts they pay a still more moderate rent. In parts of India like Madras and Bombay where the Government is virtually the landlord, the land-tax is screwed up to something near one-third of the gross produce, and the peasantry is necessarily reduced to poverty and indebtedness. In Bengal there is no such thing as enhancement of rents except on very strong and equitable grounds which landlords have to establish in Courts of Justice; in Bombay and Madras, every recurring settlement means an enhancement of the land-tax, and this uncertainty of assessments paralyses agricultural industry and impoverishes the peasantry. In Bengal I have known the cultivators of entire districts fall back on thier past savings in years of failure of crops; in Bombay and Madras there are no such savings to fall back upon, and every year of bad harvests is a year of famine and of deaths. These facts are not unknown to the authorities, and able and distinguished administrators have from time to time suggested the true remedy. As far back as 1862, Lord Canning proposed a permanent settlement for all India ; and if Lord Canning had lived five years longer, his proposal would have been acted upon, and famines in their present intense and disastrous forms would have been unknown. Lord Mayo and Lord Northbrook placed on record their view against frequent and harassing surveys and settlements ; and acting on their suggestions, Lord Ripon finally proposed a modified form of permanent settlement which seemed to meet all objections and to provide a satisfactory solution to the whole question. Lord Ripon claimed for the State the right to enhance revenue in the future on the ground of a rise in prices ; but he assured the cultivators against recurring settlements and against all enhancements except on this one equitable ground, Gentlemen, this equitble solution was accepted and acted upon in Madras, and I am informed, also in Bombay ; but Lord Ripon left India in December 1884, and his wise decision was vetoed by the Secretary of State for India in January 1885. And India has thus once more been plunged into another era of uncertain assessments, frequent enhancements, agricultural distress, and disastrous famines. We appeal, gentlemen, to the new Governor of Bombay, who comes in our midst with the best traditions of good government, to fix a moderate limit to the land-tax, which in Northern India does not exceed ten percent. of the produce. We appeal to him in this year of famine and distress to extend to us that relief which is connected with the names of Canning and of Ripon, and to proclaim that in districts which have been once surveyed and settled, and in which most of the cultivable lands are under cultivation, there shall be no further harassing surveys and settlements, and no enhancement of rents except on the sole and equitable ground of a rise in prices. Gentlemen, I thank you once more for the cordial welcome you have given me and for the kind farewell you have accorded to me. This time to-morrow, I shall be on the sea on my way to Europe, but wherever I may be, your aims and aspirations shall be mine, your endeavours shall be my endeavours, and we shall work for a common purpose and a common object—for the happiness and prosperity and good government of our common motherland.

XII. MAHA-BHARATA, THE ILIAD OF INDIA.

[*Paper read before the Royal Society of Literature, London, on June 14, 1899. Mr. Brabrook, C. B. presiding.*]

Among the many brilliant discoveries in the different departments of human knowledge for which the present century will always be remembered in the history of mankind, the discoveries in the sphere of Archæology and Ancient History are by no means the least brilliant or the least important. The successful researches of scholars and explorers in Egypt and in Babylonia, in India and in China, have effected a complete revolution in our knowledge, have widened the horizon of human history, and have broadened our ideas of the destiny of the human race. Ther are not a few of us, present here to-night, who were taught in our early school days to look for the origin of human civilisation, of philosophy, arts, and religion, in the annals of Greece and Rome, some six or seven hundred years before the birth of Christ.

But we have revised these early impressions, and we now trace the origin of civilisation from a period, not some hundred years, but some thousands of years before the birth of Christ. It almost seems as if an impenetrable mist which bounded the horizon of our knowledge has suddenly lifted, and beyond that mist, which marked the extreme limit of our historical knowledge, we now perceive for the first time long vistas of human civilisation stretching back through endless cycles and ages. This wonderful extension of our historical knowledge, almost within our lifetime, may be not inaptly compared to the experience of many a traveller who visits lofty mountains for the first time in his life. It often occurs to a traveller in the Himalayas, as it occurred to me some twelve years ago at Darjeeling, that during the first few days of his visit he sees nothing before him but the lower ranges of hills, rising to a height of eight or ten thousand feet; and he admires these graceful ranges in all their wild beauty. Suddenly one fine morning the mists clear up, and the traveller turns his admiring eyes from the lower ranges, which bounded his horizon before, to the loftiest mountains in the world—the wonderful peaks of the snow-covered Himalayas—rising to a height of 28,000 or 29,000 feet. The first sight of this lofty array of stupendous peaks strikes him speechless with wonder, and creates in him, as it created in me, an impression never to be forgotten in life. It is with something like this feeling of wonder that we turn from the civilisation of Greece and Rome to the hoary antiquity of Egypt and Babylon, of China and of India, which has now been revealed to us.

So far as we know now, the edifice of human civilisation was first reared in these four gifted lands, and curiously enough it was reared by the four great families of men of the old world. The Semitic race developed their earliest civilisation in Babylon, the Hamitic race in Egypt, and the Turanian race in China; and the great Aryan race who now rule the best portions of Europe,

Asia, and America, developed the earliest form of their civilisation in India.

The early civilisation of India must necessarily have a greater interest for all of us than the civilisation of other ancient countries, not only because India and England are at the present moment bound together by political ties, and are proud to own the sovereignty of the beloved Queen whose eightieth birthday we have recently celebrated, but also because early Aryan thought and culture must always have a deeper interest for all Aryan nations. We cannot fix the earliest date of Indian civilisation, but we know from records which have been unearthed in Babylon and Egypt, that some two or three thousand years before Christ, a Sanscrit-speaking nation, *i. e.* the ancient Hindus, lived on the banks of the Indus, and exported cotton and other products and manufactures of their land to Babylonia and to Egypt. For many centuries the Hindus lived in the Punjab, and it was there that they composed these beautiful hymns in their beautiful Sanscrit language, some of which are still left to us and are known under the collective name of the 'Rig Veda.' The period during which the Hindus lived in the Punjab is therefore known as the Vedic Age, and extended from some unknown date, two or three thousand years before Christ, to about fourteen or fifteen hundred years before the Christian era.

But to-night I wish to speak—not of the remote Vedic Age—but of the next succeeding age, the Epic Age of ancient India, extending from fourteen or fifteen hundred years B.C. to about a thousand or eight hundred years B.C. You will, therefore, perceive that the Epic Age of India partially corresponds in point of time with the Epic Age of Greece, and that the great war of the 'Maha-Bharata' was contemporaneous, within a century or two, with the Trojan War. But while the Epic Age of Greece was the very infancy of Greek civilisation, the Epic Age of India is a comparatively recent period of Indian history, and comes after a long period of an anterior and remote civilisation. India was old in her civilisation in the eleventh, twelfth, and thirteenth centuries before Christ, when Greece was in her early infancy, receiving her first nourishment from the East.

In this Epic Age, extending, roughly speaking, from 1500 to 1000 B.C., the whole of Northern India had attained a high state of civilisation, and was parcelled out into small states and kingdoms, flourishing side by side, bound together by a common language, a common civilisation, and a common religion, and thus forming a great confederation of cultured Hindu nations. Among these nations there were four which distinguished themselves above the rest by their prowess, arts, and civilisation. Two of these nations, the Kurus and the Panchalas, lived along the upper course of the Ganges, and their great war is celebrated in the great epic, the 'Maha-Bharata,' which may justly be called the Iliad of ancient India. Two other nations, the Kosalas and the Videhas, lived in the tracts of the country now known as Oudh and North Behar, and their supposed deeds are celebrated in another old

Indian epic, the 'Ramayana,' which may be called the Odyssey of ancient India. These are the two great epics of ancient India, and it is of the first of these, the Iliad of India, that I wish to give a brief account to-night.

The 'Maha-Bharata' is a vast and encyclopædic work, and is, in fact, the growth of ages. Its subject is a great war of the Kurus or Bharatas—hence the name 'Maha-Bharata,' which means the great Bharata nation,—and the authorship of the work is ascribed to to a saint, Vyasa, who is suppposed to have lived at the time of the war. But apparently the work has grown with the lapse of centuries. Songs and ballads relating to the war were composed and recited in the courts of Northern India during the centuries immediately succeeding the event, and thus the war became the centre of a cycle of poems, traditions, and legends, a thousand years before Christ, even as Arthur and Charlemagne became the centres of legends and songs in Europe a thousand years after Christ. The real facts of the war were obliterated by age; legendary or mythological heroes became the principal actors, and thus an imaginary account of an historical event grew up and became the national epic of the great confederation of ancient Hindu nations. Every succeeding generation of poets had something to add, every distant nation of Northern India interpolated some account of its deeds in the old national chronicle, every preacher of a new creed sought to have in it some sanction for the truths he promulgated. Legal codes and rules of caste were interpolated, and all the floating mass of tales, traditions, legends, and myths, for which ancient India was always famous, found shelter under the expanding wings of this wonderful epic. By the first centuries after Christ the epic had grown to nearly its present proportions, a poem of over ninety thousand couplets, in which the crystal rill of the epic itself is almost lost in a sea-like delta of religious and didactic episodes, legends, and myths, tales and traditions.

To ancient Indians this storehouse and encyclopædia of Indian thought and tradition was suitable because it was the study of their life-time But the modern reader has a wider field of knowledge and a greater variety of subjects before him ; he has to economise his time and to arrange and classify his subjects ; and in order to judge the great Indian epic he has to sift it from the mass of superincumbent matter in which he finds it embedded. Fortunately this is still possible. The leading incidents and characters of the 'Maha-Bharata' are still clearly discernible, uninjured by the mass of foreign matter in which they lie covered, even as the immortal marbles of ancient Greece and Rome remained embedded in earth or amidst ruins for centuries, and have now been recovered, and form the most valuable treasures of the museums of modern Europe. It is in this manner that the leading story of the ancient Indian epic has to be recovered, and to be judged as an epic, and as a work of art.

Judged in this way the Indian epic will be pronounced one of the greatest works of art the human mind has ever conceived. And it is in that highest form of art—the delineation of human character and the development of human incidents—that the 'Maha-Bharata' takes its pre-eminent place among the master works of the world. No work of the imagination, except perhaps the Iliad, is so rich and so true as this Indian epic in the portraiture of the human character —not in torment and suffering as in Dante, not under strong and overwhelming passions as in Shakespeare, but human character in its calm dignity, in healthy action and in healthy repose.

As we read this venerable, ancient poem, the first epic of the Aryan race, the characters live and move round us, act and suffer amid us, distinct and lifelike, and with all the simplicity and truth of ancient life. The old monarch of the Kurus, sightless and feeble, but majestic in his ancient grandeur, is the Priam of the Indian Iliad. The venerable Bhishma, righteous and truthful and unconquerable in war; the doughty Drona, a warrior priest and a Brahman fighter; the proud and fiery Karna—each of them has a distinct character of his own.

The righteous and pious Yudhishthir, the stalwart and "tiger-waisted" Bhima, and the accomplished and "helmet-wearing" Arjun, are the Agamemnon, the Ajax, and the Achilles of the Indian epic. The Kuru prince Duryodhan is proud and jealous, vindictive and relentless, and as a character of flesh and blood, as a man of undying hatred and unyielding determination, has no superior in the epic of any nation. And

Krishna possesses a character higher than that of Ulysses; unmatched in human wisdom, ever striving for justice and peace, he is unrelenting in war when war has begun. And the women of the Indian epic possess characters equally marked and pronounced. The stately and majestic Kuru queen Gandhari; the doting and loving mother Pritha; the proud and scornful Draupadi, nursing her wrath till her wrongs are fearfully revenged; and the bright and brilliant and sunny Subhadra—these are distinct images pencilled by the hand of a true master in the realms of creative imagination.

Such is the opinion which is formed from the study of the epic as an epic, separated and recovered from the mass of foreign matter in which it lies embedded.

I may perhaps be permitted to mention here that I have myself recently ventured to attempt this task, and to translate into English verse those portions of the 'Maha-Bharata' which narate the leading incidents of the real epic. My plan is very simple; I have added nothing to the original, and, except in the description of the actual war itself, I have condensed very little. I have simply selected those passages which tell the leading incidents of the epic, separated them from all episodical matter, and have placed them before the English reader in an English metre which best preserves the rhythmical movement, the sweep and majestic flow of the Sanscrit *Sloka*. I have generally rendered each Sanscrit couplet into a corresponding Engiish couplet, thereby making my translation tolerably faithful; but

I have not attempted a literal, word for word translation, but have rather sought to convey the spirit and the full import and significance of the original in my English version. I may be pardoned for making these few remarks about my own work ; it was necessary to do so, as in the brief narration of the story of the epic which I am about to undertake it will be necessary to read a few passages from my own translation. I may add that while the selected passages which I have translated virtually tell the story within the reasonable limit of about 2000 English couplets, instead of 90,000 couplets as in the original work. With these remarks I now turn to the story.

According to the epic, Pandu was the king of the Kurus or Bharatas, but died early. His brother Dhrita-rashtra became king, and brought up the five sons of Pandu along with his own hundred sons. The jealousies and wars between those cousins, *i. e.* between the five sons of Pandu and the hundred sons of Dhrita-rashtra, form the subject of the epic.

Yudhisthir, the eldest son of Pandu, was a man of truth and piety. Bhima, the second son, was a stalwart fighter, and, as I have said before, is the Ajax of the poem. Arjun, the third son, is the hero, the Achiles of the poem. On the other side, Duryodhan, the eldest son of the Kuru king, was renowned for his strength of character and his undying hatred for his cousins.

The princes were all instructed in arms, and a great tournament was held, in which the five sons of Pandu and the hundred sons of Dhrita-rashtra showed their proficiency in arms. Arjun, the third son of Pandu, excelled all others, until suddenly an unknown warrior, Karna, entered the arena, and then Arjun met his equal and his lifelong rival. The rivalry between Arjun and Karna is the leading thought of the Indian epic, as the rivalry between Achilles and Hector is the leading thought of the Greek epic.

I will quote only a few lines describing the first advent of these great rivals—the real heroes of the epic—on the field of tournament.

THE ADVENT OF ARJUN.

Gauntleted and jewel-girdled, with his bow of ample height,
Archer Arjun, pious-hearted, to the gods performed a rite;
Then he stepped forth proud and stately in his golden mail encased,
Like the sunlit cloud of evening with the radiant rainbow graced;
And a gladness stirred the people all around the listed plain,
Beat of drum and blare of trumpet rose with *Sankha's* festive strain!
"Mark the gallant son of Pandu, whom the happy Pritha bore;
Mark the heir of Indra's prowess, matchless in his arms and lore;
Mark the chief of dauntless valour, peerless in his skill of arms;
Mark the prince of stainless virtue, decked with grace and varied charms!"
Pritha heard such grateful accents borne aloft unto the sky,
Milk of love suffused her bosom, tear of joy was in her eye!

* * * * *

Now the voices of the people died away and all was still;
Arjun to his proud preceptor showed his might and matchless skill,
Towering high or lowly bending, on the turf or on his car,
With his bow and ample quiver Arjun waged the mimic war.
Targets on the wide arena, mighty tough or wondrous small,
With his arrows still unfailing, Arjun pierced them one and all;

Wild-boar shaped in plates of iron coursed the wide extending field,
In its jaws five glist'ning arrows sent the archer wondrous skilled;
Cow-horn by a thread suspended was by winds unceasing swayed,
One and twenty well-aimed arrows on this moving mark he laid;
And with equal skill his rapier did the god-like Arjun wield,
Whirling round his mace of battle ranged the spacious tourney field!

The Advent of Karna.

Now the feats of arms are ended, and the closing hour draws nigh,
Music's voice is hushed in silence, slow disperse the passers by,
Hark! like welkin-shaking thunder wakes a deep and deadly sound,
Clank and din of warlike weapons burst upon the tented ground!
Are the solid mountains splitting? Is it bursting of the earth?
Is it tempest's pealing accent whence the lightning takes its birth?
Thoughts like these alarm the people, for the sound is dread and high,
And upon the lofty gateway turns the crowd with anxious eye!

*   *   *   *

Pale, before the unknown warrior, gathered nations part in twain,
Conqueror of hostile cities lofty Karna treads the plain,
In his golden mail accoutred, in his rings of yellow gold,
Like a moving cliff in stature towering comes the chieftain bold!
Like a tusker in his fury, like a lion in his ire,
Like the sun in noontide radiance, like the all-consuming fire,
Lion-like in build and muscle, stately as a golden palm,
Blessed with every manly virtue, peerless, dauntless, proud and calm!

Karna then showed his proficiency in arms, rivalling the hitherto unrivalled Arjun. The crowds applauded him with acclamation, and Prince Duryodhan, who hated his cousins, the sons of Pandu, embraced Karna as his friend and supporter. Arjun was fired by a dark but natural jealousy on meeting this new rival, and angry words were spoken. And a fight between the two rivals was about to ensue, probably ending in the death of one of the combatants; but the day was ended. Evening fell, and the combatants parted—to remain rivals ever after in life and unto death.

The jealousy between the five sons of Pandu and the hundred sons of Dhrita-rashtra increased from day to day, and at last the Pandavs, *i.e.* the sons of Pandu, were exiled. Prince Duryodhan laid a dark scheme to kill them. They were sent to a house in a distant town, and at the appointed time fire was set to this house. But the Pandavs with their mother escaped the conflagration, and travelled unknown in distant lands in the guise of Brahmans.

In course of time they heard of the approaching wedding of the princess of the Panchala kingdom—the renowned Draupadi, the heroine of the epic. Princes and suitors came from all lands, and it was ordained that whoever could hit a distant target through a revolving disc would win the bride. The five Pandavs came to the assembly dressed as Brahmans. After days of rejoicing and feasting the bride Draupadi appeared on the scene. Her brother led her by the hand admist the assembled suitors, and introduced them to her, one by one, thus:

DRAUPADI AND HER SUITORS (*condensed*).

"Brave Duryodhan and his brothers, princes of the Kuruland,
Karna, proud and peerless archer, sister, seek thy noble hand;
And Gandhara's warlike princes, Bhoja's monarch true and bold,
And the son of mighty Drona, all bedecked in gems and gold!
King and prince from Matsya kingdom grace his noble wedding feast,
Monarchs from more distant regions north and south and west and east,
Tamralipta and Kalinga on the eastern ocean wave,
Pattan's port, whose hardy children western ocean's dangers brave!
From the distant land of Madra car-borne monarch Salya came,
And from Dwarka's sea-girt regions Valadeva known to fame,
Valadeva and his brother, Krishna, sprung from Yadu's race,
Of the Vrishni clan descended, soul of truth and righteous grace!
This is mighty Jayadratha, come from Sindhu's sounding shore,
Famed for warlike feats of valour, famed alike for sacred lore;
This is fair Kosala's monarch, whose bright deeds our heralds sing;
This is sturdy Sisupala, Chedi's proud and peerless king!
This is mighty Jarasandha, come from far Magadha's land;
These are other princely suitors, sister, eager for thy hand.
All the wide earth's warlike rulers seek to shoot the distant aim;
Princess, whoso hits the target, choose as thine that prince of fame!"

All the princes and suitors then tried to hit the target, and all failed one after another. Then Arjun, concealed in the guise of a Brahman, rose and performed the feat, and the father of the bride gave away the princess to the victor. The disappointed suitors could stand it no longer. Their humiliation and rage were redoubled when they saw a youth, apparently of the Brahman or priestly caste, win the bride whom the kings of the Kshatra or warrior caste had failed to win. And in a moment of anger they rose in tumult, determined to kill the bride's father in their wrath. I read a few lines here, as the account of the disappointed suitors in the 'Maha-Bharata' reminds one of a well-known passage in Homer's Odyssey.

The Rage of Disappointed Suitors.

Spake the suitors, anger-shaken, like a forest tempest-torn,
As Panchala's courteous monarch came to greet a Brahman-born:
"Shall he like the grass of jungle trample us in haughty pride,
To a prating priest and Brahman wed the proud and peerless bride?
To our hopes like nourished saplings shall he now the fruit deny?
Monarch proud who insults monarchs, sure a traitor's death shall die!
Honour for his rank we know not, have no mercy for his age,
Perish foe of crowned monarchs, victim to our righteous rage!
Hath he asked us to his palace, favoured us with royal grace,
Feasted us with princely bounty but to compass our disgrace?
In this concourse of great monarchs, glorious like a heavenly band,
Doth he find no likely suitor for his beauteous daughter's hand?
And this right of *swayamvara*, so our scared laws ordian,
Is for warlike monarchs only, priests that custom shall not stain!
If this maiden on a Brahman casts her eye, devoid of shame,
Let her expiate her folly in a pyre of blazing flame!
Leave the priestling in his folly, sinning through a Brahman's greed,
For we wage on war with Brahmans and forgive a foolish deed;

Much we owe to holy Brahmans for our kingdom, wealth and life,
Blood of priest or wise preceptor shall not stain our noble strife:
In the blood of sinful Drupad we the righteous laws maintain,
Such disgrace in future ages monarchs shall not meet again!"
Spake the suitors, tiger-hearted, iron-handed, bold and strong,
Fiercely bent on blood and vengeance blindly rose the maddened throng!
On they came, the angry monarchs, thirsting for revengeful strife,
Drupad 'midst the holy Brahmans fled in terror of his life!
Like wild tuskers of the jungle rushed the suitors on their foes,
Calm and bold, against the suitors, Bhima and proud Arjun rose!

The passage reminds one of the scene in the Odyssey in which the suitors of Penelope turned on her unknown husband, and Ulysses and his son were a match for them all. But in the Indian epic this tumult was not followed by actual bloodshed; Krishna, the friend and kinsman of the Pandav brothers, pacified the enraged suitors, and Arjun led away the bride. Here Krishna appears for the first time on the scene as a peace-maker, as a wise and gifted chieftain who strove for right and justice, and throughout the epic he retains his character.

A curious incident here follows, which is somewhat discordant what the customs and manners of the Hindu nation. It is said that five brothers returned with the bride to a potter's house where they were living on alms, according to the custom of Brahmans, and they reported to their mother, "We have received a great gift to-day." Their mother, not knowing what the gift was, replied,

"Enjoy the gift among you in common." And as a mother's mandate is holy in India, and cannot be disregarded, Draupadi became the common wife of the five brothers. The custom of brothers marrying a wife in common prevails in Thibet and among some hill tribes in India, but has never prevailed among the Aryan Hindus in ancient or modern times, and this legend in the Hindu epic is therefore inexplicable.

Judging from the main incidents of the poem, Draupadi might be regarded as wedded to the eldest brother Yudhisthir, though won by the skill of the third brother Arjun. For Bhima, the second brother, had already mated himself to a female in a forest, and had by her a son who distinguished himself afterwards in the great war. Arjun, too, married the sister of Krishna, and had by her a son who also distinguished himself later in the war. On the other hand, the eldest brother Yudhisthir took to himself no wife save Draupadi, and she was crowned with Yudhisthir at the imperial sacrifice which shortly followed. Notwithstanding the legend of the communal marriage, therefore, Draupadi might be regarded as the wife of the eldest brother Yudhisthir, and this assumption would be in keeping with Hindu customs and laws, ancient and modern.

After this marriage, the five brothers came out of their disguise and demanded a share of the Kuru kingdom, and their demand could no longer be gainsaid. The kingdom was divided; Prince Duryodhan retained the best portion on the Ganges, and his cousins got a wild tract of country on the Jumna. They cleared the forest, built a capital on the site of modern Delhi, and performed a great imperial sacrifice at which all the neighbouring kings, including Duryodhan himself, were present by invitation.

The cousins thus ruled two neighbouring kingdoms in peace for many years, but Duryodhan's hatred and jealousy were undying. Yudhisthir, with all his virtues and piety, had one failing—a besetting sin of the age—viz. a passion for gambling. Duryodhan knew this weakness; he challenged Yudhisthir to a game of dice, and defeated him unfairly, using loaded dice. As Yudhisthir lost game after game he was stung with his losses, and with the recklessness of a gambler staked everything and lost everything. He staked his newly acquired kingdom on the Jumna; he staked his brothers' and then his own liberty; and lastly he staked his wife Draupadi and lost her. One of the most stirring passages in the whole poem is the scene where the proud Queen Draupadi is dragged to the Council Hall as a slave woman, and insulted.

Draupadi insulted.

"Silent all? And will no chieftain rise to save a woman's life,
Will no hand or voice be lifted to defend a virtuous wife?
Lost is Kuru's righteous glory, lost is Bharat's ancient name,
Lost is warrior's warlike prowess, lost is monarch's kingly frame!
Wherefore else like painted warriors tamely view this impious scene,
Wherefore gleam not righteous weapons to protect an outraged queen?

Bhishma, hath he lost his virtue ? Drona, hath he lost his might ?
Hath the monarch of the Kurus ceased to battle for the right ?
Wherefore are ye mute and voiceless, councillors of mighty fame,
Vacant eye and palsied right arm watch this deed of Kuru's shame ?
Spake Draupadi slender-waisted, and her words were stern and high,
Anger flamed within her bosom and the tear was in her eye !
And her sparkling speaking glances fell on Pandu's sons like fire,
Stirred in them a mighty passion and a thirst for vengeance dire !
Lost their empire, wealth, and fortune, little recked they for the fall,
But Draupadi's pleading glances like a poniard smote them all !
Darkly frowned the ancient Bhishma, wrathful Drona bit his tongue,
Pale Vidura marked with anger insults on Draupadi flung
Fulsome word nor foul dishonour could their truthful utterance taint,
And they blamed Duryodhan's action when they heard Draupadi's plaint !

* * * *

Madness seized the proud Duryodhan, and inflamed by passion base,
Sought the prince to stain Draupadi with a dire and deep disgrace,
On the proud and peerless woman cast his wicked, lustful eye,
Sought to hold the high-born princess as a slave upon his knee !
Bhima penned his wrath no longer, lightning-like his glance he flung,
And the ancient hall of Kurus with his thunder accents rung :
"May I never reach those mansions where my fathers live on high,
May I never meet ancestors in the bright and happy sky,
If that knee by which thou sinnest Bhima breaks not in his ire,
In the battle's red arena with his weapon dread and dire !"

Red fire flamed on Bhima's forehead, sparkled from his angry eye,
As from tough and gnarled branches quick the crackling red sparks fly!

A tumult was oviated, and the five brothers and Draupadi were spared further insults by the intervention of the blind old King Dhrita-rashtra. He restored to them their liberty, but they were banished to forests for twelve years, to be succeeded by a year of concealment. It was agreed that if they were discovered during this year of concealment they would have to undergo another twelve years of exile by the terms of the sentence.

The hard conditions were faithfully observed. The five brothers with Draupadi spent twelve years in forests and then passed one year in concealment as menial servants of Virata, king of the Matsyas. Arjun, who was so well known, had to disguise his sex and to hide himself in the women's apartments, teaching dancing and music to the females of the royal house. A year passed away thus.

Cattle-lifting was a favourite occupation with ancient Indian chiefs as with those of Homer, and it so happened that Duryodhan came on a cattle-lifting expedition to Matsya-land where the Pandav brothers were concealed. Arjun, a true warrior in his instincts, could not stand this. He issued forth from his concealment among the women of the house; he recovered the cattle; but he was discovered. But the year of concealment had expired, the discovery brought no penalty with it, and the five brothers, having faithfully observed the conditions of exile, now boldly demanded their lost kingdom on the Jumna.

One of the most remarkable portions of this remarkable epic is the Council of War which was held by the five brothers and their many friends to determine on the course to be followed. Each chief rose and made a speech which is truly Homeric in fire and spirit, giving his views as to the plan which should be adopted to recover the lost kingdom.

At last the venerable king of the Panchalas, the father-in-law of Yudhisthir, rose and advocated that policy which has always been found to be the soundest foreign policy in ancient as in modern times. His advice was : "Endeavour to maintain the peace, but be prepared for war."

Priests and Brahmans were sent to Hastinapura in vain ; Duryodhan would not render back the old kingdom to his cousins, and at last Krishna, the wise and righteous peace-maker, went personally to the court of the Kurus to plead for peace before the sightless old monarch, the father of Duryodhan. There is something touching and sublime in this last eloquent appeal for peace on the eve of the most disastrous war of ancient times in India.

I will quote only a few lines from Krishna's long appeal :

Krishna's Speech.

"Ponder yet, O ancient monarch ! Rulers of each distant state,
Nations from the farthest reigns gather thick to court their fate,

Father of a righteous nation! save the princes of the land,
On the armed and fated nations stretch, old man, thy
healing hand!
Say the word, and at thy bidding leaders of each hostile
race,
Not the gory field of battle, but the festive board will
grace,
Robed in jewels, decked in garlands, they will quaff the
ruddy wine,
Greet their foes in mutual kindness, bless thy holy name
and thine!
Think, O man of many seasons! when good Pandu left this
throne,
And his helpless loving orphans thou didst cherish as thine
own,
'Twas thy helping, steadying fingers taught their infant
steps to frame,
'Twas thy loving gentle accents taught their lips to lisp
each name.
As thine own they grew and blossomed, dear to thee they
yet remain,
Take them back unto thy bosom, be a father once again!
Take their love, O gracious monarch! let thy closing days
be fair,
Let Duryodhan keep his kingdom, let the Pandavs have
their share!
Call to mind their noble suffering, for the tale is dark and
long,
Of the outrage they have suffered, of the insult and the
wrong!
Exiled into Varnavata, destined unto death by flame,
For the gods assist the righteous, they with added prowess
came!
Exiled unto Indra-prastha, by their toil and by their might,
They upreared a mighty empire and performed a glorious
rite!
Cheated of their realm and empire, and of all they called
their own,
In the jungle they have wandered, in concealment lived
unknown,
Once more quelling every evil, they are stout of heart and
hand,
Now redeem thy plighted promise, and restore their throne
and land!

Trust me, mighty Dhrita-rashtra! trust me, lords who grace this hall,
Krishna pleads for peace and virtue, blessings unto one and all!
Slaughter not the armed nations, slaughter not thy kith and kin,
Mark not, king, they closing winters with the bloody stain of sin!
Let thy sons and Pandu's children stand beside thy ancient throne,
Cherish peace and cherish virtue, for thy days are almost done!"

The ancient Bhishma, the warlike preceptor Drona, the wise Vidura, all advised peace. The father and mother of Duryodhan too pleaded for peace, but all in vain. Duryodhan was immoveable, and would not restore to his hated cousins their lost kingdom. His answer was plain and unmistakeable, and in keeping with his character.

Duryodhan's Speech.

"What great crime or darkening sorrow shadows o'er my bitter fate,
That ye chiefs and Kuru's monarch mark Duryodhan for your hate?
Speak, what nameless guilt or folly, secret sin to me unknown,
Turns from me your sweet affection, father's love that was my own?
If Yudhisthir, fond of gambling, played a heedless, reckless game,
Lost his empire and his freedom, was it then Duryodhan's blame?
And if freed from shame and bondage in his folly played again,
Lost again and went to exile, wherefore doth he now complain?
Weak are they in friends and forces, feeble is their fitful star,
Wherefore then in pride and folly seek with us unequal war?

Shall we, who to mighty INDRA scarce will do the homage due,
Bow to homeless sons of Pandu and their comrades faint and few ?
Bow to them while warlike Drona leads us as in days of old,
Bhishma greater than the bright-gods, archer Karna true and bold ?
If in dubious game of battle we should forfeit fame and life,
Heaven will ope its golden portals for the warrior slain in strife !
If unbending to our foemen we should press the gory plain,
Stingless is the bed of arrows, death for us will have no pain !
If in past in thoughtless folly once the realm was broke in twain,
Kuru-land is reunited, never shall be split again !
Take my message to my kinsmen, for Duryodhan's words are plain,
Portion of the Kuru empire sons of Pandu seek in vain ;
Town nor village, mart nor hamlet, help us righteous gods in heaven,
Spot that needle's point can cover shall not unto them be given !"

War, fatal war was the consequence, and into the many stirring incidents of the war, or rather the eighteen battles on eighteen successive days, I have not the time to enter. The unconquerable Bhisma led the Kuru forces for ten days and was then slain by an artifice ; the warrior priest, Drona, then led the troops for five days and was slain ; and at last the command of the Kuru army fell on Karna. He held his own for two days ; and the contest between the lifelong rivals Karna and Arjun is the crowning incident of the epic, like the contest between Hector and Achilles in the Iliad. Arjun and Karna were equal in prowess and skill, but Karna's chariot-wheel sank in the earth; he was thus taken at disadvantage, and killed on the seventeenth day of the war.

The last and eighteenth day dawned, and the preceptor Kripa still advised Duryodhan to render back the Jumna territory to Yudhisthir and to make peace with him. A melancholy interest attaches to this last appeal for peace, and to Duryodhan's last and almost sublime refusal to make peace on the eve of his death.

Kripa's Last Appeal and Duryodhan's Reply.

"Bid this battle cease, Duryodhan, pale and fitful is thy star,
Blood enough of friendly nations soaks this crimson field of war!
Bid them live, the few survivors of a vast and countless host,
Let thy few remaining brothers live, for many are the lost!
Kindly heart hath good Yudhisthir, still he seeks for rightful peace,
Render back his ancient kingdom, bid this war of kinsmen cease!"
"Kripa," so Duryodhan answered, "in this sad and fatal strife,
Ever foremost of our warriors, ever careless of thy life,
Ever in the council chamber thou hast words of wisdom said,
Needless war and dire destruction by thy peaceful council stayed,
Every word thou speakest, Kripa, is a word of truth and weight,
Nathless thy advice for concord, wise preceptor, comes too late!
Hope not that the good Yudhisthir will again our friendship own,
Cheated once by deep Sakuni of his kingdom and his throne,
Rugged Bhima will not palter, fatal is the vow he made,
Vengeful Arjun will not pardon gallant Abhimanyu dead!

Fair Draupadi doth her penance, so our ancient matrons say,
In our blood to wash her insult and her proud insulters slay,
Fair Subhadra morn and evening weeps her dear departed son,
Feeds Draupadi's deathless anger for the hero dead and gone.
Deeply in their bosoms rankle wrongs and insults we have given,
Blood alone can wash it, Kripa, such the cruel will of Heaven!
And the hour for peace is over, for our best sleep on the plain,
Brothers, kinsmen, friends, and elders slumber with the countless slain.
Shall Duryodhan like a recreant now avoid the deathful strife.
After all his bravest warriors have in war surrendered life?
Shall he, sending them to slaughter, now survive and learn to flee,
Shall he, ruler over monarchs, learn to bend the servile knee?
Proud Duryodhan sues no favour even with his dying breath,
Unsubdued and still unconquered, changeless even unto death!
Salya, valiant king of Madra, leads our armed hosts to-day,
Or to perish or to conquer, gallant Kripa, lead the way!"

I confess that passages like this, of which the great Indian epic is full, disclose to me that deep insight into human feelings, and that true portraiture of human character, which mark the greatest poets of all ages and and among all nations. For, let it be remembered that Duryodhan is not a favourite of the Indian poet; he has been depicted as cruel, vindictive, and faithless. But nevertheless a true poet does not pile on colour on his canvas like an unskilful painter; there is a certain consistency and true delineation of human impulses in all his characters. And Duryodhan, the wrong-doer and the faithless, almost commands our admiration on the eve of his death for the deep determination of his character—the unfaltering resolution of a great man, if not a good man.

The result of the day was fatal; the Kuru army was slaughtered, and Duryodhan at last ran from the field of battle and hid himself beside a lake, which is still pointed out to thousands of pilgrims in India who annually visit the scene of the battle.

Duryodhan's Death.

Far from battle's toil and slaughter, by a dark and limpid lake,
Sad and slow and faint Duryodhan did his humble shelter take;
But the valiant sons of Pandu, with the hunter's watchful care
Thither tracked their fallen foeman like a wild beast in its lair!
"Gods be witness," said Duryodhan, flaming in his shame and wrath,
"Boy to manhood ever hating we have crossed each other's path.
Now we meet to part no longer, proud Duryodhan fights you all;
Perish he, or sons of Pandu, may this evening see your fall!"
Bhima answered: "For the insults long endured not forgiven,
Me alone you fight, Duryodhan, witness righteous Gods in heaven!
Call to mind the dark destruction planned of old in fiendish ire,
In the halls of Varnavata to consume us in the fire!
Call to mind the scheme deceitful, deep Sakuni's dark device,
Cheating us of fame and empire by the trick of loaded dice!

Call to mind that coward insult, and the outrage foul and keen,
Flung on Drupad's saintly daughter and our noble spotless queen!
Call to mind the stainless Bhishma, for thy sins and folly slain,
Priest and proud preceptor Drona, Karna lifeless on the plain!
Perish in thy sins, Duryodhan, perish, too, thy hated name,
And thy dark life crime-polluted ends, Duryodhan, in thy shame!"

Bhima and Duryodhan fought, and Bhima kept the terrible vow he had taken and broke Duryodhan's knee by his mace. A midnight slaughter in the camp of the Pandavs ended the war, and Duryodhan died in the early morning.

The real epic ends with the war, and with the funerals of the deceased warriors piously ordered by the victor Yudhisthir for friends and foes alike. Yudhisthir then ascended the throne of the Kuru kingdom, and performed the ancient and august ceremony of the Sacrifice of the Horse. Afterwards, placing a grandson of Arjun on the throne, the five brothers and Draupadi retired to the Himalayas.

This is what is known as the Great Journey. Draupadi drops down dead, then Yudhisthir's brothers one by one. Yudhisthir proceeds to heaven in person.

There he meets Krishna, now in his radiant heavenly form and he meets his brothers now Immortals in the sky. The god Indra then introduces him to his wife Draupadi, to the old monarch Dhrita-rashtra, to Karna, and to Arjun's son. Indra also introduces him to his father, and to the venerable Bhishma and Drona, in these verses which are the last that I shall quote.

IMMORTAL LIFE.

"This, Yudhisthir, is thy father by thy mother joined in heaven,
Oft he comes into my mansions in his flowery chariot driven,
This is Bhishma, stainless warrior, by the *Vasus* is his place,
By the God of heavenly wisdom teacher Drona sits in grace!
These and other mighty warriors, in the earthly battle slain,
By their valour and their virtue walk the bright ethereal plain!
They have cast their mortal bodies, crossed the radiant gate of heaven,
For to win celestial mansions unto mortals it is given?
Let them strive by kindly action, gentle speech, endurance long,
Brighter life and holier future unto sons of men belong!"

This is the briefest outline of the leading story of the great epic of India, venerated in ancient times, venerated to the present day. The Hindu scarcely lives, as I have said elsewhere, man or woman, high or low, educated or ignorant, whose earliest recollections do dot cling round the story of this ancient epic. The humble manufacturer and artisan of Bengal still spells out some modern translation of this undying tale. The tall peasantry of the North-West and the Punjab know of the five Pandav brothers and the righteous Krishna. The people of Bombay and of Madras cherish with equal ardour this sacred tale. Mothers in India know no better theme for imparting instruction to their daughters than this deathless tale. Elderly men know no richer work for narrating stories to children than this great epic with its endless episodes. The *Maha-Bharata*, together with the other epic, the *Ramayana*, is more truly the national property of the Hindus than is Homer in Greece, Dante in Italy, or Shakespeare in England. No work except the Bible has such influence in forming the character of men in Christian lands as the ancient epics in India. They have been our cherished heritage for three thousand years, they are the intellectual food of a nation of two hundred millions to this day. And unless I am very much mistaken in my estimate, the Indian epics, when they are better known in Europe, shall take their rank, along with Homer and Dante and Shakespeare, as undying works of art, left for all times, for all countries, and for all mankind.

XIII. RAMAYANA, THE ODYSSEY OF INDIA.

[*Paper read before the Royal Society of Literature, London, on October* 24, 1900, *Lord Halsbury, Lord Chancellor, presiding.*]

It is little over a year ago that I had the privilege of reading in these rooms a paper on the *Mahabharata*, the Iliad of Ancient India. It gives me great pleasure to appear before you again to-night, and to read a short paper on the *Ramayana*, which may not be inappropriately described as the Odyssey of Ancient India. These two great epics, the *Mahabharata* and the *Ramayana*, comprise the whole of the epic literature of ancient India, and therefore stand apart from all the other literary productions of that country, rich and fertile as that country has always been in the highest results in every department of literature, poetry, and science.

This learned Sociey, while it very properly devotes the greater portion of its time to the literature and thought of England, has nevertheless encouraged researches into the literatures of other lands and of other times and has from time to time endeavoured to interest Englishmen in all that is best and truest in the world's literary achievements. All that interests the cultured mind in the productions of various ages and various nations has occasionly been the subject of papers which have been read within these rooms. The works of Dante and of Moliere and of Goethe are as familiar to many members of this Society as the works of Chaucer and of Shakespeare; and the works of the ancients have not unfrequently formed the subjects of discussion in this hall. I rejoice, therefore, that this Society occasionally turns its attention to the rich literature of India; and as a Fellow of this Society I consider it a proud privilege to have placed before this Society, and before English readers generally, a condensed metrical translation of the two vast Indian epics.

There are special reasons why Englishmen should feel a living interest in India's ancient literature. The beauty of ancient thought, and graphic pictures of ancient life, must always appeal to modern nations of all countries. But more than this, Great Britain and her colonies and India form to-day one great empire—the greatest that the world has yet seen. It is necessary that there should be not only community of interests, but community of thought and feeling within this great empire. And it is necessary that Englishmen should appreciate Indian thought and culture as we in India appreciate English thought. For, believe me, your greatest authors, your noblest poets, your boldest philosophers, are not more closely studied in Oxford and in Cambridge, in Edinburgh, and in London, than they are studied and appreciated in Calcutta and in Bombay. Shakespeare's matchless creations are a living world to thousands of Indian students; Milton and Wordsworth and Tennyson are studied with reverent admiration in India; the great Walter Scott fascinates, and the inimitable Charles Dickens amuses, ten thousands of Hindu and Musalman boys! Young India appreciates English thought and literature: it is necessary that Englishmen and English-women should understand ancient Indian thought, which permeates modern Indian life and institutions to a far greater extent than we generally imagine. The great past is not dead and buried in India; past traditions, past institutions, even ancient poetry and romance, are a living reality in India of the present day, in India not of the educated and cultured few, but of the millions of agriculturists and labourers who till her grateful soil, people her shady villages, and know more of Krishna and Rama than they know of all the heroes of the modern world. To be in touch with the people of modern India you must know her ancient traditions; to ignore her ancient thoughts is to isolate yourselves from modern India.

There are learned translations of oriental literature prepared by generations of devoted scholars, and which appeal mainly to scholars. It is necessary that the average reader and the busy man of work should have before him more handy and readable and attractive works, reproducing, as far as possible, the spirit, and the beauty, and the true significance of Indian poetry and Indian thought. This work has not yet been done. There is an undiscovered world for Englishmen still to explore, an undiscovered mine for literary miners to work upon; and I can assure you that the labour will not be thrown away, and Englishmen, even with a splendid literature of their own, will be all the richer when they possess themselves of Indian thought and literature. And the world will be richer in its wealth of ideas, when all that is beautiful and true in eastern culture is added to all that is fresh and vigorous in modern European thought.

India has a long, and a not inglorious, ancient history. It may be two thousand years before Christ that the ancestors of the present Aryan Hindu nation were settled on the banks of the Indus, conquering the Punjab from the aboriginal inhabitants of the soil, extending cultivation and the arts of peace, and invoking the "bright gods" of Nature in beautiful hymns which have been still left to us in that collection known as the *Rig Veda*, which is the oldest literary work now extant among the Aryan nations of the earth. For several centuries the Aryan conquerors were confined to the Punjab; their numerous petty states and kingdoms, their wars against aborigines, and their arts of peace, were all confined to that land of five rivers, or rather the land of seven rivers as it was then called; and the rest of India which lay beyond was almost unknown to them. This long period of the Aryan settlements in the Punjab is generally known as the Vèdic Age; so called from the Veda to which allusion has been already made. But I do not propose to-night to speak of this first and earliest period of Indian history.

It was in the subsequent age that the Aryan Hindus, issuing from the Punjab, spread over the whole of Northern India, and founded powerful kingdoms on the banks of the Ganges and the Jumna. It is this second period of ancient Indian history which is known as the

Epic Age, because the two epics of India described the kingdoms and the nations which flourished in Northern India during this age. It is of this second age of Indian history, this Epic Age as it is generally called, extedning from the fifteenth to the tenth century B.C., that I propose to speak to-night.

Among the many powerful nations which flourished in Northern India in this age, the Bharatas and the Panchalas were the most celebrated in the west, and the Kosalas and the Videhas were the most celebrated in the east. The Bharatas and the Panchalas lived along the upper course of the Ganges, *i. e.* in the country between modern Delhi and Kanouj: and the Kosalas and the Videhas lived further to the east, *i. e.* in those provinces which we now know as Oudh and North Behar. The deeds or legends of the western tribes, the Bharatas and the Panchalas, are described in the great epic known as the *Mahabharata*; while the deeds or legends of the eastern tribes, the Kosalas and the Videhas, are described in the other great epic known as the *Ramayana*. The *Mahabharata* may, therefore, be described as the epic of the Western Aryans; the *Ramayana* as the epic of the Eastern Aryans.

But this is not the only distinction between the two epics. The nations of North-western India have generally been known for their sturdy and warlike virtues; while those of North-eastern India have been known for their peacefulness and their culture; and this distinction pervades the two epics. The characters of the *Mahabharata* are men of flesh and blood, with the virtues and crimes of great actors in the historic world; the characters of the *Ramayana* are more often ideals of manly devotion to truth and of womanly faithfulness and love. The poet of the *Mahabharata* describes the supposed incidents of a real and sanguinary war with all its lofty heroism and chivalry; the poet of the *Ramayana* hands down the memories of a golden age with all its ideals of piety and faith and domestic love. As a heroic poem the *Mahabharata* stands on a higher level; as a religious poem, delineating the softer emotions of our everyday life, the *Ramayana* sends its roots deeper into the Hindu mind.

These remarks will be best illustrated if I narrate to you briefly the story of the *Ramayana*, as I narrated to you the story of the *Mahabharata* last year. I may remark, in passing, that the *Mahabharata* in Sanscrit consists of more than 90,000 verses, and that the *Ramayana* consists of more than 24,000 verses. In condensing these vast epics I have not attempted to tell the story in my own language; but I have selected those portions of the original which tell the leading incidents, and have translated them in full; and I have connected these selected passages by short notes so as to place the complete story before the reader. The plan has this advantage, that the main story of the epics is told, not by the translator in his own way, but by the poet himself; the passages placed before the reader are not the translator's abridgements of long poems, but are passages from the original poems. It is the ancient poets of India, and not the translator, who narrate the ancient story; bnt they narrate only the leading incidents of the story, so as to limit the poems within a reasonable compass. I may add that the *Ramayana*, like the *Mahabharata*, is a growth of ages; generations of later Indian poets adding their quota of verses through long centuries to the poem as it originally stood. It is possible, therefore, that in limiting my translation to those passages which describe the leading incidents, I have presented the great poem somewhat in the form in which it originally stood, and in which it was first recited in the Courts of Northern India. And I have generally translated each Sanscrit verse into a corresponding English verse, following the Sanscrit metre in English as far as was possible. I may be pardoned for making these few remarks about my own work; it was necessary to do so, as I shall have to quote pretty often from my own translation. And here I should also make some mention of my great predecessors in this work—of Gorresio, who completed an Italian translation of the *Ramayana* in 1867; of Hippolyte Fauche, who completed a French translation of the epic shortly after; and of Ralph Griffith, who has given us an almost complete rendering of it in six octavo volumes of English verse.

With these preliminary remarks, I will now turn to the story of the epic itself. The *Ramayana* virtually commences with a description of the kingdom of Ayodhya or Oudh, then ruled by the ancient monarch Dasa-ratha. In this description we have at once the ideal of an ancient Hindu king and of an ancient Hindu people ; and the passage is important as depicting the Hindu conception of a golden age. I will therefore read a few verses.

Like the ancient monarch Manu, father of the human race,
Dasa-ratha ruled his people with a father's loving grace,
Truth and justice swayed each action and each baser motive quelled,
People's Love and Monarch's Duty every thought and deed impelled,
And his town like INDRA's city—tower and dome and turret brave—
Rose in proud and peerless beauty on Sarayu's limpid wave!
Peaceful lived the righteous people, rich in wealth, in merit high,
Envy dwelt not in their bosoms, and their accents shaped no lie.
Fathers, with their happy households, owned their cattle, corn, and gold ;
Galling penury and famine in Ayodhya had no hold.
Neighbours lived in mutual kindness, helpful with their ample wealth ;
None who begged the wasted refuse, none who lived by fraud and stealth!
And they wore the gem and earring, wreath and fragrant sandal paste,
And their arms were decked with bracelets, and their necks with *nishkas* graced ;
Cheat and braggart and deceiver lived not in the ancient town ;
Proud despiser of the lowly wore no insults in their frown ;
Poorer fed not on the richer, hireling friend upon the great,
None with low and lying accents did upon the proud man wait!
Men to plighted vows were faithful, faithful was each loving wife ;
Impure thought and wandering fancy stained not holy wedded life.
Robed in gold and graceful garments, fair in form and fair in face,
Winsome were Ayodhya's daughters, rich in wit and woman's grace!

Like other monarchs of the East, Dasa-ratha rejoiced in a large household, and in the company of many queens, and three of these queens were the foremost in rank, and shared among them the affections of their lord. Kausalya, the eldest queen, was the mother of Rama, the hero of the epic. Kaikeyi, a young and beautiful and imperious queen, was the mother of Bharat. Sumitra, the third queen, gave birth to twins, one of whom, Lakhsman, became the faithful and devoted follower of his elder brother Rama. The names of these two loving brothers, Rama and Lakshman, are to this day household words in every Hindu home.

So far we have confined ourselves to the story of the royal family of Oudh ; let us now turn to the adjoining kingdom of Videha or North Behar. That ancient kingdom was ruled by a pious and learned king, Janaka ; and Janaka had a lovely daughter, Sita, the heroine of the epic. Suitors from distant lands came for the hand of Sita, for Janaka, like the warriors of olden times, had declared—

> "He shall win my peerless Sita who shall bend my bow of war !"

That bow was a god-given weapon, tremendous in its size and weight ; and many princes who came to seek the hand of Sita failed to bend the bow and went back humbled and disappointed. Rama and his faithful brother Lakshman came wandering from their own kingdom to the kingdom of Janaka, and the mighty weapon was produced before Rama, so that he, too, might try his strength and skill.

Wond'ring gazed the kings assembled as the son of Raghu's
race,
Proudly raised the mighty weapon with a warrior's stately
grace,
Proudly strung the bow of Rudra which the kings had tried
in vain,
Drew the cord with force resistless till the weapon snapped
in twain!

The astonished and gratified monarch of Videha kept his promise ; the lovely Sita was wedded to Rama ; and the proud and victorious prince returned with his bride to his own land amidst the blessings of Brahmans and the acclamations of the people.

Years passed away and Rama grew in grace and learning and valour ; and, according to an ancient Indian custom, his old father desired to place on him the burden of the kingdom, and to pass his few remaining years in religious rites and pious meditation. The old king's increasing feebleness, and Rama's growing worth and abilities, alike pointed to this course as the most expedient and in the poet's description of Rama's virtues we see once more a Hindu's ideal of a model prince, bold in war, rich in learning, loving and bounteous towards his people.

For his Rama strong and stately was his eldest and his best,
Void of every baser passion and with every virtue blest.
Soft in speech, sedate and peaceful, seeking still the holy path,
Calm in conscious worth and valour, taunt nor cavil waked
his wrath,
In the field of war excelling, boldest warrior 'midst the bold,
In the palace chambers listening to the tales by elders told,
Faithful to the wise and learned, truthful in his deed and
word,
Rama dearly loved his people and his people loved their lord!

To the Brahmans pure and holy Rama due obeisance made,
To the poor and to the helpless deeper love and honour paid,
Spirit of his race and nation was to high-souled Rama given,
Thoughts that widen human glory, deeds that ope the gates of heaven!
Taught by sages and by elders in the manner of his race,
Rama grew in social virtues and each soft endearing grace,
Taught by inborn pride and wisdom patient purpose to conceal,
Deep determined was his effort, dauntless was his silent will!
Peerless in his skill and valour steed and elephant to tame,
Dauntless leader of his forces, matchless in his warlike fame,
Higher thought and nobler duty did the righteous Rama move,
By his toil and by his virtues still he sought his people's love!

Dasa-ratha convened a great council, one of those great assemblages which were summoned by the Hindu kings of ancient India when great questions of State were under consideration. I will not give that council the modern name of a Parliament; but it is a fact that not only the chiefs and peers of the realm, but also representative burghers were invited from the towns and villages of Oudh to advise their king. And Dasa-ratha spake to them:

"Known to all, the race of Raghu rules this empire broad and fair,
And hath ever loved and cherished subjects with a father's care,
In my father's footsteps treading I have sought the ancient path,
Nursed my people as my children, free from passion, pride and wrath,
Underneath this white umbrella, seated on this royal throne,
I have toiled to win their welfare and my task is almost done!

Years have passed of fruitful labour, years of work by fortune blest,
And the evening of my life-time needs, my friends, the evening's rest.
Years have passed in watchful effort, Law and Duty to uphold,
Effort needing strength and prowess—and my feeble limbs are old!
Peers and burghers, let your monarch, now his lifelong labour done,
For the weal of loving subjects on his empire seat his son,
Speak your thought and from this bosom lift a load of toil and care,
On the proud throne of my fathers let me place a peerless heir;
Speak your thought, my chiefs and people, if this purpose please you well,
Or if wiser, better counsel in your wisdom ye can tell,
Speak your thought without compulsion, though this plan to me be dear,
If some middle course were wiser, if some other way were clear!"

It is needless to state that the people, by whom their prince was dearly loved, approved of their old king's suggestion, and gave their consent by acclamation; and preparations were made to decorate the city of Ayodhya or Oudh in a manner suitable to the occasion. As we read the account of these decorations we realise how much of the life and manners of ancient India survives to the present day in modern India; and every Englishman who has passed year of his life in India will realise in the following verses, written thousands of years ago, a not unfaithful description of the way in which towns and marts are decorated in India in these days, to evince the loyalty of a grateful people to those rulers whom they love to honour.

Rama shall be Heir and Regent, Rama shall be crowned to-day—
Rapid flew the gladdening message with the morning's gladsome ray,
And the people of the city, maid and matron, man and boy,
Decorated fair Ayodhya in their wild tumultuous joy!
On the temple's lofty steeple high as cloud above the air,
On the crossing of the pathways, in the garden green and fair,
On the merchant's ample warehouse, on the shop with stores displayed,
On the mansion of the noble by the cunning artist made,
On the gay and bright pavilion, on the high and shady trees,
Banners rose and glittering streamers, flags that fluttered in the breeze!
Actors gay and nimble dancers, singers skilled in lightsome song,
With their antics and their music pleased the gay and gathered throng,
And the people met in conclaves, spake of Rama, Regent Heir,
And the children by the roadside lisped of Sita, sweet and fair!
Women wove the scented garland, merry maids the censer lit,
Men with broom and sprinkled water swept the spacious mart and street,
Rows of trees and posts they planted hung with lamps for coming night,
That the midnight dark might rival splendour of the noon-day light!
Troops of men and merry children laboured with a loving care,
Woman's skill and woman's fancy made the city passing fair,
So that good and kindly Rama might his people's toil approve,
So that sweet and soft-eyed Sita might accept her people's love!

But while these preparations were made for Rama's coronation as Prince Regent, dark scheme was on foot in the palace. Among the three queens of the palace, Kausalya, the mother of Rama, rejoiced at the prospect of her son's coronation. Kaikeyi, the mother of Bharat, too, looked forward to it with pleasure, until ambition and jealousy were roused in her heart by an old nurse of the family; and this portion of the Epic has always struck me as one of the most powerful in the whole poem. The greatest of English poets conjures up three strange witches to stir up in the soul of Macbeth the first flames of a restless ambition which leads him to deeds of crime and violence; and the poet also gives him a fitting helpmate to speed his flagging purpose and stifle his scruples. With no less dramatic force and true insight into human character, the poet of the *Ramayana* brings on the stage the figure of a crooked-formed and crooked-minded old nurse, who stirs in the mother of Bharat the flames of ambition and of jealousy. She speaks with terrible effect to Bharat's mother when she urges:

"Trust me, queen, thy Bharat's merits are too well and widely known,
And he stands too near and closely by a rival brother's throne;
Rama hath a wolf like wisdom and a fang to reach the foe,
And I tremble for thy Bharat, Heaven avert untimely woe!
Happy is the Queen Kausalya, they will soon anoint her son,
When on Pushya's constellation gaily rides to-morrow's moon;
Happy is the Queen Kausalya in her regal pomp and state,
And Kaikeyi like a bond-slave must upon her rival wait!

Wilt thou do her due obeisance as we humble women do?
Will thy proud and princely Bharat as his brother's henchman go,
Will thy Bharat's gentle consort, fairest princess in this land,
In her tears and in her anguish wait on Sita's proud command?

For a time the Queen Kaikeyi repels these insinuations and answers:

"What inspires thee, wicked woman, thus to rail in bitter tone,
Shall not Rama, best and eldest, fill his father's royal throne?
What alarms thee, crooked woman, in the happy rites begun,
Shall not Rama guard his brothers as a father guards his son?

But the old nurse is importunate. She urges again and again:

"Thou hast borne the princely Bharat, nursed him from thy gentle breast,
To a queen and to a mother need a prince's claims be pressed?
To a thoughtless, heedless mother must I Bharat's virtues plead?
Must the Queen Kaikeyi witness Queen Kausalya's son succeed?
Trust thy old and faithful woman who hath nursed thee, youthful queen,
And in great and princely houses many darksome deeds has seen;
Trust my word, the wily Rama for his spacious empire's good,
Soon will banish friendless Bharat and secure his peace with blood!
Speak thy mandate to thy husband, win thy son a happy fate,
Doom him not to Rama's service or his unrelenting hate;

Let not Rama in his rancour shed a younger brother's blood,
As the lion slays the tiger in the deep and echoing wood!
With the magic of thy beauty thou hast won thy monarch's heart,
Queen Kausalya's bosom rankles with a woman's secret smart;
Let her not with woman's vengeance turn upon her prouder foe,
And as crowned Rama's mother venge her sorrows in thy woe.
Mark my word, my child Kaikeyi, much these ancient eyes have seen.
Rama's rule is death to Bharat insult to my honoured queen!"
Like a slow but deadly poison worked the ancient nurse's tears,
And a wife's undying impulse mingled with a mother's fears;
Deep within Kaikeyi's bosom worked a woman's jealous thought,
Speechless in her silent anger mourner's dark retreat she sought.

The scene which follows is tragic. The old king sought out his beautiful and imperious queen in the mourner's chamber, implored her to state her wishes, and promised with many solemn vows to fulfil them. And then, when the queen disclosed her dark purpose, that her son Bharat should be crowned, and that Rama should be banished to the woods, the feeble old king was stunned and speechless.

It is needless to add that the young wife had her own way, and the dark deed was done. Rama was sentenced to banishment, and heroic in his obedience and duty as he was heroic in feats of arms, Rama left his kingdom and his home without a word of protest.

But the banishment of Rama was the death of his old father. He never recovered from the blow, never forgot the wrong he had done to the best of sons and the best of men. For six days he suffered from the agony of grief and repentance; and, like a pious Hindu, he attributed this suffering to his own misdeeds in past years. Lying on his death-bed he narrated to the mother of Rama the story of his youth: how he had gone to hunt in a forest, how he had killed a hermit's son, how the old and sightless hermit had cursed him for that deed.

"Years have gone and many seasons, and in fulness of the time
Comes the fruit of pride and folly and the harvest of my crime.
Rama, eldest born and dearest, Lakshman true and faithful son,
Ah! forgive a dying father and a cruel action done!
Lay thy hands in mine, Kausalya; wipe thy unavailing tear,
Speak a wife's consoling accents to a dying husband's ear.
Lay thy hands on mine, Sumitra, vision fails my closing eyes,
And for brave and banished Rama wings my spirit to the skies!"

The midnight slowly passed away, and the ancient king died on the seventh morning from that of his son's banishment.

Meanwhile, Rama had not departed to the woods alone. He was followed by his wife Sita; and here the character of Sita—the Hindu ideal of a woman's devotion, faithfulness, and love—comes prominently before the reader. It may be stated without exaggeration that no creation of the human imagination —no character in the literature of ancient Greece or ancient Rome or of modern Europe—has ever had such a hold on the mind of any nation, as the matchless character of Sita among the millions of India. Her womanly love and faithfulness, her unfaltering truth and devotion, her steadfast virtue in trials and temptations—all this is not merely a literary tradition among the learned in India, but a priceless and undying heritage among the millions. There is not a Hindu woman living in that vast continent whose earliest memories of childhood do not cling around the story of the saintly Sita repeated in every Hindu nursery; whose moral education through life is not dominated by the conception of that pure and spotless woman, and whose last yearnings after righteousuess in old age are not inspired and strengthened by the lofty example of that almost divine character.

Rama, banished to the woods for fourteen years, implored Sita to stay behind until his return from banishment, but Sita repelled the idea with woman's pride and a wife's devotion.

"For my mother often taught me and my father often spake,
That her home the wedded woman doth beside her husband make,
As the shadow to the substance, to her lord is faithful wife,
And she parts not from her consort till she parts with fleeting life!

Therefore bid me seek the jungle and in pathless forests roam,
Where the wild deer freely ranges and the tiger makes his home,
Happier than in father's mansions in the woods will Sita rove,
Waste no thought on home or kindred, nestling in her husband's love!
World-renowned is Rama's valour, fearless by her Rama's side,
Sita still will live and wander with a faithful woman's pride,
And the wild fruit she will gather from the fresh and fragrant wood,
And the food by Rama tasted shall be Sita's cherished food!
Bid me seek the sylvan greenwoods, wooded hills and plateaus high,
Limpid rills and crystal *nullas* as they softly ripple by,
And where in the lake of lotus tuneful birds their plumage lave,
Let me with my loving Rama skim the cool translucent wave!
Years will pass in happy union—happiest lot to woman given—
Sita seeks not throne or empire, nor the brighter joys of heaven,
Heaven conceals not brighter mansions in its sunny fields of pride,
Where without her lord and husband faithful Sita would reside!
Therefore let me seek the jungle where the jungle-rangers rove,
Dearer than the royal palace, where I share my husband's love,
And my heart in sweet communion shall my Rama's wishes share,
And my wifely toil shall lighten Rama's load of woe and care!"
Vainly gentle Rama pleaded dangers of the jungle life,
Vainly spake of toil and trial to a true and tender wife!

Lakshman too followed his elder brother to the woods. They left the town of Ayodhya amidst the lamentations of the people ; they stole away at night, and crossed the Tamasa river to avoid the crowds of people who followed them, and they crossed first the Ganges and then the Jumna on their way to the south. The wanderings of exiled Rama through various unknown tracts, which fill a large part of the Epic, remind the reader of the wanderings of Ulysses for many a long year: but the Indian story has a far greater hold on the national mind than the story of the ancient Greeks. The illiterate modern Greeks will be at a loss to narrate the story of their hero's wanderings; but in India, thousands upon thousands of the ignorant and the illiterate make annual pilgrimages along the path which Rama and Sita and Lakshman are supposed to have traversed, thirty centuries ago. The past is not dead or buried in India, it is a living faith and a reality among the millions.

In the meanwhile, while Bharat's mother had succeeded in securing the throne for her son, Bharat himself would not accept it at the price of the banishment of his elder. He left Ayodhya in quest of Rama, crossed the Ganges and the Jumna, found out Rama in the hermitage where he was living as an anchorite, and implored him to return. But Rama's reply was worthy of him, he had received a mandate from his father, and would not violate it.

Among the many discussions which took place in this hermitage, the most remarkable are the arguments of an Indian sceptic, named Jabali. In ancient India, as in ancient Greece, various schools of philosophy flourished side by side, some of them orthodox and some of them exceedingly heterodox and even atheistic, and the greatest latitude of free thought was tolerated. Jabali was a freethinker of the broadest type, denying God, and ridiculing ideas of duty and of a future life; and he pressed Rama to return to his kingdom in words which would stagger even a modern sceptic. He said:

"Wherefore, Rama, idle maxims cloud thy heart and warp thy mind,
Maxims which mislead the simple and the thoughtless human kind?
Love nor friendship doth a mortal to his kith or kindred own,
Entering on this wide earth friendless, and departing all alone.
Foolishly upon the father and mother dotes the son,
Kinship as an idle fancy—save thyself thy kith is none!
In this wayside inn he halteth, who in distant lands doth roam,
Leaves it with the dawning daylight for another transient home.
Thus on earth are kith and kindred, home and country, wealth and store;
We but meet them on our journey, leave them as we pass before!
Ah! I weep for erring mortals, who on erring duty bent
Sacrifice their dear enjoyment till their barren life is spent;
Who to Gods and to the Fathers vainly still their offering make;
Waste of food! for God nor father doth our pious offering take!
Crafty priests have forged these maxims, and with selfish objects say—
Make thy gifts and do thy penance, leave thy worldly wealth and pray!
There is no Hereafter, Rama, vain the hope and creed of men;
Seek the pleasure of the present, spurn illusions poor and vain.

Take the course of sense and wisdom, cast all idle faith
aside,
Take the kingdom Bharat offers, rule Ayodhya in thy
pride!"

But the sophistry of the philosopher had no more influence with Rama than the affectionate pleadings of his brother: and he replied to the philosopher's reasoning in words which gave us an insight into the lofty determination of the great hero of the epic.

"Sweep aside thy crafty reasoning, Truth is still our ancient
way;
Truth sustains the earth and nations and a monarch's
righteous sway.
Mighty Gods and holy sages find in Truth their haven
shore,
Scorning death and dark destruction, Truth survives for
evermore!
Deadlier than the serpent's venom is the venom of a lie,
From the false, than from the cobra, men with deeper
terror fly;
Dearer than the food to mortals, Truth as nourishment is
given;
Truth sustains the wide creation, Truth upholds the highest
heaven!
Vain were gifts and sacrifices, rigid penances were vain
Profitless the holy *Vedas* but for truth which they
sustain;
Gifts and rights and rigid penance have no aim or purpose
high,
Save in Truth, which rules the wide earth and the regions
of the sky!
I have plighted truth and promise, and my word may
not unsay,
Fourteen years in pathless forests father's mandate I
obey;
And I seek no spacious reasons my relinquished throne to
win,
Gods nor Fathers nor the *Vedas* counsel tortuous paths
of sin!

Pardon, *rishi*, still unchanging shall remain my promise given
To thy mother Queen Kaikeyi, to my father now in heaven.
Pardon, *rishi*, still in jungle we shall seek the forest fare,
Worship Gods who watch our actions, and pervade the earth
and air;
And the deep and darksome jungle shall be Rama's royal hall,
For a righteous father's mandate duteous son may not recall!

Failing in his endeavour to induce Rama to return, the younger Bharat returned to Ayodhya; while Rama penetrated into the deeper jungles of the south to avoid fresh solicitations from his friends and relations. Accompanied by his wife and Lakshman, he travelled to the south of the Vindhya mountains, and at last chose his retreat near the sources of the Godavari river, at a place now called Nassik, not far from modern Bombay. Here the faithful Lakshman built a humble leafy cottage, thatched with reeds and jungle grass, and here Rama and his wife passed some of the happiest years of their life in the lone retreat of what was then an interminable wilderness.

The poem takes a new turn now; and we exchange the quiet life of a righteous exile in holy hermitages for the more stirring incidents of war. Ravan was the powerful and terrible king of Ceylon, and Ravan's sister, wandering the wilderness, met Rama and fell in love with him. The too forward maiden was punished by the angry Lakshman, and she went and complained to her royal brother, the king of Ceylon. Ravan meditated a deep revenge, and he lured away Rama and Lakshman from their humble cottage in order to fall on unprotected Sita.

This was the great crisis of Sita's life, when Ravan, disguised as a hermit, approached her lone and unprotected cottage, and the poet describes the critical moment in befitting verse.

Sita, in the simplicity of her heart, still believed the intruder to be a hermit and a guest, offered him the welcome due to a religious man, and narrated to him in her simple and pathetic language the story of her life, and of her husband's banishment into the woods. The scene is dramatic in the highest degree, and the simple tale told by the trustful Sita of her joys and her sorrows to the cruel and crime-polluted Ravan darkly determined on her destruction, is one of the most touching passages in the whole epic.

Ravan at last disclosed himself. And he proposed to Sita that she should leave the homeless Rama, and henceforth be his queen, and the proud Empress of Ceylon. It was then that Sita discovered the terrible nature of her situation; and her natural gentleness and sweetness gave way to the noble wrath of an insulted woman. And she repelled Ravan's proposal with the scorn and indignation of a true wife, proud of her warlike lord. And she said to Ravan:

"Sure thy fitful life is shadowed by dark and dreadful fate,
Since in frenzy of thy passion courtest thou a warrior's mate,
Tear the tooth of hungry lion while upon the calf he feeds,
Touch the fang of deadly cobra while his dying victim bleeds,
Aye, uproot the solid mountain from its base of rocky land,
Ere thou win the wife of Rama, stout of heart and strong of hand!

Pierce thy eye with point of needle till it racks thy tortured head,
Press thy red tongue cleft and bleeding on the razor's shining blade,
Hurl thyself upon the ocean from a towering peak and high,
Snatch the orbs of day and midnight from their spheres in azure sky,
Tongues of flaming conflagration in thy flowing dress enfold,
Ere thou take the wife of Rama to thy distant dungeon hold,
Ere thou seek to insult Rama unrelenting in his wrath,
O'er a bed of pikes of iron tread a softer, easier path!"

But all her threats and protests and entreaties were in vain, the cruel and relentless Ravan seized the unprotected woman, forced her into his chariot, and took her away to Ceylon. The helpless Sita, writhing in agony like a snake in the talons of an eagle, vainly called for the help of Rama and of Laksman, who were far away in the woods ; she invoked the spirits of the woodlands and of the earth and air ; and she doomed Ravan to destruction in words of terrible import and truth.

The account of the invasion of Ceylon by Rama, and of the war which followed, need not detain us long. The aboriginal dwellers of Southern India who helped Rama in this invasion are described by the poet as monkeys and bears ; and the defenders of Ceylon are described as monsters ; and the incidents of the war, though often spirited and stirring, lack the human interest of the war of the *Mahabharata*. As a heroic poem, the *Ramayana* cannot be compared with the *Mahabkarata* ; we miss in the *Ramayana* those stirring descriptions of real battles, and the encounters of real warriors, which strike us so forcibly in the *Mahabharata*. Lakshman the brother of Rama is, however, a truly fine soldier-like character; he kills the terrible son of Ravan in fair fight; and then Rama himself kills Ravan and recovers the stolen Sita.

That saintly woman, who had remained faithful to her wedded lord in all her trials and sorrows, proves her purity by an ordeal of fire, and returns to the embraces of her victorious lord, and they both return to Ayodhya with Lakhsman, the period of exile being now over.

In a fine passage the poet describes the victorious brothers and Sita, sailing over the whole continent of India in an ærial car, crossing over the mighty hills, the majestic rivers, the far-extending woods, and the towns and hamlets and smiling fields which lay beneath them spread out like a map. And when the car performed this marvellous journey from Ceylon to Oudh, the city of Oudh once more decorated herself to her returning lord and monarch.

Bharat rendered back the kingdom of Oudh to Rama, and Rama and Sita were consecrated as king and queen of a happy and joyous nation. And to this day the traditions of the people of India represent the reign of Rama as a period of felicity and happiness when

Trees their ample produce yielded as returning seasons went,
And the earth in grateful gladness never failing hervest lent,
Rains descended in their season, never came the blighting gale,
Rich in crop and rich in pasture was each soft and smiling vale,
Loom and anvil gave their produce and the tilled and fertile soil.
And the nation lived rejoicing in their old ancestral toil!

The real epic of Rama ends here. There is an *Uttara Kanda*, or supplement, which prolongs the story, and gives it a sad and mournful ending; but it is unnecessary to go into that supplemental story to-night. Enough has been said to explain the character of this wonderful ancient poem of the Hindus, embodying the highest ideals of manly devotion to truth and womanly faithfulness and love.

One word more, and I have done. I have remarked elsewhere that in India the *Ramayana* is not merely an ancient epic, but is still a living tradition and a living faith. It forms the basis of the moral instruction of a nation, and it is a part of the lives of two hundred millions of people. It is necessary to add that when the modern languages of India were first formed out of the ancient Sanscrit and Prakrits, in the ninth and tenth centuries after Christ, the *Ramayana* had the greatest influence in inspiring our modern poets and forming our modern tongues. Southern India took the lead, and a translation of the *Ramayana* in the Tamil language appeared as early as 1100 A.D. Northern India and Bengal and Bombay followed the example; Tulasi Das's *Ramayana* is the great classic of the Hindi language, Krittibas's *Ramayana* is a classic in the Bengali language, and Sridhar's *Ramayana* is a classic in the Mahratta language. Generations of Hindus in all parts of India have studied the ancient story in these modern translations; they have heard it recited in the houses of the rich; and they have seen it acted on the stage at religious festivals in every great town and every populous village through the length and breadth of India.

More than this, the story of Rama has inspired our

religious reformers, and purified the popular faith of our modern times. Rama, the true and dutiful, was accepted as the Spirit of God descended on earth, as an incarnation of Vishnu, the Preserver of the World. The great teacher Ramanuja proclaimed the monotheism of Vishnu in Southern India in the twelfth century ; the reformer Ramananda proclaimed the same faith in Northern India in the thirteenth or fourteenth century ; and his follower, the gifted Kabir, conceived the bold idea of uniting Hindus and Mahomedans in the worship of One God. "The God of the Hindus," he said, "is the God of the Mahomedans, be he invoked a *Rama* or *Ali*." "The city of the Hindu God is Benares, and the city of the Mahomedan God is Mecca ; but search your hearts, and there you will find the God both of Hindus and Mahomedans." "If the Creator dwells in tabernacles, whose dwelling is the universe ?"

The reformer Chaitanya preached the same sublime monotheism in Bengal, and the reformer Nanak in the Punjab, in the sixteenth century. And down to the present day the popular mind in India, led away by the worship of many images in many temples, nevertheless holds fast to the cardinal idea of one God, and believes the heroes of the ancient epics—*Krishna* and *Rama*—to be the incarnations of that God.

Down to the present century the lessons of the great epics are a perennial source of instruction to the people of India. Early in this century Reginald Heber, the Bishop of Calcutta, met among the wildest tribes of Western India the great Hindu reformer Swamy Narayan, who had tamed the manners of his countrymen, and preached to them lessons of purity and humanity and the love of God, under the name of Krishna. The Bishop, escorted by the East India Company's guards met the Hindu reformer surrounded by his faithful followers.

"Had our troops been opposed to each other," writes the Lord Bishop of Calcutta, "mine, though less numerous, would have been doubtless far more effective from the superiority of arms and discipline. But, in moral grandeur, what a difference was there between his troops and mine. Mine neither knew me, nor cared for me; they escorted me faithfully, and would have defended me bravely, because they were ordered by their superiors to do so, and as they would have done for any other stranger of sufficient wordly rank to make such an attendance usual. The guards of Swami Narayan were his own disciples and enthusiastic admirers, men who had voluntarily repaired to hear his lessons, who now took a pride in doing him honour, and who would cheerfully fight to the last drop of blood rather than suffer a fringe of his garment to be handled roughly."

The Bishop entered into conversation with the reformer, and this is how the reformer explained his idea of God :

"Many names there may be, and have been, given to Him who *is*, and is the *same*, but whom we also, as well as the other Hindus, call Brahma. But there is a spirit in whom God *is* more specially, and who cometh from God, and is with God, and is likewise God, who hath made known to men the will of God and Father of all, whom we call *Krishna* and worship as God's image."

These are words which the Hindu reformer uttered to the Christian Bishop early in this century; and these words describe to us accurately how the pictures of the

Perfect Man, handed down to us by our ancient epics, have enabled Indian reformers through centuries and thousands of years to rally the nations of India in the worship of one God, whose image on earth is the Perfect Man. In the teeming villages of Bengal, in the ancient shrines of Northern India, and far away in the towns and hamlets of Southern India, the prevailing faith of the million is a popular monotheism underlying the various ceremonials in honour of various images and forms,—and that popular monotheism generally recognises the heroes of the two ancient epics,—*Krishna* and *Rama*, as the earthly incarnations of the one God pervading and ruling the universe.

To know the two Indian epics is to understand the Indian people better. And to trace the influence of the Indian epics on the life and manners of the Hindu nation, and on the development of their modern languages, and religious reforms, is to comprehend the real history of the people during three thousand years. As mere literary works, the *Ramayana* and the *Mahabharata* are among the greatest and loftiest creations of the human imagination. And unless I am very much mistaken in my estimate, the two epics of India, when they are better known in Europe, will take their rank along with the work of Homer, of Dante, and of Shakespeare, as undying works of art, composed for all times, all countries, and for all mankind.

XIV. HINDU PHILOSOPHY.

[*From the Indian Review, February* 1900, *being a Review of Professor Max Muller's 'Six Systems of Indian Philosophy.'*]

An account of the six systems of Hindu Philosophy was published in the early years of this century by Colebrooke, the most careful and accurate Sanscrit scholar that England has ever produced; and Dialogues on Hindu Philosophy were afterwards written and published by the eminent Indian scholar, Rev. K. M. Banerjee. The subject has since received a great deal of attention in Europe, and earnest workers have devoted years of their life in elucidating the thoughts of Indian philosophers to the modern world. The last and greatest of these workers are Professor Deussen and Professor Garbe. Professor Deussen's great work on Vedanta Philosophy, published in 1883, has thrown a flood of new light on the subject, and is recognised as an authoritative work by philosophers in Europe. And Professor Garbe's profound work on Sankhya Philosophy, published in 1894, has assigned to that system of philosophy its proper place in the European world.

Thus the work, begun by Colebrooke early in this century, has been completed towards its close, mainly by the endeavours of German scholar. To German scholars is due the fact that Hindu Philosophy has now an assured place among the world's great systems of philosophy. To Professors Deussen and Garbe is due the credit of having placed the Vedanta Philosophy and the Sankhya Philosophy side by side with the philosophical systems of ancient Greece, and of modern Europe. No work on the History of Philosophy, no review of the philosophical systems of the world, will henceforth be recognised as complete unless it takes note of the work done in India by Indian philosophers. "And if hitherto," says Professor Max Muller, "no one would have called himself a philosopher who had not read and studied the works of Plato and Aristotle, of Descartes and Spinoza, of Locke, Hume, and Kant in the original, * * the time will come when no one will claim that name who is not acquainted at least with the two prominent systems of ancient Indian philosophy, the Vedanta and Sankhya."

Such being the work done by eminent scholars in this field of enquiry during the century which is about to close, it was necessary that the results should be placed before the general reader in a popular and readable volume; and no one was better fitted for the task than the veteran scholar, who combines a life-long familiarity with Sanscrit learning and Hindu thought with a power of lucid exposition which is not excelled by any writer of this generation. Professor Max Muller has spent his long and laborious life in the great and successful work of explaining and elucidating Indian literature and thought, history and religion for the western world; and his great work on the *Six Systems of Indian Philosophy* which is now before us is a fitting close to the labours of a true and devoted worker who will always be appreciated in Europe and gratefully remembered in India.

But the present work is something more than a bare account of the *Six Systems of Indian Philosophy.* The full scope and the object of the work is explained in the following extract from the preface.

"My object in publishing the results of my own studies in Indian Philosophy was not so much to re-state the mere tenets of each system * * as to give a more comprehensive account of the philosophical activity of the Indian nation from the earliest times, and to show how intimately not only their religion but their philosophy also, was connected with national character of the inhabitants of India."

Speaking for ourselves, we should have preferred a more handy work giving a more concise account of the six systems; and such a compilation would probably have been more useful to the student and the general reader alike. But we appreciate, none the less, the learned Professor's more ambitious exposition of the philosophical activity of the Indian nation during well nigh two thousand years, and of the influence which philosophy has exerted on the religion and thought and life of the nation in India.

We pass by about a hundred and fifty pages of preliminary and explanatory discussions, and begin with chapter IV, which deals with Vedanta Philosophy. The learned author rightly takes up this system first, because it sends its roots far back into the ancient Upanishads, and because it continues to thrive to this day, as a living faith and religion among the modern Hindus. The cardinal doctrine of the Vedanta system is explained in a few words by Hindu philosophers which Professor Max Muller has quoted :

"*Brahman is true, the world is false, the soul is Brahman.*"

The idea is, that the whole universe proceeds from Brahman, and resolves itself into Brahman ; that the visible world is fleeting and unreal ; that each soul proceeds from the universal soul, and is finally absorbed in the universal soul.

The idea is thus explained in the Chhandogya Upanishad, 10th Khanda.

1. "These rivers, my son, run, the eastern (like the Ganga) toward the east, the western (like the Sindhu) toward the west. They go from sea to sea (*i. e.*, the clouds lift up the water from the sea to the sky, and send it back as rain to the sea). They become indeed sea. And as those rivers when they are in the sea, do not know, I am this or that river.

2. "In the same manner, my son, all these creatures, when they have come back from the True, know not that they have come back from the True."

The same idea is more fully explained in another passage of the Chhandogya Upanishad, third Khanda, which should be placed before our readers, though we do not find it quoted in the work before us.

"The intelligent whose body is spirit, whose form is light, whose thoughts are true, whose nature is like ether (omnipresent and invisible) from whom all works, all desires, all sweet odours and tastes proceed ; He who embraces all this, who never speaks and is never surprised.

"He is my soul within the heart, smaller than a corn of rice, smaller than a corn of barley, smaller than a mustard seed, smaller than a canary seed or the kernel of a canary seed. He is my soul within the heart, greater than earth, greater than the sky, greater than heaven, greater than all these worlds.

"He from whom all works, all desires, all sweet odours and tastes proceed, who embraces all this, who never speaks and is never surprised. He, my soul within the heart is Brahman. When I shall have departed from hence, I shall obtain Him."

The same cardinal doctrine which is found scattered in the Upanishads, and was handed down from generation to generation and from century to century, was at last recast and condensed in the Vedanta Sutras of Badarayana, which are recognized as the authoritative text of Vedanta Philosophy. It is unnecessary to quote more than one or two short pages from these Sutras.

"The sea is one and not other than its water ; yet waves, foam, spray, drops, froth and other modifications of it differ from each other. (And thus the universal soul is one and not other from the creatures proceeding from it and differing from each other)."

Vedanta Sutra, II. 1.

"Like the sun and other luminaries, seemingly multiplied by reflexion though really single, and like space apparently sub-divided in containing vessels, in supreme Light (seemingly multiplied in creatures) is without difference or distinction."

Vedanta Sutra, III. 2.

"Having annulled by fruition other works which had begun to have effect, having enjoyed the recompense and suffered the pains of good and bad actions, the possessor of divine knowledge, on the demise of the body, proceeds to a re-union with Brahman."

Vedanta Sutra, IV, 1.

We have dwelt so long on the cardinal doctrine of Vedanta Philosophy because we cannot undertake to examine, in this brief review, the other tenets and principles of that vast system of philosophy which was reared like a mighty fabric on this simple cardinal doctrine. These tenets and principles have been explained by Professor Max Muller in a long but lucid chapter of over a hundred pages, and we refer our readers to that learned work. We can only find room to quote from that work some general remarks with which the learned author concludes his review of the system.

"It is surely astounding that such a system as the Vedanta should have been slowly elaborated by the indefatigable and intrepid thinkers of India thousands of years ago, a system which even now makes us feel giddy, as in mounting the last steps of an ancient Gothic cathedral. None of our philosophers, not excepting Heraclitus, Plato, Kant, or Hegel, has ventured to erect such a spire, never frightened by storms or lightnings. Stone follows on stone in regular succession after once the first step has been made, after once it has been clearly seen that in the beginning there can have been but One, as there will be but One in the end, whether we call it Atman or Brahman. * * We need not praise or try to imitate a Colosseum, but if we have any heart for the builders of former days we cannot help feeling that it was colossal and stupendous effort. And this is the feeling which I cannot resist in examining the ancient Vedanta. Other philosophers have denied the reality of the world, perceived by us, but no one has ventured to deny at the same time the reality of what we call the Ego, the senses and the mind, and their inherent forms. And yet after lifting the self above body and soul, after uniting heaven and earth, God and Man, Brahman and Atman; these Vedanta philosophers have destroyed nothing in the life of the phenomenal beings who have to act and to fulfil their duties in this phenomenal world. On the contrary, they have shown that there can be nothing phenomenal without something that is real, and that goodness and virtue, faith and works, are necessary as a preparation, nay as a *sine qua non*, for the attainment of that highest knowledge which brings the soul back to its source and to its home, and restores it to its true nature, to its true self-hood in Brahman."

Before leaving the subject of Vedanta system we desire to say one word about the two different interpretations of that system by two eminent commentators, *viz.*,

Sankara who flourished in the ninth century, and Ramanuja who flourished in the twelfth century after Christ. Sankara's system is *Advaita* or absolute Monism;—the Universal Soul is all that exists, individuals and the phenomenal world have no reality. Ramanuja's system is *Visishta Advaita* or Monism with a distinction:—the Universal Soul is the highest reality and is full of compassion and love with individual souls which are also real. This is the special and humane feature of Ramanuja's idea of God, as compared with the icy coldness of Sankara's idea. And if Sankara's idea has found favour with the philosophers and learned disputants, Ramanuja's idea of a compassionate God has found favour with the million, and has inspired a long line of subsequent reformers like Ramananda and Kabir, Nanak and Chaitanya, Dadu and Ram Mohan Roy. It is thus that the old and the new are connected together in India by an indissoluble chain, that the Upanishads, composed a thousand years before Christ, are connected with the teachings of the reformers of this century, that philosophy and religion have acted and reacted on each other, and that the doctrine of a Universal Soul, full of compassion for individual souls which live and move and have their being in Him, is the living faith at the present day of the Hindu cultivator and labourer as of the Hindu pandit and the devotee.

The Purva Mimansa system concerns itself mainly with religious rites, and as a system of philosophy is of minor importance. We pass it by and come to

Chapter VI of the book which deals with Sankhya Philosophy in more than a hundred pages. The Vedanta and the Sankhya stand pre-eminent among the six systems of Hindu philosophy,—the former for its noble conception of one Universal source of all objects and all beings, the latter for its fearless analysis of the mind and its faculties. As an effort of generalization,—an attempt to grasp the secret and the origin of the limitless world with its varied and varying and multitudinous creatures,—the Vedanta system has never been surpassed. As an effort of introspection,—an endeavour to analyse the senses and the mind and the phenomena which leave their impress on the unchangeable soul,—the Sankhya Philosophy has seldom been equalled.

In dealing with the Sankhya system Professor Max Muller appears to have lighted on an important discovery. Colebrooke and Wilson, Lassen and Windischmann, Pantier and St. Hilaire relied on the famous Sankhya Karikas of Iswar Krishna, the date of which is about the commencement of the Christian era. Professor Max Muller relies on the Tatwa Samasa which he considers to be the original Sankhya Sutras, and the oldest record of the Sankhya Philosophy.

Sankhya Philosophy differs essentially from Vedanta Philosophy in this that the Vedanta is strictly a system of Monism, the Sankhya is a system of Dualism. The Vedanta resolves all objects and all beings to the One Universal soul; the Sankhya maintains that Nature and Soul, *Prakriti* and *Purusha*, are eternal and co-existent.

From *Prakriti* are derived not only the subtle and grosser elements but the senses, the organs of Action, the *Manas* or faculty of Perception, *Ahankara* or Consciousness and *Buddhi* or Intellect. In the language of European philosophy *Manas* receives sensations and makes them into actual perceptions ; *Ahankara* individualises them as " Mine," *Buddhi* turns them into "concepts" or "judgments." In the language of a Hindu commentator, "As the headmen of the village collect the taxes from the villagers and pay them to the Governor of the District, as the local Governor pays the amount to the minister, and the minister receives it for the use of the king, so the *Manas* or Perception having received impressions from the senses transfers them to *Ahankara* or Consciousness; and *Ahankara* delivers them to *Buddhi* or the Intellect who receives charge of them for the sovereign *Purusha* or soul." It is remarkable that, at a time when the functions of the brain were yet imperfectly understood, Sankhya philosophers held that perception, consciousness and even intellect,—all except the soul,—derived their origin from matter. And it is still more remarkable that they traced the origin of the subtle and the grosser elements to consciousness. Hindu philosophers herein seem to have anticipated the philosophy of Berkeley and Hume that external objects are only " permanent possibilities of sensations."

Purusha or Soul has a distinct origin of its own. It is linked with Nature, *i.e.*, with corporeal body for deriving knowledge and for the fulfilment of its destiny. When that purpose has been attained, the soul is emancipated from matter, and continues to live in its isolation from matter, ever after.

Such is the nearest outline of the Sankhya Philosophy, a system of Philosophy which requires the most careful study and the deepest thought. In the words of Mr. Davies, the translator of the Sankhya Karikas, the latest German philosophy of Schopenhauer and Hartman is but a reproduction of the Sankhya Philosophy in a more elaborate form. "In this respect the human intellect has gone over the same ground that it occupied more than two thousand years ago; but on a more important point it has taken a step in retreat. Kapila recognized fully the existence of a soul in man, forming indeed his proper nature,—the absolute ego, of Fichte,—distinct from matter and immortal; but our latest philosophy, both here and in Germany, can see in man only a highly developed physical organization. "All external things," says Kapila 'were formed that the soul might know itself and be free.' 'The study of psychology is vain,' says Schopenhauer, 'for there is no Psyche.'"*

We have dwelt only on the cardinal principles of the Sankhya Philosophy, because in this brief review we cannot undertake to explain, or even to make the briefest mention of its minor tenets. We must therefore again refer our readers to the lucid exposition in Professor Max Muller's great work. The most serious charge against the system is that it is an atheistical sys-

* Davies, Preface to Hindu Philosophy.

tem, denying the existence of God. This charge against Kapila, the founder of Sankhya Philosophy, is not altogether correct, for as Professor Max Muller points out, "He simply says,—and in that respect he does not differ much from Kant,—that there are no logical proofs to establish that existence, but neither does he offer any such proofs for denying it." But even this passive negation of God was repulsive to the Hindu mind, and led to the use of a new system of Philosophy,—the Yoga system, which combines with the tenets of the Sankhya the faith and belief in a surpreme Deity.

The Yoga system, as a system of Philosophy, is based on the Sankhya system. "Yoga is indeed, as the Brahmans say, Sankhya, only modified, particularly in one point, namely, in its attempt to develop and systematise an ascetic discipline by which concentration of thought could be attained, and by admitting devotion to the Lord God as part of that discipline." We therefore pass over this subject and come to chapter VIII of Professor Max Muller's work which treats of the Nyaya system or Logic.

The four Pramanas or means of acquiring knowledge, according to the Nyaya system, are Perception, Inference, Analogy, and Testimony or word. It is under the head of Inference that we find that Hindu syllogism which has so startling a resemblance to the Greek syllogism. The Hindu syllogism consists of five terms thus:

Assertion : The mountain has fire.
Reason : For it smokes.

Instance : Whatever smokes has fire, as the kitchen.
Application : The mountain smokes.
Conclusion : Therefore it has fire.

If we omit the first two terms, which are only a statement of a proposition, the Hindu syllogism is a perfect syllogism of Aristotle. And European thinkers have naturally held that there was some communication of knowledge between the Hindus and the Greeks to make so remarkable a coincidence possible. Gorres undertook to prove that the Greeks had actually retained some technical terms of Hindu Logic, and inferred that the Greeks borrowed the syllogism from the Hindus. Niebuhr and others held, on the other hand, that the Hindus borrowed it from the Greeks. Professor Max Muller with his usual caution adopts a middle path :

"It seems to me that until it can be proved *historically* that the Greeks could freely converse with Indians in Greeks or in Sanscrit on metaphysical subjects or *vice versa*, or until technical philosophical terms can be discovered in Sanscrit of Greek, or in Greek of Sanscrit, origin, it will be best to accept facts and to regard both Greek and Indian philosophy as products of the intellectual soil of India and of Greece, and derive from their striking similarities this simple conviction only, that in philosophy also there is a wealth of truth which forms the common heirloom of all mankind. and may be discovered by all nations if they search for it with honesty and perseverance."

This is a safe way of disposing of the question which will hardly satisfy curious enquirers. As Gautama the founder of Hindu Logic lived centuries before Aristotle, and even before Buddha, and as Logic was a popular subject of study among the learned Hindus before the time of Aristotle and Alexander the Great, it is scarcely possible to deny the indebtedness of the younger to the older nation in a matter in which the coincidence so pointedly suggests one common origin.

But we must bring this brief review to a close. We pass by the system of mental philosophy included in the Nyaya system which is similar to that of the Sankhya system, but recognizes One Supreme Soul. We pass by the many technical terms of Hindu Logic, terms which have been explained and illustrated by Hindu logicians with all the acuteness and subtlety of reasoning of the European schoolmen of the Middle Ages. And we also pass by the categories of objects of knowledge,—and other important matters which are fully and lucidly dealt with in this chapter of the Professor's work.

Nor need we prolong the present review by any detailed examination of the last of the six Indian systems,—the Vaisheshika or Atomic Philosophy. The cardinal principle of the system is that the whole Universe and all material substances are aggregates of atoms. The atoms are imperishable ; the aggregates perish by disintegration.

Such are the six systems of Indian Philosophy which have now been explained to English readers in one learned and comprehensive volume by the greatest Sanscrit scholar of Europe. And we cannot conclude this review better than by quoting some general remarks from his preface on certain characteristic features which pervade all systems of Indian Philosophy.

"What I admire in Indian philosophers is that they never try to deceive us as to their principles and the consequences of their theories. If they are idealists even to the verge of nihilism they say so; and if they hold that the objective world requires a real, though not necessarily a visible or tangible substratum, they are never afraid to speak out. They are *bona fide* idealists or materialists, monists or dualists, theists or atheists, because their reverence for truth is stronger than their reverence for anything else. The Vedantist, for instance, is a "fearless idealist, and, as a monist, denies the reality of anything but the *One* Brahman, the Universal spirit which is to account for the whole of the phenomenal world. The followers of the Sankhya, on the contrary, though likewise idealists and believers in an unseen Purusha, (subject), and an unseen Prakriti (objective substance), leave us in no doubt that they are, and mean to be atheists, so far as the existence of an active God, a maker and ruler of the world is concerned. They do not allow themselves to be driven one inch beyond their self-chosen position. * * Kapila never refers to Him in his Sutras. As a careful reasoner, however, he does not go so far as to say that he can prove the non-existence of such a Being, but he is satisfied with stating, like Kant, that he cannot establish His existence by the ordinary channels of evidential knowledge.* * Whatever we may think of such views of the world as are put forward by the Sankhya, the Vedanta, and other systems of Indian philosophy, there is one thing which we cannot help admiring, and that is the straightforwardness and perfect freedom with which they are elaborated. However imperfect the style in which their theories have been clothed may appear from a literary point of view it seems to me the very perfection for the treatment of philosophy. It never leaves us in any doubt as to the exact opinions held by each philosopher. We may miss the development and the dialectic eloquence with which Plato and Hegel propound their thoughts but we can always appreciate the perfect freedom, freshness and downrightness with which each searcher after truth follows his track without ever looking right or left."

XV. HINDU RELIGION.

[*Reprinted from the Humanitarian, July* 1900].

MUCH has been written from time to time of the religious practices and observances of the Hindus, their ancient and rigid caste system, their strange celebrations and festivities, their gorgeous shrines and temples, their annual pilgrimages to holy spots and sacred streams. Much, too, has been said of the silent and uncomplaining religious devotion of their women, and the self-imposed vows and penances of their men, which remind one strongly of the practices of mediæval Europe. But in these popular and interesting accounts of the Hindu religion and customs we often miss the undercurrent of thought and philosophy which unites and holds together the people of a vast Continent like India, and which has enabled them to resist every outside influence, Greek or Persian, Moslem or Christian, for thousands of years. For it may be truly said that in India alone we see the faiths and traditions of the long past still unbroken and still instinct with life and vitality. The ancient faiths of Egypt and Babylon are now things of the past, and the religion of ancient Greece and Rome lives only in poetry and art. The doctrines of the old Medes and Persians survive among a handful of Parsees now living in India, and even the doctrines of Confucius, in China, have been transformed and changed by Buddhism imported from India. Among the Hindus only, the link between the present and the ancient past remains unbroken ; and though the forms and practices of religious worship have undergone modifications, the cardinal doctrine and the inner thought of Hinduism are the same to-day as we find them in the Upanishads and the ancient Vedas. They run through the history of thousands of years like a perennial stream, which nourishes and fertilizes the surrounding land and covers it with vegetation and life. And it is worth the while of the modern student to penetrate through the outer forms and observances of modern Hinduism, in order to obtain some glimpses of that inner thought which connects it with the earliest forms of Aryan civilisation and of Aryan religious thought.

The earliest form of religious worship in India was the worship of Nature—sacrifices and prayers offered to the Powers of Nature. The Rig Veda is the most ancient religious work of the Aryan world, and is a collection of 1,028 hymns, which were uttered at sacrifices by the ancient Hindu worshipper four thousand years ago. The sky was invoked under various names : Dyu, or the bright sky ; Indra, or the rain-giver ; Varuna, or the covering expanse of heaven. The Rain-Giver was a martial god, who helped the Aryan Hindus in their battles with the dark-skinned Aborigines, and who rent the clouds (Vrita or Ahi) by his thunderbolt in order to give rain-water to the sons of men.

"We sing the heroic deeds done by Indra the Thunderer. He destroyed Ahi and caused rains to descend, and opened out the paths for the mountain streams to roll."

"Indra slayed Ahi resting on the mountains, Twashtri had made the far-reaching thunderbolt for him. Waters in torrents flowed towards the sea, as cows run towards their calves." *Rig Veda*, I, 32, 1 and 2.

More striking and more sublime is the invocation of the sinner to the Covering Heaven, who sees all, who binds the sinner in chains, and who can free them in his mercy.

"O Varuna! Deliver us from the sins of our fathers, deliver us from the sins committed in our persons. Deliver Vasishtha like a calf from its tether, like a thief who has feasted on stolen cattle.

"Not wilfully have we sinned, O Varuna! but error or wine, dice or anger, has misled us. Even the elder leads the younger astray, even sleep leads to sin."

Rig Veda, VII, 86, 5 and 6.

The sun was similarly invoked under various names: Savitri or Surya or the Adityas, the suns of the different months of the year. Fire, which received libation and offerings, was Agni, the priest of the gods; and Soma, the libation itself, was also an object of invocation. The Maruts were the storm-winds which helped the Rain-Giver in milking rain from the clouds, and the Ushas was the lovely Dawn-goddess, who waked all creatures to life, and nourished them, and sent them to their work.

"Beauteous daughter of the sky,
Hold thy ruddy light on high,
Grant us wealth and grant us day,
Bring us food and morning's ray.
White-robed goddess of the morning sky,
Bring us light, let night's deep shadows fly!

"Fathers hailed thy glorious light,
We too hail thee, goddess bright,
For like ship that ploughs the sea,
Sky-borne chariot bringeth thee.
Come then, goddess, in thy radiant car,
Come and bring thy joyous light from far!

"Come like housewife gentle-hearted,
Tending us, for night's departed,
Grant another joyous day
Unto beasts and herds so gay.
Let all creatures to their work repair,
Birds with joyous accents fill the air!"

Rig Veda, I, 48, 1, 3 and 5.

Such was the simple invocation of the Powers of Nature in the ancient days, and such was the popular form of worship. But the sacrificers, invoking the various names, did not forget that they were the different manifestations of the One Supreme Being, who comprehended all, and who created all.

"Great is the ALL-CREATOR; He creates all, He supports all, He presides over all. The blest obtain the fulfilment of their desires in the sky where the One lives—beyond the constellation of the Great Bear.

"He is the FATHER who made us, who knows all creatures and all things. *He is One, though He bears the names of many Gods.* Others wish to know of Him."

Rig Veda, X, 82, 2 and 3.

This was the inner thought and the true philosophy of Vedic religion in India; and though we may popularly describe that religion as the worship of the various Powers of Nature under various names, it is nevertheless necessary for us to remember that the Hindu mind, even in that ancient age, penetrated beyond the visible manifestations and phenomna of Nature, and grasped the idea of that unity of power which modern science, too, teaches us to recognise as the moving and inspiring force of the universe.

This cardinal doctrine of a Unity, concealed under the changing phenomena of Nature, is more fully developed in the Upanishads, the final results of Vedic teaching. It is the All-pervading Breath, the Universal Soul, which manifests itself in all the universe, which comprehends the universe, and into which the universe will merge in the end.

"The Intelligent, whose body is spirit, whose form is light, whose thought is truth, whose nature is ether-like, from whom all works, all desires, all sweet odours and tastes proceed—He, who embraces all this, who never speaks and is never surprised.

"He is the soul within the heart, smaller than a corn of rice, smaller than a corn of barley, smaller than a mustard seed, smaller than a canary seed or the kernel of a canary seed. He also is my soul within my heart, greater than the earth, greater than the sky, greater than heaven, greater than all the worlds.

"He from whom all works, all desires, all sweet odours and tastes proceed, who embraces all this, who never speaks, and is never surprised; He, my soul within my heart, is BRAHMA. When I shall have departed from hence, I shall obtain Him."

Chhandogya Upanishad, III. 14.

And when systems of Hindu philosophy were fully developed, some centuries before the Christian era, out of the vague speculations of previous ages, the Vedanta philosophy grasped the cardinal doctrine which had been handed down from the preceding centuries, and fixed it as the abiding principle of all subsequent Hindu thought.

"The sea is one and not other from its water; yet waves, foam, spray, drops, froth and other modifications of it differ from each other. (And so all creatures differ from each other, but are sprung from one PRIMAL CAUSE.)"

Brahma Sutra, II. 1 and 5.

"Like the sun * * seemingly multiplied by reflection, though really single, and like space apparently divided in containing vessels, but really without division, the SUPREME LIGHT is without difference and without division."

Brahma Sutra, III. 2.

It must not be supposed, however, that this philosophical doctrine comprehended all the popular beliefs of the mass of the people. On the contrary, the old sacrifices to the Powers of Nature, invoked under different names and worshipped as different deities, continued from the Vedic times, two thousand years before Christ, to the centuries immediately preceding the Christian era. Indeed, the sacrifices became more elaborate and ostentatious with the lapse of centuries, and as the priests formed themselves into a separate and hereditary caste, they multiplied rules and observances, and a vast body of religious literature concerned itself with the minute details of sacrificial rites. The simple faith of the early Vedic times was, to some extent, lost in an ostentatious performance of rites and ceremonies, and all these sacred rites and observances were confined to the Aryan Hindus. The millions of the non-Aryan people who had adopted the civilsation, the language, and even the religious faith of their Aryan teachers and masters, were still jealously kept out of the pale of Vedic rites and sacred laws; and thus a great and unfortunate distinction between the handful of Aryan Hindus and the mass of Hinduised non-Aryans was perpetrated and deepened with the lapse of centuries. On the one hand, the Aryan communities, with the pride and exclusiveness of all civilised and conquering races in ancient and modern times, jealously guarded their privileges against the non-Aryans. On the other hand, the non-Aryan races, having assumed the mantle of Aryan civilisation and customs, and having risen to political power in Magadha and other provinces, demanded admission into the charmed circle. The anomaly required a solution, the times called for a leveller—and a great leveller arose in Gautama the Buddha.

This is the true explanation of the rise of Buddhism in India in the sixth century before Christ. Gautama the Buddha did not regard himself as the founder of a new religion, but as a teacher of true Hinduism, a reformer who welcomed all worshippers of all races and castes within the pale of his reformed faith. His religion is a system of self-culture—a striving after perfect holiness—to be attained, if not in this life, then after a succession of re-births. Gods and men, and all living creatures, are striving for that perfect state of holiness and are passing through a number of re-incarnations to attain it. Every deed in this life, every Karma, leads to its legitimate result in the next life, and when at last the fetters which link us to life are broken by prolonged self-culture, we attain that blessed state of holiness, that Nirvana which is the Buddhist's heaven. All these doctrines were adaptations from the doctrines of the ancient Hindu Upanishads; but Gautama the Buddha proclaimed them to all men of all nations, and thus he spread a catholic religion which eventually embraced the nations of Asia from Ceylon to Siberia, and from Kashmir to China and Japan.

As may well be conceived, this religion of self-culture and of striving after holiness, is specially rich in its moral teachings, and the precepts and maxims of Buddhism are unsurpassed in their moral elevation and grandeur. We quote a few below:

"5. Hatred does not cease by hatred at any time; hatred ceases by love; this is its nature."

"51. Like a beautiful flower, full of colour, but without scent, are the fine and fruitless words of him who does not act accordingly."

"129. All men tremble at punishment, all men fear death. Remember that you are like unto them, and do not kill, nor cause slaughter."

"130. All men tremble at punishment, all men love life. Remember that you are like unto them, and do not kill nor cause slaughter."

"183. Not to commit sin, to do good, to purify one's mind, this is the teaching of the prophets."

"197. Let us live happily not hating those who hate us. Among men who hate us, let us live free from hatred."

"223 Let one overcome anger by love, let him overcome evil by good. Let him overcome the greedy by liberality, the liar by truth."

232. The fault of others is easily perceived, but that of oneself is difficult to perceive; a man winnows his neighbour's faults like chaff, but his own fault he hides, as the cheat hides the bad die from the gambler."

"260. A man is not an Elder because his head is grey His age may be ripe, but he is called old in vain."

"261. He in whom there is truth, love, restraint, moderation, he who is free from impurity and wise, he is called an Elder."

"393. A man does not become a Brahman by his platted hair, by his family or by birth. In whom there is truth and righteousness,, he is blessed, he is a Brahman."

"394. What is the use of platted hair, O fool, what of the raiment of goatskins? Within thee there is ravening, but the outside thou makest clean."

Dhammapada.

Maxims like these appealed to the higher sentiments of men and women of many nations. Buddhist missionaries found attentive listeners in various distant lands, as far as Palestine and Egypt and Greece, in the centuries preceding the birth of Christ; and the pure-souled Jesus proclaimed once more that religion of charity, forgiveness, of love, which the pure-souled Gautama had proclaimed five hundred years before. In India the ancient and exclusive faith of the Aryan Hindus lived for a thousand years side by side with the reformed and catholic religion of Gautama. Brahmans and Aryan castes clung to their ancient privileges, while millions of the lower classes entered by the gate opened by the reformer. Hindu shrines and Buddhist monasteries flourished side by side in every town of India, from the third century before Christ to the seventh century after Christ; Hindu sacrifices and Buddhist celebrations were performed in the same villages; Hindu and Buddhist citizens lived in peace and harmony in the same localities for centuries. It is a remarkable instance of the spirit of toleration of the Hindus, that we do not read of any religious persecutions in India during the thousand years, except when some cruel warrior or invader signalised his conquest by acts of cruelty. The communities were divided in faith, but lived in harmony and peace.

It is generally believed that Buddhism has now disappeared from India, because it failed to shake the stronghold of Hinduism. The very reverse of this is the truth. Buddhism has disappeared from India, because its work is done; the Hindus are united, and Hinduism has accepted and adopted Buddhist maxims and observances. The distinction between Aryans and non-Aryans exists no longer, all Hindus from the Punjab to Travancore, although divided into profession-castes, are the followers of the same religion, and perform the same rites. The Vedic sacrifices, from which the non-Aryans were jealously excluded, have died by reason of this very exclusiveness, or survive only in marriage and funeral rites which all Hindus have an equal right to perform. Buddhist celebrations and pilgrimages were imitated and surpassed by modern Hindu celebrations and pilgrimages, and Gautama the Buddha himself found a place in the modern Hindu pantheon. It is necessary to remember these facts to understand the history of Buddhism in India; Buddhism has disappeared from India because its mission is fulfilled. Modern Hinduism has eschewed its old sacrificial rites and exclusive Aryan privileges, has adopted the joyous celebrations of the million, and has re-united Aryans and non-Aryans into one united Hindu community. These are the abiding results of the work of Gautama the Buddha in India.

Thus, in the sixth and seventh century after Christ,

Hinduism arose in India in its newer form. In all cardinal doctrines it has remained faithful to the old teachings of the Upanishads. It recognises One Supreme Being—the All-pervading Breath. It recognises the universe to be an emanation from Him, subsisting in Him, and finally resolving itself in him. It recognises rewards and punishments in future lives according to the needs of this life. And it acknowledges that all souls will be finally absorbed in the Deity—the Universal Soul. Herein the religion of to-day is the religion of three thousands years ago. But in rites and observances and popular beliefs, modern Hinduism is widely divergent from the Vedic religion. The Vedic religion insisted on the worship of the Powers of Nature; modern Hinduism inculcates belief in the threefold power of Supreme Being, known as the Hindu Trinity, under the names Brahma, Vishnu and Siva. The Vedic hymns celebrated the deeds of Nature-gods; modern Hinduism has multiplied the myths and legends of these gods until they form a vast system of popular mythology for the people. The Vedic religion insisted on sacrifices to the fire as its form of worship; modern Hindus pay worship to images and rejoice in joyous celebrations and pilgrimages.

Much has been written about the modern religious practices of the Hindus, and of the rival sects which have prevailed in India during a thousand years and more. But we miss again in these popular accounts a real explanation of that secret which has held two hundred millions of people together, a true delineation of that living faith which still inspires modern Hindus and makes them a living nation. Sects of Vishnu and of Siva have divided the millions of India for ages, but the different sects merely quarrel about a name, as they often did in mediæval Europe, and each sect worship under the name of its own popular deity the supreme Being—the personal God—who ministers to the needs of his creatures. The followers of Siva call Him by the name; the more numerous followers of Vishnu believe that he descended to earth as Rama, as Krishna, or as Buddha, for the salvation of man and the triumph of righteousness. Thus the relations of the worshipper and the Being worshipped are drawn closer; and, as in the Vedic times, men address the Deity as a personal, a beneficent, a helping friend. For the popular mind needed an object nearer to the heart and clearer to the understanding than the Universal Soul of the Upanishads; and Krishna supplied this place, which Buddha had filled for centuries with the million. The legends of Krishna gradually supplanted the birth-stories of Buddha; pilgrimages to Mathura and Brindavan and Jagganath took the place of pilgrimages to Buddhist shrines; and even Buddhist monastic life was replaced by a system of monastic life among the followers of Vishnu and Krishna. The religious Hindu mind has struggled through long centuries towards a simple and popular form of monotheism; and amidst the dissensions of rural sects, and in spite of the worship of many images in many temples, the millions of India have held to the cult of an underlying monotheism—a faith in a personal and beneficent and helping Deity whom the simple worshippnr calls by the name of Siva or Vishnu.

When the Hindus lost their national independence, and submitted to the rule of the Moslem conquerors at the close of the twelfth century, their national faith survived and burned as brightly as ever. A succession of Hindu religious reformers rose from the eleventh to the nineteenth century, repeating to the listening millions the lessons of the past, and turning their hearts to the living God, who ministered to the needs of His creatures in their sorrow and in their sufferings.

Ramanuja was the first of this glorious band of modern Hindu reformers. He lived in Southern India in the eleventh century ; he proclaimed the unity of God under the name of Vishnu ; and he preached the love of God as the way to salvation. Sectarian opposition compelled him to fly from his own country ; like other prophets he was honoured outside his country ; and in Mysore he converted the king and the people to his own faith, and established seven hundred monasteries, dedicated to the faith of Vishnu, before ne died.

Fifth in apostolic succession from Ramanuja was the great Ramanada, who spread the same simple monotheism in Northern India. He made Benares his headquarters, but wandered far and near to preach the faith of Vishnu. Unlike his predecessor, who had written in Sanscrit, Ramananda preached to the people and wrote for the people in their own modern tongue ; and the Hindi language of Northern India was enriched by the great religious movement inagurated by this gifted and popular reformer.

The history of religious reforms in India knows of no brighter name than that of Kabir, the disciple of Ramananda. He took up the work which his master had begun, and he conceived the bold idea of uniting Hindus and Mahomedans alike in the worship of one God. The God of the Hindus, he said, was the same as the God of the Mahomedans, be he invoked as Rama or Alla. "What avails it to wash your mouth, count your beads, beathe in holy streams, and bow in temples, if, whilst you mutter your prayers, or go on pilgrimages, deceitfulness is in your hearts?" "If the Creator dwells in tabernacles, whose dwelling is the universe?" "The city of the Hindu God is Benares, and the city of the Mussulman God is Mecca, but search your hearts, and there you will find the God both of Hindus and Mussulmans."

What Kabir attempted in Central India, the gifted Nanak endeavoured to achieve in the Punjab. Born in 1469, and therefore a contemporary of Martin Luther, he invited Hindus and Mussulmans to unite in the worship of one God. The great Sikh community which he founded was for a long time a peaceful religious fraternity, until the unwise persecutions of later Mahomedan Emperors turned them into the most warlike race of modern India.

Bengal had her religious reformer in the lovable and loved Chaitanya, who was born in 1486. He, too, invited Mussulmans and Hindus to unite in the worship of One God, under the name of Vishnu; and at the present day the entire population of Bengal, except the upper castes, are worshippers of Vishnu. And Gujrat, too, had its teacher in Dadu, who has left behind him a body of sacred literature extending to 20,000 lines, and whose teachings were spread all through Rajputana by fifty disciples.

The stream of religious faith has not yet dried up in India; the great Ram Mohan Roy and Dayanand Saraswati preached once more to their countrymen the faith of One God in the present century; and all over India thoughtful and earnest men are turning their eyes to the past, and are seeking for reform in religion as well as in social customs in the light of their ancient Scriptures and their ancient Philosophy.

The loyalty of India to her past is a puzzle to outsiders; the unique phenomenon presented in India of a living stream of ancient faith and tradition flowing from the dawn of history to the present time, unbroken by political revolutions, and uninterrupted by foreign influences, Greek or Turanian, Moslem or Christian, is the most wonderful fact in the history of the human race. And we can only dimly comprehend the secret of this phenomenon, if we try to grasp the underlying doctrines and the sustaining and nourishing forces of ancient Hindu thought, religion and philosophy.

XVI. THE DEATH OF PROFESSOR MAX MULLER.

[*Speech delivered at the English Goethe Society on November*, 23, 1900.]

Mr. Chairman: In response to your call I rise to perform a mournful duty, and to say a word on behalf of the people of India to express the sorrow which they feel at the death of one, who was not only one of the greatest of oriental scholars, but one of the truest friends of India. I do not exaggerate facts, Sir, when I state, that for a period of half a century, my countrymen have looked upon Professor Max Muller, not only as the best interpreter of ancient Indian literature and philosophy and religious thought in Europe, but also as the truest friend of the people of modern India. For half a century they have watched his literary labours with admiration; they have hailed his vindication of modern India with gratitude; and they have regarded him with feelings of affection and of love, heightened by the long distance from which they contemplated his sympathetic work. And the few of my countrymen who had the privilege of approaching him, and knowing him personally, have found in him a true and devoted friend.

I will not recapitulate all the life-long labours of the venerable Professor, of which my friend, Dr.

Oswald, has given a full account. The publication of the Rig Veda, which commenced in 1849, opened a new epoch in historic and religious studies in India, and helped us to turn to the past for inspiration and for guidance in solving the great religious and social problems which lie before us in the path of our future progress. Professor Max Muller's numerous contributions to the elucidation of the literature, religion, and philosophy of ancient India have helped us in this progress; and his sympathetic works on modern India have inspired us with courage, with confidence, and with hope. And lastly the splendid series of the Sacred Books of the East, which he has edited, has opened out for many of us even in India, not only a rich storehouse of ancient knowledge and wisdom, but a living stream of pure thought and learning, which sustains and nourishes and strengthens us in our conduct in life, and in our struggles for the progress and true reform.

As a personal friend, he has known and sympathised with some of the most distinguished Indians of two generations. As a young man, he knew the princely Dwarka Nath Tagore, who was in Europe fifty years ago, and who now lies buried in a London cemetery. He corresponded with his son, the venerable Debendra Nath Tagore, head of the oldest branch of the Brahma Samaj of India. He was a friend of Keshab Chandra Sen, whose earnest religious reforms and great eloquence were admired in this country thirty years ago. He frequently corresponded with Dr. Bhan

Daji of Bombay and Dr. Rajendra Lal Mitra of Calcutta; he knew Dr. Bhandarkar and Pandita Rama Bai; he was a friend of every great scholar, religious teacher, and social reformer, that India has produced within these two generations. Last and humblest among the students of ancient Indian literature, whom the Professor honoured with his friendship, was my humble self. Fifteen years ago, when I produced my translation of the Rig Veda into my own vernacular language, my work received his sympathetic recognition and his warm support. Twelve years ago, when I wrote a historical account of the Civilisation of Ancient India, I received from him encouragement and help. Two years ago, when I prepared my condensed metrical translation of the Indian Epic, the Mahabharata, Professor Max Muller kindly wrote for it that learned Introduction which graces the volume. And only last year, I had the proud privilege of dedicating my metrical translation of the other Indian Epic, the Ramayana, to him who had all his life laboured for my country and my countrymen.

Words cannot express what my countrymen feel on this mournful occasion. But, nevertheless, I am grateful to you, Sir, for having permitted me to express, however inadequately, our sorrow at the death of one of the greatest of oriental scholars, and one of the truest of our friends.

XVII. SEPARATION OF JUDICAL AND EXECUTIVE SERVICES.

[*Memorial submitted to the Secretary of State for India on July* 1, 1899. *This document is included in the present collection as it refers to and supports Mr. Romesh Dutt's scheme of the separation of the services published in* 1893. *Mr. Dutt's scheme is appended to the Memorial.*]

MY LORD,

We the undersigned beg leave to submit to you, in the interests of the administration of justice, the following considerations in favour of the separation of judicial from executive duties in India. The present system, under which the chief executive official of a District collects the revenue, controls the police, institutes prosecutions, and at the same time exercises large judicial powers, has been, and still is, condemned not only by the general voice of public opinion in India, but also by Anglo-Indian officers, and by high legal authorities. The state of Indian opinion with reference to the question is so well known as to require neither proof nor illustration. The separation of judicial and executive functions has been consistently urged throughout a long series of years alike by the Indian press and by public bodies and individuals well qualified to represent Indian public opinion. We propose, how ever, to refer briefly to some of the numerous occasions upon which the principle of separation has been approved by official authorities; next, to explain the nature of the existing grievance, and the proposed remedy; and finally, to discuss objections which have been or may be advanced against alteration of the present system. This Memorial, therefore, consists of three sections, which it may be convenient to indicate as follows:

(*a*) AN HISTORICAL RETROSPECT (Paras. 2 to 10);

(*b*) THE EXISTING GRIEVANCE, AND THE REMEDY (Paras. 11 to 14);

(*c*) ANSWERS TO POSSIBLE OBJECTIONS (Paras. 15 to 18).

(*a*)—AN HISTORICAL RETROSPECT.

2. So long ago as 1793 the Government of India, under Lord Cornwallis, recognised the dangers arising from the combination, in one and the same officer, of revenue with judicial duties. Section 1 of Regulation II., 1793, contained the following passage:

"All questions between Government and the landholders respecting the assessment and collection of the public revenue, and disputed claims between the latter and their rayats, or other persons concerned in the collection of their rents, have hitherto been cognizable in the Courts of *Maal Adawlut*, or Revenue Courts. The Collectors of the Revenue preside in these Courts as Judges, and an appeal lies from their decision to the Board of Revenue, and from the decrees of that Board to the Governor-General in Council in the Department of Revenue. The proprietors can never consider the privileges which have been conferred upon them as secure whilst the revenue officers are vested with these judicial powers. Exclusive of the objections arising to these Courts from their irregular, summary and often *ex parte* proceedings, and from the Collectors being obliged to suspend the exercise of their judicial functions whenever they interfere with their financial duties, it is obvious that, if the Regulations for assessing and collecting the public revenue are infringed, the revenue officers themselves must be the aggressors, and that individuals who have been wronged by them in one capacity can never hope to obtain redress from them in another. Their financial occupations equally disqualify them for administering the laws between the proprietors of land and their tenants. Other security, therefore, must be given to landed property and to the rights attached to it before the desired improvements in agriculture can be expected to be effected. Government must divest itself of the power of infringing in its executive capacity the rights and privileges which, as exercising the legislative authority, it has conferred on the landholders. The revenue officers must be deprived of their judicial powers. All financial claims of the public, when disputed under the Regulations, must be subjected to the cognizance of the Courts of Judicature superintended by Judges who, from their official situations and the nature of their trusts, shall not only be wholly uninterested in the result of their decisions, but bound to decide impartially between the public and the proprietors of land, and also between the latter and their tenants. The Collectors of the Revenue must not only be divested of the power of deciding upon their own acts, but rendered amenable for them to the Courts of Judicature, and collect the public dues subject to a personal prosecution for every exaction exceeding the amount which they are authorised to demand on behalf of the public, and for every deviation from the Regulations prescribed for the collection of it. No power will then exist in the country by which the rights vested in the landholders by the Regulations can be infringed, or the value of landed property affected."

3. These observations aptly anticipated the basis of the criticisms which during the succeeding century have so often been passed, as well by individuals as by public bodies of the highest authority, upon the strange union of the functions of constable and magistrate, public prosecutor and criminal judge, revenue collector and Appeal Court in revenue cases. In 1838 a Com-

mittee, appointed by the Government of Bengal to prepare a scheme for the more efficient organisation of the Police, issued its report. As a member of that Committee Mr. F. J. Halliday (afterwards Sir Frederick Halliday, sometime Lieutenant-Governor of Bengal and Member of the Council of the Secretary of State) drew up an important Minute in which, after citing at length the considerations that had been urged in favour of separating police from judicial duties in London, he stated that they applied with double force to India. The passage quoted with approval by Mr. Halliday declared that there was no more important principle in jurisprudence than the separation of the judicial from the executive ministerial functions; that a scheme to combine the duties of Judge and Sheriff, of Justice of the Peace and constable in the same individuals would be scouted as absurd as well as mischievous; that a magistrate ought to have no previous knowledge of a matter with which he had to deal judicially; and that the whole executive duty of preventing and detecting crimes should be thrown upon the police. In support of the proposition that these remarks applied with double force to India, Mr. Halliday wrote:—

"In England a large majority of offenders are, as here, tried and sentenced by the magistrates: but in the former country the cases so tried are comparatively of a trivial and unimportant nature. In India the powers of the Magistrates are much greater; their sentences extend to imprisonment for three years, and their jurisdiction embraces offences which, both for frequency and importance, are by far the weightiest subjects of the criminal administration of the country. The evil which this system produces is twofold:

it affects the fair distribution of justice and it impairs at the same time, the efficiency of the police. The union of Magistrate with Collector has been stigmatised as incompatible, but the junction of thief-catcher with judge is surely more anomalous in theory, and more mischievous in practice. So long as it lasts, the public confidence in our criminal tribunals must always be liable to injury, and the authority of justice itself must often be abused and misapplied. For this evil which arises from a constant and unavoidable bias against all supposed offenders, the power of appeal is not a sufficient remedy :—the danger to justice, under such circumstances, is not in a few cases, nor in any proportion of cases, but in every case. In all the Magistrate is constable, prosecutor and judge. If the appeal be necessary to secure justice in any case, it must be so in all: and if—as will follow—all sentences by a Magistrate should properly be revised by another authority, it would manifestly be for the public benefit that the appellate tribunal should decide all cases in the first instance. It is well known, on the other hand, that the judicial labours of a Magistrate occupy nearly all his time, that which is devoted to matters strictly executive being only the short space daily employed in hearing *thana* reports. But the effectual management of even a small police force, and the duties of a public prosecutor, ought to occupy the whole of one man's time, and the management of the police of a large district must necessarily be inefficient which, from press of other duties, is slurred over in two hasty hours of each day. I consider it then an indispensable preliminary to the improvement of our system that the duties of preventing crime and of apprehending and prosecuting offenders should, without delay, be separated from the judicial function."

4. Mr. Halliday's opinions on this subject were substantially approved by two other members of the Committee appointed by the Government of Bengal—Mr. W. W. Bird and Mr. J. Lowis. Mr. Bird, who was president of the Committee, stated that he had no objection to the disunion of executive from judicial functions. He added that he had invariably advocated the principle alike in the Revenue and the Judicial Departments, but as it was

at that time pertinaciously disregarded in one department it could not very consistently be introduced in the other. Mr. Lowis characterized Mr. Halliday's proposals as "systematic in plan, complete in detail, and sound in principle." With reference to Mr. Bird's observation, just cited, Mr. Lowis said that it was fallacious "to aver that a departure from right principle in one branch of administration requires, for the sake of consistency, a departure from it in another." It is true that Mr. Halliday, eighteen years later, held a different view, and thought that British administration should conform to the oriental idea of uniting all powers into one centre. But his personal change of opinion does not affect the force of his former arguments.

5. Again, in 1854, in the course of a letter to the Government of India, Mr. C. Beadon, Secretary to the Government of Bengal, wrote :

> "The only separation of functions which is really desirable is that of the executive and judicial, the one being a check upon the other : and if the office of Magistrate and Collector be reconstituted on its former footing I think it will have to be considered whether . . . . the Magistrates should not be required to make over the greater portion of their judicial duties to qualified subordinates, devoting their own attention chiefly to police matters and the general executive management of their districts."

In November of the same year, as a member of the Council of the Governor-General, the Hon. (afterwards Sir) J. P. Grant recorded a Minute in which he said that the combination of the duty of the Superintendent of Police and Public Prosecutor with the functions of a Criminal Judge was objectionable in principle, and the practical objections to it had been greatly aggravated by the course of legislation which had raised the judicial powers of a Magistrate six times higher than they were in the days of Lord Cornwallis. "It ought," Mr. Grant continued, "to be the fixed intention of the Government to dissever as soon as possible the functions of Criminal Judge from those of thief-catcher and Public Prosecutor, now combined in the office of Magistrate. That seems to me to be indispensable as a step towards any great improvement in our criminal jurisprudence."

6. Two years later—in September, 1856—a Despatch of the Court of Directors of the East India Company (No. 41, Judicial Department) on the re-organization of the Police in India pointed out that "to remedy the evils of the existing system, the first step to be taken is wherever the union at present exists, to separate the police from the administration of the land revenue. . . . In the second place, the management of the police of each district should be taken out of the hands of the Magistrate."

7. In February, 1857, a further Minute was recorded by the Hon. J. P. Grant, member of the Council of the Governor-General, upon the "Union of the functions of Superintendent of Police with those of a Criminal Judge." Mr. Grant, whose opinions Mr. (afterwards Sir Barnes) Peacock generally concurred, wrote :

"The one point for decision, as it appears to me, on which alone the whole question turns, is this—in which way is crime more certainly discovered, proved and punished, and innocence more certainly protected—when two men are occupied each as thief-catcher, prosecutor, and judge, or when one them is occupied as thief-catcher and prosecutor, and the other as judge? I have no doubt that the principle of division of labour has all its general advantages, and an immense preponderance of special and peculiar advantages, when applied to this particular case; and I have no doubt that if there is any real difference between India and Europe in relation to this question, the difference is all in favour of relieving the Judge in India from all connexion with the detective officer and prosecutor. The judicial ermine is, in my judgment, out of place in the bye-ways of the detective policeman in any country, and those bye-ways in India are unusually dirty. Indeed, so strongly does this feeling operate, perhaps unconsciously, upon the English minds of the honourable body of men from whom our Magistrates are chosen, that in practice the real evil of the combination is, not that a Judge, whose mind has been put out of balance by his antecedents in relation to the prisoner, tries that prisoner, but that the Superintendent of Police, whose nerve and honesty are indispensable to the keeping of the native police officers in order, abandons all real concern with the detection of crime, and the prosecution of criminals, in the mass of cases, and leaves this important and delicate duty almost wholly, in fact, to the native *darogahs*. . . . . If the combination theory were acted upon in reality—if an officer, after bribing spies, endeavouring to corrupt accomplices, laying himself out to hear what every tell-tale has to say, and putting his wit to the utmost stretch, for weeks perhaps, in order to beat his adversary in the game of detection, were then to sit down gravely as a Judge, and were to profess to try dispassionately upon the evidence given in court the question of whether he or his adversary had won the game, I am well convinced that one or two cases of this sort would excite as much indignation as would save me the necessity of all argument *a priori* against the combination theory."

Unfortunately the theory has been acted upon in reality. Actual cases—more than one or two—have excited the vehement indignation against which Mr. Grant sought in 1857 to provide. Mr. Grant added that the objections to separation of judicial and police functions seemed to him, after the best attention he could give them, to be founded on imaginary evils. He refused to anticipate "such extreme antagonism between the native public officer and the native Judge as would be materially inconvenient." "Under a moderately sensible European Magistrate, controlled by an intelligent Commissioner, who would not talk or act as if police *peons* and *darogahs* were infallible, and dispassionate judges were never right, I cannot see why there should be any such consequences."

8. These, and similar, expressions of opinion were not lost upon the Government of India, as the history of the legislation which was undertaken immediately after the suppression of the Mutiny shows. In 1860 a Commission was appointed to enquire into the organisation of the Police. It consisted of representative officers from the Nort-West Provinces, Pegu, Bengal, Madras, the Punjab, and Oudh—"all," in the words of Sir Bartle Frere, "men of ripe experience, especially in matters connected with Police." The instructions issued to the Commission contained the following propositions :

"The functions of a police are either protective and repressive or detective, to prevent crime and disorder, or to find out criminals and disturbers of the peace. These functions are in no respect judicial. This rule requires a complete severance of the police from the judicial authorities, whether those of higher grade or the inferior magistracy in their judicial capacity. When, as is often the case in India, various functions are combined in the hands of one Magistrate, it may sometimes be difficult to observe this restriction ; but the rule should always be kept in sight that the official who collects and traces out the links in the chain of evidence in any case of importance should never be the same as the judicial officer, whether of high or inferior grade, who is to sit in judgment on the case. . . . . It may sometimes be difficult to insist on this rule, but experience shows it is not nearly so difficult as would be supposed, and the advantages of insisting on it cannot be overstated."

Again :

"The working police having its own officers exclusively engaged on their own duties in preventing or detecting crime, the question is, at what link in the chain of subordination between the highest and lowest officers in the executive administration is the police to be attached, and so made responsible as well as subordinate to all above that link in the chain ? The great object being to keep the judicial and police functions quite distinct, the most perfect organization is, no doubt, when the police is subordinate to none but that officer in the executive Government who is absolved from all judicial duty, or at least from all duty involving original jurisdiction, so that his judicial decisions can never be biassed by his duties as a Superintendent of police. . . . . It is difficult to lay down any more definite rule as to the exact point where the subordination should commence than by saying that it should be so arranged that an officer should never be liable to try judicially important cases got up under his own directions as a police officer. . . . . This raises the question—Who is to be responsible for the peace of the district ? Clearly that officer, whoever he may be, to whom the police are immediately responsible. Under him, it is the duty of every police officer and of every magisterial officer of whatever grade, in their several charges, to keep him informed of all matters affecting the public peace and the prevention and detection of crime. It is his duty to see that both classes of officers work together for this end ; as both are subordinate to him, he ought to be able to ensure their combined action. The exact limits of the several duties of the two classes of officers it may be difficult to define in any general rule ; but they will not be difficult to fix in practice if the leading principles are authoritatively laid down, and, above all, if the golden rule be borne in mind that the judicial and police functions are not to be mixed up or confounded, that the active work of preventing or detecting crime is to rest entirely with the police, and not to be interfered with by those who are to sit in judgment on the criminal."

9. The Police Commission in their Report (dated September, 1860) expressly recognised and accepted

this "golden rule." Paragraph 27 of their Report was as follows:

"That as a rule there should be complete serverance of executive police from judicial authorities; that the official who collects and traces out the links of evidence—in other words, virtually prosecutes the offender—should never be the same as the officer, whether of high or inferior grade, who is to sit in judgment on the case, even with a view to committal for trial before a higher tribunal. As the detection and prosecution of criminals properly devolve on the police, no police officer should be permitted to have any judicial function."

But although the Commission adopted without question the general principle that judicial and police functions ought not to be confounded, they proposed, as a matter of practical and temporary convenience, in view of "the constitution of the official agency" then existing in India, that an exception should be made in the case of the District Officer. The Commission did not maintain that the principle did not in strictness, apply to him. On the contrary, they appear to have stated expressly that it did. But they recommended that in his case true principle should, for the time being, be sacrificed to expediency. They reported:

"That the same true principle, that the judge and detective officer should not be one and the same, applies to officials having by law judicial functions, and should, as far as possible, be carefully observed in practice. But, with the constitution of the official agency now existing in India, an exception must be made in favour of the District Officer. The Magistrates have long been, in the eye of the law, executive officers, having a general supervising authority in matters of police, originally without extensive judicial powers. In some part of India this original function of the Magistrates has not been widely departed from; in other parts extensive judicial powers have been superadded to their original and proper function. This circumstance has imported difficulties in regard to maintaining the leading principle enunciated above, for it is impracticable to relieve the Magistrates of their judicial duties; and, on the other hand, it is at present inexpedient to deprive the police and public of the valuable aid and supervision of the District Officer in the general management of police matters."

The commission recognised that this combination of judicial with police functions was open to objection, but looked forward to a time when improvements in organization would, in actual practice, bring it to an end:—

"That this departure from principle will be less objectionable in practice when the executive police, though bound to obey the magistrate's order *quoad* the criminal administration, is kept departmentally distinct and subordinate to its own officers, and constitutes a special agency having no judicial function. As the organization becomes perfected and the force effective for the performance of its detective duties, any necessity for the Magistrate to take personal action in any case judicially before him ought to cease."

10. The recommendations of the Police Commission were adopted by the Government of India and, in accordance with them, Sir Bartle Frere introduced in the Legislative Council on September 29, 1860, a Bill for the Better Regulation of Police. The debate on the second reading of this measure, which afterwards became Act V. of 1861, and is still in force, is important as showing that the Government of India regarded the exceptional union of judicial with police functions in the District Officer as a temporary compromise. Sir Barnes Peacock, the Vice-President of the Council, stated that he "had always been of opinion that a full and complete separation ought to be made between the two functions,"

while in reply to Mr. A. Sconce, who had argued that some passages in the Report of the Police Commission were at variance with the principle of separation, Sir Bartle Frere said :—

"It was one thing to lay down a principle and another to act on it at once and entirely when it was opposed to the existing system, to all existing forms of procedure, and to prejudices of long standing. Under such circumstances, it was often necessary to come to a compromise. . . . . He hoped that at no distant period the principle would be acted upon throughout India as completely as his hon. friend could desire. The hon. member had called the Bill a 'half and half' measure. He could assure the hon. gentleman that nobody was more inclined that it should be made a whole measure than he was, and he should be very glad if his hon. friend would only induce the Executive Governments to give it their support so as to effect a still more complete severance of the police and judicial functions than the Bill contemplated."

The hope expressed by Sir Bartle Frere in 1860 has yet to be fulfilled. It might have been realised in 1872 when the second Code of Criminal Procedure was passed. But the Government and the Legislature of the day were still under the dominion of the fallacy that all power must be centred in the District Magistrate, and the opportunity of applying the sound principle for which Sir Bartle Frere had contended was unfortunately rejected. In 1882 the Code of Criminal Procedure was further revised, and the Select Committee, in their report on the Criminal Procedure Bill, said :—

"At the suggestion of the Government of Bengal, we have omitted section 38, conferring police powers on Magistrates. We consider that it is inexpedient to invest Magistrates with such powers, or to make their connexion with the police more close than it is at present."

(*b*)—The Existing Grievance, and the Remedy.

11. The request which we have now the honour of urging is, therefore, that—in the words used by Sir J. P. Grant in 1854—the functions of criminal judge should be dissevered from those of thief-catcher and public prosecutor, or—in the words used by Sir Barnes Peacock in 1860—that a full and complete separation should be made between judicial and executive functions. At present these functions are to a great extent combined in India, especially in the case of the officers who in the Districts of Regulation Provinces are known as Collector-Magistrates, and the non-Regulation Provinces are known as Deputy Commissioners. The duties of these officers are thus described by Sir W. W. Hunter :*—"As the name of Collector-Magistrate implies, his main functions are twofold. He is a fiscal officer, charged with the collection of the revenue from the land and other sources ; he also is a revenue and criminal judge, both of first instance and in appeal. But his title by no means exhausts his multifarious duties. He does in his smaller local sphere all that the Home Secretary superintends in England, and a great deal more ; for he is the representative of a paternal and not a constitutional government. Police, jails, education, municipalities, roads, sanitation, dispensaries, the local taxation, and the Imperial revenues of his District, are to him matters of daily concern." It is submitted that, just as Lord Cornwallis's Government held a century ago that the proprietors of land could never consider the privileges which had been con-

* "The Indian Empire," p. 513 (3rd edition).

ferred upon them as secure while the revenue officers were vested with judicial powers, so also the administration of justice is brought into suspicion while judicial powers remain in the hands of the detective and public prosecutor.

12. The grounds upon which the request for full separation is made are sufficiently obvious. They have been anticipated in the official opinions already cited. It may, however, be convenient to summarize the arguments which have been advanced of late years by independent public opinion in India. These are to the effect (i) that the combination of judicial with executive duties in the same officer violates the first principles of equity; (ii) that while a judicial officer ought to be thoroughly impartial and approach the consideration of any case without previous knowledge of the facts, an executive officer does not adequately discharge his duties unless his ears are open to all reports and information which he can in any degree employ for the benefit of his District; (iii) that executive officers in India, being responsible for a large amount of miscellaneous business have not time satisfactorily to dispose of judicial work in addition; (iv) that, being keenly interested in carrying out particular measures, they are apt to be brought more or less into conflict with individuals, and, therefore, that it is inexpedient that they should also be invested with judicial powers; (v) that under the existing system Collector-Magistrates do, in fact, neglect judicial for executive work; (vi) that appeals from revenue assessments are apt to be futile when they are heard by revenue

officers ; (vii) that great inconvenience, expense, and suffering are imposed upon suitors required to follow the camp of a judicial officer who, in the discharge of executive duties, is making a tour of his District ; and (viii) that the existing system not only involves all whom it concerns in hardship and inconvenience but also, by associating the judicial tribunal with the work of the police and of detectives, and by diminishing the safeguards afforded by the rules of evidence, produces actual miscarriages of justice and creates, although justice be done, opportunities of suspicion, distrust and discontent which are greatly to be deplored. There is, too, a further argument for the separation, which arises out of the very nature of the work incidental to the judicial office, and which of itself might well be regarded as conclusive in the matter. It is no longer open to us to content ourselves with the pleasant belief that to an Englishman of good sense and education, with his unyielding integrity and quick apprehension of the just and the equitable, nothing is easier than the patriarchal administration of justice among oriental populations. The trial in Indian courts of justice of every grade must be carried out in the English method, and the judge or magistrate must proceed to his decision upon the basis of facts to be ascertained only through the examination and cross-examination before him of eye-witnesses testifying each to the relevant facts observed by him, and nothing more. It is not necessary for us to dwell on the importance of this procedure, nor is it too much to say that with this system of trial no judicial officer can efficiently perform his work otherwise than by close adherence to the methods and rules which the long experience of English lawyers has dictated, and of which he cannot hope to acquire a practical mastery, unless he makes the study and practice of them his serious business. In other words it is essential to the proper and efficient—and we might add impartial—administration of justice that the judicial officer should be an expert specially educated and trained for the work of the court.

13. In Appendix B to this Memorial summaries are given of various cases which, it is thought, illustrate in a striking way some of the dangers that arise from the present system. These cases of themselves might well remove—to adopt Sir J. P. Grant's words—"the necessity of argument *a priori* against the combination theory." But the present system is not merely objectionable on the ground that from time to time it is, and is clearly proved to be, responsible for a particular case of actual injustice. It is also objectionable on the ground that, so long as it exists, the general administration of justice is subjected to suspicion, and the strength and authority of the Government are seriously impaired. For this reason it is submitted that nothing short of complete separation of judicial from executive functions by legislation will remove the danger. Something perhaps, might be accomplished by purely executive measures. Much, no doubt, might be accomplished by granting to accused persons, in important cases, the option of standing their trial before a Sessions Court. But these palliatives fall short of the only complete and satisfactory remedy, which

is, by means of legislation, to make a clear line of division between the judicial and the executive duties now often combined in one and the same officer. So long as Collector-Magistrates have the power themselves to try, or to delegate to subordinates within their control, cases as to which they have taken action or received information in an Executive capacity, the administration of justice in India is not likely to command complete confidence and respect.

14. It would be easy to multiply expressions of authoritative opinion in support of the proposed reform. But, in view of the opinions already cited, it may be enough to add that, in a debate on the subject which took place in the House of Lords on May 8th, 1893, Lord Kimberley, then Secretary of State for India, and his predecessor, Lord Cross, showed their approval of the principle of separation in no ambiguous terms. Lord Cross said, on that occasion, that it would be, in his judgment, an "excellent plan" to separate judicial from executive functions, and that it would "result in vast good to the Government of India." It was in the same spirit that Lord Dufferin, as Viceroy of India, referring to the proposal for separation put forward by the Indian National Congress, characterised it as a "counsel of perfection." Appendix A to the present Memorial contains, *inter alia*, the favourable opinions of the Right Hon. Sir Richard Garth, late Chief Justice of Bengal, the Right Hon. Lord Hobhouse, Legal Member of the Viceroy's Council, 1872-77, the Right Hon. Sir Richard Couch, late Chief Justice of Bengal, Sir J. B. Phear, late Chief

Justice of Ceylon, Sir R. T Reid, Q.C., M.P., Attorney-General, 1894-5, Sir William Markby, late Judge of the High Court, Calcutta, and Sir Raymond West, late Judge of the High Court, Bombay. These opinions were collected and compiled by the British Commitee of the Indian National Congress, and, among other important indications of opinions prevalent in India, we beg to refer you to the series of resolutions adopted by the Indian National Congress—which Lord Lansdowne, as Viceroy, referred to in 1891 as a "perfectly legitimate movement" representing in India "what in Europe would be called the more advanced Liberal party." In 1886 the Congress adopted a resolution recording "an expression of the universal conviction that a complete separation of executive and judicial functions has become an urgent necessity," and urging the Government of India "to effect this separation without further delay." Similar resolutions were carried in 1887 and 1888, and the proposal formed in 1889, 1890, and 1891 the first section of an "omnibus" resolution affirming the resolutions of previous Congresses. In 1892 the Congress again carried a separate resolution on the question, adding to its original resolution a reference to "the serious mischief arising to the country from the combination of judicial and executive functions." In 1893 the resolution carried by the Congress was as follows :—

"That this Congress, having now for many successive years vainly appealed to the Government of India to remove one of the gravest stigmas on British rule in India, one fraught with incalculable oppression to all classes of the community throughout the country, now hopeless of any other redress, humbly entreats the Secretary of State for India to order the immediate appointment, in each province, of a Committee (one-half at least of whose members shall be non-official natives of India, qualified by education and experience in the workings of the various courts to deal with the question) to prepare each a scheme for the complete separation of all judicial and executive functions in their own provinces with as little additional cost to the State as may be practicable and the submission of such schemes, with the comments of the several Indian Governments thereon, to himself, at some early date which he may be pleased to fix."

A similar resolution was carried in 1894, 1895, and 1896. During recent years, also, practical schemes for separation have been laid before the Congress.

(c)—ANSWERS TO POSSIBLE OBJECTIONS.

15. The objections which, during the course of a century, have been urged against the separation of judicial and executive functions are reducible, on analysis, to three only: (i) that the system of combination works well, and is not responsible for miscarriage of justice; (ii) that the system of combination, however indefensible it may seem to Western ideas, is necessary to the position, the authority, and, in a word, to the "prestige" of an Oriental officer; and (iii) that separation of the two functions, though excellent in principle, would involve an additional expenditure which is, in fact, prohibitive in the present condition of the Indian finances.

16. It is obvious that the first objection is incompatible with the other two objections. It is one thing to defend the existing system on its merits: it is another thing to say that, although it is bad, it would be too dangerous or too costly to reform it. The first objection

is an allegation of fact. The answer—and, it is submitted, the irresistible answer—is to be found in the cases which are set forth in Appendix B to this Memorial. The cases are but typical examples taken from a large number. It may be added that, among the leading advocates of separation in India, are Indian barristers of long and varied experience in the Courts who are able to testify, from personal knowledge, to the mischievous results of the present system. Their evidence is confirmed, also from personal knowledge, by many Anglo-Indian Judges of long experience.

17. The second objection—that the combination of judicial and executive functions is necessary to the "prestige" of an Oriental officer—is perhaps more difficult to handle. For reasons which are easy to understand, it is not often put forward in public and authoritative statements. But it is common in the Anglo-Indian press, it finds its way into magazine articles written by returned officers, and in India it is believed, rightly or wrongly, to lie at the root of all the apologies for the present system. It has been said that Oriental ideas require in an officer entrusted with large executive duties the further power of inflicting punishment on individuals. If the proposition were true, it would be natural to expect that the existing system would be supported and defended by independent public opinion in India instead of being—as it is—deplored and condemned. It is not reasonable to assume that the Indian of to-day demands in the responsible officers of a civilised Government a combination of functions which at an earlier time an

arbitrary despot may have enforced. The further contention that a District Magistrate ought to have the power of inflicting punishment because he is the local representive of the Sovereign appears to be based upon a fallacy and a misapprehension. The power of inflicting punishment is, indeed, part of the attributes of Sovereignty. But it is not, on that ground, any more necessary that the power should be exercised by a Collector-Magistrate, who is head of the police and the revenue-system, than that it should be exercised by the Sovereign in person. The same reasoning, if it were accepted, would require that the Viceroy should be invested with the powers of a criminal judge. But it is not suggested that the Viceroy's "prestige" is lower than the "prestige" of a District Judge because the Judge passes sentences upon guilty persons and the Viceroy does not. It is equally a misapprehension to assume that those who urge the separation of judicial from executive duties desire the suppression or extinction of legitimate authority. They ask merely for a division of labour. The truth seems to be that the somewhat vague considerations which are put forward in defence of the existing system on the ground that it is necessary to the due authority of a District Magistrate had their origin in the prejudices and the customs of earlier times, revived, to some extent, in the unsettled period which followed the Indian Mutiny. We venture to submit that these considerations are not only groundless and misplaced, but that the authority of Government, far from being weakened by the equitable division of judicial and executive duties, would be incalculably strengthened by the reform of a system which is at present responsible for many judicial scandals.

18. The financial objection alone remains, and it is upon this objection that responsible authorities appear to rely. When Lord Dufferin described the proposal for separation as a "counsel of perfection," he added that the condition of Indian finance prevented it, at that time, from being adopted. Similarly, in the debate in the House of Lords on May 8th, 1893, to which reference has already been made, Lord Kimberley, then Secretary of state, said :

"The difficulty is simply this, that if you were to alter the present system in India you would have to double the staff throughout the country :"

and his predecessor, Lord Cross, said :—

"It [the main principle raised in the discussion] is a matter of the gravest possible importance, but I can only agree with what my noble friend has stated, that in the present state of the finances of India it is absolutely impossible to carry out that plan, which to my mind would be an excellent one, resulting in vast good to the Government of India."

The best answer to this objection is to be found in the scheme for separation drawn up in 1893 by Mr. Romesh Chunder Dutt, C.I.E., late Commissioner of the Orissa Division (at that time District Magistrate of Midnapur) and printed in Appendix A to this Memorial. In these circumstances it is not necessary to argue either (i) that any expense which the separation of judicial from executive duties might involve would be borne, and borne cheerfully, by the people of India ; or (ii) that it might well be met by economies in certain other directions. Mr. Dutt shows that the separation might be effected by simple re-arrangement of the existing staff, without any additional expense whatsoever. Mr. Dutt's scheme refers specially to Bengal, the Presidency, that is, for which the reform had been described as impracticable on the ground of cost. Similar schemes for other Presidencies and Provinces have been framed, but it was understood that the most serious financial difficulty was apprehended in Bengal.

19. In view of foregoing considerations we earnestly trust that you will direct the Government of India to prepare a scheme for the complete separation of judicial and executive functions, and to report upon this urgently pressing question at an early date.

We have the honour to be, Sir,

Your obedient Servants,

HOBHOUSE,
RICHARD GARTH,
RICHARD COUCH,
CHARLES SARGENT,
WILLIAM MARKBY,
JOHN BUDD PHEAR,
J. SCOTT,
W. WEDDERBURN,
ROLAND K. WILSON,
HERBERT J. REYNOLDS.

Scheme (Printed in "India" for August, 1893) suggested by Mr. Romesh Dutt, C.I.E., Commissioner of the Orissa Division (at that time District Magistrate of Midnapur).

The recent discussions on the subject of the separation of Judicial and Executive functions in India have given sincere gratification to my countrymen in India. They have read with satisfaction, and also with feelings of gratitude, the views expressed by Lord Stanley in the House of Lords, and the clear and emphatic opinion on the subject expressed by Lord Kimberley. They have learnt with sincere joy that the system of uniting Judicial and Executive functions in the same officer has been condemned by two successive Secretaries of State, Lord Cross and Lord Kimberley. And they entertain a legitimate hope that a policy which has been thus condemned by the highest authorities in Indian affairs will not long continue to be the policy of British rule in India.

Sir Richard Garth, late Chief Justice of the High Court of Calcutta, whose paper on this subject led to the discussions in the House of Lords, has since explained the history of the present system of administration in a clear, lucid, and forcible manner. He has shown that so far back as 1860 a commission appointed to report on the police declared that "the judicial and police functions were not to be mixed up and confounded." He has pointed out that the late Sir Barnes Peacock and other high authorities were against the union of these functions, and that the late Sir Bartle Frere, in introducing the Bill which afterwards became the Police Act of 1861, "hoped that at no distant period the principle (of the separation of Judicial and Executive functions) would be acted upon throughout India." Sir Richard Garth has also informed the public that between 1865 and 1868 the highest civilian authorities in India were again consulted on the subject, and, according to Sir James Stephen, the District Magistrates themselves were "greatly embarrassed by the union in their persons of Judicial and Executive functions." Sir Richard has further told us that under Lord Ripon's Government opinions were again collected, and the present system was only continued because the retention of Judicial powers in the hands of a District Officer was considered (and very wrongly considered, *vide* Lord Kimberley's speech) "essential to the weight and influence of his office." And, lastly, Sir Richard has quoted the words of the present Secretary of State that the present system "is contrary to right and good principle," and he has also quoted the words of the late Secretary of State, who concurs in this opinion with Lord Kimberley.

Such are the opinions of men most capable of forming a judgment on the present system of administration in India, and responsible administrators are anxious to effect a reform which will remove the evil without materially adding to the cost of administration. A practicable scheme of reform will be not unwelcome at the present moment, and many of my countrymen and some of my English friends have asked me to state my views on the subject, as I happen to be in England just now. I venture therefore to suggest the leading features of a scheme which has for many years appeared perfectly feasible to myself, and which I believe will meet the views and wishes not only of my countrymen, but of most Englishmen also, who are quite as anxious for wholesome reform on this point as my countrymen.

It is necessary for me to state that I have been employed on administrative work in Bengal for twenty-two years, and that I have had ample opportunities to observe the practical working of the present system of administration during this period. Within this period I have had the honour of holding charge of some of the largest and most important districts in Bengal—like Bardwan, with its population of a million and a half, and Bakarganj, with its population of two millions, and Midnapur, with its population of two and a half millions, and Maimansingh, with its population of three and a half millions—which is equal to the population of many a small kingdom in Europe. In these extensive and thickly populated districts I have, for years past, combined in myself the functions of the head of the Police, the head Magistrate, the head Superintendent of Prisons, the head Revenue Officer, the head Tax Collector, the head of the Government Treasury, the head Manager of Government Estates, the head Manager of Minors' States, the head Engineer, the head Sanitary Officer, the head Superintendent of Primary

Schools, and various other functions. I have, for years past, directed and watched police enquiries in important cases, had the prisoners in those cases tried by my subordinates, heard and disposed of the appeals of some of those very prisoners, and superintended their labour in prisons. And during all these years I have held the opinion that a separation of Judicial and Executive functions would make our duties less embarrassing, and more consistent with our ideas of judicial fairness; that it would improve both Judicial work and Executive work; and that it would require no material addition to the cost of administration.

Bengal is divided into nine Divisions, viz.: 1. Presidency. 2. Bardwan. 3. Rajshahi. 4. Dacca. 5. Chittagong. 6. Orissa. 7. Patna. 8. Bhagalpur. 9. Chutia-Nagpur. I think it is not feasible, nor desirable perhaps for the present, to effect a separation of Judicial and Executive functions in the Division of Chutia-Nagpur, which consists of Non-Regulation Districts. It is also, perhaps, undesirable to effect such separation in the Districts of Darjiling and Jalpaiguri in Rajshahi Division; in the Hill Tracts of Chittagong Division; and in the Santal Parganas of Bhagalpur Division. In the remaining portions of the Province it is possible to effect the separation at once.

The population of Bengal (excluding Tributary States and the States of the Maharajas of Kuch Behar, Sikkim, Tipperah), is, according to the census of 1891, *seventy-one millions* in round numbers. The population of the districts alluded to in the last paragraph, in which a separation of Judicial and Executive functions is for the present impracticable, is *seven millions* in round numbers. In the remaining portions of Bengal, having a population of *sixty-four millions*, it is possible to effect the desired separation at once.

Generally speaking, there are two senior Covenanted officers in every Regulation District in Bengal, viz., a District Judge and a District Magistrate. The District Judge is the head of all subordinate judicial officers who dispose of civil cases, and he also tries such important criminal cases as are committed to the Sessions. The work of the District Magistrate is more varied, as has been indicated above. He is the head of the police, supervises prisons, collects revenue and taxes, sells opium and settles liquor-shops, constructs roads and bridges, regulates primary education, and combines with these and other Executive duties the functions and powers of the head Magistrate of his district.

My scheme is simple. The District Magistrate, whom I will henceforth call the District Officer, should be employed purely on executive and revenue work, which is sufficiently varied, onerous, and engrossing, and should be relieved of his judicial duties, which should be transferred to the District Judge. The subordinates of the District Officer, who will continue to perform revenue and executive work only, will remain under him; while those of his present subordinates who will be employed on purely judicial work should be subordinate to the Judge and not to the District Officer.

At present the subordinates of the District officer

combine executive and revenue and judicial work. A Joint-Magistrate or Assistant-Magistrate (subordinate to the District Officer) tries criminal cases, and also does revenue and executive work. A Deputy-Magistrate (similarly subordinate to the District Officer) also tries criminal cases and does revenue and executive work. This arrangement must be changed.

I will first take the case of Joint-Magistrates and Assistant-Magistrates, who are Covenanted officers. Young civilians, as soon as they arrive in Bengal, are posted as Assistant-Magistrates; they try criminal cases and also help the District Officer in his revenue and executive work. After they have had some experience in their work and learnt something of the people, and after they have passed two examinations in Indian law and accounts, and the languages of the Province, they are promoted to be Joint-Magistrates. And the Joint-Magistrate tries all the more important criminal cases, and performs much of the important criminal work of the district. And in course of time he becomes a District Officer or a District Judge.

Referring to the Bengal Civil List for April, 1893, which is the last number that is available to me in London now, I find that the present number of Joint-Magistrates and officiating Joint-Magistrates in Bengal (excluding those acting in higher capacities, or on special duty) is only twenty-two. And the number of Assistant-Magistrates, after such exclusion, is also twenty-two. As there are over forty districts in Bengal, it is clear that on the average each District Officer has only one Covenanted

Assistant (Joint or Assistant-Magistrate) and no more. In some districts there are more than one, in smaller districts there are none.

I propose that the Assistant-Magistrates should be employed purely on revenue, executive and police work, and should be subordinate to the District Officer. And when the Assistant-Magistrates are promoted to be Joint-Magistrates, they should be employed purely on judicial work, and be subordinate to the District Judge.

This proposal will not only secure the separation of functions contemplated, but will secure two other distinctly beneficial results. In the first place, young civilians fresh from England, and wholly unacquainted with the manners and habits, and even the colloquial language, of the people of India, will be stopped from trying criminal cases until they have acquired some local knowledge and experience by doing revenue and general executive work, and watching police cases and police administration. And in the second place, such young civilians will receive a more systematic and less confused training in their duties by devoting their attention during the first two or three years to purely executive and revenue and police work, and then employing themselves for some years on purely judicial work.

I next come to the Deputy-Magistrates, who are uncovenanted officers, and generally natives of India. They also combine judicial, executive, and revenue work, and are subordinate to the District Officer. The Civil List gives their number as 305 in all; but excluding those on leave, or employed on special duty, or in sub-divisions (of which I will speak later on), there are, on an average, only four Deputy-Magistrates in the head-quarters of each district to help the District Officer. In small districts there are, perhaps, only two ; in specially large districts there are as many as six.

I propose that in each district one-half of the Deputy Magistrates may be employed on purely executive and revenue work, and be placed under the District Officer, and that the other half be employed on purely judicial work, and placed under the District Judge. In some districts, where the revenue work is particularly heavy, probably more than half the Deputy-Magistrates may be placed under the District Officer. And in other districts, where the criminal work is more important, the Judge may require more than half the Deputy-Magistrates. These details can be very easly settled. But in the main it is clear and self-evident that the officers who are able to cope with revenue and criminal work which is heaped on them in a confused manner will be able to cope with it better under the system of division of labour proposed above.

The results of the proposals made above will be these. The District Officer will still be the head executive officer, the head revenue officer, and the head police officer of his district. He will collect revenue and taxes, and perform all the work connected with revenue administration with the help of his assistants and deputies. He will continue to perform all executive work, and will be armed with the necessary powers. He will watch and direct police investigations, and will be virtually the prosecutor in criminal cases. But he will cease to try, or to have tried by his subordinates, criminal cases, in respect of which he is the police officer and the prosecutor.

On the other hand, the District Judge will, in addition to his present duties, supervise the work of Joint-Magistrates and Deputy-Magistrates employed on purely judicial work. This work of supervision will be better and more impartially done by trained judicial officers than by over-worked executive officers, who are also virtually prosecutors. And the evil which arises from the combination of the functions of the prosecutor and the judge—of which we have had some striking illustrations of late—will cease to exist when the prosecutor is no longer the judge.

The transfer of all judicial work to the District Judge will give him some additional work; but he will easily cope with it with the additional officers who will be placed under him under the proposed scheme. In important and heavy districts the Judge will have a Joint-Magistrate under him, and the Joint-Magistrate may in exceptional cases be vested with the powers of an Assistant-Sessions Judge to relieve the District Judge of his sessions work. In districts where there are no Joint-Magistrates, a senior and selected Deputy-Magistrate can do the Joint-Magistrate's work, and efficiently help the Judge in his duty of supervision of criminal work. With regard to criminal appeals, the District Judge now hears all of them from sentences passed by first-class magistrates. The few appeals from second and third-class magistrates which the District Officer now hears may also be heard by the Judge, and the addition will scarcely be felt. In exceptionlly heavy districts, like Maimansingh and Midnapur, criminal appeals did not take more than three hours of my time in a week. A trained Judicial Officer, like the District Judge, would do it in less time, and if he required help in this matter also, his subordinate Joint-Magistrate or a selected Deputy-Magistrate might be empowered to hear petty appeals.

It only remains to deal with what are called sub-districts or sub-divisions in Bengal. The Bengal districts are generally extensive in area ; and, while the central portions are managed and administered from headquarters it is found convenient to form the outlying portions into separate sub-districts or sub-divisions, and to place them in charge of Sub-Divisional Officers. Such Sub-Divisional Officers (generally Deputy-Magistrates, sometimes Assistant or Joint-Magistrates) are also completely subordinate to the District Officer, like the assistants at headquarters.

In Bengal (excluding the backward districts in which the introduction of the proposed scheme is at present impracticable) there are seventy-five sub-divisions. There is only one Sub-Divisional Officer in each sub-division, and he performs revenue and executive and judicial work in his sub-division as his superior, the District Officer, does for the whole district. The question arises, how the scheme of separation can be introduced in these seventy-five sub-divisions.

There is a class of officers, called Sub-Deputy Collectors, who are generally employed on revenue work, but sometimes perform judicial work and try criminal cases. Some of them are employed at headquarters, while others are sent to important Sub-Divisions to help Sub-Divisional Officers. For many years past the work in Sub-Divisions has been increasing, and the demand for a Sub-Deputy Collector in every Sub-Division in Bengal has been growing also. It has been urged that Sub-Divisional Officers who are mainly employed on judicial work cannot find time to perform their revenue work without help. It has also been urged, with great force, that during the absence of Sub-Divisional Officers on their annual tours Sub-Divisional treasuries have to be closed, much to the inconvenience of the Postal Department, the Civil Justice Department, and all Government Departments, as well as the public. To remove all this inconvenience, and to give the necessary help to Sub-Divisional Officers, it has been urged that a Sub-Deputy Collector should be placed in every sub-division. This should now be done.

The present number of Sub-Deputy Collectors (excluding those who are acting in higher capacities) is 97. Allowing for officers on leave, there will still be 75 officers always available for employment in the 75 sub-divisions. And when a Sub-Deputy Collector is thus posted in each sub-division, he can be entrusted with the revenue work of the sub-division, and be subordinate to the District Officer, while the Sub-Divisional Officer will be subordinate to the District Judge.

I make this proposal after a careful consideration of

the nature of the revenue work which has to be done in sub-divisions. All important revenue work connected with Land Revenue, Cesses, Income Tax, Certificates, etc., is transacted in the headquarters of the district and the revenue work of sub-divisions is light and easy. Similarly, the work of control and supervision of the Police Department is done at headquarters, and the Sub-Deputy Collector will have little to do in this line. The treasury work in sub-divisions is light, and is now often done by Sub-Deputy Collectors. On the whole, therefore, I am satisfied that a Sub-Deputy Collector will, under the instructions of the District Officer, be quite competent to manage the revenue and other work of sub-divisions, when the judicial functions have been separated and made over to the Sub-Divisional Officer.

There is only one objection which can be reasonably urged against this scheme. Many Sub-Deputy Collectors are now employed at the headquarters of districts, sometimes on important work, and to take them all away for sub-divisions may be impracticable. Some District Officers may reasonably urge that they require Sub-Deputy Collectors at the district headquarters also, and, where this is satisfactorily shown, the requisition should be complied with. It may be necessary, therefore, to appoint twenty or thirty additional Sub-Deputy Collectors, and this is the only increase to the cost of administration which appears to me necessary for effecting a complete separation between Judicial and Executive functions in Bengal.

Even this additional cost may be met by savings in

other departments. Special Deputy Collectors and Sub-Deputy Collectors are employed on excise work, and their special services are wholly unnecessary in this department. It has always appeared to me, and to many others, that the services of such trained and well-qualified officers are wasted in performing work which does not require officers of their rank. If these officers were withdrawn from the Excise Department, and if the work of that department were included in the general work of the district, as was the case some years ago, it would probably be unnecessary to appoint additional Sub-Deputy Collectors, as recommended in the last paragraph.

The scheme which has been briefly set forth in the preceding paragraphs is a practicable one, and can be introduced under the present circumstances of Bengal, excluding the backward tracts. I have worked both as Sub-Divisional Officer and as District Officer in many of the districts in Bengal, and I would undertake to introduce the scheme in any Bengal District, and to work it on the lines indicated above.

I have only to add that if the scheme set forth above—with such modifications in details as may be deemed necessary after a careful consideration of it by the Government—be introduced, it will be necessary to recast the Code of Criminal Procedure so as to relieve the District Officer and his subordinates of judicial powers in criminal cases, and to vest them in the District Judge and his subordinates, The police work, the revenue work, and the general executive work can then be performed by the District Officer with greater care and satisfaction to himself, and also to the greater satisfaction of the people in whose interest he administers the District.

Mr. Romesh Dutt wrote in INDIA for October, 1893:—

My paper on this subject appeared in the August number of INDIA. The paper has been carefully read by many gentlemen interested in questions of Indian administration, and capable of forming a proper judgment on such questions. Their opinions will help the public in forming a correct opinion on this very important subject.

The Right Hon. Sir Richard Garth, Q.C., Late Chief Justice of Bengal, has given my views his qualified support from a judicial point of view. As his remarks have already appeared in the August number of INDIA it is unnecessary for me to do more than quote one or two sentences only.

"So far," he says, "as I am capable myself of forming an opinion upon his scheme, I entirely approve of it. It seems to me the most natural and obvious means of separating the two great divisions of labour, the executive and the judicial. . . . It seems only in accordance with reason that magistrates who are employed upon executive work should be under the chief executive officer of each district, and that those who are employed in judicial work should be under the chief judicial officer."

These remarks are important, as there is no higher authority on judicial questions concerning Bengal than the late Chief Justice of that province.

In the same way there is no Englishman living who

can speak with higher authority on executive and administrative questions concerning Bengal than Mr. Reynolds, late Secretary to the Government of Bengal. He passed his official life in that province, and rose from the lowest appointments in the Civil Service of Bengal to one of the highest. He held charge of some of the most extensive and important districts in Bengal, and performed those combined judicial and executive duties which a district officer in Bengal has to perform. He rose to be Secretary to the Bengal Government, and in that capacity presided over the executive administration of the province. His opinion, therefore, has a unique value and importance.

Mr. Reynolds has suggested one modification to my scheme, and subject to that modification has entirely approved of it. I proposed to contrast sub-deputy collectors with the revenue and executive work of Bengal sub-divisons. Mr. Reynolds thinks that in the more important sub-divisions a deputy collector, and not a sub-deputy collector, should be entrusted with these duties. A suggestion coming from such an authority is entitled to respect, and I accept it in its entirety. Let deputy collectors be employed in the more important sub-divisions to do the revenue and executive work and sub-deputy collectors in the lighter sub-divisions. This modification will require the appointment of twenty or thirty additional deputy collectors, instead of as many sub-deputy collectors, whose appointment I proposed. Thus modified my scheme has Mr. Reynolds' entire support and approval.

My scheme has been read and approved by other gentlemen, who are still in the Civil Service of Bengal. One of them made to me, independently of Mr. Reynolds, the same suggestion which Mr. Reynolds has made. One the whole, therefore, I believe, I am justified in stating that my scheme suggests a practicable way of separating the executive and judicial services in Bengal, without materially adding to the cost of administration.

I have purposely refrained from saying anything on the subject of the existing rules of promotion in the Civil Service. Whether these rules will require modification in some respects after the judicial and executive services have been separated is a matter on which the opinion of the Government of Bengal must be final and conclusive. When I joined the Service in 1871 members of the Service were promoted from the rank of joint magistrates to be district officers, and from the rank of district officers to the posts of district judges. It may be considered desirable and necessary to revert to this old rule of promotion after the district officers have been relieved of their judicial duties. It may be also considered desirable to rule that an assistant magistrate will be entitled to rise to the rank and the judicial powers of a joint magistrate only after he has served as assistant for a certain number of years. Such a rule will ensure some degree of experience and local knowledge in judicial officers, and will also prevent frequent reversions from the post of a joint magistrate to that of assistant. These, however, are matters which can be best considered and decided by the Government of Bengal when the separation of the judicial and executive services has been decided upon. The Bengal Government will find no difficulty in shaping the rules of promotion in the Civil Service according to the exigencies of a just and proper system of administration.

With regard to the details of the administrative arrangements given in my previous paper, no modification except that of Mr. Reynolds has been suggested to me by my friends competent to form a judgment on the subject. I have no doubt that the scheme as modified and supported by the late Secretary to the Government of Bengal will receive the consideration which it deserves from the authorities, both in India and in England.

XVIII. LIMITATION OF THE LAND TAX.

[*Memorial submitted to the Secretary of State for India on December*, 20, 1900.]

MY LORD,

In view of the terrible famines with which India has been lately afflicted, we, the undersigned, who have spent many years of our lives among the people, and still take a deep interest in their welfare, beg to offer the following suggestions to your Lordship in Council, in the hope that the Land Revenue administration may be everywhere placed on such a sound and equitable basis as to secure to the cultivators of the soil a sufficient margin of profit to enable them better to withstand the pressure of future famines.

2.—We are well aware that the primary cause of famines is the failure of rain, and that the protection of large tracts of country by the extension of irrigation from sources that seldom or never fail has been steadily kept in view and acted on by the Government for many years past; but the bulk of the country is dependent on direct rainfall, and the pinch of famine is most severely felt in the uplands, where the crops fail simply for want of rain. The only hope for the cultivators throughout the greater part of India is therefore that they should be put in such a position as to enable them to tide over an occasional bad season.

3.—To place the cultivators in such a position, we consider it essential that the share taken as the Government demand on the land should be strictly limited in every Province. We fully agree with the views of Lord Salisbury, when Secretary of State for India, as set out in his Minute of April 26th, 1875 :—

"So far as it is possible to change the Indian fiscal system, it is desirable that the cultivator should pay a smaller proportion of the whole national charge. It is not in itself a thrifty policy to draw the mass of revenue from the rural districts, where capital is scarce, sparing the towns, where it is often redundant, and runs to waste and luxury. The injury is exaggerated in the case of India, where so much of the revenue is exported without a direct equivalent."

4.—Without going into tedious detail, we consider it very advisable that, in those parts of the country in which the Land Tax is not permanently settled, the following principles should be uniformly adhered to :—

(*a*) Where the Land Revenue is paid directly by the cultivators, as in most parts of Madras and Bombay, the Government demand should be limited to 50 per cent. of the value of the nett produce, after a liberal deduction for cultivation expenses has been made, and should not ordinarily exceed one-fifth of the gross produce, even in those parts of the country where, in theory, one-half of the nett, is assumed to approximate to one-third of the gross, produce.

(*b*) Where the Land Revenue is paid by landlords, the principle adopted in the Saharanpur Rules of 1855, whereby the Revenue demand is limited to one-half of the actual rent or assets of such landlords, should be universally applied.

(*c*) That no revision of the Land Tax of any Province or part thereof should be made within thirty years of the expiration of any former revision.

(*d*) That when such revision is made in any of those parts of India where the Land Revenue is paid by the cultivators direct to the Government, there should be no increase in the assessment except in cases where the land has increased in value (1) in consequence of improvements in irrigation works carried out at the expense of the Government, or (2) on account of a rise in the value of produce, based on the average prices of the thirty years next preceding such revision.

5.—Lastly, we recommend that a limit be fixed in each Province beyond which it may not be permissible to surcharge the Land Tax with local cesses. We are of opinion that the Bengal rate of 6¼ per cent. is a fair one, and that in no case should the rate exceed 10 per cent.

We have the honour to be,

My Lord,

Your obedient Servants,

(Signed)

R. K. PUCKLE,

Late Director of Revenue Settlement, and Member of the Board of Revenue, Madras.

(Signed)

J. H. GARSTIN,

Late Member of Council, Madras.

J. B. PENNINGTON,

Late Collector of Tanjore, Madras.

H. J. REYNOLDS,

Late Revenue Secretary to the Government of Bengal, and late Member of the Legislative Council of the Governor General of India.

RICHARD GARTH,

Late Chief Justice of Bengal.

ROMESH C. DUTT,

Late Offg. Commissioner of Orissa Division in Bengal, and Member of the Bengal Legislative Council.

C. J. O'DONNELL,

Late Commissioner of the Bhagalpur and Rajshahi Divisions, in Bengal.

A. ROGERS,

Late Settlement Officer and Member of Council in Bombay.

W. WEDDERBURN,

Late Acting Chief Secretary to the Government of Bombay.

JOHN JARDINE,

Late Judge of the High-Court of Bombay.

J. P. GOODRIDGE,

Late B.C.S., and formerly Offg. Settlement Commissioner, C.P.

SPEECHES AND PAPERS

ON

Indian Questions,

1901 and 1902.

CONTENTS.

SPEECHES AND PAPERS

ON

INDIAN QUESTIONS.

I. THE INDIAN LAND QUESTION.

[*Reprinted from the Imperial and Colonial Magazine February* 1901.]

I.

In the latter half of the 18th century, a variety of administrative problems presented themselves to the new rulers of India, but none of them was so deeply interesting or presented itself in such varied forms as the Land Question. And the servants of the East India Company, familiar only with the English system of landlords, farmers, and labourers, were fairly puzzled when Zemindars and Polygars, Village-Communities and Peasant-proprietors, appeared before their astonished eyes with all their archaic customs and ancient rights.

The Province of Bengal, the first great acquisition of the East India Company, presented the problem in its simplest form. The country was parcelled out into great estates, owned by hereditary Zemindars, who had under the Mahomedan *regime* virtually ruled their own estates, encouraged literature and arts in their courts, and often commanded troops for the Imperial service. It was obvious therefore, that any revenue settlement of Bengal, based on the ancient institutions of that land, must be a settlement with Zemindars.

For a time, however, the administration of the Province was in disorder. The battle of Plassy was won in 1757, and the Company assumed the direct administration of Bengal in 1765, but the Company's servants, bent on making large fortunes for themselves, endeavoured to take over the inland trade of the country into their own hands, and drove the traders of the country to despair. Farmers of the land-revenue were also sent to the different districts where they made collections from zemindars or tenants often by coercion, and the agriculturists were grievously oppressed. A great famine, —the greatest that is recorded in the history of India, —then occurred in 1770-71, and is estimated to have swept away one-third of the population of that rich and fertile Province.

Warren Hastings was then appointed Governor of Bengal in 1772, and became Governor-General in 1774; and the Land Question naturally came under his consideration. Hastings himself, trained in the old methods, made the harsh and unwise proposal that the estates of Bengal should be sold by public auction or farmed out on leases and that settlements should be made with the purchasers or lessees for life. A juster and a more humane view of the situation was taken by a large-minded statesman, known to English readers as the writer of the "Letters of Junius." In one of the ablest minutes ever recorded in India, Philip Francis, then a member of the Governer General's Council, dwelt on the calamities through which Bengal had passed since the British Conquest, and recommended that a permanent settlement should be made with the Zemindars. "If there be any hidden wealth still existing," he wrote, "it will be brought forth and employed in improving the land, because the proprietor will be satisfied he is labouring for himself."

When these varied proposals came before the Court of Directors in London, the Directors were fairly puzzled by the strangeness of the problem and the magnitude of the issues involved; and following a policy of drift peculiarly British, they allowed the problem time to ripen towards its own solution. On the Christmas Eve of 1776 the Directors wrote to India that "having considered the different circumstances of letting the land on leases for lives, or in perpetuity, we do not for many weighty reasons, think it at present advisable to adopt either of these modes."

For nine years more, Warren Hastings administered the affairs of India, and the Land Question in Bengal ripened towards a solution. The short leases and the prompt demands of Hastings caused much suffering to the people; ancient houses which had virtually ruled large districts in Bengal were swept away; money-lenders and auction-purchasers came in their place as new landlords; and much land went out of cultivation. When, at last, Lord Cornwallis succeeded Warren

Hastings as Governor General, he wrote, "I may safely assert that one-third of the Company's territory in Hindustan is now a jungle, inhabited only by wild beasts." With characteristic energy and benevolence Lord Cornwallis made a ten-year's settlement with the landlords of Bengal; and within a few years he made that settlement permanent in 1793. The area of cultivation has vastly extended since that date, and the additional profit has remained in the country, and promoted the prosperity of the agricultural classes.

But Lord Cornwallis' work was only a partial solution of the great question. He assured the Zemindars of Bengal against any increase of the State-demand; he also expressly retained for the State the power to protect the cultivators against undue demands on the part of Zemindars; but this power was not exercised for a long time. Lord Cornwallis has been blamed for thus leaving the actual cultivators unprotected for a long time; but the case of Ireland shows that effective legislation for the protection of tenants is not easy. It is enough to add that such legislation was undertaken in Bengal long before it was thought of in Ireland; that Lord Canning's Bengal Rent Act of 1859 was a thorough and effective measure which received the attention of Mr. Gladstone when he framed his Land Bill for Ireland in 1869; and that Lord Canning's Act has been succeeded by the Bengal Rent Acts of 1868 and 1885 which now effectually protect the cultivators of Bengal against all unjust enhancements and ejectments by landlords. It is thus after the labour of a century that

British administrators have solved in a satisfactory manner the great Land Question in Bengal, *firstly*, by extending protection to Zemindars by the Regulation of 1793, and *secondly*, by extending protection to actual cultivators by the Rent Acts of 1859, 1868 and 1885. The consequence is that Bengal cultivators at the present time are more prosperous, more self-relying, and more safe against the worst effects of famine, than the cultivators of any other Province in India.

II.

Madras was the next territorial acquisition of the East India Company. Large slices of the dominions of Mysore were acquired by the British after the wars of 1792 and 1799, and the whole of the Karnatic was taken over in 1801. The Land Question in these territories presented itself in a greater variety of forms than in Bengal; and while they puzzled the servants of the Company, they would have afforded the most interesting materials for study to thoughtful enquirers like Sismondi or Mill, like Lavelaye or Sumner Maine. For, instead of one predominating system as in Bengal, there were various systems flourishing side by side in Madras, and these may be grouped under three great classes.

(1) The Zemindars of the Northern Circars, the Polygars of the South, and the Hill Rajas of the backward tracts, were great landlords, exercising at the same time those administrative powers within their estates

which belonged in a greater or a less degree to all territorial and military lords in olden times.

(2) The Mirasi villages of the Karnatic were Village-Communities, holding the village lands in common, partitioning them among the tenants from time to time, and paying their quota of revenue to the State, like self-contained and self-governing little republics.

(3) In tracts where fighting Polygars had not extended their power, and the Mirasi Village-Communities had not grown up, Peasant-proprietors held and tilled their own soil, and paid revenue direct to the Government.

Which of these systems was the original institution of the country? Which of them should be fostered under the British rule? The Polygars being strong military chiefs were the first to be crushed. The Nawab of the Karnatic, with the help of his British allies, rooted out these local chiefs who had ruled their estates and protected their people through centuries of disorder in Southern India. The Court of Directors shed a pious tear for them. They wrote that "the native princes called Polygars should not be extirpated," that "it was repugnant to humanity to force them to such dreadful extremities." But the Governor of Madras and the Nawab of the Karnatic could afford to disregard these pious wishes; and later on, the Court of Directors reconciled themselves to what had been done!" "We entreat your Excellency," they wrote to the Governor of Madras, "to make the manufacturers the object of your tenderest care; particularly when you root out the Polygars, you do not deprive the weavers of the protection they enjoyed under them." The Nawab of the Karnatic went on merrily, with the aid of his British allies, to root out the Polygars who were strong feudatory chiefs; but the turn of the Karnatic itself came next. On the death of the Nawab, the whole of the Karnatic largely freed from Polygars, was added to the British dominions, after certain formalities, in 1801.

The Land Question was thus brought one step nearer its solution, but was not yet solved. In the Northern Circars and in other places, where there were large Zemindars, a permanent settlement had been made with them under the orders of Lord Cornwallis. What was to be done where there were no Zemindars? Colonel Read and Thomas Munro had made some settlements direct with the Ryots or cultivators, and this form of settlement is called Ryotwari Settlement. The Madras Board of Revenue, on the other hand, pressed for a settlement with the Mirasi Village-Communities which they represented as the original and ancient institution of the land. The official records of Indian Administration do not contain a more interesting controversy than this memorable discussion between the partisans or Peasant-proprietors and the partisans of Village-Communities in Southern India.

Sir Thomas Munro triumphed in the end. He gave his evidence with remarkable clearness, force, and knowledge of details, before the Commons' Committee which was enquiring into the affairs of the East India Company in 1813; and he obtained the orders of the Court of Directors for the introduction of the Ryotwari system in Madras. Except in estates where a permanent settlement has been made with Zemindars, settlement with the cultivators direct is the prevailing system in Madras at the present time. Village-Communities have been swept away, even like the Polygars of old.

But the great Land Problem in Madras still remains unsolved. Sir Thomas Murno contemplated a *permanent settlement* with the cultivators in Madras, as Lord Cornwallis had made a *permanent settlement* with the Zemindars in Bengal. His desire was that the cultivators of Madras should have their holdings as "a permanent hereditary property" of which "the assessment must be fixed." Down to 1862 the Madras Government believed and declared that "the fundamental principle of the Ryotwari system is that the Government demand on land is fixed for ever." * But within the last forty years the Madras Government has receded from their former position.

The Government demand is not "fixed for ever," but is enhanced at each recurring settlement. The Government claim of one-half the net produce of the soil, after deducting the cost of cultivation, is enforced on the basis of estimates which can never be accurate. The Government rule of fixing one-third the gross produce of the soil as the maximum of the revenue-demand is oppressive and harsh. The cultivators of Madras have no clear and adequate protection against

* Letter of the Madras Government to the Government of India No. 241 dated 8th February 1862.

the State-landlord, * as the cultivators of Bengal have against the private landlord. 11,749 cultivators were ejected from their holdings in Madras last year for inability to pay the Government demand; 60,896 acres were sold for arrears of revenue; one-half of this found no purchasers in the market and was bought up by the Government itself at a nominal value! Six millions of acres of cultivable land remain uncultivated under the present system of heavy assesment!

When the Marquis of Ripon went out to India as Viceroy in 1880, he endeavoured to remedy this state of things. With a commendable moderation and good sense he sought to effect a compromise between the principle that the State-demand should be fixed for ever, and the principle that the State-demand should be virtually unrestricted. He left a door open for the future increase of the land revenue by claiming such increase when the prices of the produce rose. And he extended protection to the cultivators by declaring that no increase would be demanded in the future except on the ground of such a rise in prices. It was an equitable rule and a reasonable compromise, and would have settled the Land Question in Madras. But the Secretary of State for India took it upon himself to set aside this reasonable compromise in 1885, in order to keep the Government-demand absolutely unrestricted. And thus it happens that the Land Question remains

* I have used the word "State-landlord" in a loose way. Strictly speaking the cultivators themselves are recognised as the proprietors of their holdings, and the State only claims a *revenue* from them, not *rent*.

unsolved in Madras, and the agricultural population remain indebted, impoverished, and subject to famines, after a century of British rule.

III.

The territory now forming the Bombay Presidency was acquired by the British later than Bengal and Madras. The last of the Mahratta Peshwas was set aside in 1817, and his dominions were annexed in that year; and the Land Question, which is the most vital question in every part of India, immediately came for consideration.

The Deccan had a well defined land-system of its own under the Mahrattas; the Village-Community-system was better organized and more general in the Deccan than in Madras. Mountstuart Elphinstone, who was the first Governor of the Bombay Presidency, was a kindly and sympathetic administrator, and sought to preserve what was good and commendable in old Hindu institutions. "I am not democratic enough," he wrote in 1822, "to insist on the Ryotwari system. I think the aristocracy of the country where it consists of heads of villages or heads of Zemindaris should be kept up."

But Mountstuart Elphinstone endeavoured in vain. When he left India, the Village-Community-system was disfavoured, and the Ryotwari system was favoured; and one of the ablest and shrewdest of the Directors of the East India Company admitted;—"It cannot be concealed or denied, I think, that the object of this (Ryotwari) system is to obtain for Government the utmost that the land will yield in the shape of rent." * The claims of the Government-revenue superseded all other claims in India ; the old village institutions were crushed or swept away in the Deccan ; the Ryotwari system or settlement with each individual cultivators was introduced as in Madras.

Settlements for thirty years have been made in Bombay in 1836, in 1866 and in 1896, each settlement showing an enhancement of the Goverment demand by over thirty per cent. But a proper solution of the Land Question, conferring clear, adequate and well-defined rights to the cultivators of the soil, has not been arrived at, because the State-landlord is unwilling to place definite limits to its powers. The State-landlord is also the Legislative power ; and it legislated in 1876 that the High Court of Bombay and the Civil Courts of that Province should have no jurisdiction over its actions in the revenue department. The consequence may be imagined ; and what the late Sir William Hunter said in 1879 from his place in the Viceroy's Council is true to this day that "the Government assessment does not leave enough food to the cultivator to support himself and his family throughout the year." In the present year of distress and famine in Western India, Lord Curzon has declared that "the weakness and incapacity for resistance of the people took the local Government

* HENRY ST. JOHN TUCKER: *Memorials of Indian Government*, London 1853, p. 113.

by surprise." That surprise is removed by a reference to the past revenue-history of the Province.

The solution that is needed in Bombay is the same that is needed in Madras. We cannot reverse the Ryotwari system after it has been established as the prevailing system in the two Provinces for generations; but we can work the system with moderation and due care. The rule laid down in 1864 by Sir Charles Wood, then Secretary of State for India, that the Government revenue should generally be limited to one-half the customary rents, should find a place in the fiscal laws of India. The rule laid down by the Marquis of Ripon in 1882, to prevent enhancements except on the equitable ground of a rise in prices, should now obtain the sanction of the present Secretary of State. And a reference should be allowed to impartial Courts of Justice against mistakes made by Settlement and Revenue Officers in Madras and in Bombay.

IV.

Northern India came under British Rule at various dates. Portions of Oudh were ceded to the British in 1801, and Delhi and Agra and other districts were conquered in 1803. The Punjab was annexed after the Sikh wars of 1847 and 1849, and the whole of Oudh was annexed in 1856.

Lord Cornwallis's successful permanent settlement of the land revenues in Bengal was extended to Benares, and proposed to be extended to other parts of Northern

India; and proclamations were made and pledges were given to the people. But after the death of Lord Cornwallis, the desire to redeem these pledges gradually lost its force. An able and exhaustive report submitted by Holt Mackenzie generally brought to the light the fact that Village-Communities were still in a fairly working order in Northern India; it was decided to make settlements with these Village-Communities as well as with landlords of large estates; and it was also decided unfortunately to make these settlements temporary and not permanent. Regulation VII. of 1822 was accordingly passed into law.

On the early mistakes of the Company's Government in the revenue-administration of Northern India it is not necessary for us to dwell; the Company's servants actually endeavoured to realize over 80 per cent., of the rental as the Government demand. A great deal of suffering and distress was caused to the people, and it has been stated that the hand of the Company's tax-gatherer was felt heavier by the agricultural population than even the occasional devastations of Afghan and Mahratta free-booters of the previous times.

A careful enquirer and a considerate administrator now appeared on the scene. Lieutenant-General Briggs, who had served under Mountstuart Elphinstone in the last Mahratta war, and had settled large districts, produced his great work on the land-systems of India in 1830. And he proved,

(1) that the integrity of private property in land had been recognized in every village in India;

(2) that the Government had no right to the land but only to a share in its produce, i.e., a land tax;

(3) that that share was limited by Hindu and Mahomedan law and could not be arbitrarily fixed;

(4) that the British Empire could be made durable only if based on the broad basis of native institutions.

A better and a more sympathetic administrator never went out to India than Lord William Bentinck who was then the Governor General, and he welcomed General Briggs' work as a help to his administration. The famous Regulation of 1833 was passed after consultation with General Briggs; the revenue-demand was reduced to two-thirds the rental; and new settlements were made between 1833 and 1849. The last great work of the Company's servants was to reduce the land-revenue still further to one-half the rental, by the Saharanpur rules of 1855, and this is the recognized rule in Northern India to the present day.

The rule of the East India Company came to an end after the Indian Mutiny of 1857, and a great famine swept over Northern India in the early years of the administration of the Crown. Lord Canning, the first and greatest Viceroy of India under the Crown, sought to pass a remedial measure which would permanently improve the condition of the agricultural classes, which would gave rise to a substantial middle class, and which would lead to some accumulation of capital among the impoverished population. Looking at the prosperous condition of Bengal under the Permanent Settlement, and after a careful enquiry into other parts of India,

Lord Canning recommended the extension of a Permanent Settlement to all the Provinces of India.

Sir Charles Wood was then Secretary of State for India ; and in his memorable Despatch of the 9th July 1862 he approved of Lord Canning's proposal as "a measure dictated by sound policy, and calculated to accelerate the development of resources of India, and to ensure, in the highest degree, the welfare and contentment of all classes of Her Majesty's subjects in that country." Lord Lawrence thoroughly supported the proposal in his Minute of the 5th March 1864 ; and Sir Stafford Northcote, who was Secretary of State for India in 1867, gave it his sanction in his letter of the 23rd March 1867 "in consideration of the great importance of connecting the interests of the proprietors of the land with the stability of the British Government."

It is a melancholy truth that the very peacefulness and loyalty of the people of India have weakened, instead of strengthening, this benevolent desire on the part of their rulers. The generation of Canning and Lawrence, of Sir Charles Wood and Sir Stafford Northcote passed away, and after a period of uninterrupted peace in India the succeeding generation of statesmen no longer thought it necessary to sacrifice a prospective rise in the land revenue to promote the welfare and contentment of the people, or to connect the interests of the proprietors of the soil with the stability of the British Rule. The people of India lost the chance of an extension of the Permanent Settlement by their silent submission, and the proposal of Lord Canning and Lord Lawrence was finally rejected by a new Secretary of State for India on the 28th March 1883.

The state of things in Northern India therefore is this. The old Village-Comunities have gradually and slowly approximated to a system of landlords and tenants. The revenue demand of the State is about half the rental, and is re-settled every thirty years. A great many local cesses, assessed on the rental, have been added to the land-revenue.

V.

It is unnecessary to prolong this article by any lengthy examination of the state of things in the Central Provinces of India. Saugor and the Narbadda Territories came under British administration in 1818, and the Nagpur State was annexed in 1853; and all these tracts were consolidated into one great Province, and called the Central Provinces of India in 1861. Sir Richard Temple's administration of this great Province from 1862 to 1866 is still remembered by the people of the Province with gratitude; the thirty years' settlement commenced in 1863 was conducted on liberal principles; the Malguzars of Revenue-payers were recognized as proprietors; and the rule of demanding one-half the rental as revenue was recognized in principle, though it was unfortunately evaded in practice.

In a country like India, where the people have no voice or share in the control of the work of administration, the principles of administration are liable to change from year to year according to the fancies of individual administrators. The history of modern India presents us with no more painful illustration of this truth than the second land-revenue settlement of the Central Provinces effected within the last decade. The Chief Commissioner who ruled the Central Provinces in 1887 considered that the rule of demanding half the rental from the landlords, as the Government revenue, was too liberal to the landlords! And that reasonable and moderate rule, arrived at after a century of bitter and painful experiments, arrived at on the experience of administrators like Lord Dalhousie, Lord Canning and Sir Richard Temple, was abrogated for the Central Provinces in 1888, without discussion in Council, without consultation with the people! Settlements have now been made in the Central Provinces in which something like 60 per cent of the rental plus 12½ per cent as local cesses have been demanded from the landlords as revenue; and the period of settlement has also been cut down from 30 to 20 years! These fatal blunders have deepened the effects of the famines of 1897 and 1900 in the Central Provinces, and have perhaps added to the loss of lives by tens of thousands.

Such, briefly, has been the history of Land Administration in the five great Provinces of India. Generally speaking, the land revenue is paid by landlords in Northern India, Bengal, and the Central Provinces; while it is paid direct by the cultivators of the soil in Madras and Bombay. To this difference in systems no objection is taken; but the people of India desire that reasonable, equitable, and intelligible limits to the State-demand should be framed. There is one clear and intelligible limit which is recognized in theory by the State itself, and which applies to all Provinces of India; and that limit is: *The Land Tax shall not exceed one-half the rental or one-half the economic rent.* This rule was recognized for Northern India by Lord Dalhousie's Saharanpur Rules of 1855; and it was recognized for Southern India by Sir Charles Wood's Despatch of 1864. Let this rule be honestly adhered to in practice.

II. INDIA AND THE NATIONAL LIBERAL FEDERATION.

Speech at the Conference of the Committee of the National Liberal Federation at Rugby on February, 27, 1901. Reprinted from "India."

THE meeting of the Delegates at Rugby was the largest of such meetings since the establishment of the Federation, and the large hall was inconveniently crowded. The South African discussions were necessarily prolonged, and it was after five o'clock when Mr. Romesh Dutt, who attended as a delegate from Lewisham, was able to move his resolution. It ran thus:

"That this meeting deplores the succession of severe famines which have caused the deaths of millions of people in India in recent years, and considers it necessary to prevent the recurrence of such severe calamities by moderating the Land Tax, extending irrigation works, and relieving as far as possible the annual burdensome drain on the financial resources of India which impoverishes the people of that country."

In moving this resolution, Mr. DUTT said that although the subjects which had been discussed by the meeting that afternoon were of the gravest importance, there was none among them which was of a higher importance in the interests of the British Empire than that which formed the subject of his resolution. They had to deplore the deaths of twenty or thirty thousand Englishmen in the South African War; but the loss of lives from the present famine in India could scarcely be much under a million; while the loss of lives from the succession of famines which had occurred in India within the present generation, or rather within the forty-two years since India had passed under the direct administration of the Crown, could scarcely be less than the entire population of England. English Liberals would ask themselves the cause of these disastrous and frequent famines in a time of profound and uninterrupted peace within the natural frontiers of India. India at present was not a great manufacturing country, nor a great commercial country, but a great agricultural country; and four-fifths of the vast population of India depended upon agriculture. If the Government demand from the produce of the soil was moderate, and placed within definite and intelligible limits, the people could be prosperous. But the Government demand was being increased at each recurring settlement every twenty or thirty years; the people could save nothing; and every year of drought was a year of famine. After the great famine of 1860, Lord Canning, then Viceroy of India, had recommended that limits should be placed on the Government demand; and Lord Lawrence, who succeeded as Viceroy of India a few years after, had supported this recommendation; but, nevertheless it was rejected by the India Office in London. The Marquis of Ripon who was Viceroy of India from

1880 to 1884 had recommended certain other limitations to the Government demand; but even his very moderate recommendation had been rejected by the India Office in London. Thus it happened that the agricultural people of India were in a state of chronic poverty and indebtedness and would continue to be subject to repeated and fatal famines, till the Land Tax was moderated and strictly limited. His second recommendation was the extension of irrigation works. On this point there was no difference of opinion, because irrigation works—tanks as well as canals—were the only possible means of saving crops in years of drought. His last recommendation was to decrease as far as possible the annual drain from India. While taxation had increased both in England and in India, there was an essential difference between the two countries. In England, the proceeds of taxation were spent in the country, and thus flowed back to the people in one shape or another to fructify their industries and help their trade. In India, an amount exceeding one half of the net revenues was annually taken away from the country, and thus rendered the people hopelessly poor. It was a drain unexampled in any country on earth at the present day; and if England herself had to send out one half of her annual revenues to be spent annually in Germany or France or Russia, there would be famines in England before long. Therefore he proposed that this annual drain should be reduced, as far as possible, from year to year, by the employment of the people of India in the administration of their own country, and by the cost of the Imperial Army in India being shared to some extent by England herself.

Miss ALISON GARLAND rose to second the Resolution and was received with cheers. She said that she had probably been asked to second it because she had been to India in 1899-1900, and had visited several famine centres, and knew what the Indian famine meant. She depicted in vivid colours the scenes she had witnessed, and concluded her description by stating that in the midst of these horrors the Government had refused to make a Parliamentary grant to India—not because the British nation were averse to such a grant, not because such a grant was not needed, but because the Indian Government and the India Office did not ask for it. The Indian Government did not ask for it because they knew that a Parliamentary grant would be followed by an inconvenient Parliamentary enquiry.

When the chairman was about to put the Resolution to the vote, one delegate rose to oppose it. He said he had been in India and had seen two famines, and he was opposed to the Resolution. The remedies suggested by the mover would not avert famines in India, for when the annual rains failed, and the crops of the two hundred million people of India failed, nothing could avert a famine. He proposed therefore that this meeting should not pass the Resolution in a hurry.

COLONEL HANNA who was in the gallery then rose to speak; and though it was getting late, his venerable appearance, his great earnestness, and his known mastery of Indian facts, ensured him a patient and respectful hearing. He said there was no such thing as the total failure of the crops in India. When crops failed in one Province there were always ample harvests in others. There always was a sufficient supply of food for the people of India. It was not the want of food supply, but it was the want of money to buy food, which caused famines in localities where the crops failed. He therefore thought that famines could be averted by improving the condition of the people. But the Government of India spent money unwisely in frontier wars, and the total outlay of such frontier wars came to eighty millions of English money. Colonel Hanna therefore supported the Resolution.

The Resolution being put to the vote was carried almost unanimously, only one or two hands being raised against it. This concluded the business of the meeting.

III. SOCIAL PROGRESS IN INDIA.

[*Speech delivered at the Annual Meeting of the National Indian Association, on March*, 25, 1901.]

MR. DUTT said: The Resolution which I have the honour to second has been explained by Sir Roper Lethbridge, and I have very little to add to what he has said, except that as an Indian myself, I feel great pleasure in seconding it. The Resolution is for making increased efforts in support of the Association's funds with the object of promoting female education in India. It is well known—speaking at least for the part of India from which I come, and with which I am most familiar—that for the last thirty or forty years or more, a great deal has been done by the people of India themselves in the cause of social progress and of female education. A great deal has been done, not ostentatiously, but by quiet work at home, to help the cause of social progress; and anything like a lasting and abiding improvement in the country must be done in the future, as has been done in the past, by the people themselves. (Hear, hear). I think many of the gentlemen present here, who have passed a great many years of their lives in India, like my friend Sir Charles Stevens who has moved the first Resolution, are familiar with the names of prominent Indian gentlemen who devoted their lives to the cause of education and of social reform. I need only mention the names of Pandit Iswar Chandra Vidyasagar and Keshab Chandra Sen of Bengal, and of Justice Ranade of Bombay whose recent death has filled the people of India with sorrow. They were prominent men in India who, in spite of various duties which they had to perform, devoted a great part of their time to the cause of social progress and social reform, and were careful to adopt methods which were consistent with our Eastern life, because they knew that all reforms in order to be abiding, must be consistent with our Eastern customs and life. (Hear, hear.) This is a point, ladies and gentlemen, which we should always remember—we who try to work in the cause of social reform. The people of India gratefully accept help from all true friends in the cause of reform; they avail themselves of the schools and teachers you provide; they benefit by your sympathy and your support; but nevertheless all abiding reforms must be worked out by themselves, consistently with the life they live. It is not desirable and it is not possible, to Europeanise Indian life. (Applause.) The people of India are well able to judge for themselves what is best for themselves, and Indian life and Hindu life has always proved itself capable of assimilating what is good for itself. It is because we have been able to assimilate all needful reforms from generation to generation and from age to age, that our ancient Hindu life still exists in India when so many phases of ancient life have passed away in other countries like Rome and Greece, like Persia, Egypt and Babylon. Therefore, Sir, our best helpers and our truest friends are those who, while they offer us their help and their sympathy, can at the same time sympathise with Eastern life and Eastern institutions. And it is because this Association is trying to co-operate with our own endeavours, to help us where we are in need of help, to provide teachers and schools for the education of our wives, sisters, and daughters, that we gratefully accept its sympathy, its services, and its help. And I have great pleasure, Sir, in seconding this Resolution, because the truest progress that we can make, and the truest line upon which we can make that progress, is the extention of female education in India. It is necessary that our women should be familiar with modern institutions, with modern knowledge, and with modern history; a sound education like this is needed to smooth the path of our future progress.

IV. THE LAND TAX, RAILWAYS AND IRRIGATION.

Speech delivered at a Conference of Indians in the Westminster Town Hall on May, 24, 1901.

Mr. Romesh Dutt moved the following Resolution :

"In view of the frequent and recurring famines which have desolated India in recent years, and the extreme poverty of the agricultural population, it is desirable that the Land Tax of India should be moderated and placed within fixed limits, and that extensive irrigation works—canals, tanks, and wells,—should be undertaken for the protection of crops in years of drought."

Mr. Dutt said : The Resolution which I have the honour to move is, properly speaking, a supplement to the Resolution which you, Mr. Chairman, have moved, and which has just been passed. You, Sir, have raised your voice to-day, as you have raised it in this country for the last forty years, against that perpetual Economic Drain which has impoverished the people of India, against that annual flow of a large portion of the Indian revenue out of India ; I desire to show how a large portion of this revenue is raised in India from the poorest of the poor, from the agriculturists and tillers of the soil. It will thus appear, Sir, that we are not speaking of two different questions, but only of two aspects of the same question ; we are not asking for two different reforms—we are demanding the same reform, shewing its need from outside and from inside. For my own opinion is that the annual Economic Drain will never be reduced until the Land Tax is moderated; and the Land Tax will never be moderated until the Economic Drain is reduced.

Sir, we stand to-day face to face with the apalling fact that famines and deaths by starvation have almost become chronic in India, after a hundred and fifty years of British Rule.

I am old enough, Sir, to remember the last years of the rule of the East India Company; and I distinctly remember the day when, 43 years ago, it was proclaimed in every town and village of India, that the East India Company was abolished, and the empire had passed under the direct administration of the Crown. During these 43 years we have enjoyed the blessings of peace, undisturbed by a single war within the natural frontiers of India. There has not been the slightest ripple of disturbance among the loyal population of that country. But peace has not brought with it prosperity to the people. On the contrary, the people of India are becoming more impoverished and resourceless from year to year, and famines and deaths are becoming more frequent and fatal. There have been 11 famines within these 43 years, and the deaths from these famines, by the most moderate computation exceed 20 millions. It is an astonishing and apalling fact, not seen in the present day in any other civilised country on earth.

The causes of these famines were not unknown to first Viceroys of India under the Crown. Lord Canning, who saved India during the dark days of the Indian Mutiny, tried also to save the country from the greater calamities of famines. He saw that our nation was a nation of agriculturists; he saw that in Provinces where the Land Tax was permanently settled, the agriculturists were prosperous; and he recommended that the Land Tax should be permanently settled all over India. He was succeeded after the interval of a few years by Lord Lawrence, another of the great saviors of India during the Mutiny, and Lord Lawrence also strongly recommended that the Land Tax should be permanently fixed all over India in order to give the agricultural people of India some means of saving in good years against droughts and failures of harvest in bad years.

These proposals came for consideration before two Secretaries of State. One of them Sir Charles Wood was a Liberal, and another, Sir Stafford Northcote was a Conservative, but they agreed in the cardinal maxim that India should be ruled for the good of the people of India. Permit me to read one or two passages from the memorable despatches of Sir Charles Wood and of Sir Stafford Northcote in which both of them approved the proposal of permanently fixing the land-revenue of India. [Passages read.]

These were the views of statesmen who ruled India during the first decade after the Mutiny, men who felt their own responsibility and who sympathised with the people of India. But that generation passed away; a less sympathetic school of statesmen were bent on eternally increasing the revenue derived from the soil; and the benevolent proposal of limiting the land-tax for the good of the people of India was finally rejected by the India Office in 1883—over twenty years after the death of Lord Canning.

Nevertheless all hope was not yet lost. A worthy successor of Lord Canning, the present Marquis of Ripon, was the Viceroy of India in 1883, and he suggested some very moderate limits to the enhancement of the Land Tax, limits which were accepted by the Government of Madras and I believe, the Government of Bombay. But Lord Ripon left India in 1884, and his proposals were rejected by the India Office in 1885. The result is that except in Provinces where it was already permanently settled, the Land Tax is being continuously raised at recurring settlements, it hangs like the sword of Damocles over the heads of Indian cultivators, it takes away the motive for permanent improvements, it paralyses agriculture, and it is accountable for the worst horrors of the succession of famines which have desolated India during these recent years.

I therefore move, Sir, that the Land Tax of India be moderated and fixed in the lines laid down by Lords Canning and Lawrence, or in those laid down by the Marquis of Ripon.

I now come, Sir, to the second part of my Resolution which concerns Irrigation works, and that will not detain me long. The necessity of Irrigation works in years of droughts to save crops is universally admitted; but it is stated that it is not possible to construct canals on high table lands and hilly tracts. My answer to this is that where canals cannot be constructed wells and tanks can be constructed; and such tanks made by old Hindu and Mahomedan rulers still exist and irrigate hundreds of square miles.

What we want is a multiplication of such useful and necessary works, and not the further extention of railways from the public revenues or under guarantee of profits from such revenues. Two hundred twenty five millions sterling have been spent on railways; and the Famine Commission of 1898 recorded their opinion that all railways required for protective purposes are done. I deplore therefore the construction of further railways in India out of the public revenues or under guarantee from public revenues. It is a misuse of public money in India under pressure from capitalists and speculators in this country. Only 25 millions sterling have been spent on Irrigation; if more attention had been paid on irrigations, famines would have been impossible today.

Sir, I have only one word more to say before I conclude. The closing years of the 19th century have revealed to Englishmen, that a greater danger than the Mutiny of 1857 has overtaken India in the impoverishment of the people and the frequency and intensity of famines. There is not an Englishman living, no matter to what political party he may belong, who does not feel grieved and humilated at this state of things in India after 150 years of British Rule. To talk to them now of the material progress of India, is an insult to their understanding. To talk to us of the recuperative power of India in the face of these repeated and disastrous famines is a mockery of our misfortunes. No Sir, we must face the broad facts which are apparent to every one, and the facts are simple enough in all conscience when we examine them honestly, for the same economic laws which create wealth or poverty in other parts of the world, create wealth or poverty in India. Prosperous industries, prosperous agriculture, a sound financial administration are the source of wealth of all nations ;—in India you have permitted our indigenous industries to perish, you have overtaxed agriculture, and your financial arrangements are so bad that you annually drain from India a sum equal to one half of her nett revenues. These are broad undeniable facts, and these are the causes of the repeated famines in a country where the land is fertile, the people are frugal and industrious, and peaceful.

It is necessary, in order to save India, that we should grasp these facts and that the people of England and the people of India should work together to remedy past blunders, and prevent future evils. My countrymen are prepared to do this. I speak without fear of contradiction when I state that there is but one feeling which pervades all ranks of the people of India, and that feeling is to support the British Government, and to help the British Government not only in the field of battle, but also in the more arduous work of civil administration. It is an unjust and an unwise policy to exclude the people of India,—as you now do,—from all control over the administration. It is unjust because it degrades the people and makes your administration fatally unsuccessful; and it is unwise because it turns the population of India into hostile critics instead of loyal parakers in the administration of their own concerns. It is only confidence and trust in the people which can maintain your Empire and make it properous. Sweep away the present policy of distrust and exclusion, concede to the people of India some control over their own laws and administration, make them cosharers in the management of their finances,—and they will be jointly responsible with you Englishman, in the eyes of the world, for the prevention of famines, and for the prosperity of the Empire.

V. RESTRICTIONS ON LAND ALIENATION.

Speech made in course of a debate on Mr. Thorburn's paper read before the East India Association at the Westminster Town Hall on June, 24, 1901; the Right Ho'nble Leonard Courtney presiding.

Mr. ROMESH DUTT said: Mr. Thorburn had spoken of the Village-Communities as owning property jointly. That was the practice up to the beginning of the nineteenth century. He looked back with regret to that old institution which was well suited to the genius of the Indian people, and was the earliest form of Self-Government in the world. But he thought Mr. Thorburn had made a mistake in saying that the right of alienation was the gift of the British Government. There never was a time when the Indian peasant had not this old customary right. What the British Government did was to legalize this ancient customary right, as could be gathered from the Blue-books of the eighteenth century and the early part of the nineteenth century. It was plain from those records that British administrators in India legalized this customary right, which was as old as the civilization of India itself. The main question raised by Mr. Thorburn had often come before the Government of India. In Bengal the prohibition of alienation had been discussed at least twice in the last twenty years. In 1883 it was discussed in connexion with the Bengal Tenancy Bill. Recommendations were then made that in the interests of the cultivators the right of alienation should be taken away from them. But enquiries, in which he himself took a part, showed that transfers were being frequently registered, and yet that the peasants were not being made the slaves of the money lenders. The reports drawn up on the matter were sent to Mr. MacDonnell, now Sir Anthony MacDonnell, who agreed in the view that the cultivator was not to be saved by being made a life-tenant for his holding. A measure of general confiscation was thus avoided at that time. But the proposal came up again from the Punjab. He would say nothing of the needs of the Western Punjab which he knew only as a tourist. But he would say that the cry of alarm rang through India, and in 1896, in Bengal, they were asked again whether it was not necessary to deprive cultivators of the right of alienation in order to save them from their own unwisdom. They were taken aback. They wondered whether they were living in the time of Haroun Al Raschid, and whether the cultivators of the soil must suffer because the Khalif's favourite wife had dreamt a bad dreamt. (Laughter.) The Bengal Government were again advised to drop the proposal. He could speak from personal knowledge of the Orissa division, where, if anywhere, the peasants needed protection against money-lenders. But he was able to show to the Government of Bengal that the peasant there had exercised the right of alienation for sixty or seventy years, and that their land was not passing to the money-lenders. Once again the proposal was rejected. But only last week he had seen from the Indian newspapers that a Bill was before the Bombay Legislative Council in which it was proposed to create a new class of cultivators who should not have the right of transferring their holdings. He would not judge a Bill which he had not seen. But on broad economic grounds he maintained that failure must attend any effort which sought to save the cultivators by confiscating their rights, and lowering the value of their property. Economic laws which operated elsewhere also operated in India. It was sometimes said that cultivators in India were like children. They might be ignorant and superstitious, but, taken generally, they were conscious of their own interests, and keen in defending them. What they wanted was a moderate assessment and clear rights which they were able to defend. He would say again that he made no remark about the Punjab Act, but the extension of this Act to the rest of India would be a calamity. (Applause.)

VI. THE ECONOMIC CAUSES OF INDIAN FAMINES.

Lecture delivered at a meeting of the Fabian Society in London on June, 28, 1901.

Mr. DUTT said: the occurrence of frequent and wide-spread famines in India in recent years was perhaps the strangest, as it was the saddest, phenomenon in modern times. India was under a civilised administration; the Indian Civil Service was an able and experienced body of administrators; the Indian people were frugal and industrious; the land was rich and fertile; the country had enjoyed uninterrupted internal peace for nearly half a century. They had all the causes which led to wealth and prosperity in other lands, and yet they were so resourceless and impoverished that every year of drought led to a famine, and deaths from each famine were reckoned not by thousands, but by hundreds of thousands, and sometimes by millions. The economic causes of this strange phenomenon were simple and obvious. The present system of administration, without popular representation, had failed to safeguard the interests of the people. All the sources of national wealth had been narrowed. Agriculture, manufactures, and a sound finance were the sources of wealth in all countries. Let them examine how these sources had been affected by the present system of administration.

Agriculture and the Land Tax.

He would begin the enquiry with Agriculture and the Land Tax of India. Four-fifths of the population of India depended at the present day on agriculture for subsistence. *Prima facie* if the land was lightly assessed, the people would be prosperous. If the land was over-assessed, the people would be reduced to a chronic state of poverty, The Land Tax therefore was a far more important question in India than in other countries, where the people were less dependent on agriculture. The system of imposing the Land Tax varied in the different provinces of India. He would not trouble them with all those details. He asked them only to remember the broad distinction that, generally speaking, the Land Tax or land revenue was paid to the State by landlords in Northern India, while in Southern India it was paid directly by the cultivators of the soil. There were large exceptions to this general rule, but it would be enough for their purpose that night to remember this general rule. The early British administrators made the fatal mistake in Southern India, as they did in other parts of India, of fixing an impossible land tax, and collecting it with a rigorous severity unknown in India before. In Madras the demand was actually fixed at 45 per cent. of the produce of the soil. In other words if a cultivator produced crops worth £10 a year—and this was a liberal estimate for an Indian cultivator—the Government demanded £4 10s. as its revenue, leaving only £5 10s. to the cultivator to support himself and his family for 12 months, and to pay for his ploughs and bullocks, his farm labour and seed grain. This naturally caused a great deal of misery and oppression and the accounts to be found in the earlier records were deplorable. [Some extracts from the records of 1818 were read.] This was the state of things in Southern India in the early days of British rule. He need hardly say that much improvement had been effected within the last 80 years. But more improvement was needed. The Land Tax had been reduced from 45 per cent. to a maximum of 33 per cent. but even this was a ruinous rate, for a cultivator could not afford to pay £3 7s. to the State out of £10 of his gross produce. The settlements were made now for long periods, generally once in thirty years, but at each recurring settlement there was a revision of the Land Tax which prevented land improvements and paralysed agriculture. Many English administrators had recommended within the last century that the State-demand should be fixed in some way in order to give the people a motive for improvements and a chance of saving. The last of these recommendations was from Lord Ripon, who proposed in 1883 that the State demand should not be increased except when there was a rise in prices of crops. All these recommendations had been disregarded. At each recurring settlement the land revenue was raised; the cultivator of Southern India did not understand on what grounds it was raised; he was not permitted to appeal to courts of justice against such enhancements made by revenue officers; and thus the strongest motive for agricultural improvements and savings was wanting.

Turning now to Northern India, there the land-revenue was generally paid by landlords—not by the actual cultivators. In some parts of India, as in Bengal, the land-revenue had been permanently fixed, once for all, and profits from improvements remained with the people. And it was remarkable that in permanently settled Bengal there had been no famine, involving loss of life, for over a hundred years, showing the beneficial effects of the Permanent Settlement. Other parts of Northern India had not been so fortunate. In the valley of the Jumna and the Ganges Permanent Settlement was promised. The Marquess of Wellesley passed two regulations, in 1803 and in 1805, in which he unreservedly gave a pledge to the people to make a Permanent Settlement. His successor, Lord Minto, pressed the Directors of the East India Company to redeem this pledge. Nevertheless, the directors of the East India Company violated the pledge, and a Permanent Settlement of the land revenue was not concluded in Northern India. The company was abolished in 1858. Three years after, Lord Canning, the first Viceroy of India under the Crown, again pressed for permanently settling the land revenues of India. Lord Lawrence, another distinguished Viceroy and able statesman, supported this proposal. Two Secretaries of State, Sir Charles Wood, a Liberal, and Sir Stafford Northcote, a Conservative, recommended this measure. Nevertheless the proposal was finally rejected in England in 1883. In the absence of a Permanent Settlement of the land revenue, the State demand had varied from time to time in most parts of Northern India. The early British administrators fixed it as high as they could—they demanded from landlords eighty percent of their rental as the Government revenue. If a landlord's rental was £1,200, the East India Company demand £1000 out of it as the Land Tax. This was found an oppressive and impossible rate. In 1833 the Land Tax was reduced to two-thirds; and in 1855 to one-half of the rental. In other words the landlord with a rental of £1,200 now paid to the Government £600 as the Land Tax. But this was not all. A new settlement was made every twenty or thirty years. In these recurring settlements the landlord's rental was ascertained after fresh enquiries. The land revenue demanded was not half the actual rental, but half the prospective rental. And to this a great many local taxes were added for local purposes.

Such was the state of things now in India. It was clear that agriculture could not flourish under such a system. There was no adequate motive for land improvements or for savings, unless there was some fixity in the Government demand. What was wanted was, (1) some clear fixed rules limiting within moderate limits the liabilities of the cultivator in Southern India, and of the landlord in Northern India; and (2) some independent Courts of Justice to which the taxpayer could appeal if these rules were violated or misinterpreted by the revenue officers. The agricultural population of India demanded such security and justice under the British rule.

Indian Manufactures.

The question of agriculture was the most important question in India. The history of Indian manufactures was equally sad. The policy of the East India Company, from the commencement of their rule, was to discourage Indian manufactures for the benefit of British manufacturers. The Company became the administrators of Bengal in 1765. Four years later they issued an order that the manufacture of silk fabrics should be discouraged in Bengal, that the people should produce raw silk in India to be woven in England, that Indian silk-winders should be made to work in the company's factories and prohibited from working outside, "under severe penalties, by the authority of the Government." The effect of this mandate, according to the Select Committee of the House of Commons was "to change the whole face of that industrious country, in order to render it a field for the produce of crude materials subservient to the manufacturers of Great Britain." This Report of the Select Committee was submitted in 1783. Let them pass over a period of thirty years to 1813, when the East India Company's charter was renewed. An enquiry was made, as usual, before the renewal of the Charter. Eminent witness like Warren Hastings of Bengal, Thomas Munro of Madras, and Sir John Malcolm of Bombay, were examined. They were asked by the House of Commons, not how Indian manufactures could be encouraged, but how they could be discouraged to make room for British manufactures. For it was found that even up to that date Indian silk and cotton goods could be sold in England at a price from 50 to 60 per cent. lower than those produced in England. What was the policy which England pursued? She imposed a prohibitive duty which killed the Indian manufactures. The following statement was made by Joseph Ranking before the House of Commons during their enquiry of 1813:

"Can you state what is the 'ad valorem' duty on piece goods sold at the East India House?

"The duty on the class called Calicoes is £3. 6s. 8d. per cent. upon importation; and if they are used for home consumption, there is a further duty of £68. 6s. 8d. per cent."

"There is another class called Muslins, on which the duty on importation is 10 per cent.; and if they are used for home consumption, of £27. 6s. 8d. per cent.

"There is a third class, coloured goods, which are prohibited from being used in this country, upon which there is a duty upon importation of £3. 6s. 8d. per cent; they are only for exportation."

"This Session of Parliament there has been a new duty of 20 per cent. on the consolidated duties, which will make the duties of Calicoes . . . . for home consumption £78. 6s. 8d. per cent.; upon Muslins for home consumption £31. 6s. 8d."

This finally killed the Indian weaving manufacture. Henry St. George Tucker, himself a Director of the East India Company, wrote in 1823:—"India is thus reduced from the state of a manufacturing to that of an agricultural country."

[Extracts from Tucker's memorandum dated 1823 were here read.]

Railways and Irrigation.

The prohibitive duties had now been abolished after they had done their fatal work. Other changes had also taken place in India. About the middle of the 19th century railways were introduced in India. Railways were beneficial everywhere in the world by shortening distances, and making journeys cheaper, quicker, and easier. But in India, unfortunately, railways had been constructed by the Government out of the public revenues, or by private companies under guarantee of profit out of the public revenues, and the economic effect of this had not been beneficial. It had been a financial loss to Indians. After deducting all earnings they had paid forty millions sterling out of the revenues of India to cover the loss; and the annual loss still continued. Capitalists and speculators and manufacturers in this country, who had votes, were putting continual pressure on the Government of India for the construction of more lines with guarantee of profits from the Indian revenues. Indians, who had no votes, were unable to resist this pressure, and railways had been overdone. The Famine Commission of 1898 reported that all lines required for famine protective purposes had been done, but still more lines were being constructed which the people did not want, and which the people were made to pay for. On the other hand, irrigation works which were needed by the people for the protection of their crops, were neglected. 250 millions sterling had been spent on railways, and only 25 millions on irrigation up to date. Yet out of 220 million acres of cultivated land in India, only 20 millions or less than one-tenth the area, were protected by irrigation works.

The people of India had struggled against every adverse circumstance, and within the last half century had endeavoured to revive their manufactures by adopting European methods, and by the help of steam and machinary. Cotton mills had been started in Bombay and in Bengal, and the products of these mills had some sale in India and out of India. No Royal Commission or Committee of the House of Commons sat to help and promote this infant enterprise; if any Government had instituted an enquiry with this avowed purpose, it was likely that British voters would have turned it out of office within a twelve-month. As it was, Lancashire voters forced the Indian Government to pass tariff rules which no national Government, responsible for the good of the people under its administration, would have passed. A small import duty used to be imposed in India on piece goods and other articles, not for the purposes of protection, but merely as a source of revenue much needed. To this the Lancashire manufacturers objected, and the Indian Government was compelled to surrender this source of revenue in 1882. But the revenue so surrendered could not be replaced; the Indian Government was in a bad way, and wished to re-impose it. A sort of compromise was then effected which was a striking illustration of how India was ruled under the dictation of British manufacturers. An import duty was re-imposed on British piece goods, and this was accompanied by a similar duty imposed on goods manufactured in India to satisfy the British manufacturers. Under the imposition of this strange duty—without parallel in any other country in the civilised world—the Indian mills which were struggling for existence had greatly declined within the last decade, especially in competition, with Japan which imposed no such duty on its own products.

FINANCIAL ADMINISTRATION.

He now turned to the financial administration of India. The entire financial policy of England in respect of India from the 18th century to the present day was to charge to India everything which could rightly, or even wrongly, be charged to that unrepresented country. England had spent hundreds of millions in acquiring and defending her colonies all over the earth. For acquiring and defending the Empire of India, she had not paid a shilling. On the contrary, during the rule of the East India Company, India paid an annual tribute to England reckoned in millions. When the company was abolished, the cost of the transfer of the Indian Empire to the Crown was charged to India. Since then they had made India pay for wars in China, Afghanistan, Persia, and the Soudan. They maintained a vast army in India, mainly for imperial purposes, at the cost of the people of India. They had virtually excluded the people of India from nearly all high offices in their own country in order to find a career for English boys in India. A Parliamentary Return was submitted nine years ago, showing all salaries and pensions of a thousand rupees and upwards paid by India. Taking Rs. 10 for a pound sterling, the total came to fourteen millions sterling to Englishmen annually, and only $3\frac{1}{4}$ millions to the Natives of India. Such had been the financial policy of England towards an unrepresented country. The result was that public debt had increased by leaps and bounds in India in a time of profound peace. The public debt, taking ten rupees for a pound, was 118 millions sterling in 1875; in 1895 it was 220 millions. In other words while the public debt was steadily decreased in England, mainly under Mr. Gladstone's influence, it nearly doubled in India within 20 years of profound peace. England paid for the Colonial Office, located in Whitehall. India paid for the India Office located in a part of the same building. In payment of the expenses of that office, and of various other liabilities, India had to make a constantly increasing annual remittance to England. As India had little manufacture and little trade, virtually the whole pressure fell on the produce of the soil—on the food of the people. Thus India was forced to export far more than she imported, and this excess was increasing at a startling rate. He compiled the following figures from a paper which an official of the India Office read before the Society of Arts in March last :—

ANNUAL EXCESS OF EXPORTS OVER IMPORTS.

FROM	Tens of Rupees.
1859 to 1863 . . .	2 millions
1864 to 1868 . . .	8 ,,
1869 to 1873 . . .	16 ,,
1874 to 1878 . . .	15 ,,
1879 to 1883 . . .	19 ,,
1884 to 1888 . . .	15 ,,
1889 to 1893 . . .	20 ,,
1894 to 1898 . . .	25 ,,

The significance of the above figures would be better understood by comparing them with the total revenues of India. The Royal Commission on Indian expenditure in their recently published Report found the net revenues of India to be 57 million tens of rupees. A sum, therefore, nearly equal to one half of the public revenues of India was annually remitted out of India without a direct equivalent. A sum representing the food of twenty-five millions of the people of India was annually remitted to England without a direct return. Was it possible that under this financial arrangement India could be other than impoverished and famine-stricken? If any of the prosperous countries of the world—America or England, France or Germany—had been subjected to such conditions, would not that country have been reduced to poverty, and visited by famines, within a few decades?

CONCLUSION.

He must now conclude. It was necessary to remember that there was no great economic effect without an economic cause. The famines in India were directly caused by the failure of rains in particular tracts, but the rains never failed over the whole of India, and there had never been a year when the total food supply of India was insufficient for the total population of India. What caused distress and deaths was that the people had been so hopelessly impoverished that they could not buy when the crops failed in any particular locality. Let them remove the economic causes of the nation's poverty and they would remove the causes of famines. In the first place they should moderate the land tax and give it some equitable limits which would be understood by the people. In the second place they should discontinue the construction of railways out of public revenues, or under guarantee of profits from public revenues, and extend irrigation works. In the third place they should encourage the industries of India, as the Government of a country ought to do, and thus multiply and add to the resources of the people. In the fourth place they should follow a just and equitable financial policy towards India, as in the case of British Colonies, relieve India from unfair charges, reduce her public debt, and reduce that annual drain which was impoverishing the nation. Lastly they should have some trust and confidence in the people, and admit them to some share in the control of the administration, for it was not in human nature that they should be able to safe-guard the interests of another people without allowing them some voice in their own concerns.

In the words of one of England's greatest philosophers and economists, Johon Stuart Mill, "The government of a people by itself has a meaning and a reality; but such a thing as government of one people by another does not and cannot exist. One people may keep another for its own use, a place to make money in, a human cattle farm to be worked for the profit of its own inhabitants." England did not wish to maintain India as a "human cattle farm," and the only way in which England could improve the condition and promote the prosperity of India was the method she had so successfully followed in all her Colonies—namely, giving the people themselves some real share in the administration of their own concerns. (Applause.)

The address, which took an hour to deliver, was listened to with the greatest interest, and frequently interrupted by cheers.

At its conclusion, numerous questions were asked, which afforded Mr. Dutt an opportunity to repeat, illustrate, and amplify his remarks. Several speakers, including Mr Pearsall, Mr. Bland, Captain St. John, and Captain Rolleston then spoke, and were followed by the Chairman, Mr. Macrosty. Mr. Romesh Dutt replied to their observations, and the meeting, which began at 8 p.m, concluded after 10 p.m., with the usual vote of thanks to the lecturer.

VII. FAMINES AND THE FAMINE COMMISSION OF 1900.

[*Speech delivered at Liverpool on October, 18, 1901.*]

On Friday afternoon, in the Common Hall, Hackins-Hey, a public meeting was held for the purpose of hearing an address by Mr. R. C. Dutt, Lecturer in Indian History, University College, London. Sir Edward Russell presided, and among an attentive and appreciative assemblage and pretty numerous attendance were Archdeacon Madden, the Rev. E. N. Hoare, Dr. Permewan, Mr. J. Hope Simpson, Mr. J. Samuelson, Mr. W. H. Russell, Mr. E. W. Cropper, Mr. Allan Bright, Mr. F. Salisbury, Mrs. Stewart-Brown, Mrs. W. H. Russel, Mr. J. W. S. Callie, Mr. Sam Reeves, Mr. and Mrs. W. C. Bonnerjee, and their daughter Mrs. Blair. As the Chairman remarked at the close of the proceedings, the demonstration and its signal success were owing to the patriotic efforts of Mrs. Blair, assisted by some English ladies. The following report appeared in *India*.

The Chairman, in his introductory remarks, said they were assembled to be instructed in a subject which deeply concerned humanity, and which as deeply concerned the interests, the reputation, and the honour of the British Empire. (Hear, hear.) He need scarcely say, both on his own account and on behalf of many in that room, that they were not there to dogmatise—in fact, that they were incapable of dogmatising on the subject upon which they were to be addressed. But they hoped instructed by a man whom they knew to be thoroughly possessed of the facts of the case, to have formed strong opinions upon it, and to have great hopes of a reform in the management of such affairs as tended to the supply of food in India and the avoidance of the catastrophes which they had so deeply to regret. The real thing they started with that afternoon, he hoped, was a disposition to increase and to cultivate in themselves the feeling of responsibility which should come to them as members of the great Empire which had India under its control. (Applause.) There was a great deal indeed to lament in the past in the apathy with which such occurrences as they had had to deplore had been regarded. It was almost a proverb in this country that Indian affairs had not received the attention to which their magnitude and the extent to which India was bound up with our honour and credit entitled them. Let them make at the very ontest the resolution that that meeting should be the beginning of a different state of things, at all events, as regarded themselves. It was impossible to listen to, or to read of, the terrible famines that had occurred in India, the loss of life, and the lives of abject misery that were led, without feeling that it was a state of things for which, if they were in any degree responsible, they should at once, as far as they could, try and devise some remedy. There were various ways of looking at the matter. They might regard famines as things to be prevented, or they might regard the occurrences during famine as evils to be mitigated and sufferings to be lessened as fas as they could. But the whole matter had been plunged into the mystery in which such great catastrophes of Nature were involved. All they could hope for was that they might be enabled, by the information they might derive, and by the impulses given to them in the direction of responsibility and in the direction of improvement, to create a real interest in the subject, which should make it a constant effort on their part, in reference to Parliament and in reference to public opinion, to produce such a change as they must all desire. (Applause). They were about to hear a lecture by a gentleman who was a master of the subject. He was not only acquainted with the subject and had studied it, but he was known to and knew all those best entitled to speak upon it. He (Sir Edward Russell) was sure they would listen with deep interest, great anxiety, and profit to all Mr. Dutt had to say on the matter. (Applause.)

Mr. Romesh Dutt said: When he was asked a few weeks ago to speak on the subject of famines in India in that great city of Liverpool, he felt some natural hesitation in undertaking the task. The subject had been so constantly before them during the last three or four years, and had been so frequently dealt with in the Press and on the Platform, that he felt some misgivings in bringing the matter before them once more. Neverthless there were grave reasons which induced him to accept the kind offer. Indian famine was an Imperial question, and the gravest of all Imperial questions. (Applause). Indian famine was a serious problem which

Englishmen would have to face again and again till it had been satisfactorily solved. There was no man or woman in that hall, or in the United Kingdom, who had not felt humiliated by the recurrence of these distressing famines under British rule in India, and who did not desire to do all that was humanly possible to avert these great and terrible catastrophes in the future.

INDIAN FAMINES DURING FORTY YEARS.

Famines were a thing of the past in all well-administered Western countries in the world. They read of famines in past centuries in France, Germany, Ireland, and other countries, when hundreds of thousands of people perished for want of food. Those days were gone, he hoped for ever, and the introduction of better government and a sounder system of finance had made famines on a large scale impossible in these countries. In India, unfortunately, the reverse was the case. Not only had famines continued after a hundred and forty years of British rule, but they had become more frequent, more widespread, and more fatal. He would not trouble them with the history of these hundred and forty years that afternoon, but he would mention that within the period which he could well remember—within the last forty years—there had been in India ten or twelve desolating and wide-spread famines, and nearly 20 millions of people had perished of starvation. He remembered the great famine of 1860, when they, as schoolboys, were asked to contribute their humble mite to save the lives of hundreds of thousands of people who were then perishing in Northern India. He remembered the famine of 1866 when the Province of Orissa lost one-third of its population, and the city of Calcutta was filled with starving emigrants from that Province, men and women with children in their arms dying in the streets, in spite of every possible endeavour to relieve them. He remembered the famine of 1874, when he had the honour of being employed as a Relief Officer, and when through the noble exertions, of Lord Northbrook, then Viceroy of India, loss of life was prevented in the stricken province of Behar. (Cheers.) Then came the more dreadful Madras famine of 1877, which in a single year carried off more than five millions of people—a population equal to that of Scotland or of Ireland perished in one Indian province in one year. Then followed the famines of 1878, 1889, and 1892; and lastly came the disastrous famine of 1897, which they all remembered, and which was more widespread than any previous famine had ever been in India. They then thought that it was the worst calamity which could happen to any country in any single year. But they were mistaken. In 1899 followed a still more widespread—and what was worse, a more continuous—famine, for it had lasted these three years, and was not quite over yet. Nothing in the history of India, or of the world, was more appalling than the recurrence of these famines claiming their victims by the hundred thousand or the million, every third or fourth year. No story of wars and invasions in modern or ancient times was more tragic than the story of deaths of twenty millions of silent uncomplaining sufferers in India, within the last forty years of British rule.

Prevention of Future Famines.

These were facts which all Englishmen would have to face. All Englishmen of all classes and all political persuasions were determined that if famines could be stopped by human wisdom and endeavour, they should be stopped in India. There was a school of writers and speakers, some of whom existed to this day, who represented that India was the natural home of famines, that famines were the work of God, and that human endeavours to prevent them were unavailing. To him such a creed appeared to be not only untrue and unmanly, but even blasphemous. (Loud applause.) There was a manlier and honester school of writers who had candidly held that these famines were mainly due to human blunders, and that they could be, and should be, prevented by human wisdom and endeavour. They pointed out that there never had been in any year a deficiency of food supply in all India; that it was the poverty of the people which had prevented them from buying food from neighbouring districts and provinces when the crops failed in any one province, and that famines could be prevented by removing this poverty and enabling the people to buy food from their neighbours in bad years as they in England did in all years. The obvious and radical remedy for famines was to improve the material condition of the people—(1) to lighten the burdens on the land, (2) to save crops by irrigation, (3) to revive the industries of the people, and (4) to reform the financial arrangements of the country.

The Land Tax.

Let them take the Indian Land Tax first. India to-day was not a great manufacturing country or a great commercial country, but a great agricultural country; and four-fifths of the population depended directly or indirectly on the produce of the soil. It followed that that if the soil were lightly taxed, the people might be prosperous; but if the soil was heavily assessed the people must be impoverished. In Northern India the cultivators generally paid their rents to landlords, and the landlords paid the Land Tax to the Government; while in Southern India—in Bombay and Madras—the cultivators paid the Land Tax direct to the State, there being generally speaking, no intervening in landlords. They had urged again and again that in Southern India—in Madras and Bombay—where the State levied the tax direct from the peasant proprietors, the assessment was too heavy; that in many cases it sweept away the whole economic rent of the land; that it made the cultivator unable to save anything even in good years against years of bad harvest; that it left him resourceless and indebted and an easy prey to famines. On the other hand the apologists of the Indian Government had denied this charge; they denied any connexion between land assessments and famines; they had denounced criticism as uninformed and foolish. Well the critics demanded a public enquiry; they asked for a Commission to enquire into the incidence of the Land Tax in India, but no such public enquiry had yet been made. However, something was conceded, a Famine Commission was appointed in December last to enquire into the methods of relief operations in India, and this Commission was permitted incidentally to enquire into the subject of land assessments. The Famine Commission, headed by Sir Antony MacDonnell, the ablest administrator now in India, submitted their report on May 8 last, and though five months had elapsed since, that report had not yet been published in England. All that they had been permitted to see yet was a summary of that report which had appeared in Indian and English newspapers; and this summary proved that their criticisms were neither uninformed nor foolish; that heavy land assessment in Bombay together with its rigorous collection was one of the main causes of the poverty and indebtedness of the cultivators of Bombay. The Famine Commissioners said that in Bombay the land tax, such as it was, could not be collected in short years without forcing the Ryots into debt. They said that the land tax was "full" in Gujrat, and that its rigidity in hard times forced the cultivators into debt. They said that "unless provision for suspension and remission of revenue and rent . . . . be an integral part of the revenue system in any province, the cultivator will be forced to borrow on conditions incompatible with his solvency and independence." And they added that "nothing can be more useful in anticipation of famine than improvements in the material condition of the cultivators whereby they may be enabled to withstand the pressure of hard times." These were admissions, made now for the first time in an official document, clearly establishing that connexion between famines in India and its Land Tax which they had urged again and again within the last few years, and which the apologists of Indian administration had hitherto ignored. He did not say that the Commission had yet arrived at the whole truth. The Commission's figures representing the produce of the soil in the different Provinces of India were admittedly guess work, and obviously incorrect ; and they could prove the produce to be vastly over-estimated if the cultivator was allowed to adduce evidence as to the average produce of his field before any Court of Enquiry, or any Commission appointed for the purpose. But nevertheless, what the Commission had stated in its report showed that public criticism was helpful to the cause of truth and of good administration in India, as it was in every other part of the world. Those who denounced all criticism on Indian administration forgot that every Government in the world needed the aid of criticism, and that the best Government on earth would degenerate into blind and blundering despotism if there was no public opinion and no public criticism. Now that the connexion between the Land Tax and famines had been acknowledged, the public would demand, not only remissions and suspensions of the tax as the Famine Commission had recommended, but also the moderating of that tax in places where it was excessive. He understood that such a revision of the land tax had already begun in the Central Provinces of India.

IRRIGATION.

Next he came to the subject of Irrigation; and here also they would find that well-informed criticism was absolutely in the right. India would have been safer from famines by this time if that criticism had more influence with the Indian Government. The old Hindu Rajas and Mahomedan Governors had left them magnificent irrigation works in all parts of India; and they had urged again and again that while railways had been overdone in India under British rule, irrigation had been neglected. Two hundred and twenty-five millions sterling had been spent on railways, while only 25 millions had been spent on irrigation; and out of over 200 million acres of cultivated land in India only about 20 millions were protected by irrigation works. Their cry had been a cry in the wilderness. Capitalists and speculators had always brought pressure on the Indian Government for more railways out of the public revenues or under guarantee of profits from the public revenues; and down to the present year the Government of India was spending more on railways than on irrigation. Let them mark what the Famine Commissioners said. Railway construction, they said, had played its part in the policy of famine insurance. On the other hand, there was a wide field for the construction of irrigation works. And, confirming the opinion of the previous Famine Commission, this Commission gave its "cordial approval to a departure in famine policy which would place irrigation works in the place that protective railways have hitherto occupied in the famine insurance programme." This was clear and emphatic. If this departure had taken place twenty years ago, when the Famine Commission of 1880 recommended it, India to-day would have been less subject to famines and deaths from starvation.

Declining Industries and the Economic Drain.

There were one or two other matters on which he would have liked to dwell at some length if time permitted, but he could only make a bare mention of them, One of the great sources of a nation's income was its industries and manufactures. For centuries before the British occupation of India, that country was renowned for its excellent manufactures which found their way to all the great markets of Asia and Europe. It was unfortunately true that under British rule Indian manufactures had declined, and the people of India had been forced to agriculture as the one remaining source of their national existence. This was a state of things which could not be good for the people of India, or of any other people, and one of the most serious problems was to find means to promote the indigenous manufactures of India, to diversify the industries of the people, and to add to their resources. Another great evil from which India suffered at present was the financial arrangement under which a large portion of the revenues of India was drained away from that country year after year. They in England were a rich and a prosperous people, and raised an immense revenue from taxation for public expenditure; but the whole of this revenue was spent in the country, flowed back to the people in one shape or another, and fructified the trades and industries of the people. But if one-half of their public revenue was annually drained out of England, and spent in Germany or France or America, England, rich as she was, would soon be a land of famines. Yet this was precisely what was happening in India; on the one hand her industries had declined and her agriculture was over taxed; and on the other hand a large proportion of the taxation so raised was not spent in India, but was drained out of that country, leaving her poorer every year. This, in the words of Lord Salisbury, who was Secretary of State 25 years ago, was the "bleeding" of India; and it was necessary to stop this process if they desired to restore to that country life and prosperity. It was an act which was enjoined by their highest ethics, to do unto others as they would others should do to them; and it was an act which was enjoined by their own interest. Their trade with India could not prosper so long as India continued in her present impoverished state. Within the last ten years the average annual import of merchandise into India had been between 47 millions and 49 millions sterling, and it was possible that about 30 millions of this was British goods. Thirty millions among a population of three hundred millions gave an average of two shillings per head of the population; and he said without hesitation that they could double this rate if India were prosperous. In this way they could easily double their exports, add a new India to their possessions, and extend their empire and trade without firing a cartridge. Their duty was the same as their interest; and as history had shown time after time the honestest policy was also the best policy, for nations as for individuals. (Applause)

THE INDIAN FAMINE UNION.

He would not detain them longer. He thanked them sincerely for the attention with which they had listened to him, and he had no doubt the subject was one which would receive their continuous and urgent attention. They would reflect with pain that the calamities which had visited their fellow subjects in India within this generation were unsurpassed, and perhaps unprecedented in the history of any period or of any country in the world. They would reflect with concern that these fatal and disastrous famines were not the work of God, but were the results of human blunders which could be rectified. There was a right way of profiting by an empire, and there was a wrong way. Honest equitable trade was the right way; to drain a subject country by annual contribution without a direct return was the wrong way. Rome pursued this wrong way; she impoverished Egypt and Sicily and other Provinces, and Rome fell at last, a victim to wealth and luxury. Spain too pursued the wrong way; she impoverished South America; and the Duke of Alva boasted that he sent a stream of gold, a yard wide, flowing from the Netherlands to Spain; the result was that Spain fell, a victim to wealth and moral turpitude. England might yet pursue the right path; she might reduce the Home Charges and the Economic Drain from India; she might establish an equation between the exports and imports of India; she might thus relieve India while doubling her own commerce. These were the salutary remedies which they recommended, the needed reforms they looked forward to. The same economic laws led to wealth or to poverty in all parts of the world, and the measures which had prevented famines in other parts of the civilised world would have the same beneficial results in India, if they had the wisdom and determination to adopt and pursue them in that country. A Union had been formed in London called the Indian Famine Union, with the object of enquiring into the causes of Indian famines and adopting measures for their prevention. A Memorial addressed to the Secretary of State for India to institute such enquiries had been signed by some of the foremost men in this country. He rejoiced to find the names of the Archbishop of Canterbury, the Bishop of Liverpool, and the Dean of Manchester among the signatories. Further action would be taken by the Famine Union in due time. The people of Lancashire were as deeply interested in the welfare of India as the people of any other part of the United Kingdom, and it was not unlikely they might wish to form a Union among themselves. He had not the least doubt that the opinions and the influence of Lancashire would effectually promote the object they all had in view—to take measures to prevent the recurrence of famines in India, and to promote the prosperity and happiness of the three hundred millions of their Indian fellow subjects. (Prolonged cheers).

The CHAIRMAN, in proposing a vote of thanks to Mr. Dutt for his lecture, said he trusted they would all feel the sympathy which the lecturer had expressed for the exertions being made in London for due enquiry into this great subject. They had felt how very broad and statesmanlike must be the policy that had to deal with the great evil they had to contend with. They had also felt that there were many aspects, even beyond that of famine, in which the statesmanship which dealt with Indian affairs needed great reformation. (Hear, hear.) It was a point for them all to keep in their minds, whether the financial arrangements with India were equitable, whether they were worthy of the boasts which we made about our Indian Empire, and whether it might not be an object for our statesmen to place the relations of India, both economically and constitutionally, on a basis more consistent with the reputation of our Empire. (Applause.) He was afraid it was a fact, as was hinted to them in the lecture, that our consciences in this country were much more active when there was anything to be got than when there was anything to give. (Laughter, and hear, hear, and a Voice : "South Africa.") Let them hope, however, that one of the consequences of the great change which had lately taken place in a sort of acceleration and intensification of the Imperial feeling would be that the conscience as well as the ambition of the country would develop—that they would not only develop the ambition which tended to increase the greatness of the country, but that with that would come a conscience for the duty which that Empire involved. (Applause.)

The Ven. Archdeacon MADDEN, in seconding the vote of thanks, said he did not think that mere charity from England was what was wanted in India. In his opinion, the remedy for these famines seemed to be in assisting to make the people of India self-supporting and self-reliant. (Applause.)

Mr. SAM REEVES expressed the belief that the government of India by English officials, whom he described as "carpet-baggers," was prejudicial to the prosperity of the country. His view was that it would be better if Native Indians were allowed to take a more responsible official part in the government of their own country. He urged that before the condition of India could be improved the people of that country would have to "kick," as the people of other countries had had to do in times gone by, before they obtained the reforms they needed.

Sir EDWARD RUSSELL here mentioned that the originators of the meeting were most anxious to hear from any one willing to assist in the formation of a branch to gain information and to stimulate public opinion. He added that that demonstration was entirely the result of the efforts of a lady—Mrs. Blair—assisted by some other ladies.

The proposition was then carried with enthusiasm.

Dr. PERMEWAN wanted to know from the lecturer whether private capitalists might not provide the desired irrigation works, considering the 5 or 6 per cent. profit spoken of.

Mr. DUTT replied that the Government would not permit of the intervention of private capitalists in irrigation works, expenditure in which received its return from an irrigation rate. Of course, this did not apply to landlords dealing with their own estates. Answering a question from another gentleman, as to more direct Parliamentary representation for the people of India, Mr. Dutt said it would be impossible for a British Parliament, even if it had more time to give, to understand Indian questions from the bottom, and to discuss with the local knowledge they ought to have. What was looked forward to was that there should be an executive council in every province, and that some representative Indian or Indians should find place in each of these, and that the legislative councils of India should be expanded. The Indian Civil Service were an able body of administrators ; the official members of the present councils were able and experienced men ; but good government was impossible in India until and unless popular opinion was fairly represented in those councils. Mr. Dutt said he had urged this to the Viceroy himself two years ago.

Mr. JAMES SAMUELSON, in proposing a concluding vote of thanks to the chairman, which was duly honoured, accentuated a remark of the lecturer as to the efficiency of the Indian Civil Service by asserting, on the authority of a personal visit to India, that the higher one got in that service the more intense became the sympathetic interest in the Native populations.

VIII. THE ECONOMIC CONDITION OF INDIA.

[*Speech delivered at the Philosophical Institution, Glasgow, on September* 4, 1901.

MR. ROMESH DUTT said : Last Monday, my esteemed and distinguished friend, Sir John Jardine, gave you a general account of that great country which now forms an important portion of the British Empire. He gave you an account of India and its people, told you of the different Provinces into which British India is divided, and also of those States which are ruled by their own Native Princes. To-night, we shall look into the state of things in India from a different standpoint. We shall enquire into the economic condition of the people—their industries, their trades, their agriculture. We shall try to ascertain how far the sources of national wealth in India have been developed by railways, and how far the annual harvests of the people have made safe by irrigation works. We shall examine the incidence of the Land Tax on the agricultural population of India, and the present state of the finances of that country. In a word the material condition of the vast population of India, forming a sixth of the hnman race, will form the subject of our enquiry this evening.

This is a subject which must always receive the attention of all thoughtful men and women in this country, but recent events in India have invested this subject with a special importance. There is not a man or woman in Great Britain who has not felt grieved by the accounts of recent famines in India. Within the memory of men who are still in their middle age, within the last 30 years, there have been no less than ten desolating famines, causing the deaths of fifteen millions of people in India. And to-night, when we are assembled in this hall, half a million of people are assembled in the different famine camps in Western India, and that country is passing through its third year of a continuous famine. It is necessary, therefore, that we should enquire somewhat minutely into the material condition of the people of India, and find out how far it is possible to prevent or minimise the effects of famines in India in the future, as they have been prevented in other parts of the British Empire.

I. Agriculture and the Land Tax.

The material well-being of the people of India, as in every other part of the world, depends on successful agriculture, on flourishing industries, and on sound system of finance. I take agriculture first, because four-fifths of the population of India depend directly or indirectly on agriculture. It is the main industry of India, the main source of subsistance for the people. This is an important fact which we should always bear in mind in speaking about India. India, today, is essentially an agricultural country. If agriculture flourishes, if the crops are safe-guarded, if the land is moderately taxed, the people are prosperous. If any of these conditions is wanting, the people must necessarily be on the verge of starvation, and must perish in years of bad harvest.

The land system of India is different from the land system of this country. Here you are familiar with the landlord who owns land, the farmer who holds farms, and the agricultural labourer who is paid by wages and has no permanent rights in the land he cultivates. In India, on the contrary, the actual cultivator, by immemorial custom, had some proprietary and heritable rights in the field which he cultivated. Sometimes, as in Bengal, he lived under his landlord, paying rent to the landlord, but owning his hereditary field from which he could not be evicted so long as he paid the customary rent. In other instances, as in Northern India and in Madras and Bombay, he lived in his village community, that ancient system of village self-government which prevailed in India for thousands of years. The landlord or the village community paid the Land Tax to the State; the individual cultivator paid his rent to the landlord or his share of produce to the community, and held his ancestral field from generation to generation, without let or hinderance. Such was the ancient land system of India—the land belonged to the nation, not to any privileged class.

How has this system been affected by British rule? In Bengal and some other places, the ancient system has been preserved and strengthened. The British Government levies the Land Tax from the landlords, and the amount of this Tax was permanently settled a hundred years ago—between 1793 and 1805. But in Northern

India, as well as in Madras and Bombay, where the village community system flourished down to the early years of the nineteenth century, that old institution exists no longer. That ancient form of village self-government has unfortunately perished under the too centralised system of British administration. In Northern India, landlords have taken the place of these communities; in Madras and Bombay, generally, the cultivators are directly under the State. Therefore, if you ask me what is the actual position and status of the Indian cultivator at the present day, I can roughly describe it in one sentence. In Northeren India the cultivator lives under landlords, and the landlords pay the Land Tax to the State; in Southern India the cultivator lives directly under the State, and pays the Land Tax to the State. There are exceptions to this general rule, but it will be enough f our purpose this evening to remember this broad distinction. In Northern India it is the landlord who pays the Land Tax to the State; in Southern India it is the cultivator who pays the Land Tax to the State.

Now what is this Indian Land Tax? You are aware that in England a Land Tax was raised during the wars of the Spanish Succession at the rate of 4s. in the £ of annual value, i. e., 20 per cent. on the rental; and that it was reduced after the Peace of Utrecht to 2s. in the £ and then 1s. in the £, or 5 per cent. on the rental.

The Land Tax in England varied between these limits, until it was made perpetual and redeemable by Pitt's Government in 1798. For a hundred years, therefore, before it was made perpetual, the Land Tax averaged between 5 and 20 per cent. on the rental in England. In India the Land Tax ranges between 35 per cent. and 100 per cent. of the rental! Let me explain this to you in a few words.

In Bengal, where the Land Tax was permanently fixed over a hundred years ago, it now bears a proportion of 28 per cent. on the rental of estates. To this should be added a newer tax of 6¼ per cent., also assessed on the rent, so that the total tax on land in this Province comes to about 35 per cent.

In Northern India, the Government of Lord Dalhousie declared as far back as 1855 its intention to limit the Land Tax to 50 per cent. of the rental. In his own words, the Government was determined "to limit the demand of the State to 50 per cent. or one-half of the average net assets." This was a heavy tax, but it was a clear and definite limit. I regret to state that even this high limit has now been exceeded. A number of new taxes are now surcharged on the Land Tax, and the Land Tax itself came to be assessed at 50 per cent., not on the actual rental, but on the prospective rental of estates. In other words, if a landlord's rental is £1,200, the Government demanded a Tax, not of £600, but may be of £700, on the ground that the rental may rise hereafter. Is this not paltering with the people of India in a double sense, keeping the word of Dalhousie's promise to the ear and breaking it to the hope?

In the Central Provinces of India, Lord Dalhousie's rule of limiting the Land Tax to half the rental was accepted in 1855, but was evaded in 1863. And then the rule was openly abandoned in 1888, and the Government demanded a Land Tax up to 60 per cent of the rental, in addition to other taxes also assessed on the rent.

Lastly in Madras and Bombay, the rule of limiting the Land Tax to half the rent was also declared in 1856 and 1864, but has been evaded in practice. The Directors of the East India Company wrote in their despatch of 1856 that the "rights of the Government is not a rent, which consists of all the surplus produce after paying the cost of cultivation and the profits of agricultural stocks, but a land revenue only." And after the Company was abolished, Sir Charles Wood, the first Secretary of State for India, wrote in his despatch of 1864 that he desired to take only a share, and generally a half share, of the rent as Land Tax. This is the rule; but in practice the Government often takes one-third of the field produce as Land Tax, and this is not 50 per cent., but approximates to 100 per cent. of the economic rent of the field. For in a small farm yielding £12 a year, the cost of cultivation and the profits of the agricultural stock generally exceed £6 or even £7 in the year; and the Government by demanding £4 as Land Tax sweeps away nearly the whole of the economic rent. How is this practice reconciled with Sir Charles Wood's principle? In this way. The Government says in effect to the cultivator: My good friend, we assume the cost of cultivation and the profits of agricultural stock to be £4; we assume the economic rent to be £8, and our Land Tax of £4 is therefore half the rent! Is this not once more, keeping the word of Sir Charles Wood's promise to the ear, and breaking it to the hope?

These details are quite enough. They will give you an idea how the Land Tax is levied in different parts of India, in Bengal, in Northern India, in the Central Provinces and in Southern India. It is the heavy incidence of the Land Tax, and especially its uncertainty, which has a depressing effect on agriculture, which prevents land improvements and any saving, and impoverishes the people. Whatever the Land Tax may be, let it be clear, definite, intelligible. Except in Provinces where it is permanently fixed, the Land Tax is recognized by the British Government, all over India, to be one-half the rent. This rate is recognized by Lord Dalhousie's rule of 1855, by the Court of Director's despatch of 1856, and by Sir Charles Wood's despatch of 1864. This rate is heavy enough in all conscience, but let us at least religiously and conscientiously adhere to this rule, and not seek to evade or exceed it. Thoughtful and moderate Englishmen demand this, and educated and public-spirited Indians desire it also. In December last, a Memorial was signed by a number of retired Indian officials pressing this recommendation on the Secretary of State for India. The Right Honourable Sir Richard Garth, late Chief Justice of Bengal, was one of the signatories; Sir John Jardine, who spoke here last Monday, was another; and several other retired officials, including myself, signed it. The unrepresented people of India demand for the British Government a faithful observance of those clear and definite rules which were laid down by the Government itself 40 or 50 years ago.

II. Railways and Irrigation.

Gentlemen, I now turn from the important subject of the Land Tax to the Railways and Irrigation Works of India. The construction of Railways has, I need hardly remark to this audience been highly benefical in India, as it is beneficial in every other part of the world. It has shortened distances, made travelling and traffic cheaper, and what is of great importance, it has made transport of food grains from one province to another in times of distress quicker and easier. Nevertheless, railways in India have been constructed with doubtful wisdom out of the revenues of the country, or under guarantee of profits out of such revenues. When the State undertakes railway construction or guarantees profits out of public revenues, the concern is never as paying as when undertaken by private companies on their own risk. And so it happens that the entire railway system in India has resulted, not in profit, but in a total loss of forty million pounds sterling to the revenues of India. This loss has added to the public debt, and the tax-payers of India are paying, year after year, a heavy tax as interest on the debt thus piled up. During the last year there was no loss, because the railway earned much by conveying vast quantities of food grains to the famine-stricken provinces. What was a wide-spread calamity for the people was a gain to the railway. We all hope the famine will not last long; and I much fear the profits of the railways will disappear with the famine. In any case it is extremely doubtful if the Indian railways will ever make sufficient profits to wipe off the past loss of forty millions ; and generations of Indian tax-payers will continue to bear the burden of taxation in consequence of this loss.

The total length of railways in India open to traffic by the end of 1898 was 22,500 miles. In that year the Indian Famine Commission stated in their published report that the lines required for famine protection purposes had been completed, and that preference should be given to irrigation works in the future. The advice was unheeded. There is a continuous pressure put on the Indian Government by capitalists and speculators for the construction of fresh railway lines out of the Indian revenues. And thus in spite of the advice of the Famine Commission of 1898 and the earlier commission of 1880, the Indian Government has shewn more activity in the consruction of railways than in irrigation works. The total length of railways open to traffic up to the end of 1900 was 25,000 miles.

The railway system does not add one single blade of corn to the food supply of the country, while irrigation works double the food supply, save crops, and prevent famines. Nevertheless, while 225 millions sterling have been spent on railways, only 25 millions have been spent on irrigation works. Irrigation works are either canals or storage tanks or wells. Canals are only possible in level tracts of the country, along the basin of large rivers. Storage tanks and wells are possible elsewhere. During a century and a half of British rule the whole country could have been covered with irrigation works. All provinces, could have been protected against the effect of droughts. The food supply of India could have been increased and made constant; famines and deaths could have been absolutely prevented; loss of revenue could have been obviated. But by a fatal unwisdom and want of foresight, railways have been fostered and irrigation neglected in India. Out of 220 millions acres of cultivated land in India not much over 20 millions are protected by irrigation works. Many of these works are the works of old Hindu Rajas and Mahomedan Governors which have been preserved up to date. If you read Dr. Francis Buchanan's narrative of his journey from Madras through Mysore to Malabar—performed just a hundred years ago—you will find mention of old canals and storage tanks, made and maintained by the old Hindu and Mahomedan rulers, in every part of their dominions. In spite of their frequent wars, in spite of rude systems of Government, they knew the value of irrigation works. If the more enlightened British Government had followed their example in this respect, they could have covered the whole of India with irrigation works within a hundred years, and they could have made famines impossible under British rule. Let us hope they will take the lesson to heart to-day; that they will henceforth devote all the available resources of the Indian Empire to irrigation works, so that famines will be impossible 20 or 30 years hence.

III. Industries and Manufactures.

I have dwelt so long on agriculture because agriculture is the one national industry of India at the present day. Fourfifths of the population of India depend upon this one industry. Other industries flourished in India in past centuries, but the history of those industries under British rule is a melancholy one; many of them have declined and some have perished altogether. If you read the account of India in the 17th century written by the eminent Frenchman, Francois Bernier, who resided there many years, you will find that in spite of the arbitrary administration of those days, the people of India were a great manufacturing nation, and exported vast quantities of cotton and silk fabrics to the markets of Asia and of Europe. And if you read the statistical account of Eastern India, recorded a hundred years ago by Dr. Francis Buchanan and edited by Montgomery Martin, you will find that one-half the women population of India found employment in spinning and weaving in those days, and earned something from day to day and from year to year, which they added to the earnings of their husbands, their fathers, or their brothers. It is a lamentable fact that practically the whole of this industry has died out in India, and the profits from this industry are lost to the people. It first declined under the illiberal and ungenerous commercial policy of England in the early part of the nineteenth century, when prohibitive duties were imposed on Indian manufactures exported to Europe, while English manufacturers were imported into Indian almost duty-free.

"It is a melancholy instance," writes Horace Hayman Wilson, the well-known historian of India, "of the wrong done to India by a country on which she has become dependent. It was stated in evidence (in 1813) that the cotton and silk goods of India up to the period could be sold for a profit in the British market at a price from 50 to 60 per cent. lower than those fabricated in England. It consequently became necessary to protect the latter by duties of 70 and 80 per cent. on their value, or by positive prohibition......British goods were forced upon her without paying any duty, and the foreign manufacturer employed the arm of political injustice to keep down and ultimately strangle a competitor with whom he could not have contended on equal terms."

Later in the century, the prohibitive duties were abolished, after they had done their fatal work. Handlooms were replaced all over the world by steam, and steam-mills were started in Calcutta and in Bombay. They prospered for a time, but the imposition of an excise duty on the production of Indian mills in recent years has greatly interfered with their success. It is a duty unknown in any other part of the civilised world; it hampers our infant steam industry, and makes it difficult for us to compete with our Asiatic competitors, Japan and China. It is an unwise and illiberal tax by which the British Government disables its British subjects in India from competing on equal terms with other Asiatic nations in the markets of the world.

What has been said about the spinning and weaving industry of India applies to some extent to other old Indian industries. Dying and the manufactures of dyes, tanning and leather work, working in iron and other metals, the weaving of shawls and carpets, muslins and brocades, the manufacture of paper and stationery articles—all have declined. Millions of the Indian population who made a livelihood from these industries are now compelled to agriculture as the one remaining source of their subsistence; and responsible statesmen in the present day, in the House of Commons and outside, and trying to think out how they can undo the mischief done in the past, and again diversify Indian industries. I have myself, during the many years of my service under the Indian Government, visited villages and towns which were once the homes of flourishing communities of weavers—those who produced that famous Indian muslin which was once the wonder of Europe. Those villages are now deserted and desolate; the great lakes excavated in the olden times are silted up; the temples and religious edifices are in decay; the streets are covered with jungle; and the old weaver families have migrated elsewhere to seek a scanty subsistance, and their old ancestral villages know them not.

Gentlemen, you hear very little in this country of this decline of the old national industries of India. Your attention is naturally attracted to those industries only in which British capital is employed. You read of tea and coffee, of indigo and jute, of coal mines and gold mines, which are worked by British Companies. We wish well to all these industries, for they give employment to hundreds of thousands of Indian labourers. But you cannot improve the condition of the people of India without fostering their own industries, carried on by themselves, in their towns and villages. You cannot add to the wealth of the Indian people except by wise legislation, tending to promote and help their own national undertakings. And unless you improve the material condition of the people of India, they will be but poor customers of your own commodities. Our interests and yours are closely allied and not divergent. If our manufactures were revived, and industrial prosperity once more restored to India, the three hundred million people of India could become the largest customers of your manufactures. But if they remain poor, resourceless, starving agriculturists, all your efforts to increase the consumption of your goods in India will utterly fail. India ought to be the greatest market for British goods ; India could be so, if her people were prosperous under British rule.

IV. Trade.

Under the present circumstances of the people of India, your imports into India show no rapid improvement. The average annual import of merchandise into India, most of which was from Great Britain, was 708 millions of rupees, or 47 million pounds, during the five years ending in 1894. In the succeeding five years ending in 1899 the average annual import into India was 736 millions of rupees or 49 million pounds. An export of 49 million of pounds to a population of 300 millions means a consumption of 3*s.* per head of the population. If the people of India consumed your goods at the rate of 5*s.* or 6*s.* a year per head of population—and this is a moderate estimate even for a poor Asiatic nation—your exports into India would be doubled, and you would carry on a trade with India exceeding your trade with any other country in the world. Therefore, I say that your trade interests and those of the people of India are closely allied and not divergent. It is not by restrictive excise duties on the manufactures of India, nor by draining her resources, that Great Britain can gain in the long run. It is by making the population of India prosperous that your trade with India can prosper.

V. Finances and the Economic Drain.

Gentlemen, I have spoken to you of the agriculture and the Land Tax of India, of her railways and irrigation works, of her industries and trade. I have only one word to add about the financial administration of India. The net revenues of India for the current year have been estimated at 42 millions sterling. Roughly speaking you can say that 20 mlllions out of this comes from Land Revenue, 20 millions from other taxes including Salt, and two millions from Opium. In other words, the trades and industries of the country bring little revenue, because the trades and industries are on the decline—one half the revenue of the country is tax on land and tax on salt, and is raised from the food of the poor. If you examine the figures thus closely, you will find how little reason there is for congratulation on the increase of revenues in India; that increase does not mean increasing prosperity, but only an oppressively increasing taxation on the food supply of the people. Twenty-six years ago, our present Prime Minister, Lord Salisbury, was Secretary of State for India, and condemned in the strongest terms this undue taxing of the food of the people. He wrote in 1876:

"So far as it is possible to change the Indian system, it is desirable that the cultivator should pay a smaller proportion of the whole national charge. It is not in itself a thrifty policy to draw the mass of revenue from the rural districts where capital is scarce...... The injury is exaggerated in the case of India, where so much of the revenue is exorted without a direct equivalent. As India must be bled, the lancet should be directed to the part where the blood is congested, or at least sufficient, not to those which are already feeble from the want of it."

These remarks of Lord Salisbury apply with greater force than they did 26 years ago. You are bleeding the agricultural population of India at a time when they are suffering from repeated, continuous and widespread famines; and you are exporting a larger portion of that revenue out of India without a direct equivalent to-day, than you did 26 years ago. You are draining India annually of sixteen millions sterling for what are called "Home charges"; while the total of charges which India has to remit annually to this country without a direct equivalent is over twenty millions! Do you think that any country can prosper under such a system of finance? Do you think Great Britain or the United States, or Germany or France or any other country could prosper if an amount equal to one half of her annual revenues was sent out of the country, year after year, to be spent in a foreign country? Do you think England is doing justice to India under a financial arrangement through which the food of 20 millions of people in India is annually sent away to England without a direct equivalent?

I have said the net revenue of India for the current year is estimated at 42 millions. The expenditure, roughly speaking is this: 17 millions for the Army, 17 millions for the Civil services, and 8 millions more for other charges. Of all these three heads the cost of the Army is felt to be most unjust and oppressive, because the great army maintained in India is not merely for the defence of India but for the defence of Great Britain's possessions in Asia and in Africa. 30,000 troops were lately sent out of India to China and to South Africa; and this proves beyond a doubt that the Indian Army is maintained as much for Imperial purposes as for India. That being so, it is only just and fair that Great Britain should pay a portion of the cost of the army maintained in India, and not try to run her empire on the cheap by throwing the whole cost of the Army on the unrepresented and famine-stricken population of India.

VI. Famines and their Remedies.

Ladies and Gentlemen, I thank you for listening so patiently and with so much interest to this account of the economic condition of India. It is a subject of the greatest importance ; I do not think there is a question of graver import connected with any part of the British Empire than the present condition of India. Called upon to deal with the subject within the limits of one speech, I should have but ill discharged my duty if I had merely gleaned some facts and figures from official reports, and placed them before you without explaining their bearing on the condition of the people of India. Great Britain can look back on the past history of Indian administration—if not with unalloyed satisfaction—at least with legitimate pride. If blunders have been committed in the past, much good work too has been well and honestly done. Great Britain has restored peace and security of property to the vast population of India after a century of disorder and disturbance. Great Britain has introduced into India Western methods of education which have had the happiest results among an ancient and intellectual people. And if Great Britain has too hastily and unwisely swept aside some of our old self-governing institutions, she is making us familiar with newer methods of enlightened administration. These are results which we can contemplate with just pride and sincere satisfaction ; but there are matters in which the success of British rule has not been so conspicuous ; and we cannot honestly feel the same satisfaction in contemplating the economic condition of the people of India in the present day. No impartial observer in India, no unprejudiced critic in this country, can think of the wretched and almost universal poverty of the vast population of India without a feeling of commiseration and sorrow, or can read of the frequent and fatal famines of that country without a feeling of pain and of humiliation. These are facts which tell their own tale; roseate pictures of Indian prosperity, so often painted and so sedulously circulated, convince no one, and deceive no one. To you, such representations of Indian prosperity appear like an endeavour to conceal defects in administration which should be remedied and not concealed; to the mass of my countrymen, who live in a chronic state of poverty of which you have no conception, such roseate pictures painted in this country appear like an unfeeling mockery of their misfortunes. The evil is undoubtedly there; Englishmen and English women desire to know the reasons of the frequent and fatal famines in the past; and they desire also to see no more of them in the future. Therefore, standing before you tonight to speak of the economic condition of my country, I have sought to lay before you, as clearly as I could within my brief limits, the causes of this undoubted evil, and the remedies which are needed. Moderate the Land Tax within reasonable and intelligible limits; extend irrigation works all over India; revive the industries and manufactures of the people; reduce the financial drain which is impoverishing India; and admit the people themselves into some reasonable share in the control of the administration of their own concerns; and you will hear as little of famines in India in the future, as you hear of famines in Great Britain or famines in the city of Glasgow. An Empire has its responsibilities as well as its glory ; and the happiness and advancement of the people of India are the highest responsibilities of Great Britain and her most glorious mission in the east.

IX. INDIAN AGRICULTURE.

[*Paper read at Mansfield House, Canning Town, London, October* 27, 1901.]

ON Sunday, October 27, Mr. Romesh Dutt, C.I.E., formerly of the Indian Civil Service, delivered a lecture at Mansfield House, Canning Town, London, upon "Indian Agriculture." There was an excellent audience, and the meeting proved most successful.

Mr. DUTT said:—The subject of my lecture this evening is Indian Agriculture. The subject is one of great importance, because, as you are all aware, India is a vast continent equal in extent and population to the whole continent of Europe, if you leave out Russia. And the people of this great continent of India is mainly agricultural. You in England were also mainly an agricultural people over a hundred years ago, and by far the greater part of Englishmen lived with their families in farms. But your splendid supply of coal and iron gave you a start in industries after the invention of steam, and long before the middle of the nineteenth century you had distanced all other countries of the earth in the extent and the excellence of your manufactures. The result was that you gradually neglected your agriculture and swarmed to towns and factories till at the present time more than half the population of England live in towns and depend on trades and industries, and you buy your corn and vegetables, and even meat, mostly from other nations. I do not myself know if this state of things is good for a nation, or if it can be permanent. Already your supremacy in trades and manufactures is threatened by the rivalry of Germany and America, and what those nations will ultimately achieve no man can foresee.

We in India have gone to the opposite extreme. If you have depended too much on your manufactures, we have depended too much on our agriculture, and four-fifths of the great population of India depend directly or indirectly on the produce of the soil. Our national industries, specially spinning and weaving, have declined within the last hundred years, firstly through the illiberal policy of the East India Company, and secondly by competition with the steam and machinery of Europe. Agriculture is our one national industry now ; if agriculture prospers, the people are well off ; if crops fail, there is famine in the land.

I myself believe that a civilised nation prospers best if it is mindful both of its agriculture and its industries. And I also believe that both England and India will need some re-adjustment of their industries in the near future. You in this country will have to be more mindful of your agriculture with the growing competition of other nations in various industries. And we in India will have to develop our manufactures by the help of steam and machinery, so as not to be entirely dependent on our crops. The soil is the gift of Heaven to each nation as well as skill in manufactures ; and it is a healthy state of things when a large proportion of a nation are engaged in cultivating the soil, while a fairly large proportion of them are also engaged in industries.

In speaking now of our agricultural system in India, I must premise by informing you that our land system is entirely different from yours in England. You are familiar with the landlord who owns his estate, the farmer who takes lease of his farm, and the labourer who tills the soil and is paid by wages. Our system is just the opposite of this. It is the tiller in India who virtually owns his holding of five or ten acres, who inherits it from his father, sells or mortgages it at will, and hands it down to his sons when he dies. Sometimes the tiller pays a rent to a superior landlord; in other instances there is no superior landlord, and the tiller pays the land tax direct to the State. But in both cases the humble tiller is the virtual proprietor of his small holding; and as long as he pays his tax or his rent, he cannot be evicted from his heritable and transferable property. I cannot but think that this ancient land system of India is better than your modern English system; for the soil in India belongs to the nation, and not to a few individuals.

Skill and Industry of Indian Cultivators.

It is generally believed in this country that the Indian tiller, whom we call a Ryot, is a thoughtless primitive creature, ignorant of his own interests, antiquated in his methods of agriculture, and altogether a poor relic of the prehistoric past whom it is necessary to instruct and to modernise. Impressed with this idea the Government of India have often been fired by the benevolent desire to teach the Indian cultivator better methods of cultivation; but before they proceeded very far, the Government discovered that they had more to learn than to teach. They found out that under the local conditions of India, it was scarcely possible to improve on the methods which the Indian agriculturist had adopted from the experience of thousands of years; and that while it was possible to improve the supply of water and the supply of manure, it was scarcely possible to improve on the art of growing wheat and rice which the Indian cultivator practised. This is generally the opinion expressed by English scientists who have carefully examined the systems of Indian agriculture. As early as 1832, Dr. Wallick, who was Superintendent of the East India Company's Botanical Gardens at Calcutta, gave his evidance before a Committee of the House of Commons to this effect: "The Bengal husbandry, although in many respects extremely simple, and premival in its mode and form, yet is not so low as people generally suppose it to be; and I have often found that very sudden innovations in them have never led to any good results. I have known for instance European iron ploughs introduced into Bengal with a view to superseding the extremely tedious and superficial turning of the ground by the common Bengal plough. But what has been the result? That the soil which is extremely superficial......has geperally received the admixture of the under soil, which has deteriorated it very much." And with reference to rice cultivation in Bengal, Dr. Wallick remarked: "If we were to live another thousand years, we should hardly see any improvement in that branch of cultivation."

This was said nearly seventy years ago; and let us turn to a more recent opinion,—the latest scientific opinion that is available to us. Dr. Voelcker, consulting chemist to the Royal Agricultural Society of England, was sent out to India in 1889 to enquire into Indian agriculture, and submitted a report which is the most valuable and authoritative work we have on that subject. And at the very commencement of his report, Dr. Voelcker bears his testimony to the skill of the Indian agriculturist in these words:—"The ideas generally entertained in England, and often given expression to even in India, that Indian agriculture is, as a whole, primitive and backward, and that little has been done to try and remedy it, are altogether erroneous.......Taking everything together, and more specially considering the conditions under which Indian crops are grown, they are wonderfully good. At his best, the Indian Rayat or cultivator is quite as good as, and in some respects the superior of, the average British farmer; while at his worst it can only be said that this state is brought about largely by an absence of facilities for improvement which is probably unequalled in any other country, and that the Rayat will struggle on patiently and uncomplainingly in the face of difficulties in a way that no one else would. Nor need our British farmers be surprised at what I say, for it may be remembered that the Natives of India were cultivators of wheat centuries before we in England were. It is not likely, therefore, that their practice should be capable of much improvement. What does, however prevent them from growing larger crops is the limited facilities to which they have access, such as the supply of water and manure. But to take the ordinary acts of of husbandry, nowhere would one find better instances of keeping land scrupulously clean from weeds, of ingenuity in device of water-raising appliances, of knowledge of soils and their capabilities, as well as the exact time to sow and to reap, as one would in Indian agriculture, and this not at its best alone, but at its ordinary level. It is wonderful, too, how much is known of rotation, the system of mixed crops, and of fallowing. Certain it is that I, at least, have never seen a more perfect picture of careful cultivation, combined with hard labour."

Mixed Crops and Rotation.

A few words will explain the system of mixed crops and of rotation, as practised in India. A grain crop like Juar is often put on the ground with a leguminous crop like Arhar. The grain crop grows rapidly and keeps the other back, and when it is reaped the leguminous crop extends itself, grows apace, and in due time is reaped. This system is followed year after year. and while to the casual observer it seems like a continuous cropping, there is really a perfect system of rotation all the time. Sometimes three or even four kinds of seed are sown at the same time, for instance, wheat, barley, grain, and rape seed. Wheat and grain often occur together, so also wheat and linseed. Sometimes again the mixed cropping is more complicated than even this. For instance there are deep-rooted plants, and there are surface feeders which grow together, drawing their nourishment from different layers of the same soil; there are plants which require shelter, and will not thrive without the friendly neighbourhood of other plants. All this is clearly understood by the Indian cultivator—the heir to the knowledge and experience of thousands of years of tilling—who to the casual British observer appears so ignorant, so improvident, so like a relic of the prehistoric past,

The one crop with which rotation is seldom practised is rice. The reason is that rice grows best on soil the fertility of which is annually renewed by the silt of inundating rivers. The Ganges and the other great rivers of India not only bring their annual supply of water to thirsty crops, but also bring a vast amount of fertilizing silt which they gently deposit on the soil—the finest and richest manure provided by Nature, over millions of acres, without the toil of man. To utilize this manure, the Indian cultivator practises surface ploughing only; any deep ploughing, such as is practised in England, and which has been sometimes stupidly tried in India, only destroys this manure, and turns up the sand below. Over this inundated and annually renewed soil, rice grows year after year without the need of mixed cropping or rotation. Yet I have seen some mixed cropping on such lands also ; the rice ripens early, and is reaped early ; and the oil seed or pulse sown with it then flourishes in the winter months, and is reaped in February and March.

These few remarks will illustrate the skill and knowledge of the Indian cultivator, and the suitability of his methods and implements to the local conditions of India. Deep ploughing would be injurious to Indian cultivation ; and steam ploughs are out of the question where the average field is from half an acre to three or four acres. And I, for one, do not wish to see these small holdings enlarged. The land in India belongs to the nation ; each petty cultivator is provided for with his three or four or ten acres ; and I would not like to see these humble cultivators squeezed out by capitalists, and small fields turned into extensive areas of cultivation.

I may only add here that where improvements are possible, consistently with the Indian land system and cultivation, they are eagerly adopted by the so-called thoughtless and primitive Indian cultivator. I have myself seen the Indian sugar-grower discarding his awkward sugar mill and adopting a mill invented by Europeans in India, which pressed the cane better, and produced more sugar. Teach him to make cheaper manure or to make better appliances for the supply of water; teach him to make a better selection of seeds, or a cheaper method of threshing ; and he will adopt your improvements quickly enough. But propose to him reforms inconsistent with the conditions of Indian agriculture and Indian peasant life, and he will decline your advice with thanks.

Geological Types of Soil.

Having spoken so far of the Indian cultivator, I wish to say one word more of his skill in distinguishing the different kinds of soil suitable for different crops. There are an infinite variety of soils in India, but nevertheless the geological types of soil may be classified into three broad classes. The Alluvial Soil predominates over the whole of Northern India, along the basin of the Indus and the Ganges, and consists of mud and sand. Away in the west, virtually throughout the province of Bombay, a basaltic formation called the Black Cotton Soil predominates, and is peculiarly fitted for the growth of cotton, for which Western India has always been famous. And all along the East and South, from the hills of Chota Nagpur and Orissa, right through the dominions of the Nizam of Hyderabad, to the undulating plains of Madras, Mysore, and Travancore, the Red Soil predominates, consisting of archæan and metamorphic rocks. These are the three grand geological divisions of the Indian soil ; but as I have said before, there are endless varieties within these three classes ; and nothing can exceed the skill with which the Indian cultivator distinguishes the different varieties of soil suitable for different varieties of crops. Chemistry and modern science have yet added nothing to the skill, acquired through the local experience of centuries.

WANT OF MANURE.

The great need for improvement in Indian agriculture is not new implements and new methods of cultivation, but a sufficient supply of manure and a sufficient supply of irrigation water. There is great apprehension in the minds of thoughtful and scientific observers that the soil of India is being exhausted, not through ignorance of rotation or proper methods of cultivation, but through the failure of manure. Cattle manure has always been, and is to this day, the universal fertiliser of Indian lands, and the only cheap and available manure. But with the destruction of forests and scarcity of firewood in these days, cattle manure is now largely dried and made into cakes for use as fuel, and thus the supply of manure for land is growing less and less. You can go to no part of India without seeing thousands of women drying these manure cakes, and taking them on their heads to towns for sale as fuel; and all that is thus consumed in towns as fuel is a loss to the country and to production. Dr. Voelcker has recorded: "As the result of my enquires I feel I may safely assert that where the practice of burning dung as fuel prevails among the genuine cultivators, it arises, in eight cases out of ten, from the scarcity of firewood." This is a serious and a growing evil; and the only possible remedy for it is in the hands of the Indian Government. Forests must be preserved, not merely for the sake of the valuable timber which is now the principal care of forest officers, but also for the supply of sufficient and cheap firewood for all the cultivators in the country. The rules of the forest department must be brought more in touch with the needs of the agricultural population ; and the people must be allowed to obtain—as they always did obtain in past centuries—an ample supply of firewood from jungles, so that their cattle manure may be saved for its proper purpose.

Another cause of the failure of manure in India is the vast exportation of oil seeds from the country to Europe. Under the present system of administration, India has to remit to England a large sum, estimated at over twenty millions annually, without any direct equivalent. This not only impoverishes the people of India directly, but it impoverishes the soil of the country, which is now virtually the sole means of the subsistence of the people. For a large portion of the remittance has to be made up by the exportation of oil seeds. If the oil was manufactured in India, and then exported, the evil would be less ; for the oil itself has no manurial properties. But to export the entire seed, or the refuse after the removal of the oil is, in the words of Dr. Voelcker, "to export the soil's fertility."

Want of Water.

Another great need for Indian agriculture is the want of a sufficient supply of water. Except in tracts of lands which are annually inundated by rivers, crops in India depend on the annual rainfall or on irrigation works. The rainfall is always uncertain, and so in old times Hindu Rajas and Mahomedan Emperors constructed vast irrigation works, the remains of which you will find not only in the basins of the Jumna and the Indus, but also in Southern India. Many of these works have been preserved and added to by the British Government; but sufficient attention has not been paid within the last hundred years to constructing new irrigation works. Too much attention has been paid to railways for facilitating the export and import trade of England with India; too little attention has been paid to irrigation for facilitating the agriculture of the people of India. 225 millions sterling have been spent on railways; and only 25 millions have been spent on irrigation works. And thus it happens that out of over 220 million acres of cultivated land in India, not much over 20 millions are protected by irrigation works. I am glad to find, however, that recent famines have at last disturbed the conscience of the India Government; and that a Commission, headed by an eminently qualified man, has just been appointed to enquire into this much neglected subject.

The irrigation works required in the different provinces of India are of different kinds. In the alluvial basins of the Ganges and the Indus, the most suitable irrigation works are CANALS fed from these rivers, and distributing their water through tributaries to the surrounding country. In many parts of Northern India not irrigated by the rivers, the most suitable works are WELLS, and some help and encouragement to their construction have lately been given to the people by that ablest of the present Indian administrators, Sir Anthony

MacDonnell. In Bengal, where the rainfall is copious, and the fields are often inundated by rivers, SHALLOW PONDS excavated in the fields are the most suitable irrigation works; and I have seen such ponds, excavated by the old Rajas of the country, two or three miles in circumference, the like of which has never been done in recent times. Away in Madras and Southern India where the soil is undulating, and the underlying rock helps the retention of water, the most suitable irrigation works are RESERVOIRS made by constructing large embankments, and thus impounding all the water descending from the hill slopes. Some of the most magnificent works of this kind, constructed by the old Polygars of Madras, were seen by Dr. Francis Buchanan in his journey through Southern India a hundred years ago. If such works had been multiplied within these hundred years, faminies would have been less frequent and less disastrous than they are to-day.

AFFORESTATION.

Gentlemen, it may sound somewhat strange, but it is nevertheless a fact, that the needed humidity of the soil is closely connected with the preservation of trees and forests. The question whether large forests and plantations cause and increase the rainfall has often been discussed, and I will not enter into that debateable matter. But there can be no doubt that forests and large plantations, by lowering the temperature, cause the rain to descend in gentle showers, where the clouds would otherwise pass on, or burst in wasteful torrents. Thus, if trees do not cause rainfall, they certainly distribute the rain; if they do not increase the quantity of rain, they certainly increase the number of rainy days. It has been noticed that in one station in southern India, that of Utakamand, the total number of rainy days in five years, from 1870 to 1874—excluding the monsoon months—was 374. This was when the station was bare of woods. Since then, trees have been planted and the place is well wooded now, and the total number of rainy days in the five years from 1886 to 1890,—excluding the monsoon months—was no less than 416. This increase in the number of rainy days is a great advantage to agriculture, even if there be no difference in the actual quantity of annual rainfall.

Want of Pasture Land.

You will see, therefore, that forests are required, not only for supplying fuel to the agricultural population, but also for distributing and utilising the rains. Another great use of forests and jungles is to supply grazing lands for cattle. In olden times, most villages in India had their adjoining jungle or waste lands for the grazing of cattle, and such lands, pertaining to each village, were used by the villagers in common. The great increase in the area of cultivation in recent times has led to the enclosing of these commons, as you would describe the process in England, until the want of sufficient pasture lands has become a real and grave difficulty. When the crops have been reaped, the cattle are let loose on the fields; but in other months they are fed on straw and fodder procured with difficulty. This growing evil has come to the notice of the Government. Up to 1880, wrote Mr. Nicholson of Coimbatore, every tenant used to hold one-fifth of his farm as pasture at one quarter the usual assessment; but this salutary rule was abolished at the new Settlement of 1880. In 1883 the Government of India recorded a resolution that the cultivated area in India had steadily increased at the expense of the grazing area. And in 1890 Sir D. Brandis recorded that in Madras the working plans for the fuel and fodder reserves should contain proposals for throwing open certain forest areas to grazing. Adequate measures, however, have not yet been taken, and the subject is one which requires the closest attention, both of the Government and of private landlords.

AN UNCERTAIN LAND-TAX.

The last evil from which agriculture suffers in India is an uncertain land-tax. You are aware that in England the Government levied a high tax of four shillings in the pound, or 20 per cent. of the rental, during the wars of the early years of the eighteenth century; and this was reduced to two shillings, and then to one shilling in the pound, or 5 per cent. of the rental, after the Peace of Utrecht. The land tax in England varied between these limits for about a hundred years, till it was made permanent and redeemable by the great minister, William Pitt, in 1798. In India the land tax was made permanent only in Bengal and a few other places. In Northern India, after many blundering and oppressive experiments, the land tax was fixed in 1855, not at 5 per cent. of the rental, but at 50 per cent. of the rental; and in Southern India, too, the same general rule of levying the land tax at 50 per cent of the rent was recognised in 1864. You will consider this rate both excessive and oppressive; but the worst of it is that even this heavy rate is not strictly adhered to. In Northern India, the Government sought to levy 50 per cent., not on the current rental, but on the prospective rental of estates; and a great many minor taxes are assessed on the land in addition to the land tax. In the Central Provinces of India the rule of levying 50 per cent of the rental as tax was evaded in 1863 and openly abandoned in 1888; and a higher tax was levied. And in Southern India, *i. e.*, in Bombay and Madras, the tax which is levied from the cultivators often approximates to 100 per cent. of the economic rent. Fresh Settlements are being continually made in different parts of India; neither the landlord nor the cultivator knows what the State demand will be after each new settlement; and this uncertainty deadens agricultural energy, and prevents agricultural improvements. What is wanted for the improvement of agriculture in India is a clear intelligible limit to the land tax—a limit which will not be evaded or altered by the whims and fancies of Settlement officers and Provincial rulers. 50 per cent. of the rental or the economic rent is the rule theoretically recognised in all parts of India where the land tax has not been permanently fixed; and it is a heavy tax for an agricultural nation to pay. But something would be gained even if this heavy rate was religiously adhered to, and was not evaded and exceeded, as it now constantly is, at each recurring Settlement in many parts of India. Nothing can be more fatal to agricultural prosperity, nothing is more destructive to agricultural improvements, than any uncertainty in the State demand from the soil.

Gentlemen, I thank you for the patient hearing which you have given me on a subject which is not altogether familiar to you. But it is a subject of the greatest importance to the prosperity and well-being of India, and to three hundred millions of your fellow-subjects. The Indian Government commands ability, knowledge, and experience, but is not in touch with the lives of the vast Indian population. There are no Indian members either in the Secretary of State's Council in London, or in the Viceroy's Executive Council in India ; and questions, involving military operations or the revenue, naturally receive more attention than questions involving the well-being and the prosperity of the unrepresented nation. It is a truism that there can be no government for the good of a people without some sort of representation ; and the Indian Government will fail to secure the happiness of the Indian people until there is some representation of the popular opinion in the Executive Councils of the Empire. The economic condition of the people of India will never be improved until the people themselves are permitted a reasonable share in the administration of their own concerns.

X. INDIAN MANUFACTURES.

[*Paper read before the Sukha Samiti London, on December 20th*, 1901.]

THE decline of Indian manufactures and indigenous industries within the last 150 years is one of the saddest episodes of British Rule in India, and presents one of the most difficult economic problems to Indian administrators at the dawn of a new century.

India was known from ancient times, not only as a great agricultural but also as one of the greatest manufacturing countries in the world. Egypt and Babylon in the palmy days of their civilisation largely imported Indian manufactures ; and Phœnycian and Arabian merchants navigated the Red Sea to convey the produce of the Indian loom into the markets of the west. Later on, Constantinople and Alexandria became the great centres of the Indian trade ; and as they declined under the rule of the Turks, Venice became the proudest seaport of Europe, and displayed before the rude barons of Germany, France and England the valuable products of Indian industry.

The success of Venice aroused the jealousy of other nations, and they endeavoured to find out a new path to India. Columbus discovered America in endeavouring to discover a new route to India, and Vasco da Gama at last succeeded in finding a way round the Cape of Good Hope. This was the main cause of the fall of

Venice and the rise of Portugal. Throughout the sixteenth century Portugal monopolised the trade of the East; and nearly all the important trade centres in Eastern Africa, in Arabia and Persia, in India and the Indian Archipelago, were in the possession of the Portuguese. Holland rose in power after the great war of independence, early in the seventeenth century, and the Dutch were the most successful traders with India in that century. A French traveller, Bernier, who resided in India for many years during the seventeenth century, speaks of vast quantities of cotton and silk fabrics manufactured by the weavers of India which were shipped annually by the Dutch merchants for the markets of Europe. Millions of Indian artisans found employment and earned an income from weaving these fabrics; and it is scarcely an exaggeration to state that there was hardly a village in India in those days where women did not earn something from spinning and weaving, in addition to what their husbands and fathers earned from agriculture and other industries.

The Dutch declined in power in the eighteenth century, and France and England strove for supremacy in India. The contest was finally decided by the peace of Paris in 1763, which left the British supreme in Bengal and in Madras, with the important port of Bombay in their possession on the western Coast. Two years after this, the East India Company obtained from the Great Mogul a formal charter as Dewan or Administrators of Bengal and the Northern Circars.

The East India Company then pursued a policy

different from what all preceding traders had done. Not content with the trade of India, they desired to discourage the manufactures of India, in order to encourage the manufactures of England.

As early as 1769, the Directors of the Company wished the manufacture of raw silk to be encouraged in Bengal, and that of silk fabrics discouraged. And they also directed that silk weavers should be made to work in the Company's factories, and prohibited from working outside "under severe penalties, by the authority of the Government."[1] This mandate had its desired effect. The manufacture of silk and cotton goods declined in India, and the people who had exported these goods to the markets of Europe and Asia in previous centuries began to import them in increasing quantities. The following figures [2] shew the value of cotton goods alone, sent out from England to ports east of the Cape of Good Hope, mainly to India, during twenty years.

Year ending 5th January.	£	Year ending 5th January.	£
1794	156	1804	5,936
1795	717	1805	31,943
1796	112	1806	48,525
1797	2501	1807	46,549
1798	4,436	1808	69,841
1799	7,317	1809	118,408
1800	19,575	1810	74,695
1801	21,200	1811	114,649
1802	16,191	1812	107,306
1803	27,876	1813	108,824

(1) *General Letter*, dated, 17th, March 1769.
(2) Return to an order of the House of Commons dated 4th May 1813.

The Company's Charter was renewed in 1813. An enquiry was made, and witnesses were examined previous to this renewal. Very important witnesses like Warren Hastings, Thomas Munro, and Sir John Malcolm were examined; and the House of Commons shewed the utmost concern for the general welfare of the people of India. But in respect of the Indian manufactures, they sought to discover how they could be replaced by British manufactures, and how British industries could be promoted on the ruins of Indian industries.

Warren Hastings who had been Governor General in India for nearly twelve years was the most important witness examined. Notwithstanding his blunders and mis-rule in India, he had carried away with him a lively idea of the many virtues of the people of that country, and he boldly stated his opinion before the Committee of the House of Lords. "I affirm by the oath that I have taken," he said "that this description of them [that the people of India were in a state of moral turpitude] is untrue and wholly unfounded. * * * They are gentle, benevolent, more susceptible of gratitude shewn them than prompted to revenge for wrongs inflicted, and as exempt from the worst properties of human passion as any people on the face of the earth." And asked by the Commons Commitee as to whether the Indian people were likely to consume British manufactures, he replied: "The supplies of trade are for the wants and luxuries of a people; the poor in India may be said to have no wants. Their wants are confined to their dwellings, to their food, and to a scanty portion of clothing, all of which they can have from the soil that they tread upon."[3]

Sir John Malcolm who had lived a good deal among the people of India, and knew them as few Englishmen have known them since, bore high testimony to the many virtues of the nation. Speaking of Northern India, he said: "The Hindoo inhabitants are a race of men, generally speaking, not more distinguished by their lofty stature * * * than they are for some of the finest qualities of the mind; they are brave, generous, and humane, and their truth is as remarkable as their courage." And replying to the question as to whether they were likely to be consumers of British goods, he replied: "They are not likely to become consumers of European goods, because they do not possess the means to purchase them even if from their present simple habits of life and attire, they required them."[4]

Grœme Mercer, who had served the East India Company as a doctor, and also in the revenue and political departments, described the people of India as "mild in their dispositions, polished in their general manners, in their domestic relations kind and affectionate, submissive to authority, and peculiarly attached to their religious tenets, and to the observance of the rites and ceremonies prescribed by those tenents." And in reference to the introduction of European goods in India he deposed that Lord Wellesley had endeavoured to find markets for such goods by instituting fairs in Rohilkhand, exhi-

(3) *Minutes of Evidence* on the affairs of the E. I. Company 1813 p 3.
(4) *Ibid*, pages 54 and 57.

siting British wollens in those fairs, and by directing the British Resident to attend the great fair at Hardwar with the same object.[5]

But the most important witness examined by the Committee of the House of Commons on this memorable occasion was Thomas Munro; and the whole of his evidence is inspired by that sympathy with the people of India, and that appreciation of their virtues, which had distinguished that gifted Scotchman during his 27 years' work in India, from 1780 to 1807.

Munro said that the average wages of agricultural labour in India were between 4 shillings and 6 shillings a month; that the cost of subsistence was between 18 shillings and 27 shillings the head per annum; that there was no probability of extending the sale of British wollen goods because the people used coarse-wollen of their own manufacture; and that they were excellent manufactures and were likely to imitate English goods. Asked if Hindu women were not slaves to their husbands, Munro replied: "They have as much influence in their families, as I imagine, the women have in this country" [England.] And asked if the civilisation of the Hindus could not be improved by the establishment of an open trade, he gave that memorable answer which has often been quoted and will bear repetition: "I do not understand what is meant by the civilisation of the Hindus; in the higher branches of science, in the knowledge of the theory and practice

(5) *Ibid*, pages 88 and 89,

of good government, and in education which, by banishing prejudice and superstition, opens the mind to receive instruction of every kind from every quarter, they are much inferior to Europeans. But if a good system of agriculture; unrivalled manufacturing skill; a capacity to produce whatever can contribute to convenience or luxury; schools established in every village for teaching reading, writing, and arithmetic; the general practice of hospitability and charity amongst each other; and above all, a treatment of the female sex, full of confidence, respect, and delicacy; are among the signs which denote a civilised people, then the Hindus are not inferior to the nations of Europe; and if civilisation is to become an article of trade between the two countries, I am convinced that this country [England] will gain by the import cargo."[6]

Munro had a high idea of the excellence of the Indian manufactures of his time. Among the causes which precluded the extended sale of British goods in India he mentioned "the religious and civil habits of the natives, and more than anything else, I am afraid, the excellence of their own manufactures." He had used an Indian Shawl for seven years, and found very little difference in it after that long use; while with regard to imitation shawls producted in England he said: "I have never seen an European Shawl that I would use, even if it were given to me as a present."[7]

The evidence of one other witness deserves mention,

(6) *Ibid*, pages 124, 127, 131.
(7) *Ibid*, pages 123 and 172.

that of John Stracey. He had served the East India Company in the Judicial department, and as Under Secretary to Government on the Bengal establishment; and he deposed that the Indian labourer earned from 3 shillings and 6 pence, to 7 shillings and 6 pence a month. How could such a nation use European goods? "I do not know that they use anything in their ordinary use from Europe, except it is some small wollens and broad cloths which they may have accidentally got at a cheap rate." [8]

Enquiries like these fairly disclosed the objects of the House of Commons Committee. It is not in human nature for any race of men to sacrifice their own interests for another race; and the British statesmen in the early years of the nineteenth century did all they could to promote British industries at the sacrifice of Indian industries. British manufactures were forced into India through the agency of the Company's Governor General and Commercial Residents; while Indian manufactures were shut out from England by prohibitive tariffs. The evidence of John Ranking a merchant, examined by the Commons Commitee, will explain this.

"Can you state what is the *ad valorem* duty on piece goods sold at the East India House?

"The duty on the class called Calicos is £3. 6s. 8d. per cent. upon importation; and if they are used for home consumption, there is a further duty of £68. 6s. 8d. per cent.

(8) *Ibid*, page 296.

"There is another class called Muslins, on which the duty on importation is 10 per cent.; and if they are used for home consumption, of £27. 6s. 3d. per cent.

"There is a third class, Coloured Goods, which are prohibited being used in this country, upon which there is a duty upon importation of £3. 6s. 8d. per cent. they are only for exportation.

"This session of Parliament there has been a new duty of 20 per cent on the consolidated duties, which will make the duties on Calicoes * * used for home consumption £78. 6s. 8d. per cent.; upon the Muslins for home consumption £31. 6s. 8d."

There was no thought of concealing the real object of these prohibitive duties. The same witness, Joseph Ranking said, further on, "I look upon it as a protecting duty to encourage our own manufactures." (9)

What was the result of these duties on Indian manufactures? Henry St. George Tucker was himself a Director of the East India Company; and he does not conceal the scope and the effect of England's commercial policy towards India. Writing in 1823, i. e. only ten years after the date of the Parliamentary enquiry referred to above, he condemned that policy in the strongest manner.

"What is the commercial policy which we have adopted in this country with relation to India? The silk manufactures and its piece-goods made of silk and cotton intermixed have long since been excluded alto-

(9) *Ibid*, pages 463 and 467.

gether from our markets; and of late, partly in consequence of the operation of a duty of 67 per cent., but chiefly from the effect of superior machinery, the cotton fabrics which hitherto constituted the staple of India, have not only been displaced in this country, but we actually export our cotton manufactures to supply a part of the consumption of our Asiatic possessions. India is thus reduced from the state of a manufacturing to that of an agricultural country." [10]

Still more emphatic is the impartial verdict of H. H. Wilson, the historian of India.

"It is also a melancholy instance of the wrong done to India by the country on which she has become dependent. It was stated in evidence [in 1813] that the cotton and silk goods of India up to the period could be sold for a profit in the British market at a price from 50% to 60% lower than those fabricated in England. It consequently became necessary to protect the latter by duties of 70% and 80% on their value, or by positive prohibition. Had this not been the case, had not such prohibitory duties and decrees existed, the mills of Paisley and Manchester would have been stopped in their outset, and could not have been again set in motion, even by the power of steam. They were created by the sacrifice of the Indian manufactures. Had India been independent, she would have retaliated; would have imposed prohibitive duties upon British goods, and would thus have preserved her own productive

(10) *Memorials of the Indian Government*, being a selection from the papers of Henry St. George Tucker. London, 1853. p. 494.

industry from annihilation. This act of self-defence was not permitted her; she was at the mercy of the stranger. British goods were forced upon her without paying duty, and the foreign manufacturer employed the arm of political injustice to keep down and ultimately strangle a competitor with whom he could not have contended on equal terms." [11]

The duties which were imposed on the import of Indian manufactures into England between 1812 and 1832 on various articles of trade are shewn in the following table. [12]

(11) *Mill's History of British India*, Wilson's continuation, Book I, Chapter VIII, *Note*.
(12) *Evidence* taken before the Commons Committee, 1832, Vol. II.

	1812	1824	1832
Ornamental Cane Work	71	50	30 Per cent on value.
Muslins	$27\frac{1}{3}$	$37\frac{1}{2}$	10 " "
Calicoes	$71\frac{2}{3}$	$67\frac{1}{2}$	10 " "
Other cotton manufactures	$27\frac{1}{3}$	50	20 " "
Goat's wool Shawls	71	$67\frac{1}{2}$	30 " "
Lacquered Ware	71	$62\frac{1}{2}$	30 " "
Mats	$68\frac{1}{3}$	50	20 " "
Raw Silk	£2-13-4. on value + 4s. per lb.	4s. per lb.	1d. per lb.
Silk manufactures	Prohibited	Prohibited	20 per cent on value.
Taffaties or other plain or figured Silks.	Prohibited	Prohibited	30 " " " "
Manufactures of Silk	Prohibited	Prohibited	20 " " " "
Sugar, (cost price about £1 per cwt.)	£1-13-0 per cwt.	£3-3-0 per cwt.	£1-12-0 per cwt.
Spirits (Arruck)	£0-1-8 per gallon + £0-19-$1\frac{1}{2}$ Excise Duty.	£0-2-1 per gallon + £0-17-$0\frac{3}{4}$ Excise Duty.	£0-15-0 per gallon.
Cotton Wool	£0-16-11 per 100 lbs.	6 per cent.	20 per cent.

Note. To what extent the unjust commercial policy of England discouraged and ruined the manufactures of India will appear from the following tables.

Exports shipped from Calcutta to United Kingdom only.

Year	Cotton Bales	Cotton Piece goods Bales	Silk Bales	Silk Piece goods Bales	Lac & Lac dye Maunds	Indigo Chests
1800	506	2,636	213	Figures not given	Figures not given	12,811
1801	222	6,341	238	,,	,,	9,928
1802	2,072	14,817	400	,,	,,	8,694
1803	2,420	13,649	1,232	,,	,,	12,986
1804	602	9,631	1,926	,,	,,	18,339
1805	2,453	2,325	1,327	,,	,,	13,486
1806	7,315	651	1,689	,,	,,	17,542
1807	3,717	1,686	482	,,	,,	19,452
1808	2,016	237	817	,,	,,	16,622
1809	40,781	104	1,124	,,	,,	8,852
1810	3,477	1,167	949	,,	,,	13,264
1811	160	955	2,623	,,	,,	14,335
1812	—	1,471	1,889	,,	,,	13,703
1813	11,705	557	638	,,	,,	23,672
1814	21,587	919	1,786	,,	,,	16,544
1815	17,228	3,842	2,796	,,	,,	26,221

Year	Cotton Bales	Cotton Piece goods Bales	Silk Bales	Silk Piece goods Bales	Lace & Lac dye Maunds	Indigo Chests
1816	85,024	2,711	8,884	Figures not given	Figures not given	15,740
1817	50,176	1,904	2,260	"	"	15,583
1818	127,124	666	2,066	"	"	13,044
1819	30,683	536	6,998	468	"	16,670
1820	12,939	3,186	6,805	522	"	12,526
1821	5,415	2,130	6,977	704	"	12,635
1822	6,544	1,668	7,893	950	"	19,751
1823	11,713	1,534	6,537	742	14,190	15,878
1824	12,415	1,337	7,069	1,105	17,607	22,472
1825	15,800	1,878	8,061	1,558	13,491	26,837
1826	15,101	1,253	6,856	1,233	13,573	14,904
1827	4,735	541	7,719	971	13,756	30,761
1828	4,105	736	10,431	550	15,379	19,041
1829	—	433	7,000 (?)	—	8,251	27,000(?)

Note. These figures will shew that while the export of raw silk held its ground, that of silk piece goods shewed a decline. The export of cotton too was on the decline, but the most marked decrease was in that of cotton piece goods. In the early years of the nineteenth century, in spite of all prohibitions and restrictive duties, six to fifteen thousand bales were annually shipped to the United Kingdom. The figure fell to less than 1000 bales in 25 years.

The preceding figures shew the decline in the exports to the United Kingdom only. A similar decline took place in the export of Indian piece goods to the other countries of the world, notably to America, Denmark, Spain, Portugal, Mauritius, and the markets of Asia. The export to America declined from 13,633 bales in 1801 to 258 bales in 1829; Denmark which took 1,457 bales in 1800 never took more than 150 bales after 1820; Portugal which took 9,714 bales in 1799 never took a thousand bales after 1825; and the exports to the Arabian and Persian Gulfs which rose to between four and seven thousand bales between 1810 and 1820, never exceeded two thousand after 1825.

On the other hand, as India lost her manufacturing industry, she began to import British and other foreign piece goods, paying for it in food grains. The following figures are interesting. [14]

(14) *Ibid.* Appendix 33.

Some British and foreign goods imported through Calcutta into Bengal.

Year	Broad Cloth Pieces	Cotton Yarn lbs.	Cotton Twist lbs.	Mule Twist lbs.	Piece goods Value in £ sterling	Liquors Value in £ Sterling.
1813	3,381	Figures not given	Figures not given	Figures not given	Figures not given	52,253
1814	4,635	"	"	"	"	57,201
1815	3,908	"	"	"	"	59,462
1816	3,707	"	"	"	"	56,411
1817	2,355	"	"	"	"	53,157
1818	5,633	"	"	"	"	36,712
1819	9,244	"	"	"	"	20,988
1820	5,546	"	"	"	"	26,949
1821	7,590	"	"	"	"	30,382
1822	5,108	"	"	"	"	46,235
1823	7,346	"	"	"	64,449	30,129
1824	5,401	"	"	"	43,030	22,439
1825	13,981	"	"	"	158,076	14,223
1826	9,629	"	"	"	178,481	56,058
1827	5,430	82,738	432,878	339,234	296,177	80,595
1828	7,609	149,076	642,306	464,776	235,837	41,142
1829	11,838	98,154	398,930	918,646	197,290	31,311

Some British and Foreign Goods imported through Madras into the Madras Province.

Year	Chintz	Long Cloth	Muslin	Piece Goods	Satin	Silk Piece Goods	Broad Cloths	Shawls	Wollen Apparel	Wollens
	£	£	£	£	£	£	£	£	£	£
1824	—	—	—	—	—	—	—	181	—	—
1825	—	—	—	—	—	—	—	920	—	—
1826	—	—	342	903	312	—	835	1,159	—	614
1827	510	470	941	536	637	—	2,176	754	601	915
1828	219	380	789	958	593	—	915	1,115	481	1,310
1829	352	348	598	474	853	644	1,417	409	581	844
1830	372	—	224	1,121	577	136	1,158	476	365	457

Note. Public men and public writers in England never spoke or wrote of this policy pursued in India. The great Political Economists of the time, headed by Ricardo, had nothing to say on the subject. Later Political Economists, headed by John Stuart Mill, were equally silent on the subject. Down to the present time no popular English writer on India has dealt adequately with the greatest fact of modern Indian history,—the extinction of Indian Industries under British rule.

Englishmen in England were engaged in the Thirties and Forties in carrying on the agitation against the Corn Laws to a successful issue. Sir Robert Peel, who repealed those Laws in 1846, trusted that his name would be remembered by Englishmen who would "recruit their exhausted strength with abundant and untaxed food, the sweeter because no longer leavened with a sense of injustice." But the bread of the Indian artisan and manufacturer is still leavened with a sense of injustice; and no statesman has yet seriously endeavoured to protect, foster, and revive their old and ruined industries. Lancashire would not permit any such an endeavour if it was made.

Continental economists were able to take a more unbiassed view of the situation, and to speak more openly and freely. In a great work on Political Economy written in Germany in 1844, while the injustice of the Corn Laws was occupying the minds of English Economists, a German Economist pointed out the graver injustice which had been perpetrated in India.

"Had they sanctioned the free importation into England of Indian cotton and silk goods, the English cotton and silk manufactories must of necessity soon come to a stand. India had not only the advantage of cheaper labour and raw material, but also the experience, the skill, and the practice of centuries. The effect of these advantages could not fail to tell under a system of free competition.

"But England was unwilling to found settlements in Asia in order to become subservient to India in manufacturing industry. She strove for commercial supremacy, and felt that of two countries, maintaining free trade between one another, that one would be supreme which sold manufactured goods, while that one would be subservient which could only sell agricultural produce. In the Northern American Colonies, England had already acted on these principles in disallowing the manufactures in those colonies of even a single horse shoe nail, and still more, that no horse shoe nails made there should be imported into England. How could it be expected of her that she would give up her own market for manufactures, the basis of her future greatness, to a people so numerous, so thrifty, so experienced and perfect in the old systems of manufacture as the Hindus?

"Accordingly, England prohibited the import of the goods dealt in by her own factories, the Indian cotton and silk fabrics. The prohibition was complete and peremptory. Not so much as a thread of them would England permit to be used. She would have none of these beautiful and cheap fabrics, but preferred to consume her own inferior and more costly stuffs. She was however quite willing to supply the Continental nations with the far finer fabrics of India at lower prices, and willingly yielded to them all the benefit of that cheapness she herself would have none of it.

"Was England a fool in so acting? Most assuredly, according to the theories of Adam Smith and J. B. Say, the Theory of Values. For according to them, England should have bought what she required where she could buy them cheapest and best; it was an act of folly to manufacture for herself goods at a greater cost than she could buy them at, elsewhere, and at the same time give away that advantage to the Continent.

"The case is quite the contrary, according to our theory, which we term the Theory of the Powers of Production, and which the English Ministry, without having examined the foundation on which it rests, yet practically adopted when enforcing their maxim of importing produce and exporting fabrics.

"The English Ministers cared not for the acquisition of low priced and perishable articles of manufacture, but for that of a more costly and enduring *Manufacturing Power*"[15]

The above extract will shew that while English political economists professed the principles of free trade from the latter end of the eighteenth century, the English nation declined to adopt them till they had crushed the Manufacturing Power of India, and reared their own Manufacturing Power. Then the British Ministry turned free traders, and invited other nations to accept free trade principles. The other nations, including the British Colonies, knew better, and are now rearing their Manufacturing Power by protection. But in India the Manufacturing Power of the people was stamped out by protection against her industries; and then free trade was forced on her so as to prevent a revival.

(15) *The National System of Political Economy* by Friedrick List. Translated by Sampson S. Lloyd M. P., London 1885, P, 42.

But is it Free Trade which has been imposed on us? Thrice within the present generation has the Indian tariff been altered, not in the interests of Free Trade, but in the interests of Lancashire. The Indian Government used to impose a small import duty on foreign goods imported into India, not as a protective measure, but simply as a needed source of revenue which did not operate as a protection to her industries. To this insignificant duty, Lancashire objected. Lancashire had twenty or more votes in the House of Commons, and was in a position to coerce the Indian Government and the Secretary of State. The Indian Government yielded against the strong protest of their ablest advisers like Whitley Stokes and Rivers Thompson, afterwards Lieutenant Governor of Bengal; and the import duties were abolished. A legitimate source of revenue was thus sacrificed some 20 years ago.

But the Indian Government could not do without this source of revenue. Endeavours were made to conciliate the Lancashire voters,—in vain! Appeals were made to their generosity,—in vain! At last a remedy was found which was worse than the evil. An Import duty was reimposed on goods imported into India; but in order to conciliate Lancashire importers, an Excise Duty was also imposed on cotton duties manufactured in India. The ablest officers of the Indian Government, including Charles Stevens afterwards Lieutenant Governor of Bengal protested, but the *mandate* had come from England, that official members must not vote against the policy decided upon by the

Home Government. And thus an Excise Duty on cotton manufactures,—unknown in any other part of the civilised world,—was imposed on Indian manufactures. While every other Government on Earth is helping and encouraging its manufacturers in the great international competition, the Indian Government hampers and obstructs Indian manufacturers by an Excise Duty on Indian fabrics. Is this Free Trade? Is this administration of India for the good of the Indian people?

But, gentlemen, I go further than this. I do not pin my faith to Free Trade, and I do not pin my faith to Protection. I hold that the policy most conducive to the prosperity and happiness of the people of India is the policy which should be adopted for India.

My conclusion is therefore this:

(1) That whatever trade policy conduces to the prosperity of the Indian people is the policy which should be adopted for India.

(2) That it is more advantageous to the general well-being of India to encourage and revive her native industries and manufactures than to obtain articles manufactured in other countries for the consumption of her population.

(3) That seeing that every country in the world takes measures to promote home manufactures and industries by measures needed for the purpose, India would be doubly justified in adopting similar measures to revive her Manufacturing Power crushed by injust and unfair methods, and to give varied employment to her population who are now almost entirely dependent

on agriculture and therefore subject to frequent and devastating famines.

(4) That it is the duty of every Indian to do all that he can, all through his life, to help in the revival of Indian industries and manufactures, so as to diversify the occupations and add to the resources of the people of India.

XI. BOMBAY LAND REVENUE AMENDMENT ACT.

[*Memorial to the Secretary of State for India, presented in November* 1901.]

A CONFERENCE of Indians residing in the United Kingdom was held at 84, Palace Chambers, Westminster, on the afternoon of November 23, Mr. Dadabhai Naoroji in the chair, the object being to adopt a Memorial to the Secretary of State for India in regard to the Bombay Land Revenue Amendment Act. Among those present were Messrs. Romesh Dutt, C. I. E., Martin Wood, J. M. Parikh, E. Hellier, O. P. Vaidya, H. L. Ahuja, N. B. Wagle, and K. H. Singh. The following report apeared in *India*.

The CHAIRMAN called upon Mr. Dutt to move the first resolution, remarking that there was no one more competent to treat with the subject under debate than that gentleman.

Mr. DUTT moved:—"That this Conference adopts this Memorial, printed copies of which have been circulated, and requests Messrs. Naoroji, Dutt, and Harnam Singh, to forward the same to the Right Hon. Lord George Hamilton, M. P., Secretary of State for India in Council, for his kind and careful consideration." He said that the Memorial itself fully explained the object for which they were assembled. It began by describing the state of the cultivators of Bombay in the early days of British rule, as well as under the Mahratta rule which obtained immediately prior to 1817. They were told that during the first four of five years after the Bombay Presidency came under British rule, very able and benevolent officers like the Hon. Mountstuart Elphinstone and Mr. Chaplin went into the land question, and ascertained what was the status of the cultivators under the old Mahratta rule; and extracts were given from their recorded opinions.

The Hon'ble Mountstuart Elphinstone, who became Commissioner of the Deccan in 1818, submitted, in October, 1819, a long report on the territories conquered from the Peshwa, in the course of which he said:—"A large portion of the Ryots are the proprietors of their estates, subject to the payment of a fixed land tax to Government," and that "their property is hereditary and saleable." Two years afterwards the whole question was gone into by the different Collectors in the Bombay Presidency; and Captain Robertson, the Collector of Poona, said in 1821, that the Bombay cultivator was "in no way inferior in point of tenure on its original basis as described in the quotation to the holder of the most undisputed freehold estate in England." Another Collector, Captain Pottinger of Ahmadnagar, wrote in 1822: "The Mirasi tenure has existed in this part of India from time immemorial, and when I have asked about the period of its establishment, I have been told I might as well enquire when the soil was made." Again, Mr. Commissioner Chaplin, in his report of August, 1822, stated that "the Mirasi tenure is very general throughout the whole of that part of the conquered territory which extends from the Krishna to the range of Ghats which divides Gungterre from Khandesh," and "a Ryot having once acquired the hereditary right of occupancy, is together with his heirs entitled to hold it by sale, gift, or mortgage, and, according to the usage of the Deccan, without previously obtaining the permission of the Government."

These extracts from reports written by the ablest officials of the Bombay Presidency proved, that at the time when the Peshwa's dominions came under British rule, the fixed tenants of the Bombay Presidency were possessed of the rights of sale and mortgage and inheritance, and paid a fixed land tax. The Mahratta Government, no doubt, from time to time imposed additional taxes to meet war and other expenses, but the land tax was a fixed tax. During the first years of British rule there were many experimental land settlements, failures more or less, but at last Captain Wingate and other officials, who were employed to make a more satisfactory land settlement, issued their joint Report in 1847. The principles advocated in that Report, and adopted by the Government, were, firstly, that separate settlements should be made with individual cultivators; secondly, that leases for thirty years should be substituted for the short leases which had preceded; and thirdly, that the estimated value of lands should be accepted as the basis of assessment. The heritable and transferable rights of the tenants were recognised, but the principle of a fixed land tax was abandoned in favour of a land tax to be settled at each recurring settlement. Thus the British Government accepted and continued the rights of inheritance and of sale and mortgage which the Bombay cultivator had previously possessed, but they discontinued the right of paying a fixed land tax.

The Survey Officers fixed a new land tax according to their own judgment, and called upon the cultivator to accept his holding on condition of paying the tax, or in the alternative to give it up. While that settlement was still going on, the East India Company's Charter came under consideration, and in 1853 a Committee of the House of Commons held an enquiry into the Bombay Land Settlement, at which Mr. W. A. Goldfinch, one of the officers who had been working under Captain Wingate, was examined. He was asked the following question by Sir T. H. Maddock :—"After the survey was finished when you found a field—say No. 11—of five bigas of land in the possession of some particular person, did the Collector assess the revenue upon it arbitrarily, or did he ask the occupant or proprietor whether he was willing to pay the amount?" He answered; "The assessment was fixed by the Superintendent of the Survey, *without any reference to the cultivator*, and when those rates were introduced the holder of each field was summoned to the Collector, and informed of the rate at which his land would be assessed in future; and if he chose to retain it on those terms he did; if he did not choose, he threw it up." Thus it was clear that on the question of the land tax the cultivator was placed entirely at the mercy of the

Survey Officer, and was not consulted at all. It was a contract between two parties—the Government and the cultivator—in regard to which one party had no chance of expressing an opinion. Where a man had inherited land from his forefathers, dating back it might be for many generations, and even centuries, the land tax was assessed solely on the judgment of the Survey Officer, and the man's retention of his holding was made to depend on his willingness to pay the new tax; refusal, in fact, involved forfeiture of the land. Thus, the great fault of the system introduced by the British administrators in the forties and fifties was the arbitrary fixing of the land tax without consulting the views and wishes of the cultivators. It was acknowledged that the cultivators had certain rights of sale and mortgage, and that those rights passed with the transfer of the inheritance; the only thing that was not acknowledged was the right to a fixed land tax.

Nine years later—in 1862—Lord Canning caused an exhaustive enquiry to be made into the cause of the famine which had desolated Northern India in 1860. Col. B. Smith conducted it, and he came to the conclusion that, for the benefit of the people of India, it was necessary to fix a permanent limit to the land tax, so that, in future, addition to agricultural income might go to the people themselves and not be made the basis for additional taxation. Lord Canning thereupon consulted the Bombay and Madras Governments. The latter replied that their settlement was virtually permanent, as they did not ask for any increase in the land tax unless waste lands were brought into cultivation. On the other hand, the Bombay Government said they did not agree as to the propriety of a fixed land tax, as prices of food were going up and there was no reason why the Government should not increase its taxation accordingly. These were the words of the Bombay Governor :—"As the prices of the produce are yearly increasing, I see no infringement of the original conditions of the settlement, nor will such be felt by the Ryot, if on the expiration of this experimental settlement the Government land tax should be re-adjusted according to those increased prices, and to other circumstances." Lord Canning's proposal for a permanent settlement received the support of both Lord Halifax and Sir Stafford Northcote; and had Lord Canning lived five years after his retirement, no doubt the people of India would have got a permanent settlement. But, unfortunately, he died shortly after his retirement. The question consequently hung fire for about 20 years, and at last, in 1883, the proposal was absolutely rejected.

At that time the Marquis of Ripon was Viceroy of India, and he, made another suggestion, giving some sort of security to the cultivators of India against an unreasonable increase in the revenues. He suggested that in all districts which had once been surveyed and settled, there should not be any increase in the land tax except on the ground of an increase in prices. That proposal, which was rejected by the Bombay Government, was accepted by the Madras Government, and for a year or two was acted upon, but Lord Ripon having retired from India in 1884, it was vetoed by the India Office in 1885. That brought them back to the old state of things; the cultivators had absolutely no voice in fixing the land tax; there was no appeal from the decision of the Survey Officers—who he was willing to admit were experienced considerate men—and the contract was altogether one-sided.

What had been the result of this state of things which existed up to last year? The land tax had gone on increasing, and it had been estimated that in the survey commenced in 1866, the revenue increased 32 per cent.; and so far as the 1896 survey had proceeded there had been a further increase of 30 per cent. These continuous increases necessarily left the cultivators poorer after each settlement. They would all remember the opinion expressed by the late Sir William Hunter that the difficulty of improving the condition of the cultivator of Bombay was attributable to the fact that the land tax was so heavy as not to leave the cultivator sufficient money to support his family and himself for twelve months. And no doubt most of them had read the report in which Sir A. MacDonnell's Commission declared that in Gujrat the land tax was so "full" that its rigorous collection necessarily drove the cultivator into debt, and put him under the thraldom of the money-lender. What was the remedy for this state of things? It was to make an enquiry into the circumstances of the land tax and to reduce it where it was too heavy. That had been urged from time to time, but so far no enquiry had been held. The Government claimed that their desire was to rescue the cultivator from the thraldom of the money-lender, but they had adopted a wrong remedy.

For they were now taking power in the Act, to which the Memorial took exception, to withdraw from the cultivator his ancient right of holding his fields in perpetuity, as recognised under the old Mahratta rule, and under British rule from 1835 to 1900. The Hon. Mr. Mehta, speaking before the Bombay Council, thus described that ancient right: "The combined operation of Sections 68 and 73 shows that every occupant of land has an heritable and transferable right in it, and if the Survey Settlement is applied to that land, the occupant is entitled to the use and occupation in perpetuity. It is impossible to explain away the final words of Section 73—'the right of occupancy shall be deemed and heritable and transferable property, etc., and shall immediately pass to the person whose agreement to become occupant shall have been accepted by the Collector.' The last words would never have been allowed to form part of the Act unless it was deliberately intended to render impossible annual or short term tenancies of land brought under settlement. My hon. friend (Mr. Monteath) has told us a great deal in his speech about individual existing occupants and their vested rights and interests. But he quietly gives go-by to the fact that leaving individual occupants alone, the effect of Section 73 is to permanently impress the land with occupancy rights, the tenure in perpetuity being the most essential in them. Individuals may hold and individuals may relinquish it, but the land itself can be held only, whenever held by a tenure, in perpetuity. It is this deliberate character impressed upon the land that this Bill is framed to destroy."

Under the system which existed in Bombay down to 1900, certain rights attached to the land itself. The system was similar to what prevailed in Bengal, where, when an estate was sold, the purchaser acquired it with the right of paying the old land tax. The same principle obtained, too, in England. Under this Bill the Government, however were taking power to confiscate the right which had so long attached to the land in Bombay. What were the words of Mr. Monteath in regard to this proposal? "There are strong reasons for believing that it was not the intention of the Code to deprive the Government of the power to grant land in special cases." Surely, if the Government only proposed to apply this new power to special cases there might be some justification for it. But the special cases were not even indicated in the Act itself, and that was one of its vital defects. It might the necessary, for political reasons, to restrict the right of sale, mortgage, or inheritance, in the case of certain hill tribes. But the Bill enabled the power to be exercised wherever the Bombay Government liked in the whole Presidency. Of course there was no intention to apply it universally, but surely a limit should be placed in the Act itself. Their objections to the Act then were: Firstly, that it confiscated a right which existed under the Mahratta rule and which had been respected under British rule, and for the withdrawal of which there was no sufficient justification; and, Secondly, that the Act was too vague, enabling the Goverment to withdraw the right in any part of the Presidency without giving any details or assigning any reasons. The Memorialists, therefore, asked the Secretary of State to veto the Act, or at any rate to exclude from its operation all lands to which the Survey Settlement had been extended, and in which, therefore, the heritable, transferable, and perpetual right of the cultivator has already been recognised by British legislation; and the Memorialists believed that the effect of the Bill would be to deepen agricultural distress and create a political danger. (Cheers.)

Mr. GADGIL seconded the resolution. Resonable men, he said, looked upon this piece of legislation as a defective and retrograde step. It would not achieve the object which the Government professed to have in view; it would not improve the position of the poor down-trodden agriculturist of the Bombay Presidency; but pernicious results were bound to follow from it. It was a small piece of legislation, but it had created great consternation throughout the Presidency. He particularly desired to direct their attention to Section 68, which read :—

"Provided that nothing in this or any other Section shall make it, or shall be deemed ever to have made it, unlawful for the Collector at any time to grant permission to any person to occupy any unalienated unoccupied land, for such period, and on such conditions as he may, subject to the orders of the Government, prescribe, and in any such case the occupancy shall, whether a survey settlement has been extended to the land or not, be held only for the period, and subject to the conditions so prescribed."

Now, until this Act was passed, a tenant, immediately he entered into possession of a piece of land, became entitled to all the rights attaching to it in perpetuity; but the effect of Section 68, read with Section 73, would be to make the cultivator absolutely dependent on the will of the Collector, who would impose his own conditions and make the tenure for any period he pleased—short or long. This was a very large power indeed. What were the reasons advanced by the Government for making this change? It was alleged that they desired to prevent the cultivator being overburdened and falling into the hands of the money-lender, who was said to have brought him into his present distressful condition. But how was it proposed to do it? They took away from the agriculturist the power to transfer or mortgage his piece of land, which he held in perpetuity; the money-lender would consequently refuse to lend him any money because the security was gone; and the man would become absolutely dependent on the Government even for his living. Failure to pay the land tax would lead to forfeiture, and the land would only be re-granted on entirely new conditions. They were told by Mr. Monteath that the occupants on the restricted tenure would have the same right of holding in perpetuity as other occupants, and the guarantee of the survey assessment would be as binding in their case as in any other case. That in itself was a very good assurance, but what was there to prevent any future officer of the Bombay Government giving full force to the Act irrespective of that assurance? What was desirable was to make the Act thoroughly explicit. He would especially like to draw their attention to the first sentence of Section 68. That gave retrospective effect to the Act. Then again Section 73 gave absolute power to the authorities to deal with the proprietary rights of the cultivators, and he ventured to urge in conclusion that the general effect of the Act would be to detract from the desire of the occupant of the land to improve the soil, because he would never be sure that his descendants would be allowed to benefit by his improvements.

Mr. VAIDYA said that undoubtedly the Bombay holders were hampered by their indebtedness, but it was curious that the Government should take this opportunity of introducing fresh legislation calculated to make their position worse. He did not think the Act would remove the evil at which it was aimed. He looked upon it as a suicidal policy and regretted to say that it was only another illustration of the tendency of the Government, whenever it dealt with the land question, to further restrict the rights of the land owners. If they wanted to deal with the money-lending evil, let them put some limit on the operations of the money-lending classes.

Mr. J. M. PARIKH said the new Act gave the Government complete dominion over the land which they had never before possessed. The indirect effect of the legislation was to legalise the position of the Government as absolute owner of the land in the Bombay Presidency, and it constituted a deprivation of the rights of the occupants for the time being without any compensation whatever. They were promised that the Act should not be applied at random, but they wanted a clear statement in it of the intentions of the Government, so that in the future the evils which they feared might not be brought about. The past history of the British administration in India did not give them confidence that the promises now made would be fulfilled, and hence the necessity for clearly limiting the operation of the Act. Collectors were bound to fill the coffers of the Treasury as completely as possible, and in the days to come the Act would be construed not according to the utterances of Mr. Monteath but by the canons of statute law.

The resolution was then put and carried unanimously, and the proceedings closed with hearty votes of thanks to Mr. Naoroji and Mr. Dutt, proposed by Mr. Ahuja and seconded by Mr. Patker.

Text of the Memorial.

To the Right Hon'ble Lord George Hamilton, Secretary of State for India.

My Lord,—We, the undersigned, have been empowered at a Conference held on November 23, 1901, to forward to your Lordship in Council this memorial on the subject of the Bombay Land Revenue Code

Amendment Act, known as Bombay Act VI of 1901, which received the assent of His Excellency the Viceroy and Governor-General of India on the 24th September 1901.

2.—We desire, at the commencement, to submit to your Lordship that the Bombay cultivator's right of inheritance, sale, and mortgage, with regard to his holding, is an ancient right, and is not a creation of British legislation. The dominions of the last Mahratta Peshwa were annexed by the British Government in 1817, and two years after, the Hon'ble Mountstuart Elphinstone wrote thus in his "Report on the Territories conquered from the Peshwa," submitted in October, 1819 :—

"A large portion of the Ryots are proprietors of their estate, subject to the payment of a fixed land tax to Government; that their property is hereditary and saleable, and they are never dispossessed while they pay their tax, and even then they have for a long period (at least thirty years) the right of reclaiming their estate, on paying the dues of Government. Their land tax is fixed, but the Mahratta Government loaded it with other impositions."

3.—Captain Robertson, who was Collector of Poona in 1821, bore his testimony to the rights of the Mirasi or hereditary cultivator in the following terms :—

"He is in no way inferior in point of tenure on its original basis, as described in the quotation, to the holder of the most undisputed freehold estate in England." "The ancestors of many of the present occupants of the lands of the Deccan were probably holders of land antecedent to the Mussalman conquest of the country, on condition of paying a 'reddendum' equal to a sixth part of the produce." "Every original paper relating to Thalkaris [Mirasi tenants] and their occupation of the land, every return I have obtained from the districts concerning them and the ancient distribution of land, proves beyond a shadow of doubt that at a former time the whole of the arable land of each village was apportioned out among a certain number of families." "Their descendants collectively are termed a Jutha; they are inferred to possess the whole of the original estate among them; they are responsible as a body corporate for the payment of whatever is due to Government." Captain Robertson also showed that the Mirasi tenure was heritable and transferable and existed in all villages in Poona district.

4.—Captain Pottinger, the Collector of Ahmadnagar, wrote in 1822 that the Mirasi tenants "can dispose or mortgage their lands when they like." "The Mirasi tenure has existed in this part of India from time immemorial; and when I have asked about the period of its establishment, I have been told I might as well enquire when the soil was made."

5.—These and other reports were enclosed by Mr. Commissioner Chaplin in his exhaustive and famous report of the 20th August, 1822. And with regard to the Mirasi tenure he recorded that it "is very general throughout the whole of that part of the conquered territory which extends from the Krishna to the range of Ghats which divides Gungterre from Khandesh."

"A Ryot having once acquired the herditary right of occupancy is, together with his heirs, entitled to hold it by sale, gift, or mortgage, and according to the usage of the Deccan, without previously obtaining the permission of the Government." A Mirasdar "has a voice in all the village councils, has a right of pasture on the village commons, can build a house or dispose of it by sale." "The Collector [of Poona] is very properly an advocate for preserving the rights of Mirasdars, a line of policy which he strenuously recommends in several places; but as nobody, I trust, has ever thought of invading their rights, the discussion of the question at any length would be superfluous."

6.—We have made these extracts from the reports of the first five years after the Mahratta dominions came under the British rule, in order to show the position of the majority of the cultivators under the old Mahratta rule. It is too often assumed that the cultivators had no heritable and transferable rights under the old regime; that their heritable and transferable rights were the creation of British legislation. The extracts we have made will show that the very opposite of this is the truth. Laws were not passed by Legislative Councils, nor recorded in published Acts under the Hindu rule, but were embodied in the customs and usages of the land, which were more durable and less variable than the Acts and Laws of modern times. And the testimony of Elphinstone, Robertson, Pottinger, and Chaplin, quoted above, will show that the usages and customs of the land recognised the right of inheritance and transfer in the

Bombay cultivator, and also respected his right to hold his land on payment of a fixed land tax.

7.—The Government of Bombay, after many experimental land settlements, at last based their policy on the famous Joint Report of 1847. The principles advocated in this report, and adopted by the Government, were, firstly, that separate settlements should be made with individual cultivators; secondly, that leases for thirty years should be substituted for the short leases which had preceded; thirdly, that the estimated value of lands should be accepted as the basis of assessment. The heritable and transferable rights of the tenants were recognised, but the principle of a fixed land tax was abandoned in favour of a land tax to be settled at each recurring settlement.

8.—From that date, the heritable and transferable rights of the Bombay cultivators have been uniformly recognised up to the present year. In the Bombay Land Revenue Code of 1879 (Bombay Act V of 1879), Section 68, runs thus:—

"An occupant is entitled to the use and occupation of his land for the period, if any, to which his occupancy is limited, or if the period is unlimited, or a survey settlement has been extended to the land, in perpetuity conditionally on the payment of the amounts due on account of the land revenue for the same, according to the provisions of this Act, or of any rules made under this Act, or of any other law for the time in force, or on the fulfilment of any other terms lawfully annexed to his occupancy."

And Section 73 runs thus :—

"The right of occupancy shall be deemed an heritable and transferable property, subject to the provisions contained in Section 56, or otherwise prescribed by the law, and shall immediately pass to the person whose agreement to become occupant shall have been accepted by the Collector."

9.—Thus stood the law in 1879. The law of 1901 empowers the Bombay Government to extinguish at its pleasure these ancient and customary rights of the cultivators, hitherto recognised by British legislation.

In Section 68, the following Proviso has been added, by the new Act :—

"Provided that nothing in this or any other Section shall make it, or shall be deemed ever to have made it, unlawful for the Collector at any time to grant permission to any person to occupy any unalienated unoccupied land, for such period, and on such conditions as he may, subject to the orders of Government, prescribe, and in such case the occupancy shall, *whether a survey settlement has been extended to the land or not*, be held only for the period and subject to the conditions so prescribed."

And after section 73, the following new Section has been added by the new Act :—

"(1) Notwithstanding anything in the foregoing Section, in any tract or village to which Government may, by Notification published before the introduction therein of an original survey settlement under Section 103, declare the provisions of this Section applicable, *the occupancy or interest of the occupant in the land shall not after the date of such Notification be transferable without the previous sanction of the Collector.*

"(2) Government may, by Notification in the Bombay Gazette, from time to time exempt any part of such tract or village, or any person or class of persons, from the operation of this Section."

10.—The italics in the foregoing two paragraphs are our own, and indicate the principal changes introduced by the new Act. The new Act empowers the Government

(1) to abolish the tenant's right "in perpetuity" in tenures to which the survey settlement had been extended, and empowers it to make temporary settlements;

(2) to restrict the right of transfer hitherto recognised in all tenants of lands to which the survey settlement had been extended.

11.—We do not believe that it is the intention of the Indian Government to confiscate tenant rights which are based on the ancient customs of India, and which have been recognised by British rulers and by British legislation for more than two generations. It is intended, as we learn from the assurances of the Bombay Government, to exercise the power taken by the Government only in exceptional cases. The fatal defect of the Act just passed is that it does not indicate these exceptional cases. It empowers the Bombay Government to withdraw old and legalised rights by a simple Notification, i.e., by a simple exercise of the executive power of the Government. It invests the Bombay Government with a more unlimited power in this respect than is possessed or claimed by the Government of any Province in India. Laws are made to indicate, as nearly as possible, the powers which they vest in the Executive, and the rights which they assure to the people; and the Land Revenue Codes of other Provinces of India and the Rent Laws of Bengal have been framed on this plan. Laws which vest in the Executive unlimited powers to extinguish or to preserve tenant rights fail in their primary object, and have hitherto been unknown in India.

12.—It is remembered in Bombay that the rights of holding land "in perpetuity" and of sale and transfer were legally conferred by the British Government on tenants as substitutes for the same rights which they enjoyed previous to the British rule, and which were observed and recorded by Elphinstone and Chaplin. It is politically unwise now to withdraw the legal assurance to these ancient rights, and to make them dependent on the will of the Executive. It is politically unwise to empower the Executive to preserve or to extinguish those tenant rights which have been customary in Western India for centuries, and which have hitherto been legally recognised by the British Government.

13.—No laws made by British rulers in India affect the interests and the lives of the great mass of the Indian population more intimately than the laws relating to tenant rights. The laws attaching certain rights to survey tenures in Bombay have been keenly appreciated by millions of cultivators in that Province, and these rights have been recognised since the dawn of British rule. The new Act making these rights dependent in the future on the will of the Executive has created alarm and consternation. There has been a strong, unanimous, and vehement opposition against the new Act on the part of the Indian public such has never before been witnessed in Bombay. To keep the Act on the Statute Book will create a feeling of unrest among the agricultural population of Bombay.

14.—We therefore pray that your Lordship, in Council, will, after due consideration, veto the Act which has lately received the sanction of the Indian Government. In any case we trust and hope that your Lordship will exclude from the operation of the Act all lands to which the survey settlement has been extended, and in which, therefore, the heritable, transferable, and perpetual right of the cultivator has already been recognised by British legislation.

The Memorial was signed by Mr. Dadabhai Naoroji, Mr. Romesh Dutt, and Mr. K. Harnam Singh, on behalf of the Conference.

XII. ENQUIRY INTO THE ECONOMIC CONDITION OF INDIA.

[*Memorial submitted to the Secretary of State for India in January 1902. It was prepared by the Indian Famine Union, and is included in this volume as Mr. Dutt was one of the signatories.*]

My Lord,

We, the undersigned, being interested in the welfare of India, and grieved on account of the sufferings of the Indian people from recurring famines, desire to approach you with reference to an investigation of the causes of these famines and the promotion of all practical means of prevention.

We recognise the energy and success with which the Government of India have through several visitations of famine performed their stupendous task of feeding millions of starving sufferers scattered over vast areas, and we believe that the various Famine Commissions, by careful scrutiny of past results, are gradually bringing our system of famine relief to the highest point of efficiency. The methods of famine relief do not therefore appear to us to press for enquiry. But there remains the question of famine prevention. Here all possible help is needed to collect facts and mature practical suggestions. And we believe that such as we can offer will be welcomed by the hard-worked officials in India, whose time is fully occupied by the current duties of administration.

Many means have been suggested for strengthening the position of the Indian agriculturist and rendering him more capable of resisting the effects of drought, such as the more rapid extension of irrigation, agricultural banks, village and other industries, re-afforestation, migration, grain storage, export duties on grain, technical education, arbitration courts, besides administrative reforms, such as timely remissions of land revenue during periods of famine, and the limitation of land alienation. These various remedies appear to us to deserve careful enquiry, and we doubt not that, as each comes under investigation, your Lordship will favour us with information from the India Office showing what has been done by the Government in the directions indicated up to the present time. But we are most strongly impressed with the conviction that the problem of checking famine in India cannot be usefully considered without further special knowledge of the different circumstances of its extended territories and of their inhabitants. What is beneficial in one area may be useless and even mischievous elsewhere. An exact diagnosis of the patient must precede the application of remedies. Our request therefore is that the Government will be pleased to cause a detailed enquiry to be made into the economic condition of a limited number of selected villages in each of the provinces which have been afflicted by famine. It is suggested that in each province the local administration should select typical villages, and appoint suitable persons, including officials and non-officials, Europeans and Indians, to make a complete enquiry into their condition, ascertaining the exact financial position of each cultivator, with the history and causes of his difficulties. When the economic record of these villages is complete, approved experiments in their management might be entrusted to administrators of proved capacity and discretion. Different groups of villages will doubtless be found to require different treatment; and the remedies, administrative and legislative, found efficacious in the typical villages, could be afterwards cautiously extended to the groups existing under similar economic conditions.

We ask with the more confidence for the detailed local enquiries above indicated because we find that precedents exist in which the Government of India have based remedial agrarian legislation upon the results of such enquiries. As important instances we would refer to the labours of the Dekkhan Riots Commission, which led to the Dekkhan Ryots Relief Act of 1879; and to the Punjab Alienation of Land Act, 1900, which was based upon a village-by-village and holding-by-holding enquiry carried out in 1895-6 by Mr. Thorburn in typical tracts in the Western Punjab. This enquiry, which was both minute and comprehensive, extending to 742 villages, was completed within six months, and involved an extra expense of only £300.

We are, of course, aware that valuable information regarding the economic condition of the agriculturists has been collected by the Government from time to time, especially by means of the enquiries initiated in 1881 and in 1887, and we hope for much enlightenment from a study of the information thus made accessible. But we desire to point out that, although this information is most valuable for purposes of comparison, it is based on enquiries having no direct connection with famine questions; it belongs to a period before the great famines of 1897 and 1900 had seriously affected the condition of so large a portion of the agricultural population; and it was not generally based, as we believe, on such local enquiries as we suggest. It appears to us, therefore, that fresh enquiries of the kind asked for are urgently necessary, in order to determine the economic condition of the cultivators with reference to their present power of resisting the attacks of famine.

In conclusion, we desire to state that this movement is of a purely scientific character, that it is unconnected with party politics, and that our wish is to support the Indian Government in its efforts to deal with a great national calamity.

For the *Indian Famine Union*,

LEONARD H. COURTNEY, *Chairman.*
W. WEDDERBURN
S. S. THORBURN
M. M. BHOWNAGGREE } *Joint Hon. Secretaries.*

The Hon. Secretaries have been authorised to add the following names to this Memorial:

The Archbishop of Canterbury.	The Marquis of Ripon.
	The Earl of Aberdeen.
The Cardinal Archbishop of Westminster.	The Earl of Dunmore.
	The Lord Hobhouse.
The Archbishop of Armagh.	The Lord Kinnaird.

The Bishop of Carlisle.
The Bishop of Liverpool.
The Lord Leigh.
The Lord Radstock.
The Lord Stanley of Alderley.
Sir Auckland Colvin, K.C.S.I.
Right Hon. Sir Richard Garth, K. C.
Sir Lepel Griffin, K.C.S.I.
Sir John Jardine, K.C.I.E.
Sir William Markby, K.C.I.E.
Sir William Muir, K.C.S.I.
General Sir Henry Norman, G. C. B.
Sir W. Comer Petheram.
Sir John Budd Phear, K.C.I.E.
General Sir J. W. Sneider.
Sir Raymond West, K.C.I.E.
Mr. G. B. Chapman.
Mr. T. Hart Davies.
Mr. T. A. Denny.
Mr. E. C. Ozanne.
Dr. A. D. Pollen.
Mr. J. R. Reid, C.I.E.
Mr. H. J. Reynolds, C.S.I.
Mr. Alex. Rogers.
Mr. G. W. Vidal.
Mr. C. W. Whish.
Mr. T. Gair Ashton, M.P.
Mr. T. Burt, M.P.
Mr. John Burns, M.P.
Mr. T. Bayley, M.P.
Mr. J. Brigg, M. P.
Mr. W. S. Caine, M.P.
Mr. D. Brynmor Jones, M.P.
Mr. J. Herbert Lewis, M.P.
Sir John Leng, M.P.
Mr. J. Herbert Roberts, M.P.
Mr. Thomas Shaw, K.C., M.P.
Mr. H. J. Wilson, M.P.
Mr. J. H. Yoxall, M.P.
The Dean of Durham.
The Dean of Lincoln.
The Dean of Llandaff.
The Dean of Manchester.
The Principal of Jesus College, Oxford.
The Warden of Keble College, Oxford.
The Principal of Manchester College, Oxford.
The Master of Pembroke College, Oxford.
The Principal of Somerville College, Oxford.
The Master of Catherine College, Cambridge.
The Master of Clare College, Cambridge.
The President of Queen's College, Cambridge.
The Principal of Aberdeen University.
The President of Queen's, College, Belfast.
Rev. Canon Ainger.
Rev. R. A. Armstrong.
Rev. W. T. A. Barber.
Rev. Canon Barnett.
Mr. Bramwell Booth.
Rev. Dr. John Clifford.
Rev. E. D. Cornish.
Rev. J. Estlin Carpenter.
Rev. Dr. Glasse.
Rev. Canon Gore.
Rev. Canon Hicks.
Rev. J. Page Hopps.
Rev. A. O. M. Jay.
Rev. Canon Knox-Little.
Rev. J. T. McGaw.
Rev. Dr. Mair.
Rev. Dr. Marshall.
Rev. F. B. Meyer.
Rev. J. H. Moulton.
Rev. Dr. Paterson.
Rev. J. E. Radcliffe.
Rev. Dr. Rigg.
Rev. T. G. Selby.
Archdeacon Sinclair.
Rev. T. Spurgeon.

Rev. Dr. Taylor.
Rev. H. A. Thomas.
Rev. S. Vincent.
Rev. H. Russell Wakefield.
Rev. Principal Whitehouse.
Ven. Archdeacon Wilson.
Sir Arthur Arnold.
Sir Thomas Barlow, M. D.
Dr. Karl Blind.
Mr. P W. Bunting.
Mr. Wilfrid Scawen Blunt.
General Sir William Butler.
Mr. W. P. Byles.
Mr. Jas. Carter.
Mr. Donald Crawford.
Mr. Wm. Digby, C I.E.
Mr. J. Passmore Edwards.
Mr. A E. Fletcher.
Sir Douglas Fox.
Rt. Hon. Sir Edward Fry.
Sir Theodore Fry.
Professor Wm. Graham.
Mr. Frederic Harrison.
Mr. T. E Higham.
Mr. C. H. Hopwood, K. C.
Mr. J. Seymour Keay.
Mr. Bertram Keightley.
Mr. C. S. Loch.
Right Hon Sir Massey Lopes.
Mr. Fred. Maddison.
Professor Alfred Marshall.
Mr. George Meredith.
Mr. H. S. Murray.
Professor S. J. Owen.
Mr. H. D. Pearsall.
Sir H. Gilzean-Reid.
Mr. G. Bernard Shaw.
Mr. J. Bamford Slack.
Mr. Robinson Souttar.
Mr. Herbert Spencer.
Sir W. P. Treloar.
Sir E. H. Verney.
Mr. Alfred Wallace.
Professor John Westlake.
Mr. A. J. Wilson.

Mrs. G S. Barnett.
Miss E. A. Bayly ("Edna Lyall").
Mr. Bramwell Booth.
Mrs. W. P. Byles
The Countess of Carlisle.
Miss Alison Garland.
Madame Sarah Grand.
Mrs. Eva M'Laren.
Mrs. Chas. Mallet.
Mrs. F. Max Muller.
Mrs. Russell Rea.
Mrs. Flora Annie Steel.
The Countess of Warwick.
The Lord Mayor of Bristol.
The Lord Mayor of York.
The Mayor of Barnsley.
The Mayor of Barrow in-Furness.
The Mayor of Birkenhead.
" " Blackburn.
" " Bootle.
" " Bradford.
" " Cheltenham.
" " Coventry.
" " Gateshead.
" " Grimsby.
" " Huddersfield.
" " Ipswich.
" " Maidstone.
" " Newport (Mon.)
" " Nottingham.
" " Shoreditch.
" " Stepney.
" " Sunderland.
" " Warrington.
" " Wigan.
The Provost of Ayr.
" " Melrose.
" " Montrose.
" " Paisleya.
The Chairman, Blackburn Chamber of Commerce.
The Chairman, Cardiff Chamber of Commerce.

The Lord Aberdare.
The Lord Keane.
The Marquis of Winchester.
The Lord Wrottesley.
Sir George Birdwood, K.C.I.E.
General Sir Andrew Clarke.
Mr. Romesh C. Dutt, C.I.E.
Mr. Robert H. Elliot.
Colonel H. B. Hanna.
Sir Robert G. Head.
Mr. J. Knox Wight.
Mr. Edward Bond, M. P.
Mr. R. Cameron, M. P.
Mr. Alfred Emmott, M. P.
Mr. Samuel Evans, K.C., M.P.
Sir Michael Foster, M. P.
Sir Walter Foster, M. P.
Mr. J. P. Farrell, M. P.
Mr. M. J. Flavin, M. P.
Sir W. Brampton Gurdon, M.P.
Mr. J. Keir Hardie, M. P.
Mr. A. H. Heath, M. P.
Mr. J. D. Hope, M. P.
Mr. P. J. Kennedy, M. P.
Sir James Kitson, M. P.
Colonel Hon. Heneage Legge, M. P.
Mr. Maurice Levy, M. P.
Mr. Chas. McArthur, M. P.
Dr. T. J. Macnamara, M. P.
Mr. J. Lloyd Morgan, M. P.
Mr. Chas. Morley, M. P.
Mr. T. W. Nussey, M. P.
Mr. J J O'Shee, M. P.
Mr. A. C. Humphreys Owen, M. P.
Mr. D. V. Pirie, M. P.
Mr. H. J. Reckit, M.P
Mr. S Forde Ridley, M.P.
Mr. Edmund Robertson, K.C. M.P.
Mr. C. P. Scott, M.P.
Mr. Chas. E. Shaw, M.P.
Mr. J. W. Spear, M.P.
Mr. T. Courtenay Warner, M.P.
Mr J.K. Wingfield-Digby, M.P
Mr. Samuel Young, M.P.
The Dean of Glouchester.
Rev. Dr. G. S. Barrett.
Rev. Canon McColl.
Rev. Wm. Dale.
Rev. Hugh Price Hughes.
Rev. Vernon Staley.
Rev. Chas. Voysey.
Comptoir National D'Escompte (Mr. E. Lazarus, Manager).
Councillor Fielding Johnson.
Sir Wm. Bruce.
Sir Alfred Newton.
Mr. A G. Symonds.
Mr. Edgar Speyer (Messrs. Speyer Bros.)
Dr. R. Spence Watson.
Mr. Alex. Wedderburn, K.C.
Mr. Spencer Wilkinson.
Mr. W. Martin Wood.
Mrs. H. Bradlaugh Bonner.
Chairman, Cambridgeshire County Council.
Chairman, Merionethshire County Council.
The Mayor of Glouchester.
The Chairman, Bradford Chamber of Commerce.

XIII. SPEECH AT MADRAS.

[*Delivered in the rooms of the Mahajana Sabha, on February* 4, 1902.]

Gentlemen,—I received your telegram a few days ago at Colombo, kindly inviting me and my gifted fellow-passenger, sister Nivedita to speak at a Public Meeting on our arrival at Madras. I felt an unspeakable joy that you should have thus accorded your hearty greetings to a lady who is now one of us, who lives our life, shares our joys and sorrows, partakes our trials and troubles, and labours with us in the cause of our motherland. I also felt gratitude at the honour you had done me personally by giving me this welcome after my prolonged absence. At the same time, I will not conceal from you that your request filled me with grave misgivings. After a somewhat severe course of work in England, I had looked forward to rest and cessation from labours on my return to India, and to a quiet life among those who are nearest and dearest to me. Nothing was farther from my mind than the idea of appearing before the public during my stay in India; and you will believe me when I tell you, that I opened your telegram at Colombo with some degree of terror. Nevertheless, your invitation was so kind that it was difficult to decline; and when you added the wortheir name of sister Nivedita to mine in your telegram, you skilfully closed the gates behind me, and made a retreat on my part impossssible. At the same time you also lightened my task; for in appearing before you on the platform to-day, I feel that I am like the door-keeper of the Sanskrit Drama, who comes on the stage, opens the palace door, introduces the princess, and then retires. I will take care, therefore, not to detain you long; for I am sure you will all be as anxious as I am to listen to her who follows me. She appears before you not as the partisan of any particular sect or creed, but as belonging to all India, cherishing a noble pride in India's past, labouring with a loving heart for India's future. Therefore, you will recognise in her, as I recognise in her, a beloved countrywoman devoted to the cause of India, and you will listen to her, as I shall listen to her, as to a sister working for all of us in this her adopted country.

NO SIGN OF PROGRESS.

Gentlemen, I cannot adequately express to you my feelings on an occasion like this, when we meet after an absence of years. We have been divided by seas and oceans, but have not been divided in our aims and endeavours. The same cause has enlisted our sympathies, and the same objects have inspired our efforts. Therefore, although I have been absent from you for five years,—except during the winter months of 1899-1900,—my thoughts have been your thoughts, my endeavours have been your endeavours, and my aspirations have been your aspirations, all this time.

India has seen little change during these five years. A century has ended and a new century has begun, but we have seen no sign of progress,—rather the reverse. There is no sadder chapter in the economic history of India than the story of these five years, commencing with the famine of 1897, and proceeding on to the famine which has not yet ended. Never in India's history were the mass of the people more resourceless, more crippled as manufacturers, more indebted as agriculturists. Never were greater misfortunes and deaths crowded together within so brief a space. Never did a civilised, fertile, and industrious country present a scene of more widespread poverty and desolation.

But, gentlemen, when we have narrated the story of famines and pestilence, we have not told the whole story of our misfortunes during these five years. Unfortunately, the administration of these years has not made for progress. It is unnecessary for me on an occasion like this to recall to your minds those repressive acts of Government which have engaged your attention so long, and which are still fresh in your memories. I doubt very much if there is any thoughtful and responsible man in India who can look back on these repressive measures to-day with gratification and pride. A feeling of sadness and of despair comes over us as we think of these measures. But, gentlemen, we should never yield to such despair. I for one, have never believed, and will never believe, in this dark future for India. The British Government, in spite of its occasional lapses into repressive and retrograde measures, cannot permanently accept a policy which is so fatal to the good of the people and so fatal to the Empire.

SELF-GOVERNMENT.

More than this, the future of India depends on us, and on us alone. I am old enough to be able to took back thirty or forty years, when a few solitary voices in a few remote places, disconnected with each other, asked for some feeble concessions for the people. I have lived to see the whole of the educated people of India united by one common aim, striving for one common object, demanding that priceless boon of Self-Government which no civilised Government can for ever deny to a civilised nation. I have heard the same note sounded in Madras and in Bombay, in Calcutta and in Lucknow ; I have seen the best, the foremost, the most moderate and thoughtful men in India banded together to obtain for their countrymen a real share in the administration of their own concerns. You cannot travel in any part or province of India, you cannot visit any town or village in India, where the engrossing idea of the most influential and best educated men is not the idea of progress and Self-Government. And this idea which pervades tens of thousands to-day is spreading to hundreds of thousands and to millions. Do you think this fact has no significance ? Do you think that the spread of this feeling, this idea, this ambition, among the entire body of our educated men,—which has taken place within our own memory,—means nothing ? Why, gentlemen, I see in this one fact the strongest promise for the future, the strongest guarantee for administrative reform and political advancement. It is this slow, silent, steady, irresistible advance which makes nations,—not particular Acts of legislation or measures of administration. The most liberal Acts would be useless and valueless and even hurtful if we had no strength, no faith, no capacity of progress. The most retrograde Acts will fail to impede us, if we have trust and faith in ourselves, if we are true to our country and our cause.

Exhortation to his Countrymen.

Therefore, my friends, and countrymen, my first and last word to you is this : Let us have faith in ourselves ! Our future depends on us ; our fate is in our own hands ; our destiny rests on our labours ! Do not, for one moment, despond, for despondency in such a cause is a sin. Do not be intemperate and violent, for hysteric spasms are the signs of weakness, not of strength. Strong in our determination, calm in our conviction, let us speak temperately, clearly, and unmistakably ; and let us work steadily and silently, swerving neither to the right nor to the left from the path of our duty to our country.

Gentlemen, we have candid friends who are always telling us that our agitation is useless and futile ; that our activity does more harm than good ; that our endeavours had better be abandoned. But the path which they thus point out to us is not the path of progress, but the path of death ! The remedy which these physicians prescribe is that the patient, in order to be cured, should commit suicide! If you ever study the Economic History of India during the last 150 years, you will clearly comprehend how much we have lost in every way by our inactivity in the past. And if you have watched carefully the course of recent events, you will understand how much of our economic disasters at the present time is due to the exclusion of the people from all share in the management of their own concerns.

Government by Co-operation.

There never has been, and there never can be, any good Government in any great and civilised country without the help and the co-operation of the people themselves. And to advise us to refrain from all endeavours to secure self-Government for India, is to perpetuate that economic distress and suffering and misery which unhappily distinguishes India at the present day among all great and civilised country in the earth. No gentlemen, our duty demands it, the good of our country requires it, and the prosperity of British Rule depends on it, that we should have some real share in the administration of our own concerns.

Our Destiny is in our hands.

For, myself, I would rather that we should endeavour and fail, than not endeavour at all. It is national life to pursue great and worthy objects; it is national death to stand still and stagnate. But with us, at the present moment, it is not a question of failure; it is a question of certain triumph in the end. We may be beaten back, once and again; we may labour a whole life-time without attaining our end; but, rest assured, the endeavour will not be made in vain. Our sons will press forward when we sink in the struggle; the cause of our country will prosper when our ashes are cold; and before half a century is over, before a quarter of this new century is over, the people of India will have secured a real and valuable share in the administration of their own affairs,—like all the great and civilised nations of the earth. Let us have faith in ourselves, let us be true to ourselves, and our political future is assured, our destiny is in our own hands.

The Land Assessment Resolution.

Gentlemen, I thank you again for the welcome you have accorded to us on our arrival in India. In the few words I have addressed to you I have purposely refrained from alluding to the important Resolution which the Government of India have recorded on the subject of the Indian land revenue. I feel greatly honoured by the reference which has been made to my humble work in this very important Resolution; and the courtesy with which His Excellency's Government has dealt with my suggestions almost disarms criticism. The paper was placed in my hands only this morning, and I have not read even a tenth part of the Resolution yet, and you will pardon me therefore if I am wholly unable on the present occasion to express any opinion on this most important subject. I shall conclude by reiterating my thanks to the Government of India for the earnest attention which they have bestowed on this subject which is all important in reference to the economic condition of the people of India.

XIV. FIRST REPLY TO LORD CURZON'S LAND RESOLUTION.

[*Appeared in the "Pioneer" March* 12, 1902.]

SIR—A SIRIES of Letters on the land tax in the different provinces of India were addressed by the present writer to Lord Curzon, Viceroy of India, in the course of 1900, and were subsequently published under the title of "Open Letters to Lord Curzon on Famines and Land Assessments in India." The views expressed in my Letters were also the views of many distinguished Englishmen who had retired after long and meritorious work in India; and a joint Memorial was submitted towards the close of 1900 to the Secretary of State for India. Among the signatories were the Right Hon'ble Sir Richard Garth, late Chief Justice of Bengal, Sir John Jardine, late Judge of the High Court of Bombay, Mr. R. K. Puckle, C. S. I., late Director of Revenue Settlement in Madras, Mr. H. J. Reynolds, C. S. I., late Revenue Secretary of Bengal, Mr. A. Rogers, late Member of Council in Bombay, and Mr. J. H. Garstin, late Member of Council in Madras. I betray no confidence in informing you that the draft of the Memorial was made by the most experienced revenue officer among us, Mr. Puckle, and that his draft was adopted with some slight modifications after several conferences.

The Secretary of State forwarded this Memorial to

the Government of India for consideration, and Lord Curzon's very able Resolution on the subject has just appeared.

Lord Curzon has approached the subject with a statesmanlike conviction of its vast and national importance. He has obtained reports from the Local Governments of the different Provinces; he has recognised the question as transcending the sphere of party or sectional controversy; and he has dealt with his critics with that courtesy which is a part of him. A few extracts from the opening paraghaphs of the Resolution will indicate the spirit in which the Viceroy has approached the subject :—

"The Government of India welcomed the opportunity thus afforded to them of instituting renewed enquiries into a matter that has, for more than a century, been the subiect of anxious discussion. The well-being of the agricultural community in India, constituting as it does so overwhelming a proportion of the entire population of the Indian Continent, and contributing so large a quota to the Indian revenues, cannot fail to be to the Government a matter of the most intimate concern; nor can it be denied that upon the incidence of the land revenue collections must the prosperity of those classes in a great measure depend. The question may be recognised, therefore, as one of the highest national importance, transcending the sphere of party or sectional controversy, and demanding at once the most exhaustive scrutiny and the most liberal treatment. . . If prevention of the inevitable consequences of drought be an ideal incapable of attainment, mitigation is manifestly an object worthy of the closest attention of the Government. It cannot but be their desire that assessments should be equitable in character and moderate in incidence, and there should be left to the proprietor or to the cultivator of the soil—as the case may be—that margin of profit that will enable him to save in ordinary seasons, and to meet the strain of exceptional misfortune."

In these passages, the Government of India have fully recognised the cardinal principle which I have urged so often in recent years that, in an agricultural country like India, the prosperity and well being of the nation greatly depend on the incidence of the land revenue being moderate and equitable; and that land assessments should be so made as to leave to the proprietor or the cultivator of the soil a margin of profit which will enable him to save in ordinary years to meet the strain of exceptional bad harvests. I could not wish for a more emphatic confirmation of the opinions which I have so frequently advanced; and I gratefully acknowledge that there is no difference, in principle, between the views I have urged and the views so authoritatively laid down in this Government Resolution. And if I still press for land reforms in India, it is because the prevailing practice in India is *not* in conformity with this principle; the incidence of land revenue is *not* moderate and equitable; and a sufficient margin is *not* left to landlords and cultivators to meet the strain of occasional bad harvests.

The Permanent Settlement.—The question of permanent settlements does not arise in this discussion. Believing as I do, that a permanent settlement of the land revenues would be in the highest degree beneficial to the people, and would add to their wealth, prosperity, and staying power, I nevertheless refrained from urging such a settlement in my Open Letters, because the India Office had rejected the proposal so late as 1883. And the retired officers who submitted their Memorial to the Secretary of State did not ask for a permanent settlement. We asked for such concessions as were probable, and were consistent with the present land policy of the India Office and the Indian Government. Nevertheless, Lord Curzon has, in his Resolution, dwelt at considerable length on the question of permanent settlements, and the following extracts from his Resolution will explain His Excellency's views:—

"The Government of India indeed know of no ground whatever for the contention that Bengal has been saved from famine by the permanent settlement, a contention which appears to them to be disproved by history, and they are not, therefore, disposed to attach much value to predictions as to the benefits that might have ensued had a similar settlement been extended elsewhere.

"As regards the condition of cultivators in Bengal, who are the tenants of the land owners instituted as a class in the last century by the British Government, there is still less ground for the contention that their position, owing to the permanent settlements, has been converted into one of exceptional comfort and prosperity. It is precisely because this was not the case, and because, so far from being generously treated by the zemindars, the Bengal cultivator was rack-rented, impoverished, and oppressed, that the Government of India felt compelled to intervene on his behalf, and by the series of legislative measures that commenced with the Bengal Tenancy Act of 1859 and culminated in the Act of 1885, to place him in the position of greater security which he now enjoys. To confound this legislation with the permanent settlement, and to ascribe even in part to the latter the benefits which it had conspicuously failed to confer, and which would never have accrued but for the former, is strangely to misread history."

In other words, Lord Curzon holds *firstly*, that the permanent settlement of Bengal has not prevented the worst effects of famines; and *secondly*, that the prosperous condition of the Bengal cultivator is due, not to the permanent settlement, but to the land legislation of 1859 and 1885. An examination of the facts of the case does not support His Excellency's views.

Bengal in 1770 was visited by the worst famine that has ever afflicted India, and one-third of the population of that rich and fertile province, estimated at ten millions or more, was swept away within twelve months. Bengal was permanently settled in 1793; and since that date famines have been rare in Bengal, and *there has been no famine within the permanently settled tracts causing any loss of life.* The agricultural people are generally prosperous and resourceful; and with some help from the Government they have tided over the worst calamities without the most lamentable result of famines,—a ghastly tale of deaths. They very reverse of this has been the case in every other province of India not permanently settled. The agricultural people are so resourceless and impoverished, that the most liberal relief measures have failed to save lives; and the uniform story of deaths by the million has been told in every famine year. These are facts that tell their own tale. Within a period of over a hundred years there has been no famine in permanently settled Bengal causing loss of life; while loss of life has been lamentable and frequent in every other province of India in spite of all relief operations. The contention, therefore, that the permanent settlement has saved Bengal from the worst results of famines is not disproved, but proved by history, as completely and unanswerably as any economic fact can be proved.

But it has been urged in the second place that the comparative prosperity of the Bengal cultivators is due not to the permanent settlement but to later legislation, *i. e.* to the Rent Act passed between 1859 and 1885. I myself rendered some humble assistance in the framing of the Rent Act of 1885, and my services on the occasion were kindly acknowledged in the *Calcutta Gazette* by the then Revenue Secretary of Bengal, Mr. Antony MacDonnell, now Sir Antony MacDonnell, the most distinguished Indian administrator of the present generation. I shall be the last person, therefore, to deny that the Rent Acts of Bengal were needed for the protection of cultivators, or that they completed the good work done by the permanent settlement. But to maintain that the permanent settlement did no good until the Rent Acts were passed is to discredit the testimony of the ablest officers and the most distinguished statesmen who lived and worked in India during three generations. Their recorded opinions have been quoted on my work on the *Economic History of British India*, which is expected to appear next month, and need not be fully recapitulated here. There were men among them like Colebrooke, who had served in India for over forty years, who had known Bengal before the permanent settlement and after, and who declared in 1808 (long before the Rent Acts were passed) that "the reviving prosperity of the country, its increased wealth and rapid improvements are unquestionably due to the permanent settlement." There were thoughtful observers like Bishop Heber who wrote in 1826 (long before the Rent Acts) that "in Bengal where independent of its exuberent fertility there is a permanent settlement, famine is unknown." Lord William Bentinck, as Governor of Madras, recommended a permanent Ryotwari settlement; and Sir Thomas Munro insisted on this all through his life, and stated before the House of Commons that there was no difference between the Zemindari settlement of Bengal and the Ryotwari settlement of Madras as regards permanency. One Governor-General, the Marquis of Wellesley, was so convinced of the benefits of the permanent settlement that he pledged the word of the British Government, in 1803 and 1805, by Legislative Acts and Proclamations, to extend it to Northern India. His successor Lord Minto recorded his opinion in 1813 that "to ameliorate generally the conditions of the natives, it is our firm conviction that no arrangement or measure will tend so speedily and effectually to the accomplishment of those important objects as the establishment of a permanent settlement." Lord Minto's successor, the Marquis of Hastings, once more urged in 1820, that "it is, then, our unanimous opinion that the system of a permanent settlement of the land revenue, either upon the principle of a fixed *jumma*, or of an assessment determinable by a fixed and invariable rate, ought to be extended to the ceded and conquered Provinces." The Directors of the East India Company rejected the proposals of the three successive Governor-Generals, and broke the pledge given by Legislative Acts and Proclamations, not because the permanent settlement in Bengal had borne no fruit, but because a trading Company would sacrifice nothing of their own prospective profits and dividends for the happiness of the people of India. The Company was abolished in 1858; the first Bengal Rent Act was passed by Lord Canning in 1859; and the same Viceroy urged once more the extension of a permanent settlement to all provinces of India for the prevention of such famines as he had witnessed in Northern India in 1860. Sir Charles Wood, then Secretary of State for India, (afterwards Lord Halifax) accepted the proposal and described it as "a measure dictated by sound policy, and calculated to accelerate the development of the resources of India, and to ensure in the highest degree, the welfare and contentment of all classes of Her Majesty's subjects in that country." Sir John Lawrence, (afterwards Lord

Lawrence) wrote in the same year, "I recommend a perpetual settlement, because I am persuaded that however much the country has of late years improved, its resources will be still more rapidly developed by the limitation of the Government demand." And Sir Stafford Northcote, Secretary of State for India, approved of the proposal in 1867 "in consideration of the great importance of connecting the interests of the proprietors of the land with the stability of the British Government."

Such were the opinions of three generations of distinguished administrators and able statesmen in India, —of men who built up the Empire, and valued the contentment and happiness of the people. But unfortunately, the desire to promote the welfare of the people did not ultimately shape the action of the Government; the desire to conciliate the people lost its force when the empire became stable; the desire to continuously add to the land revenue prevailed; and the proposal of extending the permanent settlement into all provinces of India was rejected by the India Office in 1883.

Since then the Indian Government have tried to persuade themselves, and to persuade others, that the permanent settlement is a useless and a hurtful institution. English landed proprietors, who themselves enjoy and appreciate the benefits of a permanent settlement in England under Pitt's Act of 1798, learn to repeat, when they arrive in India, that what is good for themselves is not good for the people of India. Young men, fresh from schools, when they come out as administrators to India, learn to sneer at the opinions of Cornwallis and Sir Thomas Munro, of Wellesley and Lord Hastings, of Canning and Lawrence, of Lord Halifax and Sir Stafford Northcote, as the "school of thought" of an earlier period which is now out of date and out of fashion. And the people of India are asked to believe, with all the eloquence of official persuation, that the grapes which are now placed beyond their reach are sour, and that they will thrive best under a continuous increase of the State demand from the soil. All this is very intelligible, however sad. But the impartial student of history will occasionally turn from the made-to-order opinions of modern times to the freer discussions of past generations; to the opinions of men who watched the operation of the permanent settlement from the earliest period, judged its merit from the highest stand point, viz. that of the happiness of the people of India, and recommended its extension with greater freedom than has been enjoyed by any Viceroy since 1883.

Remedies proposed in the memorial of 1900.—But as has been stated before, the question of a permanent settlement does not arise in the present discussion. The extension of the permanent settlement to other provinces of India was not urged in my Open Letters to Lord Curzon; and it was not recommended in the Memorial submitted to the Secretary of State for India in 1900. The Memorialists made some exceedingly moderate proposals for placing reasonable limits on the land tax, limits which are consistent with the present land policy of the India Office and the Indian Government. The proposals were: (1) Half net produce rule for cultivators paying the land-tax direct. (2) Half rental rule for landlords paying the land tax. (3) Thirty years settlement rule. (4) Limitation of enhancements from cultivators to the ground of increase in prices. (5) Limitation of cesses to 10 per cent. of the land revenue.

With your permission I propose to examine on a future occasion how far Lord Curzon has found it possible to accept these proposals, and on what points His Excellency has not found it possible to adopt them.

XV. SECOND REPLY TO LORD CURZON'S LAND RESOLUTION.

[*Appeared in the "Pioneer," March* 28, 1902.]

SIR—In my last letter which appeared in your issue of the 12th March, I made mention of the five rules which were suggested in the memorial of 1900, to limit the land tax within reasonable and intelligible limits. I propose in the present letter briefly to examine how these rules have been dealt with in the Government Resolution.

(1) *Half net produce from cultivators.*—The first rule suggested by the memorialists was worded thus: "Where the land revenue is paid directly by the cultivators, as in most parts of Madras and Bombay, the Government demand should be limited to 50 per cent of the value of the net produce after a liberal deduction for cultivation expenses has been made, and should not ordinarily exceed one-fifth of the gross produce even in those parts of the country where in theory one-half the net is assumed to approximate to one-third the gross produce."

The first part of the rule, limiting the Government demand to one-half the net produce, is based on Sir Charles Wood's despatch of 1864, and is accepted, in theory, by the Madras Government. "It is now forty years," says Lord Curzon's Resolution, "since the alternative standard of half the net produce was introduced in Madras." The Memorialists, therefore, suggested no new rule, but only recommended that the accepted rule should be fairly and universally worked wherever the land tax was paid by the cultivators direct. In Bombay, no endeavours are made to limit the land tax to one-half the net produce; in Madras the calculations are often so made that, according to the testimony of many revenue officers, the land tax approximates sometimes to the whole of the net produce. What the Memorialists urged was that the rule, accepted in theory, should be strictly and universally carried out in practice; and that the cultivator should be saved, in every single case, from an assessment exceeding one-half the net produce of his field. His Excellency the Viceroy must feel, as stongly as we do, that such protection is needed by each individual cultivator; but nevertheless the Government Resolution provides no such protection, and leaves the incidence of the land tax on the peasant proprietors of Madras and Bombay as uncertain as before.

The second part of the rule quoted was meant as a further limit, and provides that the land tax, estimated at half the net produce, should not exceed the maximum of one-fifth the gross produce. Lord Curzon has declined to adopt this limit also, and deals with the proposal in these words: "The gross produce standard recommended by the Memorialists would, if systematically applied, lead to an increase of assessment all round. The Report from the Central Provinces shows that the proportion to produce of the gross rental ranges from one-sixth to one-fourteenth, and that the enforcement of any such standard would double the liabilities of the raiyats. The Bengal Report gives statistical reasons for believing that rents are generally much below one-fifth of the gross produce, and indicates that raiyats on Government temporarily settled estates are, judged by this standard better off than under proprietors with a permanent settlement. The Madras reply says that 'if Government took one-fifth of the real gross produce from its raiyats, it would fully double its present land revenue. The Governor-General in Council is unable to accept a proposal which could only have consequences the very opposite of those which are anticipated by its authors."

The reference to the tenants of private landlords in Bengal and the Central Provinces is out of place, because the rule framed by the Memorialists was intended for tracts "where the land revenue is paid directly by the cultivators, as in most parts of Madras and Bombay." Tenants of private landlords are protected by the Rent Acts of the different provinces, and the more complete the protection, the more thorough will be the support which those Acts will receive from all true well-wishers of Indian cultivators. In the rule now under consideration the Memorialists explicitly confined themselves to the cases of the cultivators who paid the land tax direct to Government, and it is a matter of regret that the rule framed by them has been completely misapprehended by Government. For the Memorialists did not suggest one-fifth the gross produce as the standard of land tax; they suggested it as the maximum which should never be exceeded. As far back as 1883, one-fourth the gross produce was suggested as the maximum rent payable by Bengal raiyats to their private landlords, and in reducing this proportion to one-fifth Sir Antony MacDonnell, then Revenue Secretary of Bengal, recorded the following remarks : "It was never pretended that all landlords were justified in claiming one-fourth of the produce as rent, or that the proportion should be looked on otherwise than as the farthest limit which under circumstances most favourable to the landlord his claims might reach. ...The result of the information collected by these officers was to induce the Lieutenant-Governor to advocate the substitution of one-fifth for one-fourth of the gross produce in the Tenancy Bill now before the Legislative Council of India." The Memorialists had this rule before them when they framed a similar rule for tenants paying direct to Government ; and in suggesting the maximum of one-fifth the produce, they did not pretend that "the proportion should be looked on otherwise than as the farthest limit which under circumstances most favourable" to the Government, its claim might reach.

As a matter of fact, Government very often exceeds this limit. It was in evidence before the Famine Commission of 1880 that the land tax in some Talukas in Madras was as high as 31 per cent. of the gross produce ; and the Madras Board of Revenue now explains that this high rate referred to a small area, and that "a truer idea is given by the figures 12 to 28 per cent." It was in evidence before the Famine Commission of 1900 that the land tax in some districts of Gujerat was 20 per cent. of the gross produce; and it is obvious, therefore, that this full rate must have been exceeded in many particular villages and Talukas in those districts. The object of the Memorialists was to prevent such excessive assessments in any single case. Their intention was that the land tax, necessarily varying according to the different qualities of the soil, should in no case exceed 20 per cent. of the gross produce. They hoped that the maximum limit proposed by Sir Antony MacDonnell for the tenants of the Bengal zemindars would be fixed by the Government for rayats paying the land tax to the State direct. The Government has misapprehended this suggested rule; has described the evil consequences of another rule which the Memorialists did not propose; and has declined to place any maximum limit on the land tax payable by cultivators. I deplore this decision. It was eagerly hoped that the revelations made by the Famine Commissions of 1880 and 1901 would induce Lord Curzon to place some clear, workable, intelligible maximum limit on the State demand from the present proprietors of India. Not only is it necessary that Revenue and Settlement Officers should be moderate in their demands, but it is also necessary—in India more than in any other country in the world,—that the cultivators should know and understand clearly what the State demands, and what they are entitled to keep. Uncertainty in the State demand paralyses agriculture. And this fatal uncertainty will hang on the agricultural industry of India until some future ruler, in closer touch with the people and with a firmer determination to protect them at all costs, will declare to them in language which they can understand, how much the Government claims from the produce of their fields, and how much is assured to them, untouched by the Settlement and the Revenue Officer.

(2) *Half the rental from landlords.*—The second rule suggested by the Memorialists was thus worded; "Where the land revenue is paid by landlords, the principle adopted in the Saharanpur rules of 1855, whereby the revenue demand is limited to one-half of the actual rent or assets of such landlords, should be universally applied." Rule XXXVI of the Saharanpur Rule laid down that "the Government have determined so far to modify the rule laid down in para. 52 of the Directions to Settlement Officers as to limit the demand of State to 50 per cent or one-half of the average net assets." Revenue Officers have from time to time sought to place on these clear words an interpretation which they do not bear on the face of them; and have sought to realise as land revenue one-half of the prospective and potential rental of estates. Mr. J. B. Fuller, who was Secretary to the Chief Commissioner of the Central Provinces in 1887 described such procedure (in his letter of the 18th May, 1887) as an attempt "to evade the operation of the half-assets rule." By his singular ability and talents, as well as by his unsurpassed experience in settlement work, Mr. J. B. Fuller has deservedly won the high rank which he now occupies. But alas! one of the first duties of his high office has been an attempt to justify in 1902 what he himself described in 1887 as an evasion of a Government

rule by Government officers. As Secretary to the Government of India, he signs Lord Curzon's Resolution, and he writes that "the construction placed on the word assets at the time, and for many years later, permitted the Settlement Officer to look beyond the actual cash rental, and to take into consideration prospective increases of income." I would not like to compare these words too closely with what Mr. Fuller wrote in 1887. It is pleasanter to know that the old practice, whether an evasion of rules or a misapprehension of them, has now been abandoned. Lord Curzon proceeds to say :—

"In the North-Western and other zemindari provinces prospective assets have been excluded from consideration. . . In the resettlement of Oudh, now on the point of completion, the average falls below 47 per cent. . . Already as pointed out in the Report from the Central Provinces three of the districts in the whole of the Provinces have recently been reassessed . . at less than 50 per cent. of the rental . . . In Orissa the gradual reduction of the government proportion has been even more striking. In 1822 it was authoritatively declared to be 83·3 of the assets, in 1833 it was lowered to 70-75 per cent., in 1840 to 65 per cent. with a permissive reduction to 60 per cent., while in the resettlement just concluded it has been brought down to 54 per cent."

I can scarcely flatter myself that His Excellency meant the last words as a compliment to me personally : but I may say, in passing, that the last resettlement of Orissa went on under my supervision in 1896 ; and that my recommendations were before the Government when the settlement was finally concluded in 1897. Generally speaking, the Government of India recognises the rule proposed in the Memorial without formally laying it down. "While the standard of 50 per cent. has nowhere been laid down as a fixed and immutable prescription, there has been and there is, a growing tendency throughout temporarily settled zemindari districts to approximate to it." The Memorialists may feel satisfied that this virtually proclaims the abandonment of the practice of assessing estates on prospective rentals, or at over half the rental; and they are grateful for this to Lord Curzon.

(3) *Settlements for thirty years.*—The third rule suggested by the Memorialists was thus worded: "That no revision of the land tax of any province or part thereof should be made within thirty years of the expiration of any former revision." The name of Lord William Bentinck is honoured in India for doing away with short settlements and introducing settlements for thirty years. The great settlement of Northern India, effected between 1833 and 1849 was for thirty years. The first great settlement of Bombay, effected in 1837 was for thirty years. Settlements made in Madras have been for thirty years during over half a century. The Orissa settlement of 1837 was for thirty years, and when the period expired in 1867, Lord Lawrence, then Viceroy of India, continued the old settlement for another thirty years instead of harassing the people with a fresh settlement in the year of the Orissa famine. The advantages of long settlements are obvious. In spite of all precau-

tions, every re-settlement is a harassment of the people; short settlements take away all motives for improvement; long settlements give some assurance and encouragement to the people, and promote enterprise in the landed classes. These facts were forgotten or ignored in the last years of the 19th century; and in 1895, Lord George Hamilton ruled that while thirty years should continue to be the ordinary term of settlement in Madras, Bombay, and the N. W. Provinces, twenty years should be the general rule for the Punjab and the Central Provinces. Against this ungenerous departure from a healthy rule I raised my voice in my Open Letter to Lord Curzon on the Central Provinces; and it is against this departure that the rule proposed by the Memorialists is meant to be a protest. The Government Resolution defends this departure in the following words; "Where the land is fully cultivated, rents fair, and agricultural production not liable to violent oscillations, it is sufficient if the demands of Government are re-adjusted once in thirty years, *i. e.* once in the lifetime of each generation. Where the opposite conditions prevail, where there are much waste land, low rents and a fluctuating cultivation, or again where there is a rapid development of resources owing to the construction of roads, railways, or canals, to an increase of population or to a rise in prices, the postponement of resettlement for so long a period is both injurious to the people who are unequal to the strain of a sharp enhancement, and unjust to the general tax-payer who is temporarily deprived of the additional revenue to which he has legitimate claim."

A moment's examination will show that this defence of Lord George Hamilton's action of 1895 is unsound. The Punjab and the Central Provinces were not less fully cultivated and not less developed in 1895, after half a century of British rule, than the Bombay Province was in 1837, after twenty years of British rule, or the N. W. Provinces were in 1833, after thirty years of British rule. It is possible that the Government of India sees this; for the closing sentence of Lord Curzon's Resolution on this subject is hopeful. His Excellency writes: "Whether these considerations justifying a shorter term of settlement than thirty years apply with sufficient force to the Punjab and the Central Provinces at the present time, and if they do apply at the present time, whether the force of their application will diminish with the passage of time, are weighty questions to which careful attention will be given by the Government of India upon suitable occasions." The last words inspire me with hope; and if Lord Curzon succeeds, before laying down his office, to extend the thirty years' rule to the Punjab and the Central Provinces, His Excellency will have satisfied the Memorialists, and earned the gratitude of millions of cultivators in those Provinces.

(4) *Limitation of enhancements from cultivators.*—The fourth rule proposed by the Memorialists was thus worded: "Where the land-revenue is paid by the cultivators direct to the Government, there should be no increase in the assessment except in cases where the land has increased in value (1) in consequence of im-

provements in irrigation works carried out at the expense of the Government, or (2) on account of a rise in the value of produce based on the average prices of the thirty years next preceding such revision."

The object of the Memorialists was to define the grounds on which the land tax paid direct by cultivators would be enhanced. As between private landlords and their tenants the Rent Acts of Bengal lay down clearly and definitely the grounds of enhancement, and Courts of Justice will allow no enhancement of rent except on those specific grounds. As between the State and the peasant proprietors no such definite grounds of enhancement of the land tax are laid down, and no appeal to Courts of Justice is allowed. The result is that the cultivators paying the land tax live in a state of perpetual uncertainty, they do not know on what grounds the State will claim an enhancement at the next settlement, they do not comprehend to what extent the enhancement will be made. As I am writing these lines, I find from the reply of a Member of the Madras Council that in the recent Malabar settlement, the assessment was raised 85 per cent. at Palghat, 55 per cent. at Calicut, 84 per cent. at Kurumbranad, and 105 per cent. at Walavanad. Such enhancements, made on grounds which the cultivators never fully comprehend, must deaden agricultural enterprise, and keep the cultivating population in a state of chronic poverty.

As far back as 1882, the Marquis of Ripon endeavoured to remove this uncertainty, and made a rule, with the concurrence of the Madras Government, that in districts which had been surveyed and setteled, there should be no increase in the land revenue, except on the equitable ground of a rise in prices. Lord Ripon left India in December, 1884, and in Januany, 1885, the India Office cancelled his rule and plunged the tenantry of India once more into a state of uncertainty. It was the object of the Memorialists to remove this deadening uncertainty; to place the tenants of the State in the same position in which the tenants of private landlords have been placed; and to let them know the clear and definite grounds on which the State claimed an enhancement of the revenue at resettlements. They therefore framed a rule similar to Lord Ripon's rule, and they hoped and believed that Lord Curzon would see the necessity of extending to the cultivators, paying revenue to the State, something of that protection which has been extended by law to cultivators, paying rents to private landlords. Lord Curzon's decision on this point is disappointing.

"To deny the right of the State" writes Lord Curzon "to a share in any increase in values except those which could be inferred from the general table of price statistics, in itself a most fallacious and partial test, would be to surrender to a number of individuals an increment which they had not themselves earned."

This decision is disappointing. Increase in values is indicated by the table of prices. Lord Ripon's rule suggested, and the rule framed by the Memorialists also suggested, that the Government should obtain an enhancement of revenues when there was such increase in prices. And they reasonably urged that the Government should claim no increase when prices had not increased. All the real advantages which the cultivator secures from new roads or lines of railway are shown in a rise in prices. I was a District Officer in Midnapur ten years ago, when there was no railway line in the District. I am writing the present letter from the same place, which is the now connected by rail with Calcutta, Bombay, and Madras. And prices have increased owing to this connection. A high official who has been here all these years informs me that rice was selling at 16 seers the rupee ten years ago, and is now selling at 12½ seers the rupee. When such increase takes place in temporarily settled tracts, it is a legitimate ground for enhancement of revenue at the next settlement. When no such increase has taken place, the cultivators have derived no advantages; and to claim an increase of revenue at a settlement is to drive them deeper into debt and poverty. And not to define, clearly and intelligibly, the grounds on which the State is entitled to an increase of revenue from lands, is the most efficacious method that human ingenuity could devise for keeping them eternally in the gloom of uncertainty and the slough of despond.

(5) *Limitation of Cesses.*—The fifth and last rule proposed by the Memorialists was worded thus: "That a limit be fixed in each Province, beyond which it may not be permissible to surcharge the land tax with local cesses. We are of opinion that the Bengal rate of 6¼ per cent. is a fair one; and that in no cases should the rate exceed to ten per cent."

In my Open Letter to Lord Curzon on the Central Provinces, I made the mistake of stating that local cases amounting to 12½ per cent. were assessed on the rental. The Government Resolution on the Nagpur Settlement, published a year ago, corrected my mistake, and pointed out that the cesses amounting to 12½ per cent, were assessed on the revenue, and therefore came to about 6¼ per cent, on the rental. The Memorialists had the facts and figures for Bengal Madras, Bombay and other provinces before them, but their rule is somewhat obscurely worded. What they meant was that in a permanently settled province like Bengal, where the cesses are imposed on the rental, the rate of 6¼ per cent. on the rental is fair; and that in temporarily settled provinces, like Bombay, Madras and the N.-W. Provinces, the cesses, calculated on the land revenue, should not exceed ten per cent. of the land revenue. The decision of the Government in this subject is stated in this following words, and gives us some grounds for hope :—

"The general conculsion of the Government of India is that there is no reason for thinking that local taxation if properly distributed is on the whole either onerous or excessive. But there are grounds for suspecting that the distribution is often unfair. . . The question presents itself whether it is not better, as opportunities occur, to mitigate imposts which are made to press upon the cultivating classes more severely than the law intended. The Government of India would be glad to see their way to offer such relief."

I have now travelled over the entire ground covered

by the Memorial, and have shewn how the five proposals made therein have been dealt with by the Government. Lord Curzon has approached the subject with a statesmanlike conviction of its importance. He has virtually affirmed the principle, which we urged, that in temporarily settled estates held by landlords, the Government revenue should generally be limited to one-half the *actual* rental. He has given us hopes that the rule of thirty years settlement, which we urged, will be extended to the Punjab and the Central Provinces. And he has also given us hopes that the pressure of local cesses will be mitigated. If to all this His Excellency had added some clear and workable limits to the Government demand in Ryotwari tracts, and defined some intelligible and equitable grounds for enhancement of revenue in such tracts, the Government Resolution would have given to millions of cultivators the assurance and the protection they need so much. The subject is one of national importance, and not one for sectional controversy. Personally, I have never written or spoken on the subject, and I will never write or speak on the subject, merely to carry on an idle debate or to prolong a needless controversy. I have felt, and I feel, that the happiness and well-being of an agricultural nation largely depend on some clear, definite, intelligible, and workable limits being placed on the land tax in Ryotwari tracts, as limits have been placed on Zemindari tracts by the Saharanpur rules. And the land question in India will not be solved, and India will know no rest, till this is done.

XVI. THIRD REPLY TO LORD CURZON'S LAND RESOLUTION.

[*Appeared in the "Hindu" March* 29, 1902.]

On landing at Madras, last month, I saw for the first time the Viceroy's famous Resolution on the Indian Land Revenue, published in January last. And while I sincerely appreciated the courtesy which distinguished that document, I was unable to agree in many of the conclusions to which His Excellency had arrived. The ground covered by the Resolution, however, was so vast that I found it impossible to touch on all the points within the limits of my previous letters. I propose in the present letter to deal with some remarkable statements which have found a place in the Resolution and with some remedial measures which Lord Curzon had announced.

Famines and the Land Revenue.—The Governor-General in Council is unable to accept the theory that: "Were the assessments diminished, famine would be less frequent, or that at least when they do occur, they would cause infinitely less suffering." And yet if we take entire provinces and large tracts of country into consideration, this theory is proved beyond a question. Permanently settled Bengal is lightly taxed, and has known no famine attended with loss of life since 1793. Madras and Bombay under the Ryotwari system bear a heavier and more uncertain land-tax, and the worst famines during the last quarter of the century have been in Madras and Bombay. The Central Provinces had its assessment enormously increased at the last Settlement, and suffered from a desolating famine with a few years. In Northern India the cruel land assessments of the early years of the 19th century were reduced by Bentinck and Dalhousie, and famines within the present generation have been less fatal than those of 1837 and 1860. No statesman outside India questions the theory that moderate taxation helps the people, and heavy taxation impoverishes them. We all hope that Lord Curzon will take his place as a statesman in England after he retires from India; and if he does not accept a peerage, he will seek the votes of some constituency to enter the Parliament again. Will His Excellency promise his constituents that he will keep up a heavy rate of taxation, because, according to his Indian theory, heavy taxes do not interfere with the prosperity of the people? It would be interesting to watch the result of the Election.

But let us confine ourselves to India. If moderating the taxes and rents does not improve the condition and the staying power of the people, what was the object of the long line of statesmen from the time of Munro and Elphinstone in pressing for moderation? Why did Lord William Bentinck reduce the land revenue to two-thirds the rental, and Lord Dalhousie reduce it further to one-half the rental, if such reduction was a needless and foolish sacrifice of the Government revenue? Why did Lord Canning place restrictions on enhancements by private landlords in Bengal, and why has that policy been followed by Rent Acts in every province of India, if it is a useless loss to landlords and does not benefit the tenants? British legislation has striven since 1859 to place equitable and intelligible limits on the power of private landlords to enhance rents; and yet the moment we propose such limits on the power of the State in provinces where the State is virtually the landlord, a cry is raised in the official world, and even the Viceroy permits the statement to find a place in his Resolution that to diminish assessments would not promote the prosperity and the staying power of the people.

Money-lenders and the land revenue. Another fallacy which has found place in the Resolution is this: "Neither in the past nor in the present circumstances of the country can any warrant be found for the belief that the revenue so relinquished by Government would constitute a famine relief fund in the hands of the people. Experience has shewn that excessive leniency of the kind in question reacts prejudicially upon the industry of the agricultural classes, while it encourages the transfer of soil to moneylenders and middlemen."

The experience of every revenue officer in Bengal directly contradicts this theory. Within my memory,—within the last 43 years since the first Rent Act was passed in Bengal,—the indebtedness of the Bengal cultivators and the power of the moneylenders have decreased in consequence of the provisions against the undue enhancement of rents; and this has been so even in Behar since the passing of the last Rent Act. It is excessive assessment and rigorous collection, not leniency, which drive the cultivators to serfdom under moneylenders, and this is proved by the report of the last Famine Commission.

In 1876 a cyclone and storm-wave destroyed the crops of many districts in Eastern Bengal, and I was sent as a Sub-Divisional officer to an island which had suffered the most. I knew that the people had no food, and I was prepared to open relief operations when needed, without acting in haste. What was my surprise when I found that the people needed no relief and asked for none! The cultivators had paid light rents for years before, and had invested all their savings in silver jewellery for their women, and in other valuable articles. In the year of disaster they sold their silver things, bought shiploads of imported rice, and helped themselves till the next harvest. A small number of orphans and helpless old men who had lost their relations by the cyclone were relieved; the mass of the people supported themselves through the crisis. What was this silver jewellery of the cultivators but "a famine relief fund in the hands of the people?" And if the State treats its ryots in Madras and Bombay as leniently as the private landlords treat their cultivators in Eastern Bengal, the ryots of Madras and Bombay would naturally have "a famine relief fund" in their own hands, in some shape or other, for years of drought and distress. For the ryots of Bombay and Madras are not less thrifty and provident, but notoriously more so, than the cultivators of Eastern Bengal. But the State virtually repeats the words of the landlords of the old school:—"Squeeze the tenants well in order to prevent them, poor things, from getting into bad ways!"

Native Rule and the Land Revenue. Another fallacy which has found place in Lord Curzon's Resolution is that the defects of the present Land Revenue system of India are inherited from the old Native Rule. "The Government of India," says the Resolution, "would not desire to claim for the Land Revenue system of British India an exactitude or freedom from blemish to which it cannot pretend. Historically, it owes its immediate origin to practices inherited from the most decadent period of Native Rule."

The decadent period of Native Rule has many sins to answer for; but in respect of over-assessment of the soil, the East India Company were the worst sinners. This is abundantly manifest from the Blue Books and official records of the early years of the 19th century which I have summarized in my *Economic History of British India*, and need not recapitulate here. It is in evidence that the Company's servants swept aside Village Communities, Jaigirdars, and Polygars, in order to come in direct touch with the cultivators, and they raised a land revenue such as was never known in India before. In Bengal the actual collection during the last three years of the Nawab's administration varied between six and nine million Rupees; in the first year after the Company obtained the Dewani, they screwed up the revenue to nearly 15 million Rupees; and in less than thirty years they made it 27 millions, by 1793. In Bombay the revenue of the territories acquired from the last Peshwa in 1817 was increased within a few years from 8 millions to 15 millions of Rupees. In Madras, the Company's servants were actually taking about half the produce of the field as *Land Tax* at the very time when, according to the testimony of Dr. Francis Buchanan, private landlords in Bengal were taking less than one-fourth the produce as *Rent.* And in Northern India, the land revenue of the Districts ceded by the Nawab of Oudh in 1801 was raised from 13½ million Rupees to 17 million Rupees in three years.

This policy of continuously screwing up the lanc revenue to a higher figure than was ever known in Indi before under any Native Rule, was steadily pursued b the Company's servants under the sanction of th Company's Directors; and all thoughtful and moderat Englishmen of the time deplored the policy. Verelst Governor of Bengal, replied in 1768 to the Director' fresh demands for increase by stating that: "It is totall beyond the power of your administration to make an material addition to your rents." Warren Hasting reported in 1772 that: "Notwithstanding the loss c at least one-third of the inhabitants of that provinc (Bengal) and the consequent decrease of the cultivatior the nett collections of the year 1771 exceeded even thos of 1768." Colebrooke, writing in 1808, proteste against "grasping at the highest revenue and wringin from our peasants the utmost rent." The Madras Boar of Revenue raised its voice in 1818 against "bindin the ryot by force to the plough, compelling him to ti land acknowledged to the overassessed, dragging hi back if he absconded, * * taking from him all that could be obtained." Bishop Heber, writing in 1826 said : "The peasantry in the Company's Provinces are, on the whole, worse off, poorer, and more dispirited than the subjects of the Native Princes ;" and that "no Native Prince demands the rent which we do." Lieutenant Colonel Briggs, writing in 1830 said that: "A Land Tax like that which now exists in India, professing to absorb the whole of the landlord's rent, was never known under any Government in Europe or Asia." Robert M. Bird, the Father of Land Settlement of Northern India, said before the House of Commons in 1832, that: "In Madras and other places* * the revenue was fixed too high at the beginning, and impoverishes the people." And the Hon'ble Mr. Shore, writing in 1837 said : "Every successive province, as it has fallen into our possession, has been made a field for higher exaction; and it has always been our boast how greatly we have raised our revenue above that which the Native Rulers were able to extort."

Protection needed in Madras and Bombay. Much has been done to remedy these abuses since the early years of the Company's Rule. Bengal was saved by the Permanent Settlement. Northern India obtained some relief from Lord W. Bentinck's two-third-rental rule, and subsequently from Lord Dalhousie's half-rental rule. The cultivators of Bengal obtained protection from Lord Canning's Rent Act of 1859, and the tenants of private landlords in the different provinces of India have obtained similar protection from the Rent Acts of the different provinces. But it is a remarkable and a lamentable fact that the Government has not granted to the peasant proprietors of Madras and Bombay the protection which it has granted to the tenants of private landlords under these Rent Acts. The Bengal ryot knows and understands the clear and definite grounds on which his Zemindar may claim an enhanchment. The Bombay and Madras ryot does not know and does not understand the grounds on which the State will claim an enhancement at the next revised settlement. The Bengal ryot can reckon beforehand the limits of the Zemindar's claims. The Madras and Bombay ryot cannot calculate beforehand what the Settlement Officer's claims will be. The Bengal ryot can appeal to Civil Courts against unjust claims on the part of his landlord. The Madras and Bombay ryot is allowed no appeal to any independent tribunal against the mistakes of the Settlement or Revenue officer. Certainty and definiteness in the rental make the Bengal ryot confident in his own rights and prompt him to save. Uncertainty and indefiniteness in the State-demand at each revised settlement demoralize the Madras and Bombay ryot and take away from the motive to save. We had hoped that Lord Curzon would on the present occasion introduce some definite rules and limits on the enhancement of revenue in Madras and Bombay, (as Lord Ripon did in 1882), so as grant to the Madras and Bombay ryot the protection and the assurance which the Bengal ryot enjoys. Lord Curzon has allowed the opportunity to pass, and has not granted the needed protection.

The land question in India will know no satisfactory solution until some future ruler, more in touch with the people, and more truly realizing the position of the cultivating population, will grant to the Madras and Bombay ryot that assurance and protection which the Bengal ryot enjoys, and without which agricultural prosperity is impossible in any country in the world.

Protection granted by Lord Curzon. Three remedial measures are proposed by Lord Curzon. They are (1) progressive and gradual imposition of large enhancements; (2) greater elasticity in the revenue collection; (3) reduction of assessments in case of local deterioration. These remedies are excellent, so far as they go, but they do not go far enough. They will obviate temporary hardship, but will not promote the prosperity of an agricultural nation. Large enhancements should certainly be progressively imposed when made ;—but they should *not* be made at all except on these clear grounds and under those strict rules which the Government has provided in the case of private landlords. In, the recent Malabar Settlement, the assessment has been raised 85 per cent. at Palghat, 55 per cent. at Calicut, 84 per cent. at Kurumbranad, and 105 per cent. at Walavanad. Private landlords in Bengal stand amazed at these enormous enhancements, and ask themselves under which of the prescribed grounds in the Bengal Rent Act they could induce Courts of Justice to grant them such enhancements of the rental from their ryots ! And it is quite clear that if such enhancements are permissible in Madras and

Bombay, on the opinion of the Settlement Officer, the condition of cultivators can never be other than one of perpetual poverty and wretchedness. Greater elasticity in revenue *collection* is also necessary in hard times, but the revenue *assessment* should be light to enable cultivators to save in good years. To screw up the land-tax to the "full" amount, and then to allow remissions when harvests fail, is to keep cultivators always on the brink of famines and starvation. Lastly, the reduction of assessments in case of local deterioration is of course necessary, or the country will be depopulated; but will no reduction be made except to prevent depopulation?

The remedial measures proposed by Lord Curzon indicate the desperate condition of cultivators in Southern India, and the desperate cases in which the Government proposes to relieve them. Wiser statesmanship should go further, and should permanently improve the condition of the cultivators, should give them clear, definite and intelligible rights, and should provide them with a complete protection against enhancement except on clearly defined legal grounds. This is what Lord Canning's Act of 1859 and subsequent Rent Acts have done for the Bengal cultivator. This is what Lord Curzon's Resolution has failed to do for the Madras and Bombay cultivator.
